THE RACING - CRUISER

THE RACING-CRUISER

written and illustrated by

RICHARD HENDERSON

REILLY & LEE BOOKS
a division of Henry Regnery Company
Chicago, Illinois

Dedicated to my father
William L. Henderson

Acknowledgments

More than a few knowledgeable sailors have been helpful and generous in expressing their opinions and supplying me with specific information. First of all, I would like to thank Dr. Roger P. Batchelor for his help, interest, and encouragement in each of my nautical book projects. A very special thanks goes to Harold R. (Buzz) White, manager of the Gibson Island Yacht Yard, for allowing me to drop in and "gam" with him about our favorite subject. I owe a debt to Clayton Ewing, Commodore of the Cruising Club of America, for lending me an advance copy of the new IOR measurement rule, and I am most grateful to Reid A. Dunn and the Fishing Bay Yacht Club of Virginia for allowing me to reprint their handy time allowance tables. Thanks to designers and/or yacht measurers—Paul F. Fitzgerald, Robert S. Blumenstock, Robert G. Henry, Jr., and Richard D. Carlson; and also to sailmakers—Allan MacKenzie, Walter Flynn, Owen C. Torry, Jr., James Meehan, and especially Wallace C. Ross. Other sailors who have been helpful in one way or another include: Bruce Smart, Dwight Webb, Charles F. Stein, Jr., James A. Potter, Frederick C. Grell, David and Richard F. Jablin. I am very appreciative of the fine job done by my typist, Patty M. Maddocks, and my thanks go to Judith Pownall of Reilly and Lee for efficiently handling so many details in connection with this book's production. Finally and most especially, I am indebted to Roger C. Taylor, President of the International Marine Publishing Company, for his interest, suggestions, and thorough job of editing the manuscript.

Contents

Author's Introduction

Many fine books have been written on the subject of yacht racing. The vast majority of these books have concentrated on small racing sailboats of a particular kind, the *one-design classes* or boats of as nearly as possible identical hulls and rigs which race boat-for-boat (one boat of a certain class competing against sisters of the same class).

In general, this book deals with the subject of yacht racing, but in particular, it specializes in selecting and racing fairly large boats and also those having at least some cruising accommodations, those sailing yachts sometimes described as *racing-cruisers*. These boats usually (but not always) race against each other on a handicap basis. I have chosen to concentrate on racing-cruisers for several reasons. First of all, this is the area of racing in which I feel most at home and have the most experience. Second, it is the area least covered by other books — especially the area of handicap racing *on-soundings* (near shore); and third, it is an area of tremendous growth and greatly increasing popularity.

Several factors account for the increasing interest in racing-cruisers. New materials and methods of production have brought the price of moderate sized boats within the grasp of many dedicated sailors. In recent years boat designers have developed a great variety of high performance craft that incorporate surprisingly comfortable accommodations at very little sacrifice to speed. In fact, it is not uncommon to see racing-cruisers overtake out-and-out racing boats of comparable size when they are sailing over the same race course. Many skippers of small one-design boats are finding that they can enjoy high performance sailing in larger racing-cruisers and the same keen competition as is found in small boat classes. Indeed, many small boat class champions who have moved up to big boats have been surprised to find that the "pickins" are not so easy, that the new found competition is more than bargained for. Of course, much of this competition is due to the accumulation over the years of top talent from the many competitive small boat classes. At any rate many small boat sailors are coming to realize that they can enjoy fairly economical racing of high quality in versatile boats that can also serve as comfortable family day-sailers and over-nighters or even offshore cruisers.

Other newcomers to the racing-cruisers are first boat owners who have improved their sailing skills to the point where they wish to begin racing, crew members who have acquired a great deal of racing knowledge and wish to try their hand at being skippers, and devotees of cruising who want fast cruising boats that will be competitive for occasional racing.

This book is directed primarily to the following: (1) sailors in general who wish to begin racing, (2) experienced small boat racers who wish to race bigger boats, (3) all prospective buyers of racing-cruisers, especially those for whom racing is a prime objective, (4) those who wish to crew on racing-cruisers, and (5) experienced racing-cruiser sailors who want a handy compendium of reference material. The book attempts to cover boat selection, equipping, safety and accommodation features, hull and rig tuning, sails, basic tactics, strategy, and sailing techniques. Furthermore, it discusses in simple terms such semi-technical subjects as yacht design, aerodynamics, and handicap measurement rules. In addition, the book strives continually to point out major and minor differences between racing large and small boats.

It is assumed that the reader already knows the basic principles and terminology of sailing. In a sense this book is a sequel or a somewhat more advanced companion to *Hand, Reef, and Steer,* one of the author's former books published by Reilly & Lee Books. In the present book, not all nautical terms are defined, but rather those words pertaining to racing, those that are unusual or semi-technical, and those that have not been defined in *Hand, Reef, and Steer.* The system used for defining or explaining nautical terms and nomenclature is the same in both books. All new terms are italicized when first used and are followed by an explanation in the text. In addition, there is an index of the terms at the back of the book.

Here's wishing the reader satisfaction in selecting, tuning and racing his racing-cruiser. May he have his fair share of challenging windward legs, steady winds, and well-set starting lines.

1

An Introduction to Racing

Why Race?

Sailboat racing might be considered as both a means to an end and an end in itself. In the latter case it is racing for the love of racing as a sport; for the competition, excitement and stimulation; for the mastery of sailing skills; for the team spirit and crew camaraderie; and even for the almost unparalleled visual beauty of racing boats in action. In addition, of course, there is the great satisfaction to be gained by the acquisition and application of a great variety of knowledge that includes boat behavior, sails, wind, weather, tide and much more.

As a means to an end, racing rounds out the sailor's life and exposes him to many fine points of the art that, without competition, he might never come to know. Admittedly, formal racing is not everyone's cup of tea. There are those who like to cruise whether they be the offshore passage makers or the gunkholers, those who quietly push from one shallow creek to another. Cruising is a truly wonderful way of life, but for those who want to get the most from a balanced sailing life and to live sailing to the hilt, racing is a must even if it is only done occasionally. Racing does not merely broaden our range of experience, it sharpens our awareness, develops efficiency, and improves our seamanship. For example, after a lengthy period of leisurely cruising, many of us are satisfied with complacent and lethargic sailing, seldom bothering to improve a sheet lead or to set a light sail when there is a need for it. An occasional diet of racing will shake us from such lethargy, make us more aware of the need for rigging adjustments or sail trim, make us alert to changing conditions of the wind or tide, give us confidence to set the spinnaker or drive the boat in heavy weather. Thus is racing a means to an end: it will give us more pleasure and a better sense of values in all forms of sailing.

There are some sailors who profess a distaste for formal racing, but when these people own fast boats, they seldom shy away from a subtle brush or informal race. Although they may not care to admit it, most boat owners take pride in their skill as sailors and especially in the performance of their boats. Even the rare sailor who openly decries every form of racing can often be seen slyly changing course or improving sail trim when he finds his boat alongside another of similar size. Occasionally he can be caught casting a furtive glance in the direction of the other boat to judge the relative performance of his own craft. This is almost irresistible for a devoted sailor who owns a smart sailing boat. Chances are that any true sailing buff who never can be tempted to race owns a sluggish tub of a boat (but of course, he'll claim his boat is wonderfully comfortable or seaworthy).

With formal racing, a proper mental attitude has a marked effect on full enjoyment from the sport. First of all, newcomers to yacht racing must accept certain responsibilities. They must learn and abide by the rules of the game. They must familiarize themselves with the measurement rules and the racing rules, principally those which have to do with right of way situations. Impeccable honesty and sportsmanship are important in any sport, of course, but they are especially so in yacht racing, for there are no actual umpires or referees in this sport.

In boat racing there should be a balance or happy medium between levity and seriousness. There is no doubt that the top racing skippers have a determined and earnest desire to win; but when racing becomes grim, it ceases to be fun. Then, there is little point in doing it. However, a certain degree of calm seriousness from skipper and crew alike during a race is essential for the necessary concentration and attention to details.

We need never feel humiliated for simply losing a race. The main considerations should be to avoid unnecessary mistakes and to learn something from the mistakes we do make. After all, what we are really after is complete enjoyment of the sport, and the greatest rewards come from gradual improvement and the challenge of trying to approach perfection in sailing skills and seamanship.

Kinds of Races

Although there are several variations in the way that sailboats can race, the two basic forms of competition are boat-for-boat and handicap racing. In the former case, identical boats or boats of similar speed potentials race over the same course.

With this form of competition, the boat that finishes first, or has the least *elapsed time,* the actual time from start to finish, is the winner.

Handicap racing, however, involves boats of different sizes and different speed potentials competing against each other, and therefore the first boat to finish is not necessarily the winner. Performances of handicap racers are predicted by actually measuring various features of each individual boat and applying these measurements to a *rating formula.* As a result of this, each boat is given a *rating* or *rated length* which is assigned a *time allowance* in seconds per mile. The allowance one boat receives from another in a given race is the difference between their time allowances, as shown in standard tables, multiplied by the distance in miles of the race. The elapsed time of each boat is taken and time allowances are applied to give each boat a *corrected time.* The boat with the lowest corrected time is the winner.

Rating measurements are the principal dimensions and characteristics of a boat which have a direct bearing on her potential speed or performance. These include length, beam, draft, *displacement* or weight, sail area, and certain propeller measurements. Measurement rules are rather complex, so most of chapter seven will be devoted to them.

Most racing-cruisers compete under handicap systems, but if there are enough boats of the same stock class (identical boats of the same design), they may race each other as a class on a boat-for-boat basis. Examples in the United States are the Alberg 30 and Cal 40 classes. Of course these boats may and usually do participate in handicap racing as well.

A relatively new development in racing-cruiser competitions is the *One Ton Cup* (and *Half Ton Cup*) concept. This kind of racing, named after a historic trophy but only recently competed for by racing-cruisers, pits boats of various designs with almost identical ratings against each other boat-for-boat. One Ton Cup racing may well gain in popularity, but it has at least one drawback in that the owner of this type of racer cannot try to improve the speed of his boat with any physical changes that would increase her rating above the allowed limit.

What we have been talking about thus far might be termed *fleet racing* where individuals in a fleet of boats race against every other boat in the group.

This is the usual form of racing, but on certain occasions boats *match race* or *team race.* Match racing is limited to a pair of boats, one boat against another. Although this type of competition is relatively infrequent, it has been brought to the public's attention through the America's Cup races where, in recent times, one twelve meter boat has been matched against another.

Team racing matches a team of boats, usually a small group of preferably four or five boats, against another team or, in rare instances, several teams having the same number of boats. This kind of competition is most often seen when one yacht club challenges another to race in identical or nearly identical boats. Sometimes an interclub competition involving many clubs will use class boats to fleet race in a *round robin series* with one club using one boat. In this case there is an exchange of boats with each crew sailing a different boat in each race.

Both match racing and team racing involve special tactics or actually subtle variations of standard tactics. Chapter 10 will be devoted to boat-vs-boat tactics and general course strategy, and there will be an occasional mention of match racing but, for the most part, the chapter will concentrate on the tactics of the most common form of competition, fleet racing.

Race Courses

All race courses can be considered as belonging to one of two broad classifications: the *closed course* or the *point-to-point* course. The latter involves racing from one geographic location to another. The race distance may be great or small as long as the start and finish are not in the same general locality. Points of sailing during this kind of race depend to a large extent upon the vagaries of wind direction, but many courses include intermediate turning marks to give legs of varying directions, thereby increasing the chances that there will be at least some windward work and/or downwind sailing suitable for carrying spinnakers. Most distance and ocean races are point-to-point.

Closed courses have their starts and finishes in the same or nearly the same general locality. The usual day race over a fairly short closed course is often referred to as a round-the-buoys race. In this kind of race, the courses are laid out to vary the points of sailing, to give reaches, runs and especially beats to windward. Courses are usually

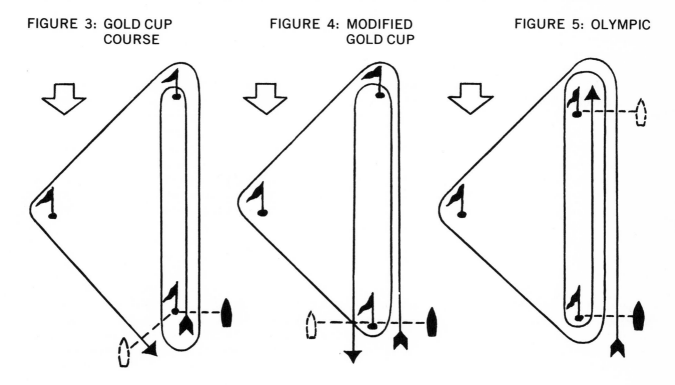

FIGURE 1: WINDWARD-LEEWARD COURSES

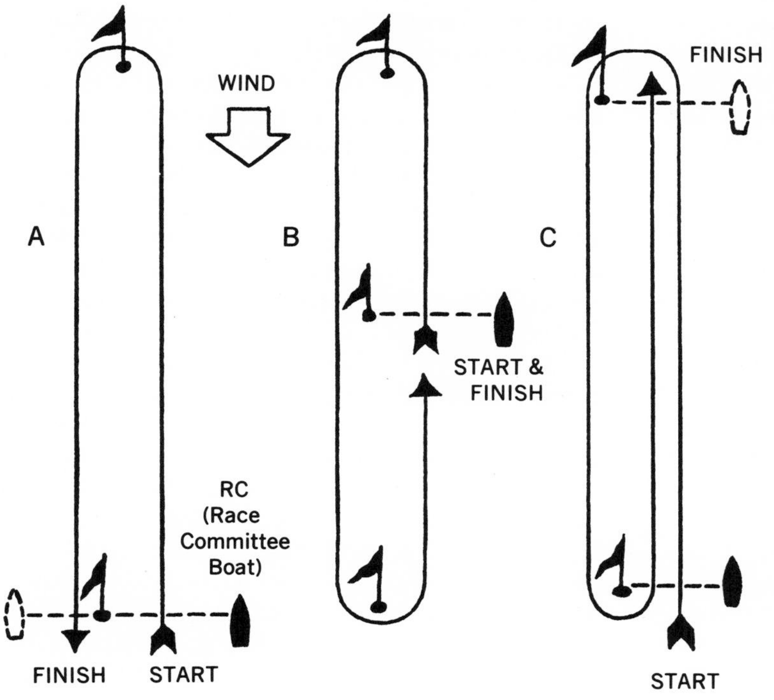

WIND

A

B

C

RC
(Race
Committee
Boat)

FINISH   START

START &
FINISH

FINISH

START

FIGURE 2: TRIANGULAR
COURSE

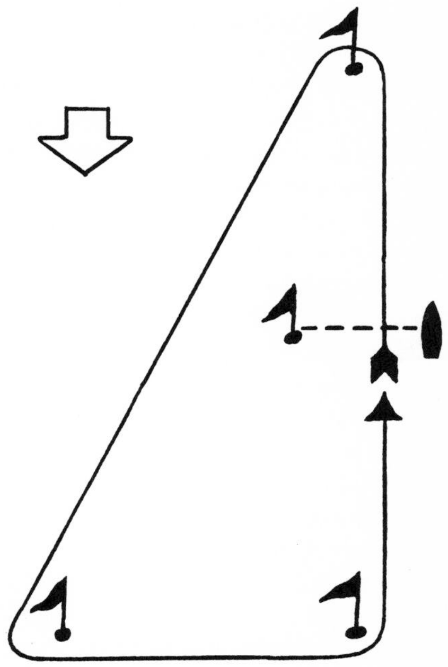

FIGURE 3: GOLD CUP
COURSE

FIGURE 4: MODIFIED
GOLD CUP

FIGURE 5: OLYMPIC

planned to keep beam reaches and close reaches to a minimum because boats are least likely to change positions on these points of sailing. A race comprised of reaching legs that are too close to the wind for effective spinnaker sailing is very likely to end up as a "parade" with each boat being unable to pass the next boat ahead of her. Most closed courses are laid out to give long windward legs for it is generally agreed that working to windward gives the greatest test of ability in helmsmanship and tactics, in non-planing boats at least. Whenever possible, the course should be planned so that the first turning mark lies dead to windward.

Short, closed courses are nearly always planned to be *windward-leeward, triangular,* or some combination of both. The most common forms of these courses are illustrated in figures 1 through 5. These figures show typical windward-leeward, triangular, *Gold Cup, modified Gold Cup,* and *Olympic* courses. Figure 1 shows three windward-leeward variations with "A" being the simplest form of an acceptable course. Variation "B" involves an extra turning mark and places the starting line in the middle of the beating leg to give an initial short beat followed by a long run and another short beat to the finish. "C" is similar to "A" except that there is an extra windward leg which puts the finish line at the first turning mark. Figure 2 shows a typical triangular course, having a right angle, but such a course may be equilateral or any other triangular shape as long as it gives the desirable points of sailing. The Gold Cup course, Figure 3, has a windward-leeward round followed by a triangular round, while the modified Gold Cup, Figure 4, puts the triangular round first and the windward-leeward second. The Olympic course in Figure 5 is similar to the modified Gold Cup with an extra windward leg.

All turning marks should be left on the same *hand* (side) unless participants are instructed to the contrary. Port turns, as shown in Figures 1 through 5, are preferable since they allow boats to round the windward mark on the starboard tack, which gives them the right of way. However, in the interest of safety when the course is laid out so that boats have to cross their own tracks soon after rounding a mark, there may be a mixture of rounding designations with some marks being left to port and others to starboard. Turning marks may be government marks such as channel markers, buoys, beacons, lighthouses, etc., or they may be partially or entirely privately owned club marks. The latter type may be flags mounted in row boats or brightly painted styrofoam buoys on pylons. Often these markers will be fitted with pieces of shiny metal to increase visibility.

Very often certain locales are geographically restricted so that perfect windward-leeward and triangular courses cannot be laid out. In such cases it becomes necessary to sail irregular courses, but these are usually oriented to the prevailing winds, and they can nearly always be planned to give at least one good windward leg per race with some variety in points of sailing on the other legs.

Starting and Finishing Lines

Figure 6 shows three types of starting or finishing lines. For racing-cruisers "A" is the most usual type. Each line is imaginary and runs between two marks, or between a mark and a white flag on a *committee boat*. This boat, usually displaying a flag marked "RC" (for race committee), may be any kind large enough to accommodate several of the sponsoring club's committeemen but not so large that she blocks the starting boats or interferes with their wind. She needs a rig for hoisting signals. Each contestant attempts to cross the starting line headed towards the first turning mark with full way on, precisely as the starting signal is given.

As shown in Figures 1 through 6A, it is customary to set up the starting line so that the starting mark is left on the same hand as are the other marks of the course. If marks are left to port as shown in the diagrams, then the starting mark is on the port-hand end of the line when heading towards the first turning mark), and the committee boat is to the starboard. Although this practice is customary it is by no means invariable. Some race committees prefer to place the committee boat at the port-hand end of the line because boats often tend to jam up on the starboard side of the line. This crowding occurs because many skippers like to start at the windward end of the line on the starboard tack. However, a port-side committee boat can be dangerous on a windward start, because it can create a trap, often called *coffin corner,* for starboard tack boats on the extreme port-side of the line when there is a last minute heading wind shift. This is explained in Figure 7. If boat "A" sails into the shaded area she is trapped because she cannot bear off sufficiently to clear the committee boat, and she cannot tack because of

FIGURE 6: TYPICAL STARTING LINES

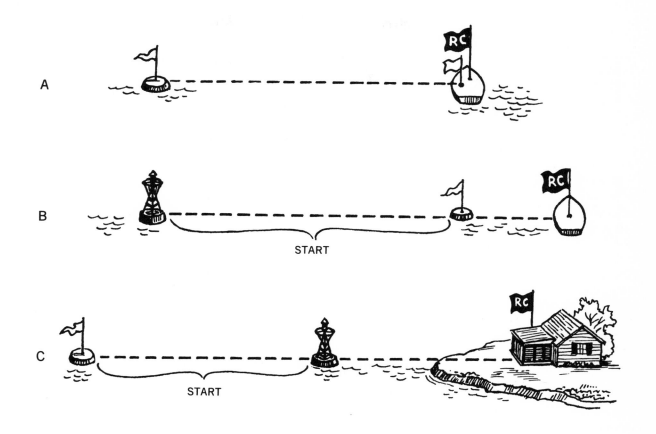

A

B

START

C

START

the proximity of boat "B". "A" must bear off as shown by the curved arrow, before she reaches the shaded area.

It is also customary (but optional) to set the finish line so that the finishing mark is passed on the same hand as the other marks. It can be seen in Figures 1, 3, and 4 that the committee boats have changed positions relative to their accompanying markers for the sake of mark passing uniformity. Of course, this method requires moving the committee boat, but quite often she must be moved anyhow if the line's mark is a fixed buoy, because in most cases the finish line should be no more than half the length of the starting line. Of course, a finish line in the middle of the windward leg, as in Figures 1B and 2, makes it unnecessary to move the committee boat unless shortening the finish line is the consideration. The finish line is usually set at

right angles to the last leg, as shown in Figures 1 through 5.

Most competent race committees try to set the starting line in such a way that the first turning mark lies dead to windward and the line lies nearly at right angles to the wind. Of course, this is often not possible. On many point-to-point races, for example, reaching and running starts are necessary, but whenever possible, the start should be to windward. Even if the course cannot be planned so that the first turning mark is dead to windward, *the line should be set nearly square to the wind*. The reason for this is that such a setting tends to spread contestants fairly evenly along the line. The object of such a line is to avoid bunching or jams near the line's mark or committee boat. Theoretically, every point on the perfectly set line should be equally attractive. An argument in favor of windward

FIGURE 7: COFFIN CORNER

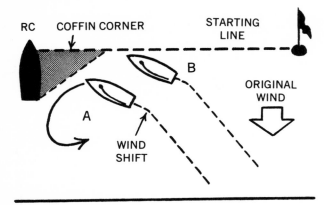

FIGURE 8: RECOMMENDED LINE FOR WINDWARD STARTS

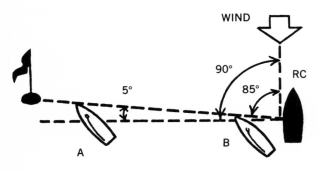

Boat A is slightly ahead of Boat B

starts is that beating tends to spread the distance between contestants so that boats do not arrive simultaneously at the first turning mark.

In attempting to achieve the ideal windward starting line, some race committees slant the line slightly away from the right angle by about five or even ten degrees with the port end slightly closer to the first turning mark (see Figure 8). The reason for this is that, given a line exactly ninety degrees to the wind, many starboard tack starters will crowd the starboard end of the line, trying to get to windward of their adversaries. Also with a perfectly square line, those starboard tack starters to leeward will lack the right of way after tacking and thus will be unable to tack if they so desire immediately after the start. This tends to make the starboard end of the line slightly more attractive.

6

Slanting the line away from the perpendicular makes the end that is closer to the first mark more favorable (see Figure 8). This will be explained in greater detail when we discuss starting tactics in Chapter 8. Line slanting on windward starts should be very slight because overdoing it would overly favor the port end and cause boats to crowd at that end.

It is interesting to note that in old editions of the *Race Committee Handbook,* published by the *North American Yacht Racing Union* (our national organization that sets up rules and standards for yacht racing), a ten degree slant is recommended, while the latest edition (1965) recommends an approximate five degree slant. Actually the degree of slant should be determined by a judgment of all factors that would favor either end of the line, such as tide, wind, anticipated courses of most boats, and so forth.

With reaching starts, line slanting is (or should be) much more drastic when the line is cocked as much as fifteen to thirty degrees away from a perpendicular to the course of the first turning mark with the leeward end considerably closer than the windward end to the first mark. This increases the attractiveness of the leeward end, which prevents crowding at the windward end. With running starts, however, the line is approximately square to the course to the first mark.

The length of the starting line is determined by the size and number of boats participating. A general rule of thumb is that for windward starts, the line should be slightly more than the product of the number of boats times the over-all length of the largest boat. For example, if there are twenty boats racing with the largest being forty feet, the line should be at least 800 to perhaps 1000 feet long.

Starting System

Races are started with both visual and audible signals. The audible signals are traditionally made with guns or signal cannons, but nowadays the extremely loud freon horns are often used. Visual signals are in the form of flags or various geometric *shapes,* usually cylinders or cones, that are raised or hoisted a short distance up the committee boat's mast.

The following starting system is customary: at ten minutes before the start a *warning signal* is made, audibly and visibly at the same instant. Four minutes and thirty seconds later, the visual warn-

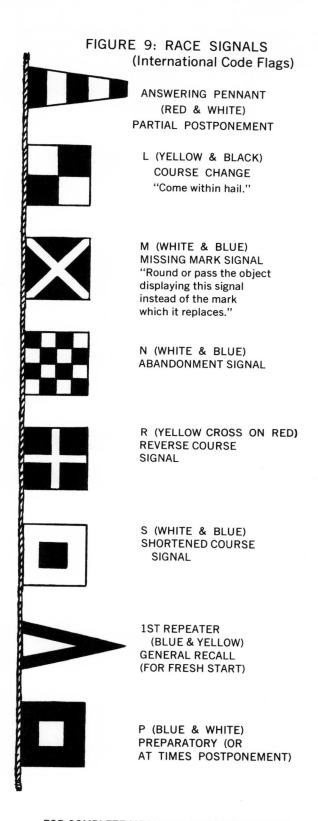

FIGURE 9: RACE SIGNALS
(International Code Flags)

ANSWERING PENNANT
(RED & WHITE)
PARTIAL POSTPONEMENT

L (YELLOW & BLACK)
COURSE CHANGE
"Come within hail."

M (WHITE & BLUE)
MISSING MARK SIGNAL
"Round or pass the object
displaying this signal
instead of the mark
which it replaces."

N (WHITE & BLUE)
ABANDONMENT SIGNAL

R (YELLOW CROSS ON RED)
REVERSE COURSE
SIGNAL

S (WHITE & BLUE)
SHORTENED COURSE
SIGNAL

1ST REPEATER
(BLUE & YELLOW)
GENERAL RECALL
(FOR FRESH START)

P (BLUE & WHITE)
PREPARATORY (OR
AT TIMES POSTPONEMENT)

FOR COMPLETE MEANINGS SEE NAYRU RULES

ing signal is lowered, and thirty seconds later a *preparatory signal* is given audibly and visibly. Four minutes and thirty seconds later the preparatory signal is lowered, and thirty seconds after this, the *starting signal* is made, again by sight and sound. Because guns can misfire and horns can fail, the visual signals govern, and the exact time of the start is judged by the raising of the flag or shape. The customary visual signals (especially for racing-cruisers) are: a white flag or shape for the ten-minute warning signal, a blue flag or shape for the five-minute preparatory signal, and a red flag or shape for the start.

Frequently, many different classes of boats use the same starting line. A large fleet of racing-cruisers is often divided into classes designated as A, B, C, etc. according to number and size or measurement ratings. Class A is generally made up of the largest boats. In such cases, one class usually starts after another, and very often the starting signal for class A will be the warning signal for class B, the start of B will be the warning for class C, and so forth. Most race committees explain the exact system used in race instructions, mailed or otherwise distributed before the race.

Other signals used frequently by the race committee are shown in Figure 9. These include postponement, abandonment, missing mark, reverse course, shortened course, and recall signals. When code flag "P" is used for a preparatory signal, the warning signal is usually the class flag or another distinctive signal, and the start is signified by lowering both the warning and preparatory signals. All these signals are explained in greater detail in the NAYRU (North American Yacht Racing Union) Racing Rules. The usual reasons for the postponement or abandonment of a race have to do with the weather—either too much wind, too little wind, or fog. The general recall signal is given when many boats have crossed the line before the starting signal and all boats are recalled for a fresh start on the next gun. When only one or a few boats cross the line early only these boats are recalled and there is no new starting signal. Usually the committee boat will give one horn blast for each early starter, then the committee will endeavor to notify each yacht recalled by signaling or hailing, but it is the responsibility of each yacht to make a proper start. An early starter must recross the line and start over again. In order that they command attention, flag signals (except for "R" and "S" before the warning signal) are accom-

7

panied by sound signals.

Race Instructions, Requirements, and Equipment

Race instructions are usually in the written form of a circular, mailed or handed to each contestant before the race. Sometimes these written instructions are accompanied by oral instructions given at a skippers' meeting held prior to a race or series. The race circular contains vital information such as the race date, racing rules under which the race is being sailed (nearly always the NAYRU rules in the United States), the course, marks, signals, time and location of the start, the location of the finish line, scoring system, method of breaking ties, any special instructions or exceptions to standard NAYRU procedures, length of course, time limit if any, protest procedure, prizes, postponement or abandonment procedure, etc. Many race circulars even include a rough chart of the area showing location of marks and the course.

Most race committees require that participants fill out entry forms before entering a race. This is especially important for handicap races in order that the committee has all the proper rating information. Reproduced in this chapter is a typical entry blank, in this case a form used by the Chesapeake Bay Yacht Racing Association. The racing number required in the form is the large number, for identification purposes, sewn on the sails of each participating boat. These numbers should be on both sides of mainsails and spinnakers, and overlapping jibs. Numbers are assigned according to area location by the NAYRU directly or often by the NAYRU through the local yacht racing association.

The word "class" in the entry form means any particular group (one-design or handicap) to which the entering boat belongs and for which there is a race scheduled, as shown in the race circular. The space on the form devoted to ratings is for handicap racers. The blank after the word "cruising" is for the rating of an entering racing-cruiser which, for CBYRA events, uses the *Cruising Club of America* measurement rating. "MORC" stands for *Midget Ocean Racing Club* and this is a national measurement rule for small racing-cruisers. The word "racing" refers to strict racing type boats with few if any cruising accommodations, which race under their own handicap measurement rule. "Deltas" are a local Chesapeake Bay class which also have their own handicap rule. As can

be seen in the entry form, valid and up-to-date rating certificates are required, and also participants usually must belong to a recognized yacht club. Details and explanations of the most frequently used measurement rating rules will be given in Chapter 7.

The following is a partial check list of recommended racing equipment to be carried aboard: (1) race circular, (2) NAYRU Racing Rules, (3) stop watch and clock, (4) detailed charts of the area, (5) compass, (6) binoculars, (7) current tables, (8) class rules or handbook of local racing organization containing local regulations and list of competitors with their ratings, (9) parallel rules or course protractor, (10) dividers, (11) protest flag, code flag "B" or a solid red flag, (12) spare parts and extras such as battens, sail tape, assortment of shackles, pins, turnbuckles, blocks, line, sail stops, sewing gear, marline, ribbon and thread for tell-tales, etc., (13) masthead wind sock or indicator, (14) small anchor and line, (15) lead line, (16) basic tools—screw driver, pliers, etc., (17) safety equipment.

The last item, 17, requires extensive comment so it will be considered in Chapter 4 where there will be equipment lists for both short on-soundings races and offshore races. Many items in the preceding list should be carried on board whether racing or not, but all are listed with the prime consideration of usefulness during a race. For example, the extra items are to replace gear that may be carried away so that the boat can continue racing, and the small anchor is of great importance in light air when sailing against a strong foul current. The protest flag is flown when a boat has been fouled in a right of way situation, or when it is desired to protest another yacht for any racing rule infringement or violation of the race instructions. Racing rules will be discussed in Chapter 7.

C·B·Y·R·A

STANDARD RACE ENTRY BLANK

TO: ....
SPONSORING CLUB

Race .... Date ....

Class .... Racing Number ....

Name of Yacht .... Rig ....

Color of Hull ....

Owner .... Address ....

....

Skipper .... Address ....

....

This Yacht conforms in every way to her class requirements and possesses a valid Mesurement or Registration Certificate. ....
YES/NO

OFFICIAL C. B. Y. R. A. RATING

Cruising .... Racing .... Delta .... M O R C ....

Date of Latest Measurement Certificate ....

Name of Measurer ....

Since date of latest measurement, has any change of any kind been made which might affect the rating? ....
YES/NO

I agree to abide by all rules established for this Regatta or

Race, and I release the ....
SPONSORING CLUB
its officers, members and employees, and the members of the Regatta or Race Committees from all liability by reason of injury either to the Yacht above entered or to myself or my crew

SKIPPER ....
SIGNATURE

CLUB AFFILIATION ....

1. Print all entries except for signature.
2. Send to Race Committee of sponsoring club.

2

Thoughts on Hull Design

Some sailors seem to have the attitude that since hulls are the way they are and existing hulls can't be changed drastically, they might as well leave hull design to the naval architect and not bother to investigate the subject. This thinking falls short for several reasons. First of all, hull design is a fascinating subject and should be of real interest to sailors, especially those who race or sail offshore. The study of hull shape teaches us about the performance and behavior characteristics of boats, and this is not only important in getting to know your own new boat but in understanding the boats of competitors. This latter point is of real importance in handicap racing when boats of various designs are competing (more will be said about this later when we discuss competition tactics).

As for your own boat, a little understanding of hull design will help guide you in such important matters as determining the best angle of heel, best fore-and-aft trim, amount and distribution of ballast, obtaining favorable measurement ratings, managing your boat in heavy weather, helm balance, selection of propeller, centerboard adjustment, optimum sailing angles, fairing and minor hull modifications, steering control, amount of gear to be carried and stowage of same, placement of tanks, and so forth. The new boat buyer has a great variety of hulls to choose from, and often he will have to make many design judgments after simply looking at boats, plans, dimensions, advertising information, and written data. These judgments will include such vital characteristics as stability, seaworthiness, speed in various winds, behavior in head seas, performance to windward, steering tendencies, general racing competitiveness, and more.

As a final argument for knowing some of the principles of hull design, it seems logical that the more we learn about all aspects of sailing, the more successful we will be and the more fun we will get from it.

Today, sailing yacht design has ostensibly reached a high degree of scientific sophistication. A great deal of theoretical research is being done, and much use is being made of computers, wind tunnels, and model testing tanks. Most stock hulls are thoroughly tested in the tank before they are produced. Yet despite advanced technology sailboat designing remains an art as well as a science. In fact, several of our most successful designers are men who have little if any formal training as naval architects. Tank tests give guidance and verification to a designer largely through comparative data, but the original concept is born in his mind. The designer still must make use of his "eye" for form, his intuition and empirical knowledge developed through observation and sailing experience.

It is little wonder that the tank cannot, at present at least, "design" a boat or give the naval architect all the answers. Imagine the complexity of forces and resistances working on a yacht offshore, beating against a head sea. The hull is being pushed through the water in a forward direction while *yawed,* or turned askew and at varying angles of heel, while simultaneously it is *swaying* (being moved bodily sideways), *heaving* (rising and falling), yawing (being turned from its forward direction), rolling, and pitching. Meanwhile, the helmsman is constantly changing the rudder angle to vary the effect of lift and drag forces acting on the hull.

There is really very little that is radically new in sailing yacht design. Many of the fads and trends of today were tried and used in only slightly different ways by such designers as Nathaniel Herreshoff, Starling Burgess, F. D. Lawley, William Gardner, Clinton Crane, and others. To be convinced of this, all one has to do is leaf through the design sections of the yachting books or periodicals of just before or after 1900. Of course many gradual improvements in boat designs have come through slow evolution and step-by-step refinements.

The greatest changes in recent years influencing yacht design are new construction materials, changes in rating rules, and the yachtsman's and designer's concept of what constitutes a cruising or racing type. Let me elucidate on this last point. Around forty or so years ago a cruising boat was usually thought of as a heavy, rugged, seakindly,

FIGURE 10: HULL DESCRIPTIVE & DIMENSIONAL NOMENCLATURE

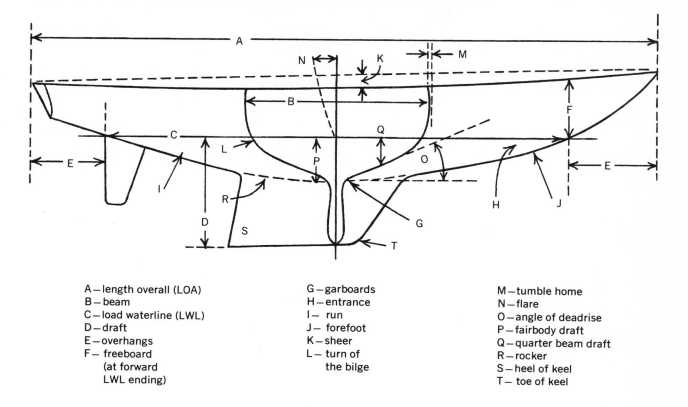

A — length overall (LOA)
B — beam
C — load waterline (LWL)
D — draft
E — overhangs
F — freeboard
(at forward
LWL ending)

G — garboards
H — entrance
I — run
J — forefoot
K — sheer
L — turn of
the bilge

M — tumble home
N — flare
O — angle of deadrise
P — fairbody draft
Q — quarter beam draft
R — rocker
S — heel of keel
T — toe of keel

not especially *weatherly* (close-winded) craft. These boats were built for comfortable cruising and they were intended to be raced only rarely and then only in a relatively informal way against boats of similar type. By comparison, many of the modern, so-called cruising boats that are racing today, especially those light displacement types with dinghy-shaped hulls and fin keels, are out-and-out racing machines. At least such boats probably would have been so considered if they had been put into the cruising divisions of the past. With most popular cruisers racing today, great emphasis is put on racing ability. Although this type of boat is often designated as a "cruising" class boat in contemporary race circulars, perhaps the more accurate appellation is racing-cruiser because she has been designed at least as much for racing as for cruising. (This name should not be confused with the European *International Cruising-Racer classes,* which are divided into 7, 8, 9, 10.5 and 12 meter classes. These boats race each other on a boat-for-boat basis.)

Since boat designing nearly always involves compromise or the accentuation of some qualities at the expense of others, it might be assumed that a boat designed specifically for cruising is more seaworthy than one designed for both racing and cruising. However, this is not necessarily true. The modern racing-cruiser is designed for offshore sailing, and she may be light and fast, but she is also strong and able. Compared with the cruiser of yesteryear, the modern counterpart is not even sacrificing much in the way of space below deck. What she probably does sacrifice, however, is a certain ease of handling and *seakindliness,* a word that has a very different meaning than seaworthiness. The latter has to do with a vessel being able to "take it" at sea regardless of the crew's comfort, but a seakindly boat has a relatively easy and comfortable motion and is relatively easy to steer. A tough, modern, fiberglass racing-cruiser of light displacement with flat bilges may pound into a head-sea hard enough to rattle the teeth of her crew, but they won't care about a few days of discomfort if the boat holds together and there's a chance of doing well in the race. That's all part of the game.

Preliminary Terms and Definitions

Before discussing the basic principles of hull design, let us review some descriptive terms and definitions. Figure 10 illustrates many basic dimensional terms and most of these are self explanatory. A few might require a brief comment or two.

Strictly speaking, *garboard* means the plank, or *strake,* next to the keel, but the word is also used to refer to that part of the hull that is next to the keel on metal or molded boats. The word *rocker* is used to describe the fore-and-aft upward curvature, from amidships toward each end, of the bottom of the keel, but may also refer to the fore-and-aft curvature of a boat's bottom or bilge. *Fairbody draft* refers to the depth below the water's surface of the deepest part of the hull's actual body (not including the keel). The *turn of the bilge* is the athwartships curve where the boat's bottom turns into her topsides. A *slack bilge* makes a slow, gradual turn, while a *hard bilge* makes a sharper, tight turn. The *angle of deadrise* refers to the upward slanting of the bottom from the keel to the turn of the bilge. A boat with an extremely low angle of deadrise would have a nearly flat bottom. *Flare* is the outward slanting of the topsides while *tumble home* refers to the topsides turning inward near the rail. *Sheerlines* are of several types, *concave* or conventional (shown in Figure 10), straight, *reversed* or *hogged* (having a humped-backed appearance), and *powder horn sheer* (being concave aft and reversed forward).

Figure 11 is a perspective sketch of a hull to show her lines. *Water lines* are the horizontal lines representing planes passing through the hull parallel to the water's surface. The *load water line* (LWL) is the actual contact line of the water's surface and the hull when the boat is floating upright. *Sections* are the lines formed by vertical planes passing through the hull at right angles to the fore-and-aft centerline. They usually divide the LWL into ten equal parts. The *midship section* is at the midpoint of the LWL and is usually numbered station five. *Buttocks* are the lines formed by vertical planes slicing the hull parallel to the fore and aft centerline. The *diagonals* (not shown in Figure 11) are lines formed by oblique, longitudinal planes which, from the fore-and-aft view, run from the centerline downward and outward and cut the sections approximately at right angles. Plans are shown in three views. The side view, called the *sheer plan,* shows the sections as straight vertical lines, the waterlines as horizontal straight lines, and the buttocks as curved fore-and-aft lines. The fore and aft view, called the *body plan,* shows the buttocks as straight vertical lines, the waterlines as horizontal straight lines, and the sections as curves (usually "S" type curves in a round-bottom keel boat). The view looking down on the hull, by convention usually showing half its width, is the *half-breadth plan,* and this shows the sections as straight lines at right angles to the centerline, the buttocks as straight lines parallel to the centerline, and the waterline as curves running fore-and-aft.

Most of the following definitions are short and simple. In some cases these may not be entirely adequate for complete understanding, but elaborations will be made later in the chapter.

Displacement–actual weight. As Archimedes discovered, a floating object displaces its own weight.

Center of Gravity (CG)—the point at which the entire weight of the hull may be considered as concentrated.

Buoyancy—upward pressure of the water exerted on the hull equal to the hull's displacement.

Center of Buoyancy (CB)—center of gravity of the volume of water displaced by the hull. When the hull is upright, the CB and CG will lie on the same vertical line both laterally and *longitudinally* (fore and aft).

Metacenter (transverse metacenter)—the point of intersection of a vertical line through the hull's CB when it is floating upright with a vertical line through the new CB when the hull is heeled at a small angle (See Figure 34).

Stability—tendency of a boat to return to an upright position after being heeled. A *stiff* boat is very stable, while a *crank* or *tender* boat heels easily.

Directional stability–tendency to hold a straight course or not *yaw,* swing from side to side around the vertical axis.

Yaw Angle, also *angle of leeway*–the angular difference between a boat's centerline and her actual course made good owing to her making leeway or crabbing but not including any effects of current. Yaw angle is not a constant factor for a given

FIGURE 11: LINES & PERSPECTIVE SKETCH

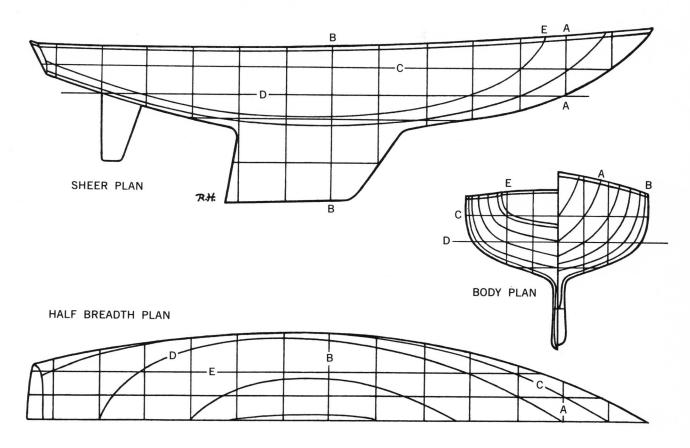

SHEER PLAN

BODY PLAN

HALF BREADTH PLAN

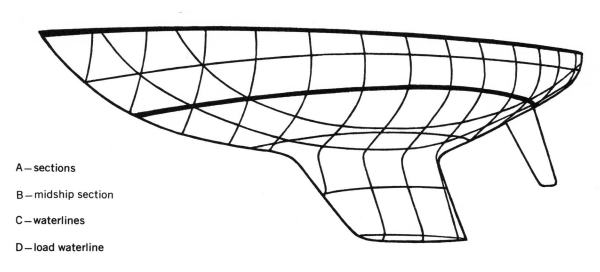

A — sections

B — midship section

C — waterlines

D — load waterline

E — buttocks

13

hull design, of course, but varies for any hull according to conditions of wind and sea.

Helm balance–relating to *weather helm,* when a boat turns into the wind, or *lee helm* when the boat turns away from the wind with the helm unattended in both cases.

Lateral plane–the immersed profile area or underwater, fore-and-aft, vertical plane.

Center of lateral resistance (CLR)–the geometric center of the lateral plane or the theoretical point at which the hull could be pushed sidewise without turning.

Center of effort (CE)–the geometric center of a sail's silhouette or that of the entire sail plan where the wind's side force theoretically is concentrated. Helm balance has to do with the relationship of the CE of the sails that are set to the CLR.

Wave-making resistance–waves caused by the hull's forward movement which become increasingly harmful to speed the faster a heavy boat moves. In general, designers try to shape the hull so that as little propulsion power as possible will be wasted in forming waves. Wave-making resistance depends on hull shape, displacement, and length.

Form resistance–additional resistance, apart from wave making, due to the formation of eddies.

Induced drag–increased resistance arising from heeling and making leeway.

Wetted surface resistance–the skin friction between the *wetted surface* or immersed surface area of the hull, and the water. Designers often lump wave, form, and induced resistance into one category called *residual resistance*. Residual resistance can be found from tank testing by measuring total resistance after model towing and then calculating skin friction and subtracting this from the total resistance.

Planing–high speed sailing when the hull rides up on its bow wave and partially escapes from its own wave system. Planing requires a planing hull, one that is fairly flat and of light displacement, in conjunction with good winds. Following seas are definitely helpful. The opposite of a planing hull is a *displacement hull* which cannot plane and is limited in speed by its own wave system.

Speed-length ratio–The speed of a boat is relative to her length. The speed-length ratio compares a boat's speed with her length and is expressed in the formula

$$R = \frac{V}{\sqrt{L}}$$

R is the speed-length ratio, V is velocity in knots (nautical miles per hour), and L is the load waterline length in feet. For example, a boat making four knots with an LWL of sixteen feet has a speed-length ratio of 1.0, the same as a twenty-five foot boat making five knots. Most racing-cruisers have a maximum speed length ratio of about 1.35.

Displacement-length ratio–

$$\frac{D}{(.01L)^3}$$

D is the displacement in tons and L is load waterline length. This ratio is useful in estimating resistance and for determining a boat's proper weight for her length or visa versa.

Sail area-displacement ratio–comparing sail area (SA) in square feet to displacement in cubic feet is expressed as

$$\frac{SA}{d^{2/3}}$$

a guide in determining amount of sail for a hull of given weight.

Sail area-wetted surface ratio–

$$\frac{SA}{WS}$$

gives a good indication of light weather performance.

Ballast-displacement ratio–

$$\frac{B}{D}$$

comparing weight of keel with displacement, gives some indication of stability.

Lift-drag ratio–L/D. Although this is usually associated with aerodynamics, the same principle is involved in hydrodynamics. The keel is a hydrofoil which alters the direction of water flow to create a *lift* force at right angles to the direction of flow and *drag,* or resistance in the direction of flow. The price for obtaining lift is drag, and the lift-drag ratio measures the efficiency of the hydrofoil.

Aspect ratio–a comparison of height and width of an airfoil or hydrofoil expressed by the formula:

14

$$AR = \frac{(height)^2}{area}$$

or often simply luff length divided by foot length for sails.

Moment—a tendency to produce motion especially about an axis. Examples are, heeling moment, its opposite, righting moment, and moment of inertia, all of which relate to a hull turning on its axis. The moment of a force is the force times the lever arm or distance from the axis.

Scantlings—specifications for construction, minimal sizes and weights of structural parts such as frames, beams, and planking for various types and sizes of vessels.

Basic Design Considerations

At the risk of great over-simplification, it might be said that the designer of a sailboat's hull is primarily concerned with two major factors, (1) axial turning and (2) resistance. The hull turns around three axes: the vertical, longitudinal, and transverse as shown in Figure 12. Turning on the vertical axis relates to steering control, yawing, and helm balance. Longitudinal axial turning relates to rolling, heeling, and righting, or transverse stability. Transverse axial turning relates to such matters as pitching and hull trim.

The second major factor, resistance, can be divided into two categories, lateral and forward. Lateral, of course, is concerned with reduction of leeway and includes such considerations as draft, shape of the underwater lateral plane, and hydrodynamic lift. Forward resistance affects the speed of the hull through the water, and this is concerned with wetted surface resistance, wavemaking resistance, form resistance, induced drag, and windage, the last of which may help or hinder depending on the point of sailing. A hull's axial turning characteristics and its forward and lateral resistance will depend on its dimensions, sail plan, form, and displacement.

Displacement

In this country, the gradual trend has been towards moderately light displacement racing-cruisers. Although a fairly recent change in the CCA measurement rule has been somewhat discouraging to the trend, it will probably continue because there are many advantages in moderately

FIGURE 12: AXIAL TURNING

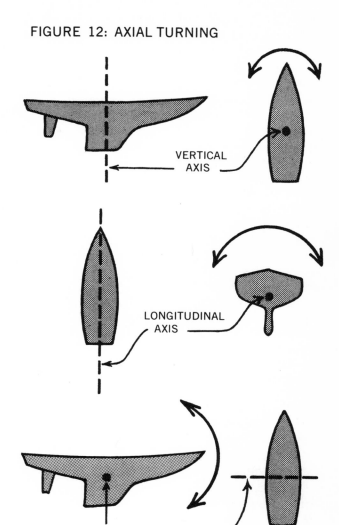

VERTICAL AXIS

LONGITUDINAL AXIS

TRANSVERSE AXIS

light designs. Some of the principal advantages are good performance over a wide range of conditions, generally lower cost, racing competitiveness over the most frequently sailed short and middle distance courses, and certain special qualities for cruising and offshore racing. These special qualities are: (1) relatively great space in length and breadth because a light displacement boat gives more useable space for a given weight, (2) relatively great buoyancy which is essential to seaworthiness and dryness, and (3) the fact that only a relatively small rig, light gear and consequently a smaller crew are required. It is generally agreed that a good quality light displacement boat is somewhat less expensive to build than one of heavy displacement because cost is roughly proportional to weight. The light boat is also generally cheaper to maintain. In races that are not extremely long, most light displacement boats are quite competitive provided their ratings are reasonably good, because their hulls are easily driven, and they are capable of especially high speeds in good winds on the frequently encountered reaching and running points of sailing. However, these boats may be at a disadvantage in long distance races when they are deeply loaded with gear and supplies.

As an argument for heavy displacement, there have been some high performing moderately heavy boats, and these do not seem to suffer as much from heavy loading. Some sailors mistakenly assume that light boats are better than heavy ones in light airs, but more often than not, the opposite is true, because the heavy boat has the larger rig. The height of the rig is especially important in light going. In addition, the heavy boat has more momentum to carry her from one patch of breeze to the next. The light boat will pick up faster in puffs, but she will be stopped quicker by seas when the breeze is light. Actually, a great criterion of light weather performance is the sail area to wetted surface ratio, which will be discussed briefly when we consider sail area.

Compared to her heavy sister, a light displacement boat usually performs best when it blows, because she has less form resistance. One performance criterion for moderate to heavy winds when the hull moves at high speeds is the displacement-length ratio which varies according to boat size, but which gives figures generally ranging from 240 to 400 for moderate size, smart racing-cruisers. Those on the low side, the lighter boats, will probably have less resistance at high speeds. However, in heavy weather sailing there are other important factors to consider such as stability and the ability to carry sail.

America initiated the trend towards light displacement offshore cruising boats when young Olin Stephens designed the *Dorade* back in 1930. She has been hailed as the first truly modern ocean racer, and she was quite light by the standards of those times. Immediately after World War II, however, the British took over leadership in this design trend when certain loopholes in the RORC (Royal Ocean Racing Club) rating rule were exploited. First and most famous of these new, light racing-cruisers was the Laurent Giles designed *Myth of Malham,* a magnificent performer especially in strong winds.

With the exception of a few ultra light types developed by enlarging dinghies or small racing hulls, America produced racing-cruisers of medium displacement during the late forties and the fifties. In fact, the trend towards lighter boats received a slight setback in 1954 with the appearance of *Finisterre,* an Olin Stephens designed keel-centerboarder of moderately heavy displacement. *Finisterre's* success in ocean racing is well known, and she exerted a great influence on the design of racing-cruisers in subsequent years. Reasons for her success, besides the obvious one that she was very well sailed, were that she could be deeply loaded at little sacrifice to speed; she had a deep, fairly efficient centerboard that gave her good performance to windward but reduced wetted surface downwind when the board was retracted; she had above normal beam and unrated ballast, such as heavy bronze floors, to give her great sail-carrying power in strong winds; and perhaps most important, early in her career, she had a very low handicap rating in comparison with her performance under the weather conditions to which she was usually exposed. Today, the rating rule has caught up with her, and no matter who sails her, she seems to be much less competitive in 'round-the-buoys racing at least. This can also be attributed to the fact that today's competition includes many high performance types of moderately light displacement.

In America, light racing-cruisers were pioneered by such designers as Farnham Butler, William Tripp, and particularly William Lapworth, who first got a lot of attention when a controversial boat of his design, the *Flying Scotchman,* entered the 1950 Bermuda Race from Newport, Rhode Island to Bermuda. Lapworth boats have been extremely successful racers, particularly the "Cal" classes and especially the light displacement Cal 40s which have dominated ocean racing in recent years. These boats are still considered the design "target" or boat to beat when new cruisers are built for racing.

The object of this brief discussion of displacement has not been necessarily to advocate either light or heavy boats, but to give a little background on displacement consideration in racing-cruiser design, and to show a few of the

FIGURE 13: BOUNDARY LAYER

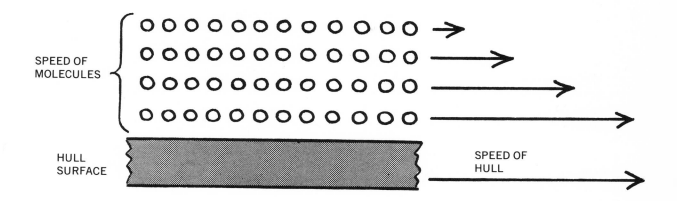

SPEED OF MOLECULES

HULL SURFACE

SPEED OF HULL

ways in which displacement affects performance.

Another important factor in the consideration of displacement is strength of the hull. Light hulls must be lightly built, yet usually they must take strains greater than those to which cruisers of the past were exposed. This is due to the greatly increased popularity of offshore racing today and the fact that modern sails do not readily blow out nor does modern rigging easily stretch. The solution to this problem is construction that is light but tremendously strong. To achieve this end, new construction methods and techniques have been developed, and some of these will be mentioned very briefly later on.

Forward Resistance

A hull's total forward resistance may be divided into various kinds of drag forces. For the sake of this nontechnical discussion we prefer the system of division mentioned earlier: (1) resistance due to wetted surface, (2) wave-making, (3) form, (4) induced resistance due to leeway and heeling, and (5) windage, or wind resistance. Total windage comes from the rig and the part of the hull above the water, so this will be discussed briefly in Chapter 5 which deals with rigging.

WETTED SURFACE: When designing a modern racing-cruiser, the naval architect puts a great deal of thought into the non-sacrificial reduction of wetted surface. He does this because wetted surface area causes most of the forward resistance at low to medium speeds, those speeds at which most boats in most localities travel the majority of the

time. By non-sacrificial, it is meant that there is little sacrifice of characteristics associated with good performance to achieve a low wetted surface area.

Wetted surface causes skin friction between the hull's surface and the water, or, to be more accurate, friction between water molecules which cling to the hull surface and molecules a slight distance away from the hull surface. The molecules that cling or partially cling to the surface and move along with the hull are referred to as the *boundary layer*. This layer varies in thickness, and it is considerably thinner forward than aft. Figure 13 shows, in a simple way, how the boundary layer is built up of rows of molecules with the inner rows, next to the hull, moving along at the same speed as the hull and the rows out from the surface moving progressively slower the further away from the hull they are. To be convinced of the boundary layer's existence, one need only drop a small floating object such as a wooden match in the water next to a moving hull and watch the object be pulled along with the boat for a brief period of time.

Obviously the way to reduce skin friction is to reduce wetted area but this is not so easy to do without increasing some other form of resistance or detracting from some desirable characteristic. Some sailors seem to judge wetted area entirely by the shape of the lateral plane, but actually the fore-and-aft view gives as much or more indication of wetted surface. Figure 14 shows four types of midship sections. The triangular form shown in section A was frequently used over a century ago. In fact

17

FIGURE 14: MIDSHIP SECTIONS

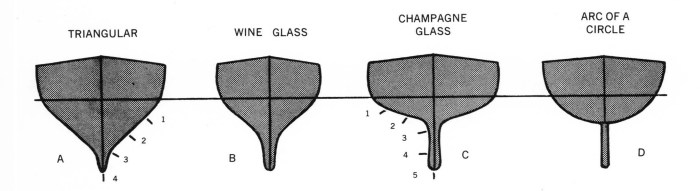

TRIANGULAR   WINE GLASS   CHAMPAGNE GLASS   ARC OF A CIRCLE

the section is typical of the famous yacht *America* which beat the British yachts in 1851. The champagne glass, section C, is typical of some of the light displacement racing-cruisers of today such as the *Myth of Malham* or in a very general way, some of the "Cal" classes, Tripp designed "Galaxies," Richard Carlson designed "Cutlass" class, Butler-Edgar "Coronado 25," Bruce King "Islander 37," or the less extreme Graves "Constellation" classes. As can be seen in the illustration, the wetted surface of the triangular section is much less than that of the champagne glass section. The scale drawn on the bilge and keel of each section shows the same unit of measurement.

In order to compensate for the unfavorable wetted area in section C, it is necessary to reduce drastically the area of its lateral plane. Figure 15 shows in A, the lateral plane of a hull similar to the *America* and in C and D two drastic reductions of lateral plane wetted surface that could be used for the champagne glass section. As a net result, C and D might have slightly less total wetted area than A, and at the same time C and D will have keels that are more efficient for windward sailing, but we will talk about this consideration of the lateral plane later. Choosing between C and D, the latter seems preferable, in one very important respect at least, in that the rudder separated from the keel and moved aft, gives the longest possible distance from a completely submerged rudder to the boat's vertical turning axis. This increases the length of the lever arm, as shown in the diagram, for easier steering. More will be said about this in the specific discussion of rudders.

Sections D in Figure 14 and E in Figure 15 show another approach to the wetted surface problem. These sections are arcs of circles, and the bottom of the immersed hull profile in 15E is an arc also. This hull shape is based upon the well known fact that the sphere has the smallest area for a given volume, thus, by making the hull conform to arcs of circles, wetted surface is reduced. This type of section often works well for fin-type keels or short keels (having little distance from the leading to trailing edges), where the hull is considered the main body and the keel a separate appendage. If the keel were long, running the entire length of the hull, the total wetted area would be high, because we would have to consider the girth around the hull and keel together over the whole water line length. This is the same kind of problem we faced with the champagne glass section. Examples of the arc of a circle section are the Charles Hunt designed "Melody 34" class and Richard Carter's RORC and One-Ton Cup designs, such as *Rabbit* and *Tina*. Some of Ted Hood's latest designs have an immersed hull profile similar to E in Figure 15.

The wine glass section shown in Figure 14B might be considered a compromise between the triangular and arc sections. This section is not appropriate for a fin keel because of the fullness at the garboards. The keel for this type, which we might call an *integral keel*, should be considered as an integral part of the hull. The lateral plane often associated with this section is shown in Figure 15B. Reduction of wetted area has been accomplished by trimming down the forefoot and raking the rudder. Up to quite recently, this kind of profile was used very successfully on the majority of Sparkman and Stephens racing-cruising keel boats. The rudders on some of these boats are raked as much as forty-five degrees. As can be seen, the wetted area is not large on the lateral plane—also see the sectional view shown in Figure 14B.

Another very important aspect of skin friction is the fairness and smoothness of the hull. Rough seams, paint and any indentations or protuberances especially, cause resistance. However, this aspect will be considered in Chapter 4 when we discuss tuning the hull.

WAVE-MAKING. Next to wetted surface friction the most significant resistance is that caused by wave-making. This is the dominating drag at high speeds, whereas wetted surface drag dominates at low speeds. Figure 16 gives the approximate curves of the two kinds of resistances for a displacement hull. Of course, exact curves would depend on the form and dimensions of the particular hull. However, these curves show the general character of resistances for a racing-cruiser. Notice that the skin friction curve is almost straight and slopes up slowly as speed is increased, whereas the wave-making curve starts very low on the resistance scale and curves up with increasing rapidity until at high speed, it comprises most of the total resistance.

As a displacement hull moves forward it pushes up a mound of water at the bow and sets up complicated pressures which propagate several wave systems. These are transverse bow wave and stern wave systems and divergent wave systems as shown in Figure 17, but we are primarily concerned with the transverse waves which have their crest lines almost at right angles to the boat's centerline. These waves move in the direction of the boat and at the same speed. The faster the boat moves, the faster will be her transverse waves and the longer they will become, because the speed of a wave is in proportion to its length from crest to crest.

Wave-making takes energy and thus causes resistance. When a hull travels at so great a speed that the transverse wave length corresponds to the load water line length, there is such resistance that the hull can theoretically go no faster. This is the maximum speed for a displacement hull, and the only way it can overcome this natural speed bar-

FIGURE 15: LATERAL PLANES

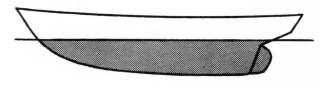

A—LONG KEEL

B—TRIANGULAR PLANE

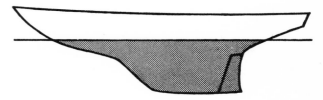

C—TRAPEZOIDAL

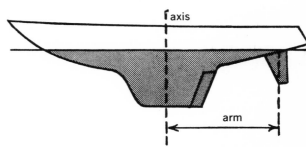

D—SHORT FIN—SEPARATED RUDDER

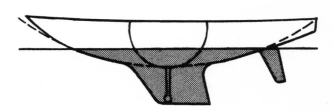

E—ARC OF A CIRCLE

FIGURE 16: RESISTANCE CURVES

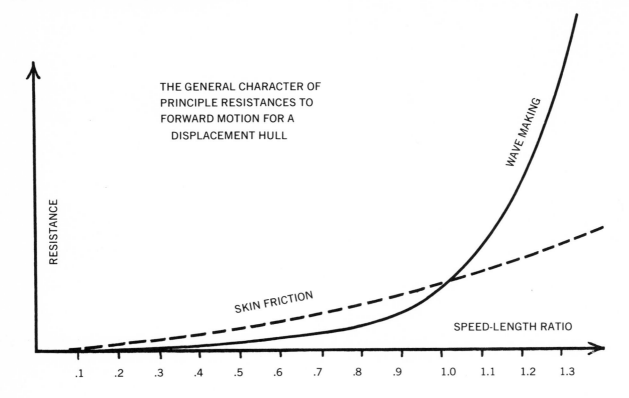

THE GENERAL CHARACTER OF
PRINCIPLE RESISTANCES TO
FORWARD MOTION FOR A
DISPLACEMENT HULL

WAVE MAKING

RESISTANCE

SKIN FRICTION

SPEED-LENGTH RATIO

.1   .2   .3   .4   .5   .6   .7   .8   .9   1.0   1.1   1.2   1.3

FIGURE 17: WAVE SYSTEMS

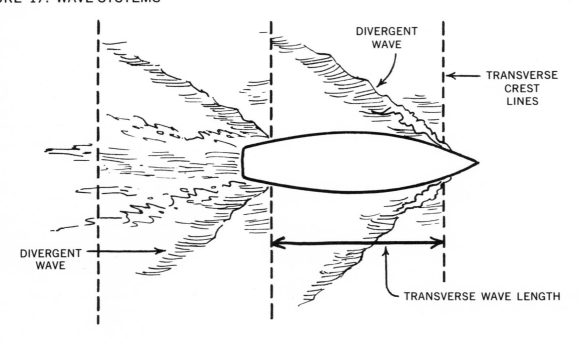

DIVERGENT
WAVE

TRANSVERSE
CREST
LINES

DIVERGENT
WAVE

TRANSVERSE WAVE LENGTH

rier is to lift up and partially plane. This would require enormous power for a heavy displacement boat, and it could only be accomplished momentarily running before strong winds with long following seas. The maximum speed-length ratio for an average fast racing-cruiser would be approximately 1.35, and beating to windward in ideal conditions it would be about 1.0. A twenty-five foot LWL boat, for example, could make just under seven knots reaching and about five knots to windward.

Of course, some of the small, light-displacement racing-cruisers, such as "Sharks," "Nomads," "Shock 22s," and "Mustangs" can exceed a speed-length ratio of 1.35 because they can partially plane under ideal conditions. Even large yachts of good hull form and light displacement can, for brief periods, partially plane down long ocean waves. This is often called *surfing,* and it is one of the most exciting and demanding forms of sailing. However, the occasions are quite rare when a displacement boat can exceed her *hull speed* or speed-length ratio of 1.35, and the most critical factor in high speed sailing is length of the LWL.

Another factor concerning wave formation is displacement. A heavy boat, displacing more water than a light one, has a fuller, deeper underbody which depresses the water into a deeper wave system. Even though the heavy boat has a similar LWL to the light one and the waves of each are the same length, the deeper hull causes more resistance. This is shown in Figure 18.

One of the reasons why a non-planing hull has such difficulty exceeding the speed of a wave equal in length to its LWL, is the correspondence or superimposing of the bow wave upon the stern wave. As the hull speed increases the second transverse wave abaft the bow wave moves aft. When it reaches the stern, at hull speed, it is reinforced by the independently formed stern wave (often called quarter wave). This is explained in Figure 19. Notice in boat A the second bow wave has not reached the stern and it partially negates or cancels out the effect of the quarter wave, but when the two waves reinforce each other there is enormous resistance.

Another consideration in hull-made wave length is bow and particularly stern overhang. A boat with long overhangs can increase her waterline length at good speeds and often considerably so when heeled in a good breeze. She then actually has a new load water line which is often called her

FIGURE 18: DISPLACEMENT & WAVES

wave length A = wave length B
depth C is greater than D

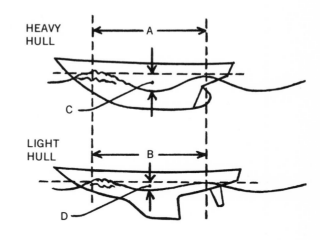

FIGURE 19: WAVE CORRESPONDENCE

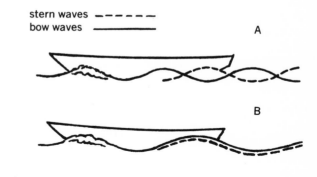

FIGURE 20: SAILING LENGTH

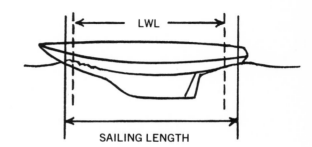

21

sailing length. See Figure 20.

FORM RESISTANCE (HULL SHAPE, BALANCE & APPENDAGE DRAG). Although form resistance is often considered under the wave-making category and there is interaction between all underwater resistances, it seems convenient to think of the drag caused by the form or shape of the hull as a distinct and separate kind of resistance. A submarine moving deep below the surface makes no waves and thus has no resistance from this source; and if wetted surface friction were the only consideration, the submarine would be ball-shaped. However, as we all know, a submerged spherical submarine could not move very fast, and this is because of the existence of another type of drag caused by the form of the hull.

The search for the ideal hull form has been going on for sometime. It is not surprising that the multi-talented Leonardo Da Vinci even tried towing models to determine optimum hull form. The Da Vinci ideal was the so-called "cod's head and mackerel tail," or *fish form.* Some designers feel that Da Vinci's conclusions retarded the progress of naval architecture because of improper use of the fish form on so many vessels for so many years. However, this form with its greatest body fullness forward of amidships is not always bad. In fact, it is often effective at low or *ghosting* speeds in light airs. Captain Illingworth's successful, light displacement *Mouse of Malham* has a slightly fish-shaped hull.

The fish form exerted a strong influence on the design of sailing vessels until the middle 1800's; but after this, yachts began to take a different shape. Scott Russell had developed his *wave-line theory* which proposed that a hull should fit or conform to the outline of a wave, and this produced a hull having a fine bow and maximum fullness abaft amidships, the so-called *wedge form.* The yacht *America,* designed by George Steers, had this kind of form, and it is not surprising that she had a great influence on designs of that period. Another promoter of the wedge form was the famous Norwegian, Colin Archer. He developed a wave form theory differing from Russell's in that the *curve of areas* or the distribution of displacement should conform to the wave (as opposed to the actual curve of the hull's body conforming to the wave).

One of the main problems with either a fish or wedge form is improper balance. As every sailor knows, a rudder turned hard to one side to correct for poor balance causes great drag. When heeled, the wedge form tends to round up into the wind, while the fish form may tend to fall off or bear away from the wind as shown in Figure 21. As a result of trying to achieve good balance, most modern yachts are a compromise form having somewhat similar ends. The hull is often shaped, very roughly, to be in accord with the *metacentric shelf theory,* an analysis developed in 1931 by Rear Admiral Alfred Turner. This rather complex analysis estimates how the immersed volume of a heeled hull is disposed symmetrically with respect to a vertical fore-and-aft plane passing through the metacenter. This theory predicts that a *symmetrical hull* will not trim down by the bow or stern on heeling and will be well balanced. Another balance analysis was made by D. A. Rayner. This compares the increase and decrease of immersed and emersed sectional areas for a given angle of heel as seen on the body plan. Figure 22 shows the immersions or emersions of a heeled hull at three different sections. In the Rayner analysis, a curve is plotted from the differences between the areas of immersed and emersed wedges at all sections on the waterline. This curve can then be interpreted by a designer or experienced observer to predict hull balance. Usually, when wedge differences in the bow and stern are similar, the plotted curve is quite symmetrical, and this indicates the boat will have good balance. In other words, a boat with symmetrical ends or with her displacement distributed somewhat the same way in the hull's forward half as in the after half, should balance reasonably well when heeled.

In actual practice, it is not that simple, because a completely symmetrical hull sometimes has bad qualities. Quite often such a hull is either not sharp enough at the entrance or lacks buoyancy in her after sections. This latter point is particularly important with a small racing-cruiser, because crew weight is largely concentrated around the cockpit; so this is just the area where fullness and buoyancy is needed. Also many light displacement boats capable of semi-planing need a slightly hollow entrance and a wide flat run, a partial dinghy shape. This type of boat, therefore, must sacrifice a certain amount of balance and she must be sailed on her feet, at low angles of heel. In sailing yacht design, compromises nearly always have to be made. The hulls of most modern racing-cruisers

FIGURE 21: BALANCE OF FISH & WEDGE FORMS

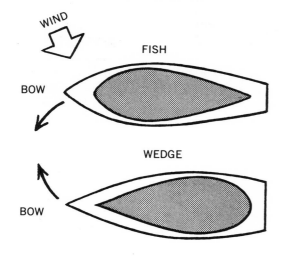

are, in varying degrees, compromises between wedge and symmetrical forms. Examples are shown in Figure 23. Slightly wedge-shaped forms often have a little less resistance then symmetrical forms between the speed-length ratios of 0.5 and 1.0.

Beam, fairbody depth, displacement, and shape of the ends all contribute to wave-making and form resistance. As the hull moves ahead, the water must be moved aside and divided, and of course, this takes energy. The flows on either side of the hull reunite, and this action together with disturbances caused by various appendages in the form of the rudder, keel, or centerboard, and propeller can cause turbulence and harmful eddies. This type of drag is significant at all speeds, but it might be said that surface friction dominates at low speeds, wave-making at high speeds, and form resistance gains its greatest relative importance at the middle to high speeds.

FIGURE 22: BALANCE WHEN HEELED

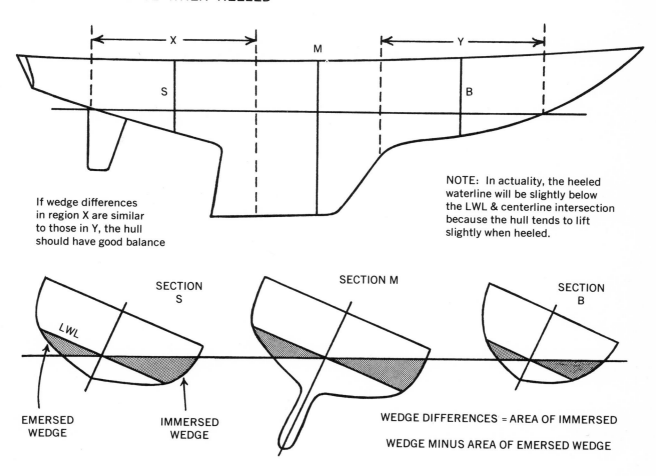

If wedge differences in region X are similar to those in Y, the hull should have good balance

NOTE: In actuality, the heeled waterline will be slightly below the LWL & centerline intersection because the hull tends to lift slightly when heeled.

SECTION S

SECTION M

SECTION B

EMERSED WEDGE

IMMERSED WEDGE

WEDGE DIFFERENCES = AREA OF IMMERSED

WEDGE MINUS AREA OF EMERSED WEDGE

In the interest of reducing turbulence and eddies, appendages should be streamlined, sharp angles and corners should be avoided, waterlines should not be excessively full or blunt at the ends, nor should entrance angles be excessively sharp, and buttocks should have an easy sweep and not be excessively steep. It is usually better to have the garboards faired smoothly into the keel (as in sections B and C of Figure 14), although the garboard area would have to be very small and tight in a finkeeler.

A recent design development is the use of *kicker fins* or streamlining skegs (also called *bustles*), as shown by the shaded area in Figure 24. These appendages were used with apparent great success on the twelve meter boats involved in the 1967 America's Cup races. Also, they have been used to a minor extent on some of the latest racing-cruisers. Although kickers can help the directional stability of a boat, their main purpose is to fine the waterlines aft and to reduce the quarter wave and wake turbulence. The skeg is faired into the hull and extends to, or even beyond, the LWL ending. This seems to help the flow move in smooth streamlines past the hull's afterbody. Part of the turbulence ordinarily found around the region of a yacht's quarter is often due to water flowing under the keel and afterbody from the lee side to the windward side as a result of making leeway. A well-designed kicker cannot only help with this problem and reduce the size of the quarter wave, but when faired into the hull, it can distribute some of the buoyancy further aft. Distributing the buoyancy by this means can raise the capability for high speed performance, and furthermore this helps support the weight of the crew in the cockpit. The rudder may hinge from the kicker's after end, hang from the kicker (as shown in Figure 24), or attach in the conventional way to the keel. It can be seen that the addition of the skeg appendage increases wetted area, but if the kicker is a buoyant type faired into the hull, the area increase will be very small.

Propeller drag is a great problem for sailboats with auxiliary engines. Some of the small racing-cruisers use outboard motors which either attach to the transom or protrude through a motor well in the boat's counter. In these cases, the outboard may be removed when under sail in order to eliminate the drag. A boat with an outboard well is usually equipped with a flush-fitting hatch which

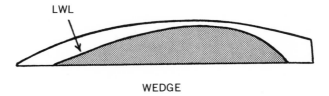

WEDGE

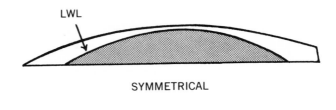

SYMMETRICAL

FIGURE 24: INTEGRAL STREAMLINING SKEG

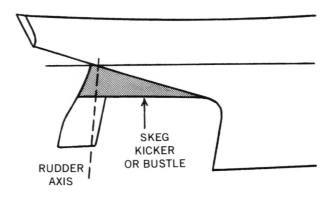

RUDDER AXIS

SKEG KICKER OR BUSTLE

closes the opening through the counter and virtually eliminates any resistance from water entering and sloshing around in the well.

With racing-cruisers having inboard power, there will always be at least some prop drag, but this can be minimized. Ways of doing so include the use of two-bladed props with movable, folding or *feathering blades*. A three-bladed prop causes tremendous drag and is almost unthinkable for any racing boat. The feathering prop has blades that twist so that, in effect, the blade width can be reduced. On the folding type, which has the least resistance by far, the blades are hinged and fold back against each other (see Figure 48). More will be said of this in Chapter 4 when we discuss tuning the hull.

Figure 25 shows several propeller installation arrangements. Type A is probably the most common, but each arrangement has advantages and disadvantages. A and B have *apertures,* or holes, cut out of the lateral plane, and these in themselves cause a great deal of drag. Type A will probably have the best steering control under power because the prop wash is directed onto the rudder. However, a rudder with an aperture loses efficiency when under sail because it loses area, and the aperture allows some water flow to leeward of the keel to escape to windward. Installation B, seen on many William Tripp designed boats, has an advantage in that the aperture is forward in the thick area of the keel where the prop, when vertical, may hide behind the deadwood to reduce drag. Installations C, D, E and F are without apertures and each can be fitted with a *solid prop* (having non-movable blades) or one with movable blades. The boat owner will have to weigh the advantages of a low drag prop against the increase of measurement rating it gives him.

The off-center propeller, C, is usually put on the port side to offset the *torque* (tendency for a propeller to move the stern sidewise and thus turn the boat) of the normal right hand prop going ahead. Despite the torque, however, it is often necessary to angle the shaft so that it does not run exactly fore-and-aft in order to counteract the off-center propeller push which would ordinarily make the boat turn to starboard. A shaft angled to the direction of water flow adds to the making of eddies. Then considering the drag of the shaft strut and the fact that there is no way to hide the prop behind the deadwood, it is evident that the offset propeller creates a large amount of drag especially if the prop is solid.

Propellers D, E, and F are on center and therefore may partially hide behind the keels, but even when vertical, the props are partially exposed to the water flow, because at these locations, the keels are relatively thin. The arrangement of E, similar to a "Cal 40" and others, has the prop

FIGURE 25: PROP LOCATIONS

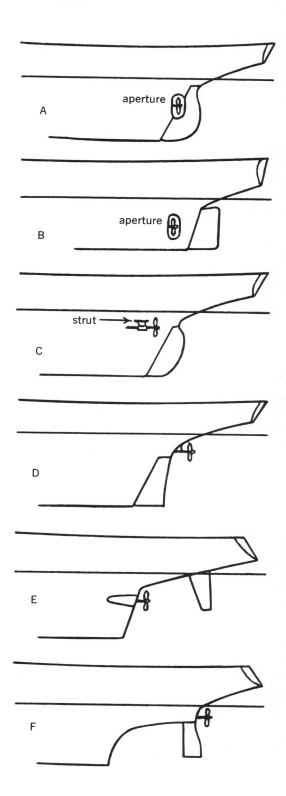

forward of the rudder which may assist in steering under power. In arrangement D, similar to a "Cal 30," and especially E, similar to some of Bruce King's designs, the propeller is very near the water surface which makes for some inefficiency under power but low resistance under sail.

More will be said about propeller drag, streamlining, and fairing appendages when we talk about tuning the hull in Chapter 4. Keels and rudders will be discussed further later in this chapter when we deal with lateral resistance and steering.

PRISMATIC COEFFICIENT. Although this is a non-technical discussion of yacht design, it seems unavoidable in the interest of necessary coverage to introduce occasionally a frightening term from the jargon of naval architects. The prismatic coefficient (often called simply the prismatic) tells how displacement is distributed longitudinally. It is a measure of how fine or full the ends are in comparison to the midship section. Technically, the prismatic coefficient (C_p) is defined as the ratio of displaced volume to that of a prism equal in length to the LWL and having a cross-section area equal to the immersed midship section. This definition is illustrated in Figure 26. The immersed hull is shown by dotted lines, the immersed midship sections are shaded, and the prism is shown by the solid lines. The C_p is a comparison of the volume within the dotted hull to the volume within the area defined by the solid lines.

The prismatic has a significant effect on form resistance and especially wave-making. For displacement racing-cruisers, the C_p may vary from .51 to .58 with the lower coefficients indicating the yacht has relatively fine ends while the higher figures indicate full ends. An extremely full-ended craft was Captain Joshua Slocum's famous *Spray* with a prismatic of .65. It is generally agreed that the higher coefficients indicate good performance at high speeds, whereas low coefficients are better at low speeds in light winds. Optimum prismatics might be .52 or .53 for speed-length ratios of below 0.8 but .58 or higher for speed-length ratios of over 1.0. At the highest planing or semi-planing hull speeds, .60 or higher coefficients would be more suitable. Selection of a suitable C_p depends to some extent on where the boat will be sailed and whether heavy winds or light airs will predominate in her locality.

INDUCED DRAG. The additional resistance due to a boat's angle of yaw (or angle of leeway) and her

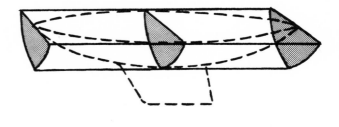

FIGURE 26: PRISMATIC COEFFICIENT

FIGURE 27: HEELED RESISTANCE

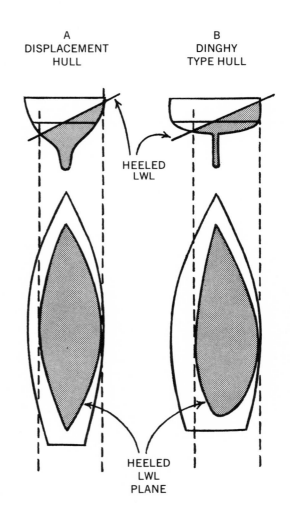

A
DISPLACEMENT
HULL

B
DINGHY
TYPE HULL

HEELED
LWL

HEELED
LWL
PLANE

angle of heel is called induced drag. Both yaw angle and heeling cause drag, but there seems to be a tendency for some sailors to underrate the former and overrate the latter, at least insofar as racing-cruisers are concerned. The truth of the matter is that the yaw angle causes far more drag than moderate heeling in most well-balanced, displacement yachts. Although admittedly, under actual sailing conditions, drag from these two sources is combined, and it is difficult to differentiate and determine exactly what percentage is due to leeway alone or heeling alone.

When considering the resistance from heeling only, tests have shown that there is some additional drag at very low angles of heel but beyond this, until medium angles are reached, there is very little increase in resistance. Tests on the yacht *Gimcrack,* made in 1936, showed that increased resistance from heeling was significant up to five degrees of heel, but then there was little more increased drag until nearly twenty-five degrees, at which time the *Gimcrack* immersed her rail. These results have largely been verified by later tests. These include recent computer experiments at M.I.T. and tests on a full size 5.5 meter boat at the David Taylor Model Basin near Washington, D.C.

Of course, we know that heeling causes some drag in most boats because the heeled waterline is usually asymmetrical; thus, it is puzzling why many tests show so little additional drag with heeling. The English designer-author, D. Phillips-Birt, offers the explanation that the increased sailing length from overhangs gives additional speed which partially cancels out the increased drag due to heeling. Then also, many of the experiments have been performed on narrow, displacement racing hulls with rather symmetrical ends and heeled waterlines. Nevertheless, many dinghy sailors moving into racing-cruisers who have been brought up on the dictum "keep your boat flat," don't always realize that there are times when it may pay to sail certain boats at a definite angle of heel. Heeling affects the set of the sails, helm balance, waterline length, air flow loss at the foot of sails, stability, wetted surface; and of course if some heeling proves beneficial in these areas it might more than compensate for the slight drag it causes.

Figure 27 shows two entirely different types of hulls. A is a displacement, symmetrical type with a deep fairbody and round bilges. B is a light displacement dinghy type with flattish shallow bilges.

The heeled waterline plane of each is shown by the shaded areas. A will probably have good balance and little heeled resistance because her ends are quite symmetrical and also the windward side (the emersed side) of the waterline plane is not too dissimilar from the leeward side. On the other hand, B will undoubtedly have considerable weather helm and considerable heeled resistance because of her wedge-shaped waterline plane and the fact that the windward waterline is entirely dissimilar to the leeward waterline. We can see, therefore, that A can be sailed at moderate angles of heel at very little cost in drag, and she may benefit by (1) increasing her waterline length, (2) possibly decreasing her wetted area slightly, (3) increasing weather helm slightly for effective steering in light airs, (4) probably increasing stability because of hull shape and the effect of keel ballast, and (5) increasing effectiveness of sails in light air at slight angles of heel. Points 3, 4 and 5 will be discussed later when we deal with sail plan balance, stability, and sail trim. Boat B, on the otherhand, should be sailed very flat in most winds on account of her high resistance when heeled. However, even she could be given a slight angle of heel in light airs to improve the set of her sails and for reduction of wetted surface which might be considerable in this case.

There will be further discussions of heeling in the sections on lateral resistance and stability, but before leaving the subject of heeling in connection with forward resistance, it should be stressed that any time the lee rail becomes submerged (usually just before or after 30° of heel), resistance increases tremendously. This is due not only to greater hull resistance and sail inefficiency at the higher angles of heel but to the fact that the rail, shroud turnbuckles, jib sheets, blocks, winch bases, cleats, and the like become submerged and obviously cause great drag.

Drag caused by a wide yaw angle can be very considerable, up to perhaps forty percent more than upright unyawed resistance, because the hull is crabbing or moving forward while being turned askew. Of course, a certain amount of leeway is essential for windward performance in order that the keel or centerboard can act as a hydrofoil and exert transverse lift to windward and thus counteract the side force in the opposite direction exerted by the sails. The lift and drag forces acting on the keel of a boat beating to windward are diagrammed in Figure 28. Increasing the angle of yaw will increase the lift but will also increase the drag. Yaw angles will vary between two and five and one-half degrees on racing-cruisers, but angles over five degrees will usually produce excessive drag in proportion to lift.

Lateral Resistance

Up to this point, for the most part, we have been talking about resistance to forward movement, but in the sailing yacht, consideration of lateral resistance is of equal importance. This is especially true for a displacement racer, because it is probably still true that the more weatherly of this type win the majority of races over the average closed course.

LEEWAY AND THE HULL. Lateral resistance is supplied by the keel or centerboard, but the hull itself may have considerable influence on leeway. Of course, the degree of influence depends on whether the keel is an integral part of the hull or a separate fin. It also depends on the shape of the hull and the angle of heel. There is a great deal of interaction between heeling and leeway. One of the obvious interactions is the relation between angle of heel and draft. A hull draws less when she heels for two reasons. First, the angle away from the perpendicular reduces the vertical distance from the water surface to the keel's bottom. Second, the hull has a tendency to float higher when the immersed volume begins to exceed the emersed volume.

Another interaction, not so obvious, between heeling and leeway can be seen by comparing the hull forms shown in Figure 29. The hull itself (not including the keel) can act as a hydrofoil. Notice the arrows shown on the hulls in the diagrams. These show the direction the hulls tend to move due to the hydrofoil shape of their heeled waterlines. On hull B in Figure 29, the heeled waterline on the leeward or low side is a pronounced curve while the windward waterline has very little curvature. This causes the water flow on the leeward side to move faster than the flow on the windward side, and therefore (in accordance with the physical law known as Bernoulli's principle which states that the higher the velocity of a moving fluid the lower will be its pressure) there is less pressure on the boat's leeward side than her windward side. Naturally this imbalance of pressures will tend to force the hull to leeward.

28

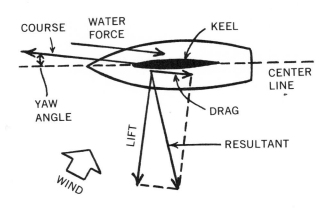

FIGURE 28: KEEL-WATER FORCE

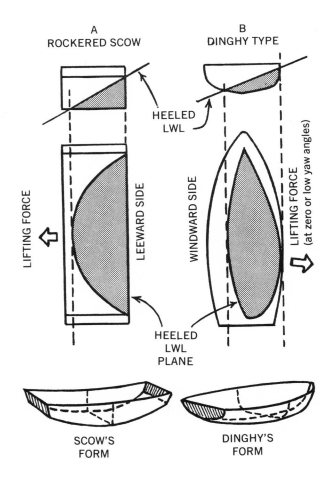

FIGURE 29: HULL LIFT

Hull A has a very unusual form. As can be seen, she is a scow with straight sides and a very pronounced rocker at the bottom. A friend of mine learned the basics of sailing in such a boat which had neither rudder nor keel nor centerboard. Steering was accomplished by the movement of crew weight fore-and-aft in order to relocate the center of lateral resistance. Lateral resistance for windward performance was supplied by the immersion of the leeward chine. But there was probably another reason why the boat could be sailed to windward without a keel or centerboard. Looking at hull B, it is plain to see that this heeled waterline plane has the opposite shape of hull A. The scow (her owner prefers to call her a punt) has her waterline curve on the windward side and this lowers the pressure on that side which tends to pull the boat to windward. Actually this force cannot counteract the opposite lateral force from the wind on the sails, but the net result is a slight reduction of leeway.

Also, compare these two hulls with the normal displacement hull A in Figure 27, and observe how the low pressure force works on the three hulls. The scow with straight sides and rocker bottom has the force to windward. The dinghy with curved sides and flattish bottom is forced to leeward, and the displacement hull with curved sides and rocker bottom is pulled very slightly to leeward, but it is affected very little by the force. This substantiates our conviction that there is little harm done, and there may be some benefits, in sailing the displacement boat at moderate angles of heel; but on the other hand, it is often very harmful to sail the dinghy type or wedge-shaped hull having little deadrise at pronounced angles of heel to leeward. In moderate winds it may even pay to sail a true dinghy with a slight heel to windward.

KEELS. Although the hydrofoil action of the hull is part of the picture, the keel or centerboard has the far greater effect on lateral resistance. The efficiency of a keel depends on its area, aspect ratio, sectional form, profile shape, depth, and location on the hull. Of course the latter two considerations are more closely related to stability and balance which we will discuss separately later on.

Area together with aspect ratio have the greatest effect on leeway. The area is primarily determined by the draft, LWL length, displacement, wetted surface, and hull form. Draft in a keel boat is usually fixed by certain practical considerations

such as rating rule penalties and the depth of water in the sailing locality. Also, the draft is roughly in proportion to the LWL length. The normal, medium-sized, racing-cruiser with keel is about five times as long on the waterline as she is deep. Smaller boats are slightly deeper, but large boats have proportionally less draft.

The grey area in Figure 30 shows a typical racing-cruiser's immersed lateral plane. The ratio of a boat's lateral plane to a rectangle formed by her LWL length and draft, as indicated by the black and grey area in the diagram, is called her *lateral plane coefficient*. This usually varies from about .45 to .65 for keel boats of the kind we have been discussing. A light displacement type might have the lower figure and a heavy boat the higher figure. Hull form and beam as well as displacement will make a difference in the coefficient partly because the lateral plane might be composed mostly of an efficient, thin keel in a light boat, but it might be composed mostly of an inefficient (for lateral resistance) full, fat hull on a heavy, integral-keel boat. However, these coefficient figures can serve as a rough guide concerning the needed amount of lateral area. To put it very simply, the area of a keel boat should be roughly fifty percent, or slightly more, of the rectangle under the waterline.

A very important consideration concerning keel area and aspect ratio is wetted surface. The optimum is the least wetted area for the most lateral plane efficiency. Referring back to Figure 14, we can see that a triangular midships section, A, with an integral keel will lower wetted surface, but this will give a thick, angular-sided hydrofoil which will not be as efficient as a fin-type keel which more nearly resembles a vertical airplane wing. However, if we use a champagne glass section which gives a more efficient keel, we increase wetted surface. One answer to this dilemma is use of the latter section with a very short fore-and-aft length. This gives us a high aspect ratio keel, deep in proportion to its length, and this is by far the most effective type of keel for a given area.

Of course a high aspect ratio keel is not the most suitable type for every boat. If draft is limited, the high aspect ratio must be achieved by reducing the keel's length, and this has its point of diminishing returns on some racing-cruisers. An overly short keel reduces the lateral plane and may very well increase the yaw angle. On a light displacement, fin-keeler, a slight increase in yaw angle might be tolerated, because the lower friction of the short keel could more than compensate for a slightly greater induced resistance caused by the additional yaw. However, on a full-bodied heavy displacement boat, the yaw angle should be kept low, because any yawed resistance will probably be high, and it is doubtful that this could be compensated for by the reduction in wetted surface of a short keel. In other words, heavy boats of limited draft should generally have longer keels than light boats. Directional stability is a related consideration we will discuss later.

The profile shape of the keel is not only determined by the area and aspect ratio but by certain practical considerations. For instance the leading edge of the keel should be raked, as shown by the various keel configurations in Figure 15. This is a very important antifouling measure to prevent the snagging of various kinds of flotsam, floating seaweed, and the lines from lobster pots or crab traps. In many areas boats are especially troubled with eel grass and kelp. In fact, some skippers of one-design class boats having nearly vertical keels, have found it necessary to install glass windows in their boats' bottoms to aid in the detection of keel fouling.

Of course, the keel's after edge need not be raked for antifouling reasons, but it is sometimes raked in the opposite direction (as shown in Figure 15B) to move the rudder's center of pressure further aft for better steering leverage at a minimum cost in wetted surface area when the rudder is attached to the keel. When the rudder is separated from the keel, it may pay to have the after keel edge fairly vertical or even raked slightly in the same direction as the forward edge.

Tank tests have shown that a straight trailing edge and a sharp angle at the heel of the keel gives good lateral plane efficiency. Of course, other considerations affect the shape of the keel's trailing edge such as the distribution of keel area in such a way as to produce maximum length for directional stability at a minimum cost in the wetted area when the draft is fixed. With this in mind, the keel could have a trapezoidal shape with the fore-and-aft edges raked the opposite way similar to a Cal 40's keel (see figure 15D). A further advantage of this keel shape is that the opposite raking edges tend to raise the CLR, which minimizes heeling (see Figure 57).

Another factor that affects the keel's profile and sectional shape is the amount and location of ballast. On most boats, the ballast must be placed far forward on the keel in order that the boat be properly trimmed fore-and-aft. Of course, this will depend on the fore and aft location of the keel which in turn will depend on the position of the sail plan's center of effort. However, most modern racing-cruisers must have their keel ballast well forward to float on their designed waterlines, and this is especially true with small boats which are easily affected by the concentration of crew weight in the cockpit. If such is the case, when the keel is triangular, without a toe (Figure 15B), then the ballast must be moved up to a higher position where it will contribute less to the boat's stability than if it were at the keel's bottom. This is one advantage of a keel with a toe (Figure 15C). In this case the ballast can be kept low.

Induced drag caused by the yaw angle creates a kind of turbulence at the bottom of the keel often referred to as tip, or *end vortices*. These are similar to the vortices at the end of airplane wings that are occasionally visible at high altitudes. When a boat reaches or sails to windward some of the high pressure flow on the keel's leeward side escapes under the keel's bottom to its low pressure, windward side. This creates the swirling eddies somewhat similar to those shown in Figure 31. These vortices not only detract slightly from the keel's lateral resistance, but also they can cause a considerable increase in forward resistance. In recent years there has been a good deal of experimentation with variations in the shape of keel bottoms in an effort to minimize this type of turbulence. The V'd bottom has been used with apparent success in helping to reduce cross flow under the keel while at the same time it has a favorable shape for low forward resistance. This shape may also have some advantages when pitching while sailing into head seas. V'd keels have been used on the twelve meter cup defenders, and they can be seen on some Olin Stephens and Charles Morgan racing-cruiser designs.

Some recent designs, notably those by William Crealock, have made use of the *end plate fin* which has a flaring section at the keel's bottom as shown in Figure 31. This does not seem to differ radically from some of the old bulb fins which had the ballast concentrated in a more or less streamlined lump at the keel's bottom. End plate keels of the type illustrated may help prevent cross flow, and at the same time, they enable the ballast to be placed at the lowest point for a given draft.

A debate could probably be started between proponents of the thin, all-metal fin bolted to a boat's bottom, and advocates of the thicker integral fin which is blended into the hull. However, it seems to me, for moderately light racing-cruisers above the smallest sizes at least, the latter type of keel has many more advantages. To begin with, a flat keel causes more resistance to yawed forward motion than a streamlined keel with a certain amount of thickness. Tank tests have shown that a practical, high lift, streamlined keel should be roughly twelve times as long (or slightly longer) as it is thick with maximum thickness about twenty-five to forty percent abaft the leading edge. The trailing edge should be quite fine while the fore edge should be slightly thicker and rounded. A sharp leading edge often causes turbulence at certain yaw angles.

Other arguments for the integral fin would include greater strength at the juncture of hull and keel, less maintenance on account of the corrosion associated with many flat metal keels, space in the keel for a water tank and bilge water sump, and a sectional shape permitting the use of curved garboards to mitigate turbulence. In addition, part of the boat's displacement could be put into her keel in order to allow a less full, bulky, and deep hull to lessen form resistances.

CENTERBOARDS. Most of the basic principles we have discussed in regard to keels apply also to centerboards, but there are differences. With centerboards draft, aspect ratio, and area are not fixed. We may choose a very efficient high-aspect ratio

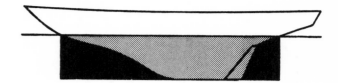

C_{LP} = GRAY AREA/black + gray area

board with little consideration for depth of water in the sailing locality or concern over wetted surface area. Up wind, we can lower the board for great draft and efficiency and down wind pull it up for a great reduction of wetted area, and by raising or lowering the board, we can move the center of lateral resistance to improve balance. However, with all the advantages that centerboarders have, they have disadvantages, too. There are maintenance problems which include difficulties in cleaning and painting the board, worn pins, and broken pendants (see figure 32). In addition there is often the thumping of a centerboard in its well when in rough seas. Furthermore, metal centerboards can be bent after a hard grounding while heeled with the board fully down. For this reason, it is often advisable to keep the board partly housed when sailing in shoal waters.

Centerboard boats require ample beam for stability, and it is nearly always necessary that their

FIGURE 31: KEEL END VORTICES

END PLATE OR
FENCE TYPE FIN

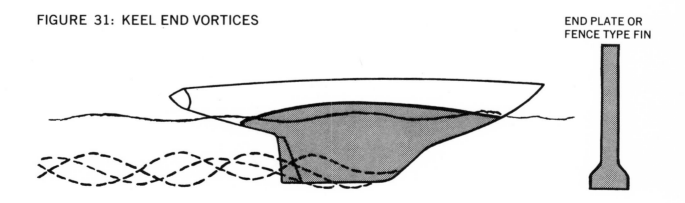

rudders are shallow. Unless a boat is fitted with a *lifting rudder* (one that pivots up or retracts as shown in Figure 32) which is very rare for a large boat, her rudder cannot extend below her keel, because it could be broken or damaged by grounding. This means that centerboarders can have steering problems when running before fresh winds and following seas. Furthermore, the broad beam can compound the problem if there is any excessive heeling, because balance is disturbed by the asymmetrical heeled waterlines due to the beam, and the lee side supplies buoyancy which tends to lift the shallow rudder further from the water.

Disregarding helm balance and susceptibility to snagging seaweed, there might be an advantage in a centerboard that can be lowered to rake forward of the vertical (with the bottom of the leading edge ahead of the top of the leading edge). Such a rake will cause lift to act in a more lateral (rather than an upward) direction when heeled, and if the board should twist from water pressure, added lift will force the hull to windward. Twist or bending of an after-raking board will be harmful to lift. This is one reason why it seldom pays to raise the board at all when beating except possibly in very light airs to reduce wetted surface or in heavy winds to improve helm balance or to reduce heeling.

It is not my intention to sound discouraging about centerboards but merely to point out some of the potential problems. There have been some outstanding centerboarders such as *Finisterre,* the Philip L. Rhodes designed *Carina,* and the Charles Morgan designed *Paper Tiger* to name just a few, but boats of this type can be very demanding under certain conditions. Perhaps the most important characteristic that any keel-centerboard offshore racer should have is sufficient depth of ballasted keel. She should have (1) sufficient ultimate stability to prevent capsizing at sea, (2) a sufficiently long, deep keel to prevent yawing and steering problems, and (3) enough lateral plane so that she can be sailed to windward fairly well with the board fully housed. A very general rule of thumb is that the draft of a small to medium sized yacht with board up should be no less than one seventh of the LWL length.

TWIN KEELS. Before leaving the subject of keels and centerboards, a mention should be made of twin keels. These are side by side fins, each being attached to the hull approximately half way be-tween the boat's centerline and her LWL as shown in Figure 33. Notice that on this fore-and-aft view the keels are angled away from the LWL vertical. The obvious advantage of the design is that the upright hull gives minimal draft, but heeling gives maximum draft to prevent leeway. Twin keelers have enjoyed some popularity in England, and now they are beginning to catch on in this country in the smallest sizes of racing-cruisers. A desirable feature is that a twin keel boat can be beached and easily put on a boat trailer, because she can stand upright on her two fins.

Advocates of this design claim that, despite the low aspect ratio of the usual twin keel, the fin can be made very efficient by means that are not possible with a conventional single keel. For instance, a twin keel can be angled to the hull's centerline in order to give it an angle of yaw without the hull being yawed. The keel on one side can be yawed for one tack while the opposite keel can be yawed for the other tack. Then, too, the keels can be made asymmetrical if this is deemed an advantage. Twin-keelers are said to have great directional stability and resistance to pitching when the boat is heeled, at which time the forces created by the weather keel act in a more up and down rather than a lateral direction.

Some claim that twin keel boats are the up and coming designs of the future. However, at the present time, it is doubtful that they have approached their full potential. One aspect of the design that might be of some possible concern is the matter of ultimate stability. Should a twin keeler be knocked down far enough to lift her windward keel clear of the water, an unlikely occurrence but a possibility, a beam sea could break under the exposed keel and exert a great capsizing force. However, at such an angle of heel, the righting moment of the windward keel is considerable, so probably this would offset the wave force. At any rate, in most twin keelers, it might be advisable to ride out a storm head to or stern to the seas.

Axial Turning

The main considerations relating to axial turning are transverse stability, turning about the longitudinal axis; steering and directional stability, the turning related to the vertical axis; and pitching, turning on the transverse axis.

STABILITY. There are several kinds of stability,

longitudinal which has to do with turning on the transverse axis, and directional which is concerned with turning on the vertical axis, but when we speak of "stability" alone, we are talking about transverse stability, the tendency of a vessel to return from a heeled position to an upright position. Of course all sailboats must have sufficient stability for sail carrying power. They need stiffness to stand up to their rigs and sail at low or optimum angles of heel in fresh winds. Furthermore, racing-cruisers need the reserved or ultimate stability for safety, to prevent capsizing or rolling over at very high angles of heel.

The characteristics that affect a boat's stiffness are the area and height of her sails, sectional form of the hull, draft, displacement, beam, and ballast. The latter two are the most significant for hull stability. Figure 34 illustrates the importance of beam and ballast and shows the righting forces at work. The center of gravity (CG) is fixed on the boat's centerline, but the center of buoyancy (CB), also on the centerline when the boat is upright (at CB1), moves to the side (to CB2) when the boat is heeled. The distance between the upward force acting through the heeled center of buoyancy (CB2) and the downward force acting through the center of gravity, is the righting arm. This arm changes in length as the angle of heel changes and the CB moves towards or away from the boat's centerline. The longer the righting arm, the more righting force is exerted on the hull. It can be seen by studying the diagram that there are actually two ways that the arm can be lengthened: (1) by increasing the beam or changing the hull shape to make the CB move outboard, because the CB is the geometric center of the immersed hull, or (2) by lowering or increasing the keel ballast to lower the center of gravity.

The actual measure of stability is the *righting moment* which is the length of the righting arm times the displacement of the boat. Thus it is possible for a light displacement boat with a slightly longer lever arm than a heavy boat, to be more tender than the heavy boat. The metacentric height (GM), shown in the illustration, varies according the height of the CG and the lateral location of the CB. The GM on most keel racing-cruisers measures, depending on size, between less than 2.5 feet to more than 3.5 feet with the smaller boats having the lower heights. The figures for centerboarders are usually somewhat less. The CG is

FIGURE 32: CENTERBOARDER & ITS RUDDER

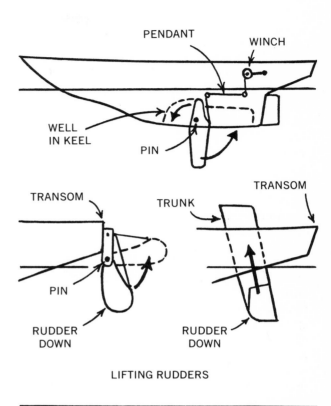

LIFTING RUDDERS

FIGURE 33: TWIN KEELS

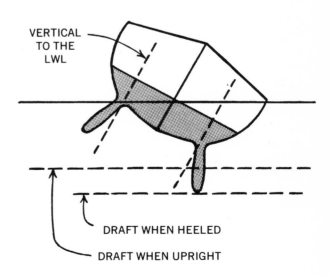

slightly above, on, or slightly below the LWL on most racing-cruisers.

Hull form also has its effects on stability. Hard bilges and low angles of deadrise usually contribute to stiffness, while slack bilges with higher angles of deadrise are often associated with initial tenderness at low angles of heel. Boats with high prismatic coefficients are usually relatively stiff in good breezes, partly because their full ends allow support by the bow and stern waves when there is little support amidships at the hollow between the waves. The hull form also has some affect on dynamic stability (meaning, in this non-technical discussion, stability or lack of it due to the boat's forward motion) at high speeds. The asymmetrical heeled water lines have an influence on heeling as well as on the lateral forces we mentioned in the discussion on lateral resistance, because those forces act in a downward as well as a lateral direction when the boat is heeled. High freeboard and flaring topsides give good reserve stability at the higher sailing angles of heel, and a slight tumble home near the rail will often delay dragging the rail.

Stability due to beam is most effective at normal sailing angles of heel but stability from keel ballast is what is needed for ultimate stability. A boat designed for offshore sailing should be able to recover from at least a 110 degree knockdown. Ballast-displacement ratios on most racing-cruisers vary from about thirty-three to fifty percent, meaning that percentage of their total weight has been consigned to ballast.

The relationship of stability to the sail area will be brought up when we discuss sails in Chapter 6.

RUDDERS AND STEERING. Innovations in the refinements of yacht design often seem to develop into fads. Most innovations have real merit, but they are not always suitable for every type of boat.

Several years ago, there was a vogue for *Constellation rudders* (named for the famous twelve meter cup defender). Tank tests have shown that rudders of this general kind, with concavely curved or straight after edges, with wide bottoms, narrow tops, and angular heels (see Figure 35A), are highly effective for steering and reduction of leeway at a minimum cost in area. The current rage, however, is for the so called *spade rudders*. These are separated from the keel, underhung, and moved to the extreme after end of the LWL (see Figure 35 B & D).

FIGURE 34: HULL STABILITY

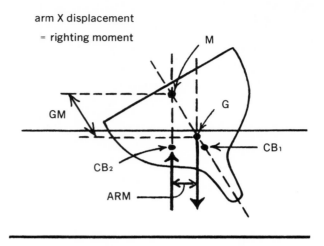

arm X displacement

= righting moment

FIGURE 35: CONTEMPORARY RUDDER STYLES

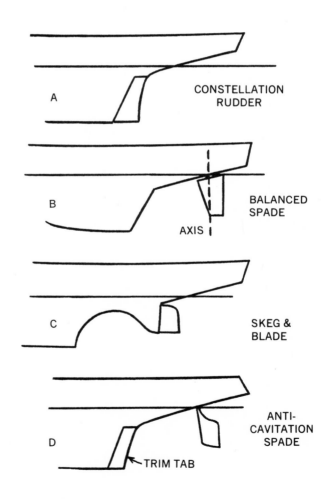

A — CONSTELLATION RUDDER

B — BALANCED SPADE — AXIS

C — SKEG & BLADE

D — ANTI-CAVITATION SPADE — TRIM TAB

34

The chief advantage of a spade rudder is that its location gives the maximum distance between the boat's vertical turning axis and the rudder's center of pressure, and this distance means a long lever arm for effective rudder power and control. The spade rudder is not suitable for every type of boat, however. It seems most appropriate for: (1) a boat having a short keel in a forward location, (2) a boat that will spend a large percentage of her time running or broad reaching in high winds and seas especially with a spinnaker set, and (3) a fairly large boat that steers with a tiller. As to the first point, many sloops which concentrate their sail area forward, in conformance with another modern trend of large headsails and short main booms, need a forward keel location for proper balance. If these boats have short keels or fins with rudders attached, they could have real steering problems under certain conditions; thus the rudder should be separated from the keel and moved aft.

As to the second and third points concerning the appropriateness of spade rudders, running or broad reaching at top speeds under the spinnaker puts enormous demands on steering. Under these conditions, instant helm response and immediate power is required. For boats that participate in offshore, downwind races (the Transpacific Race is an example), the spade rudder or skeg-attached rudder located well aft certainly fits the bill. For instant helm response, tiller steering is hard to beat, but with large boats this requires great physical effort. One solution offered by the spade rudder is the fact that it is often *semi-balanced,* that is, the turning axis lies slightly abaft the leading edge, so that water force will assist in the turning (Figure 35B).

On the other side of the coin, there are often problems with spade rudders, and for some boats there are advantages in having conventional rudders attached to the keel. Some of the advantages of a keel-hung rudder are: (1) it can contribute considerably to keel lift, (2) it requires less area than a spade rudder for a given length of lever arm because of the keel directing water flow against the rudder, (3) it causes less drag when yawed and it *stalls* (causes turbulence and a sudden loss of lift) at a wider angle than a spade, (4) there is less chance of fouling seaweed or other flotsam, and (5) there may be greater inherent strength in a properly-hung keel rudder as compared with a frees-tanding spade.

To elaborate on the first point, a slight amount of weather helm is a definite asset to a boat with a keel-hung rudder, because the helm gives extra side force and the effect of *camber* or curvature to the keel-rudder combination (see Figure 36). The water flow on the keel's windward side moves faster than the flow on the leeward side, and therefore the relative pressure is lower on the windward side, resulting in a force to windward. The slightly turned rudder thus contributes to the lift caused by the yawed keel. Optimum helm angles vary between three and five degrees as a rule. Angles beyond this cause too much drag in proportion to lift.

Free-standing, spade rudders should have very little weather helm. They must be almost perfectly balanced, because their drag contributes nothing to keel hydrofoil shape. Furthermore, a semi-balanced rudder with its leading edge turned away from the centerline, causes more drag than if the edge were on the centerline; and with the edge being separated from the keel or skeg, there is some danger of early stalling and *flow separation.* This means that the flow cannot make the abrupt turn without breaking away into turbulence. Many spade rudders are especially subject to stalling and loss of control when heeled, reaching in a blow. Under these conditions it is often necessary to reef the main and slack the mainsheet during puffs. Another point that should be mentioned is that perfectly balanced helms often make windward sailing difficult, because the helmsman has no consistent pressure, or helm "feel". This may not be a serious point when one becomes accustomed to such helms, but it takes considerable getting used to.

A questionable practice seen occasionally, is the positioning of a spade rudder well abaft the end of the LWL. Of course the stern wave will usually cover the rudder's top at high speeds, but if its top should emerge, the rudder could *cavitate,* or suck air down from the surface, which would hurt its effectiveness. This might happen on a reach in a strong wind when the boat is heeled and has a strong weather helm. Improvements were made to early models of a certain class boat having this problem, by adding *cavitation plates,* thin horizontal plates on the rudder similar to those found on some outboard motors. These form a barricade to help prevent bubbles being pulled down from the surface. Of course, the best solution is to have the rudder positioned where it is well submerged in non-turbulent water, usually little if any distance abaft the after end of the LWL, or else have the rudder type shown in Figure 35D.

Some of the problems connected with a spade rudder can be avoided with the use of a skeg ahead of the rudder (Figure 35C). In this case, the rudder can be aft, the rudder can be smaller than if it were free standing, and there is often not as much eddy-making resistance. Also the skeg may add considerably to the boat's directional stability, and stalling is delayed. On the other hand, the skeg adds to the wetted surface area, and the rudder does not augment keel lift.

One solution to the problem of no keel lift with a separated rudder is the installation of a trim tab on the trailing edge of the keel. This concept got a lot of publicity after the 1967 America's Cup races in which the *Intrepid* used a trim tab. The progressive Dutch designer E. G. Van de Stadt has used keel trim tabs for many years, and Richard Carter has recently used them with apparent success on his designs. The well-known Robert Derecktor designed *Vamoose,* now in stock production as the "PT 40", and some new Sparkman Stephens designs feature keel trim tabs. At the present time, however, these devices are still somewhat in the experimental stage for most U. S. racing-cruisers at least. The theory on their use is that the boat is balanced to have a slight weather helm, and then the trim tab is adjusted to remove the weather helm causing the helm to be almost perfectly balanced. This should enhance keel lift, but of course, it causes drag and adds to the complications of boat tuning. A trim tab can help delay spade rudder stalling when weather helm becomes excessive as, for example, when heeled on a beam reach.

Rudders attached to keels are often sharply raked, up to forty-five degrees for the primary purpose of reducing wetted lateral plane area, but there may be a beneficial side effect on certain points of sailing. Figure 37 shows the principal forces at work on a rudder. Notice that when the raked rudder is turned there is a downward force component, but when the boat carries weather helm while heeling, the resultant of the downward force and upright side force is converted to mostly side force. On boat B, having a vertical rudder, the side force is directed upward when she carries weather helm when heeled. This force could be harmful to a shoal draft centerboarder because it

could lift the stern, decrease rudder draft, and add to the rudder's ineffectiveness. The upward force due to heeling can also add to spade rudder control problems. It should be said, however, that when the boat is upright, a vertical rudder is more effective than one that is raked, because it is acting in one plane only.

Directional stability is related to the length of keel as well as the length of the lever arm between the rudder and the boat's turning axis. It is generally conceded that boats with long keels are steadier on the helm and do not yaw back and forth as much as boats with short keels. However, on modern racing-cruisers, short keels are needed not only to reduce wetted surface, but for quick turning and good helm response. Although a short keeled boat may have a tendency to start yawing fairly quickly in a following sea with a spinnaker set, she needs a short keel combined with a correctly positioned rudder of the proper size and shape to counteract the yawing and to prevent broaching to. As Phillips-Birt has pointed out, the inertia of a yaw is more easily overcome in a boat having a moderately short keel. Long keels are probably more suited to offshore cruisers having special steering devices or twin headsails especially designed for short-handed cruising or easy downwind sailing.

When the hull is heeled, directional stability is largely a problem of helm balance as a result of the hull's form relating to the rig and sail plan. Much more will be said about this in Chapter 5.

PITCHING. A vessel is pitching when she moves up and down, turning around her transverse axis. If the pitching becomes very severe, she is often said to be *hobbyhorsing.* Some racing yachtsmen have been accused of making a fetish over gear stowage and ballasting in the interest of minimizing pitching, but these yachtsmen know the disastrous effect that hobbyhorsing can have on speed to windward in a head sea.

It is generally agreed that pitching is usually minimized when weights are concentrated amidships. This means the keel ballast, tanks, inside ballast, and all major weights should be located as near as possible to the boat's longitudinal center of gravity when doing so has no adverse affect on trim, balance, or any other important aspects of the hull's behavior. Most designers are very conscious of weight placement. Several recent racing-cruiser designs by Olin Stephens even have their engines placed almost amidships in the main cabin instead

36

FIGURE 36: KEEL-RUDDER HYDROFOIL ACTION

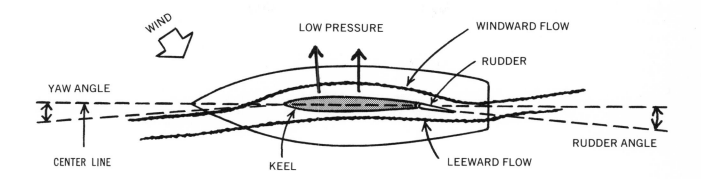

WIND

LOW PRESSURE

WINDWARD FLOW

RUDDER

YAW ANGLE

RUDDER ANGLE

CENTER LINE

KEEL

LEEWARD FLOW

of in the usual location under the cockpit. The advertising literature for one of these boats says that this characterizes the designers' and builders' desire to keep major weight components amidships.

The boat's resistance to turning about its axis, described as the *moment of inertia,* is weight times the square of its distance from the axis. Thus the spread of weights can be very critical. This is not only true in the fore-and-aft direction but in the vertical direction as well. Excessive weight up the mast and even excessive keel ballast in a very deep location can contribute to hobbyhorsing. Richard Carter has written that he prefers low ballast-displacements ratios on some of his designs for

this reason. Of course his designs have good form stability to compensate for any lack of ballast.

Spreading the weights from a boat's center can adversely affect her motion by increasing the pitching period to the point where it nearly corresponds to the period of the waves, the time period between the passing of two successive crests. A short pitching period can help keep the bow from burying in the seas, and if this happens, the light ended boat has a relatively quick recovery.

Of course, there are other factors that affect pitching, perhaps the most important being the shape of the bow sections. The bow must have enough buoyancy to prevent burying but not so much as to cause excessive quickness. V'd and

FIGURE 37: RAKED VS VERTICAL RUDDERS

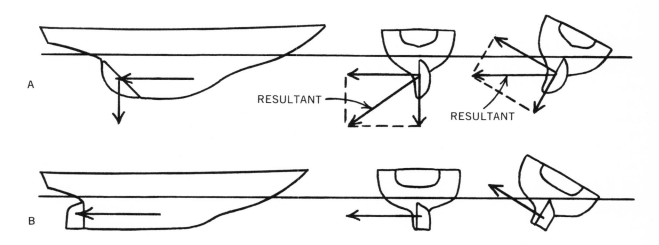

A

RESULTANT

RESULTANT

B

flaring sections forward are often very suitable to cut through the seas clearly and throw them aside. Slightly rounded bow sections are often good in light airs but not when pounding into head seas. There are indications that for heeled resistance, it is important for the bow to be fine in the general region just under the forefoot where the hull joins the keel. Stern sections should generally be fuller, with more U-shaped sections, to help damp pitching, but the designer has to be careful that the ends are reasonably matched for good balance. A boat with flat bilges, having little deadrise, will tend to pound in head seas, but if pitching is not excessive this may not have much effect on speed, and the main question becomes whether the boat and crew can take it for a lengthy period.

For the best performance in these conditions, racing-cruisers should not have excessive overhangs. This seems especially true for small light displacement boats, as they usually have sufficient buoyancy in the ends, and with long overhangs, they would tend to pound and hobbyhorse. However, some heavy boats might need moderate overhangs for pitch damping and reserve buoyancy.

In this chapter, we have not talked about rolling, but this is not an especially important point for a racing-cruiser. An out-and-out cruising boat might need a fairly short metacentric height for sea kindliness, but a boat that will be raced needs power to stand up to large sails, and she usually needs all the stability she can get without paying too large a price in rating. Another fact to be considered is that large racing sails are often effective roll dampers.

3
Hull Selection

In choosing a racing-cruiser, careful thought must be given not only to the primary but secondary purposes for which the boat is intended. Of course, this is a subjective matter that will vary with individuals. However, if prospective buyers plan to do a fair amount of racing, they might list the main considerations in the following order of importance: (1) price and upkeep, (2) seaworthiness and safety, (3) racing potential, (4) versatility and accommodations, (5) looks.

Price and Upkeep

Boat costs are listed first because this is the foremost concern for most buyers. The first step before shopping for the boat is obviously to figure how much can be spent on the initial purchase. It should be realized that most advertised or listed prices represent a fairly bare or stripped boat. A few are advertised to be equipped completely, with the basic price including everything down to the eating utensils. However, the buyer will usually find he needs more, and often that he would prefer different equipment. Standard fittings and sails are not always the best, and in some cases they are not even adequate. It is probably fair to say that the buyer of an average new racing-cruiser should be prepared to pay at least a fifth more than the basic boat price to adequately equip his boat for racing.

Extras and optional equipment often include such desirable or necessary items as working sails, racing sails, spinnaker gear, compass, winches of ample number and size, life lines, *pulpits* (metal railings) at bow and stern, a gimballed stove, extra sheets and blocks for racing sails, awning, sail covers, spreader lights, and much more. Usually all Coast Guard safety equipment such as fire extinguishers, fog horn, life preservers, proper ventilation, and the like are standard. Extras and optionals vary tremendously with individual boats.

New boat prices change rapidly, so there is no point in quoting exact current prices, however,

there are a few general rules of thumb for relative pricing. The cost of a boat is roughly in proportion to her displacement. Also, the larger a boat, the greater will be her cost per foot of overall length. For instance, an average new twenty-foot boat might cost $150 per foot of LOA, a twenty five-foot boat $300 per foot, a thirty-foot boat $450 per foot, and a thirty five-foot boat $600 per foot. Generally speaking, stock, molded fiberglass boats are the least expensive. To mold one boat by standard methods would be very expensive, but when a great number of boats are made from the same mold, costs go down. Conventional wood construction in this country is in general quite high, but in many foreign countries where labor is cheap, prices of wooden boats are competitive with molded boats, and quite often the quality of work is excellent. However, the buyer should be wary of some foreign fittings and fixtures such as electrical systems, rigging, and so forth. Some of these items are very good, but others are definitely not.

Frequently, bargains can be found in the used boat market. Sound, fully equipped boats only a few years old often can be bought very cheaply because their design has been only slightly outmoded for racing. Also, it is not uncommon for a boat owner to buy a new boat before the old one is sold, and this often results in a desperation sale. Many sound, beautiful boats of wood can be bought at bargain prices because of the current vogue for boats of fiberglass or other low maintenance materials. In many areas it may pay to shop for a used boat at the end or even just before the beginning of the sailing season rather than in mid-season.

The old rule of thumb concerning annual costs and maintenance was ten percent per year of the initial cost. On first impression this figure seems a little high, but it is, based on all costs including insurance, yacht club, and storage fees. Annual costs today may be somewhat less than ten percent, because many modern boats have substantially less upkeep than those of former times. Of course, there is a direct relation between upkeep and appearance. The more bright work, areas that need varnish or metals that need polishing, the greater will be the upkeep. Boats with fiberglass, or even painted cabin trunks having a minimum of varnished wood trim, or having teak trim that is allowed to weather, will be relatively maintenance-free above the water; but most people might agree that these boats suffer in appearance. Anodized aluminum spars do not need paint or varnish, and in some localities where boats are left afloat, masts can be left in the boat the year around. In fact, where this is possible, it is often preferable, because it saves the spars from getting scratched or bent from improper storage. Yearly maintenance for a fiberglass boat with aluminum spars and no bright work might be about five percent or slightly more of initial cost.

Seaworthiness and Safety

After the prospective buyer has decided what size boat he can afford to buy and maintain, his next consideration should be for seaworthiness and safety. This is especially true if the boat is to be raced, because in the heat of competition, boats are often driven beyond the point when sails would ordinarily be reefed or other precautionary measures would be taken.

The Midget Ocean Racing Club has a minimal set of safety rules for racing-cruisers under thirty-feet LOA and, of course, if the new boat will be raced under MORC rules, she must meet those safety requirements. These rules state that a boat must be self-righting and in some cases where a boat's stability is questionable, a self-righting test is performed. This consists of heaving the boat down on her beam ends after all hatches and openings have been closed. From this position, the boat must be able to right herself with the mast weighted with her working sails attached at the jib halyard block. The cockpit must be either self-bailing or watertight, and it should not be of excessive volume. The reason for this is that there is always the possibility of a sea breaking into and filling the cockpit, and the larger the cockpit volume, the more the stern will be sunk down by the weight of the water before it can drain or be cleared. The MORC formulas for maximum allowable cockpit volume are:

$$\frac{100V}{FB\left(LWL \text{ plus } \frac{LOA-LWL}{2}\right)}$$

equals 7 or less, for watertight cockpits; or

$$\frac{100V}{FB\left(LWL \text{ plus } \frac{LOA-LWL}{2}\right)}$$

equals 12 or less, for self-bailing cockpits,

where V equals cockpit volume in cubic feet, F equals average freeboards at waterline endings in feet, and B equals maximum beam in feet.

The Annapolis to Newport Race, run every two years under the CCA rules specifies that "the cockpit shall have a volume, measured to the lowest point in the coaming over which water can escape, not exceeding six per cent of 'L' times measured beam times freeboard aft—all from your measurement certificate." 'L' is the measured length or sailing length, obtained from the boat's CCA rating. The new NAYRU equipment lists recommend certain hull safety standards, and these include a cockpit volume formula which will be given in the discussion of the NAYRU lists near the end of Chapter 4.

The MORC safety rules further specify that "all hatches and/or locker doors leading from the measurable cockpit volume to the interior of the hull must be so constructed and secured as not to admit dangerous quantities of water in the event of knockdown or swamping of cockpit." It is best to have a bridge deck between the cockpit well and the companionway, but if not, the bottom of the companionway hatch should be raised to prevent water from flowing below should the cockpit be flooded. Some boats without this feature have short, removable, sliding hatch panels that fit in the lower part of the companionway hatch, but this is not as desirable from the standpoint of safety.

Some small keel boats with open or non-watertight cockpits lack flotation. In my opinion this is positively dangerous. A capsizable centerboard boat with flotation is far more safe. It is preferable that all small keel boats be fitted with flotation, but this is especially important for boats with open cockpits.

The MORC states that: "A rigid, non-sinkable dinghy or raft or inflatable raft with bottle inflation must be carried, the combined capacities of such being sufficient to support the maximum crew to be shipped. All such must be carried secured above decks or accessible from companionway. As an alternative to the above, the yacht may be provided with means for positive flotation in the event of being filled, capable of floating the hull, ballast, crew, stores, and a 250 pound reserve. Use of plastic foam for this purpose is encouraged. If inflated or inflatable bags or tanks or similar devices are used, they must, in the opinion of the measurer, be adequately secured and protected against puncture."

The MORC rule further states that: "All hatches, ports, or other openings giving access to the cabin or interior of the hull shall be so constructed and secured as not to carry away or admit dangerous quantitites of water in the event of a knockdown or swamping."

There are other safety features not especially required by the MORC, but which seem important. For small, offshore boats, it is best that freeboard be over twelve percent of the LWL length at the forward end of the LWL. Large boats need proportionately less freeboard than small boats. Overhangs should not be excessive. The Annapolis-Newport Race instructions limit combined overhangs to one third of LOA. Extremely light displacement boats are sometimes barred from certain distance ocean races, but I think the really important criterion is constructional strength.

For standard methods of construction aluminum and fiberglass are among the lightest weight hulls, and these hulls are immensely strong in most respects. However, after hearing reports of certain failings and damages to these hulls as a result of several rugged ocean races, one might wonder why they are not reinforced in certain vulnerable areas. Aluminum bows have been dented in by head seas, and fiberglass hulls have flexed and prevented taut adjustment of the rigging. Some of the late model fiberglass boats are being strengthened and made more rigid with a greater use of constructional bulkheads, metal backbones, stems, strapping, and also by the utilization of lockers, stowage shelves, and integral tanks to serve double duty as constructional stiffening members.

Quite a few steel hulls are being built today and some of these are covered with fiberglass. In theory this sounds very satisfactory, because the steel gives the hull rigid strength while the fiberglass checks corrosion, but the construction is relatively heavy, and probably only time will tell how successful the method is in coping with the problem of rust.

A relatively new construction in this country is *ferro-cement* (a type of reinforced concrete construction) whereby thin layers of cement are applied to both sides of a wire mesh and metal pipe skeletal form of the hull. Ferrocement has many advantages in cost, upkeep, strength, and non-deterioration, but this construction method must

also stand the test of time.

Wood as a hull material can still be very satisfactory, especially the strip plank and edge glued construction. This gives a smooth, strong, bottle-tight hull that can be completely free of rough, leaky seams caused from alternate drying out and swelling of the wood. However, this type of construction is probably best in cool climates and where there are not great extremes of temperature. Molded plywood construction gives excellent strength and rigidity for light displacement hulls.

Other highly recommended safety features are: seacocks (barrel-type valves in pipes where they go through the hull) installed on all through-hull openings below or near the waterline; dogs or latches for all opening ports, hatches, and cockpit seat locker lids; a means of closing all ventilators in stormy weather; proper gas tank installation with the fill pipe connected to a deck plate, the fill pipe running to bottom of the tank to form a liquid seal, the vent pipe above deck, baffles in the tank, and a shut-off valve near the tank with a control outside the tank's compartment (see Figure 39); head (WC) bowl located above the LWL in order that the boat will not flood in the event of a stuck or faulty valve, and the discharge hoses (on the WC and fixed bilge pump) should be looped and vented to prevent back siphoning (see Figure 38); approved Coast Guard ventilating system for the engine compartment which requires a large vent and duct bringing air into the bottom of the compartment and a large vent and duct taking the air out (see Figure 38); dog house or cabin windows of safety glass or preferably plexiglass having moderate areas to reduce their vulnerability to being broken by boarding seas; mast, chainplates, stem head, and permanent backstay, if possible, electrically grounded to the keel ballast or a ground plate for lightning protection (see Figure 39); a strong rudder of ample size at an after location for good steering control; skid-proof decks either of teak or fiberglass having a molded pattern, or a smooth surface painted with abrasive paint; bow and stern pulpits; life lines higher than knee level with through-bolted stanchions spaced no further than seven feet apart (see Figure 39); all fittings through-bolted whenever possible, a forward hatch large enough for an alternate exit; ample through-bolted grab rails; and electric wiring of good-grade, stranded copper with an impervious cover, installed high out of the bilge, and with the

FIGURE 38: HULL SAFETY SUGGESTIONS FOR RACING-CRUISERS

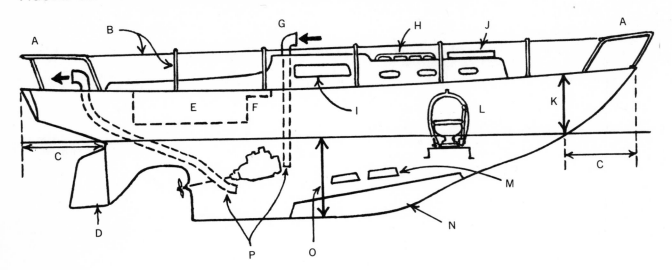

A—bow & stern pulpits. B—lifelines above knee level & bolted stanchions. C—moderate overhangs (less than 1/3 LWL). D—rudder of ample depth & located well aft. E—draining cockpit fairly deep but of small volume. F—bridge deck (or raised companionway). G—removable or watertight vents. H—ample strong grab rails. I—small, unbreakable doghouse windows. J—latching hatches permitting exit. K—freeboard at least 12% of LWL length. L—head above LWL & discharge hose with vented loop above LWL at greatest angle of heel. M—inside ballast secured or well wedged. N—keel ballast sufficient to right boat at 110° heel (at least 30% displacement). O—draft at least 1/7 LWL length. P—Coast Guard approved gas engine installation and ventilation.

FIGURE 39: SOME HULL SAFETY DETAILS

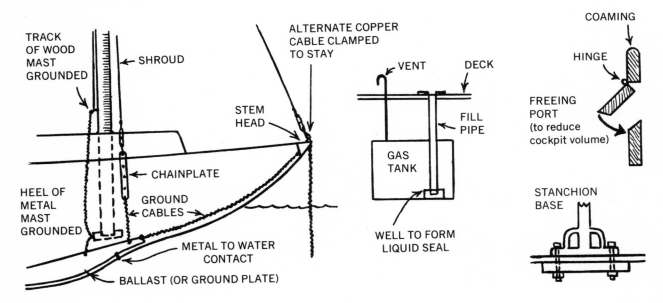

electrical system protected with fuses or circuit breakers and having a master shut-off switch.

The question often arises about the seaworthiness for offshore sailing of centerboarders as compared with deep keel boats. This is a somewhat controversial question, and of course it depends on the individual design. There have been very unseaworthy keel boats and some very seaworthy centerboarders. One hears occasional reports of centerboarders being rolled over at sea, but of course this has happened to keel boats also. The important point with the safety of a centerboarder's design is that its stability should not be overly dependent on beam, because beam contributes little to stability at extremely high angles of heel.

For ultimate stability, to prevent a capsizing or roll over, a boat needs ample and deeply located keel ballast. A keel-centerboarder can meet this requirement if she has sufficient depth of keel and keel ballast. As said in the last chapter, a general rule of thumb for draft is that it should be at least one-seventh of the LWL for the smaller racing cruisers. This ratio is also important for sufficient rudder depth (because the rudder usually cannot extend below the keel) and also for sufficient lateral plane for windward sailing in the event the centerboard is put out of service due to jamming or a broken pin or pendant. As a general rule, the ballast displacement ratio should be at least thirty percent. If there is any doubt about a centerboarder's ultimate stability, and if she will be sailed at night and/or offshore, then a heaving down test, as described earlier, should be performed, or on a large boat, the stability should be calculated by a naval architect.

In one respect, a keel-centerboarder may have a safety advantage over a deep keel boat. In extremely heavy weather at sea the shoal draft boat will be less subject to being knocked down as a result of tripping on her keel (having excessive lateral resistance) when she is *lying a-hull* (lying nearly beam to the seas while stripped of sail). She will make considerable leeway and give to the seas.

A brief summary of safety features for racing-cruiser hulls is as follows:

● Hull self-righting from a position on her beam ends with the weight of the sails on her mast. It is preferable that a boat have recovery from a 110 degree angle of heel.

● Strong construction with ample frames, strapping, and stiffening bulkheads.

● A watertight or preferably self-bailing cockpit having minimal volume. If the volume exceeds the limit specified in the formulas given in this chapter, it might be reduced by means of rigid flotation bodies securely fastened in the cockpit or by putting scuppers or clearing ports in the cockpit coamings. (See Figure 39.)

● Flotation to prevent the hull from sinking in the event of a capsizing or swamping. This is essential if the boat has an open cockpit. If she has a watertight or self-bailing cockpit but no flotation, a non-sinkable dinghy or an inflatable life raft with bottle inflation capable of supporting the entire crew should be carried.

● All hatches, ports, vents and seat lockers capable of being closed and secured. Don't put ventilating holes in the sides of seat lockers unless the vents can be closed, or unless the lockers are an integral part of the watertight cockpit.

● Bottom of companionway hatch raised high off cockpit floor or a bridge deck at fore end of cockpit.

● Adequate freeboard (over twelve percent of LWL at forward end of LWL for small boats).

● Overhangs not excessive (perhaps no more than one-third of LOA).

● Sufficient draft (perhaps no less than one-seventh of the LWL for small boats).

● Seacocks installed on all through-hull openings below or near the LWL.

● Proper gas tank installation and ventilation. Exact requirements should be obtained from the Coast Guard (see CG pamphlet No. 395).

● Head above the LWL, and discharge hoses looped and vented.

● Moderate size port lights or windows of safety glass or plexiglass mounted in strong rigid metal frames.

● Pulpits and life lines with bolted stanchions, and all fittings through-bolted whenever possible.

● Forward hatch large enough to permit exit. All hatches should have *dogs,* or strong latches.

● Skidproof decks and ample through-bolted grab rails above and below decks.

● A strong rudder of ample size at an after location, as far as possible from the boat's vertical turning axis.

● Proper electrical grounding approved by a qualified marine electrician for electrolysis and lightening protection.

The prospective buyer of a used, second-hand boat should have her thoroughly surveyed by a professional marine surveyor before purchase is made. Regardless of the hull material, it should be carefully examined for deterioration, strains, corrosion, or any constructional weaknesses. All fittings, rigging, piping, electrical wiring, and gas tank installations should be checked. A survey will not only give the buyer assurance that he is getting his money's worth, but also that he is getting a basically safe and sound boat. In this section we have merely talked about hull safety. Safe rigging practices will be discussed in Chapter 5, and safety equipment lists will be given in Chapter 4.

Racing Potential

The third item on our list of considerations for buying a new boat is racing potential. If the boat will be raced at all, raceability is an important consideration, almost without regard to how often she will be raced. To begin with, if the boat has the potential for doing well in races, this will affect her resale value. Then too, if she is to be raced at all, she should be able to stay up reasonably well with the rest of the boats, otherwise, she will merely be trailing the fleet around the course, in which case there is hardly any point in racing. Today's racing skipper cannot afford to handicap himself in any way. He must not only have ability himself, but a fast boat with a low rating, a capable crew, and good sails (and a little luck doesn't hurt). That is the formula for success and the boat herself is an important part of it.

A great deal can be learned about a boat's potential performance by studying her plans and looking at her out of water. However, it is often difficult to judge racing potential by appearance only. Experienced sailors and even designers have been fooled trying to do this. One way to improve the chances of getting a competitive boat is to look at the records of sister boats being raced *in your area*. But even this can be deceptive, because a successful boat might do well at times on account of unusual weather conditions or as the result of an occasional tactical gamble that happened to pay off. On the other hand, a potentially fast boat might have a poor record because she is being badly sailed, or is not properly tuned, has poor sails, or for some other reason. Judgments of a design's raceability should be made only after a study of all data and information from all available sources. These might include a study of racing records over a period of time, estimates of the skipper's ability, notations of circumstances affecting their performance, performance records of competitors, discussions with owners, a comparative study of handicap ratings, a study of plans and dimensions, and a careful examination of the actual boat with a trial sail, if possible.

With a brand new design, however, it is often impossible to study performance records or to take trial sails, and so judgments must be based on the designer's reputation and boat plans alone. Of course, it is the safest policy to wait until a new design has been proven before buying; but frequently, when a new design is first introduced, its price is lower than a year or so later after the boat has been proven.

The risk of getting a poor racing performer is greatly minimized, even though the design is unproven, if complete data and plans are available. Unfortunately, this is seldom the case. Many designers will not release line plans, presumably for fear that the plans will be lifted or copied. This is especially true if good racing potential is anticipated. Many advertising brochures for new designs do not even show a midship section of the hull, and a lot of useful information is often missing, such as the centerboard area and aspect ratio, sail area to wetted surface ratio, prismatic coefficient, metacentric height, location of the longitudinal center of buoyancy, and sometimes even the weight of ballast and estimated handicap rating.

To get a fair appraisal of a boat's racing potential the prospective buyer should have the following information:

● LWL length. This is the most basic determinant of big boat performance, because it imposes a limit on the speed of a displacement hull. Most handicap ratings are fundamentally based on or closely related to either upright LWL or heeled LWL while the boat is under way.

● Displacement. This is important because it is directly related to form and wave resistance, stability, and sail area. Advertising literature nearly always gives the displacement in pounds or tons. The displacement-length ratio, discussed briefly in the last chapter, is a useful aid in estimating speed potential. Light boats tend to be fast off the wind in strong breezes.

● Sail area. This information, always given out, is obviously essential because it is the motivating power. Advertising literature usually gives the square footage of sail area of the working sails but with the headsail area counted as 100 percent of the *fore triangle* (the area bounded by the foremost mast, jibstay, and foredeck). Sail area is proportional to length, stability, displacement, and wetted surface. The latter information is almost never published (although it might be obtained from the designer, builder or sales agent); thus it can only be approximated by looking at the hull or complete plans. A sail area to wetted surface ratio can be most helpful in determining light weather performance, as previously stated. A competitive boat should usually have well over twice as much sail area as wetted area but preferably 2.5 times as much. The relationship of sail area and displacement is commonly expressed by the ratio of sail area (in square feet) divided by the cube root of the displacement (in cubic feet) squared (displacement to the two-thirds power). The CCA ideal for sloop-rigged, racing-cruisers of all sizes is 15.4 but this may be on the low side for many stiff boats. In plain, simple language, sail area should be as large as possible without overburdening the boat in a strong breeze and without imposing a significant penalty in rating. Careful consideration should be given to the prevailing winds in the racing locality, whether they are predominantly heavy or light.

● Wetted surface. This factor is vital to performance in light and even moderate winds. Many prospective buyers make the mistake of judging wetted area by looking at a profile plan only. This tells very little unless the midship section can be seen at the same time. As said in the last chapter, triangular type sections or those full at the garboards may have relatively long keels without creating excess wetted surface, but champagne glass sections with low angles of deadrise must have short, almost fin type keels, in the interest of keeping wetted area low. In the absence of sectional plans or the designer's calculation of wetted surface, this area can only be estimated by looking at the hull out of water.

● Beam and ballast. These are the greatest indications of sail carrying ability in good breezes. Beam is relatively more important at low angles of heel and ballast at high angles of heel. Waterline beam varies from less than twenty five percent of the LWL for a large keel racing-cruiser to more than forty percent of the LWL for a small centerboarder. Small boats need relatively more beam

than large boats, and centerboarders need more beam than keel boats. The beam given in sales literature is maximum beam at the rail. Waterline beam usually must be estimated after measuring or observing a plan view or the actual boat, noting flare and tumble home. Although ample beam is very important for sail carrying, excessive beam increases form resistance and wetted surface, and can be harmful when beating in a light wind against choppy seas. Ballast-displacement ratios vary between approximately thirty and almost fifty percent. Ballast and beam are not only relative to a boat's length and weight but especially to her sail area.

● Draft. This dimension together with the lateral plane area has a great effect on windward performance. Sufficient keel depth with an appropriate lateral plane coefficient, as discussed in the last chapter, is needed to prevent excessive leeway. High aspect ratio keels or centerboards of deep draft are most efficient, and streamlining them increases lift and decreases drag. Centerboard depth and description is not always published in promotion literature, but the information can be acquired from the dealer or builder. Centerboards should be fairly light (to avoid rating penalties and lifting difficulties), strong, short fore-and-aft, and deep.

● LOA. This basic dimension sometimes determines what class a boat can race in, and when LWL is known, it gives the length of overhangs. These factors have an effect on the boat's rating, her seaworthiness (as discussed previously), and on her sailing length or heeled LWL. MORC rating rules tend to encourage fairly short overhangs, while the CCA rule favors straight bow overhangs (often with a fairly sharp turn or *knuckle* near the LWL) as opposed to *spoon* bows with slow curving convex stems. Concave counters (often seen on Sparkman-Stephens and Morgan designed boats) help reduce wetted area when the boat is upright in light airs but lengthen the waterline when she is heeled. Some boats with rounded sterns (without transoms) or with deep, reversed transoms (see Figure 43) have enjoyed a slight but temporary rating advantage.

● Shape of the hull. This can only be judged by a study of lines plans, photographs, and/or preferably an examination of the boat out of water. On a non-planing boat, the run can be moderately steep, but it should be easy and sweeping, without an abrupt upward turning of the buttocks. The entrance at the bow should not be excessively full, or windward performance in a head sea will suffer. Flattish, hard bilges give good form stability while slack, rounded bilges with high angles of deadrise generally give less initial stability but less wetted surface. The form of the bilges should be compared with the keel length for evaluation of wetted surface and compared with beam and ballast for evaluation of stability. Integral keels with lead ballast are usually easier to maintain and keep smooth than iron fins or integral keels with iron ballast.

In general, the hull should have smooth, flowing lines with a minimum of sharp angles or hard edges. Maximum beam and depth of fairbody should not be far abaft or forward of amidships and hull lines at the bow and stern should not be too dissimilar for good balance. As said in the last chapter, a slightly wedge-shaped hull with the center of buoyancy slightly abaft amidships is usually more suitable for most of today's hulls, especially the small ones, to offset crew weight in the cockpit. There should be extra beam above the waterline for reserve stability and good flare at the bows for reserve buoyancy and dryness.

● Propeller installation. An evaluation should be made of propeller drag. It is important to know the prop's lateral location (on or off center), its depth below the surface, its diameter and blade width, the aperture size and location, and whether or not a feathering or folding type can be used. These factors, discussed in the last chapter, affect the rating and speed under sail.

● Rating. In judging a boat's racing potential, it is essential to have an approximation of her rating for the handicap rule under which she will sail. It is not enough to feel reasonably sure that the boat will be good performer; because, even though she might do well with her competitors boat for boat, she might have a considerably higher rating that would make her non-competitive after the figuring of time allowances. When there is a difference of one foot in rating between very small boats of similar speed, the higher rated boat will have to finish as much as five minutes or more ahead of her lower rated competitor over a race course of about twenty miles.

The rating of an untried boat can be compared with the rating of a competitor to be, whose performance is known. If the new, untried design compares favorably in sail area, LWL, and other vital measures of speed with a successful com-

petitor of similar rating, the chances are that the new boat will be successful also.

If possible, several ratings of sister boats should be acquired, because there are often substantial variations. Differences in sail sizes, ballast, and propellers can make a foot or more difference in the ratings of otherwise identical boats. Advertising literature for most boats gives low ratings based on the boats having solid propellers and headsails that are not penalized for overlap.

The prospective buyer should be acquainted with all the handicap rules used in his area, for he might want to race under several or one of several rules if the boat qualifies. He should also decide in which class of the cruising division (the division for racing-cruisers) he would prefer to race. Classes are composed of boats within the same rating range (having roughly similar ratings). If a boat's rating happens to be near the dividing line between classes, it might be possible to move up or down into the next class by making a slight change in the boat's rating. Thus it is important to find out whether a new boat will rate near the top, middle, or bottom of her class. Preference for a class should be based on such factors as the class assignment of sister boats, of boats similar in size and type, and the quality of competition in general. More will be said of this and other aspects of rating when we discuss handicap rating and measurement in Chapter 7.

Versatility and Accommodations

This is the fourth item on the list of considerations in selecting a boat. Versatility and accommodations might be listed ahead of racing potential, if racing were not the primary consideration.

By versatility, it is meant that the boat can be used successfully for a number of purposes, racing, day sailing, and cruising. Such combinations are quite possible and even commonplace, but quite often some compromises are necessary. The boat's primary purpose is often accentuated at a slight expense to the secondary purposes. An example can be seen in many small boats whose design emphasizes day sailing as opposed to cruising qualities. The day sailer will have the longer, roomier cockpit while the cruiser will have part of the cockpit space allocated to the cabin.

All racing-cruisers must have at least minimal cruising accommodations. For boats under thirty feet LOA racing under the MORC rules, the min-

FIGURE 40: ACCOMMODATIONS ARRANGEMENTS

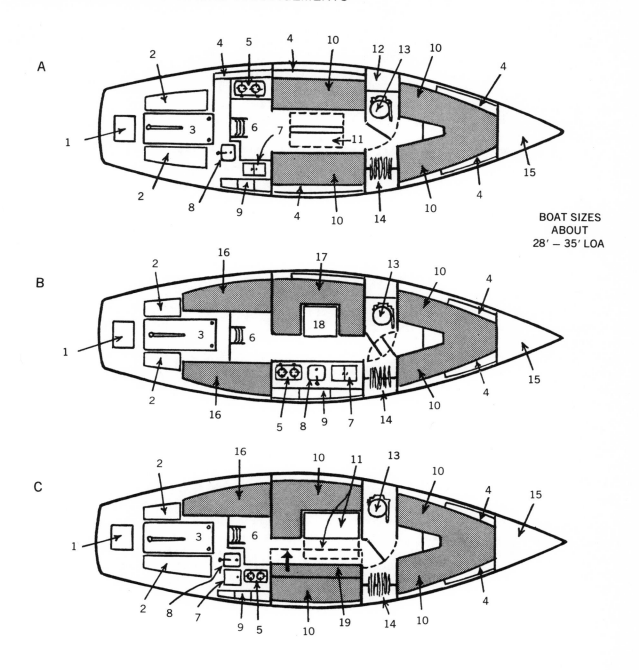

BOAT SIZES
ABOUT
28' — 35' LOA

1—LAZARET (STOWAGE), 2—COCKPIT SEAT LOCKERS, 3—COCKPIT, 4—SHELVES, 5—STOVE, 6—COMPANION LADDER, 7—ICE BOX, 8—SINK, 9—CUPBOARD, 10—SINGLE BERTH, 11—DROPLEAF TABLE, 12—LOCKER, 13—WC, 14—HANGING CLOTHES LOCKER, 15—FOREPEAK (STOWAGE), 16—QUARTER BERTH, 17—DINETTE, 18—TABLE (LOWERS TO MAKE DOUBLE BERTH, 19—TRANSOM EXTENSION BERTH (SLIDES OUT).

imum accommodations requirements are simply, "two full size berths not less than six feet long, a stove capable of safe operation at sea, and an adequate head or fitted bucket."

Figure 40 shows three popular accommodations arrangements for small to medium size boats, perhaps twenty eight to thirty five feet LOA or slightly larger. Most other arrangements are variations of these three. There are many reasons for having the all important galley in an after location. When aft, it is in a position near the boat's maximum beam for room, it is near the companionway hatch for best ventilation, it is near the transverse turning axis for least motion, and it is near the cockpit for the greatest convenience and accessibility. Also, one of the galley counter tops can often be made to double as a chart table which must be located near the cockpit, in a position of minimal motion, and where there is good light and good headroom.

The head is usually located in the forward central position shown in the drawings because this affords maximum privacy, being away from the cockpit and forward of the main saloon (main cabin). On small boats the head door is often designed to close two ways, to close off the head or to separate the head and forward cabin area from the main saloon as shown in arrangement A. Sometimes there is an additional door between the head and the forward cabin as in B. The advantage of these double-duty door arrangements is that the entire width of the boat may be used for the head area, yet privacy is maintained. Large boats can have an enclosed head as illustrated in C. This head is large enough to hold a person when the door to the compartment is closed; thus no double swinging door arrangement is necessary. On very small boats the head is usually put between the two forward bunks, and it is often hidden with a seat cushion. A curtain or door between the forward and main cabins provides privacy.

Plan A is the traditional and perhaps the most commonly seen arrangement for berths, but plan B seems to be growing in popularity and for good reason. It provides more bunk space (even though there might be too much emphasis put on how many a boat can sleep), and the quarter berths utilize space which is partially wasted on the conventional arrangement shown in A. The usual quarter berth often makes an excellent bunk for overnight sailing or racing, because it is in a position of minimum motion, and its sides prevent the occupant from being rolled out at substantial angles of heel. For harbor sleeping, quarter berths can be hot and cramped in very small boats when these bunks are put in excessively after locations under the cockpit seats. It is sometimes possible to install at the after ends of the quarter berths, ventilation holes with removable doors that will permit a through circulation of air when the cockpit seat locker lids are raised (see Figure 42). These doors should be watertight, however, and fitted with dogs for the sake of safety when at sea or in rough weather.

Another feature considered desirable by many is the dinette (sometimes called settee) arrangement shown in plan B. The table lowers to form a double berth. If there are only four people living aboard (an ample number in a small boat for any period of time), the quarter berths can be used for sleeping, and the table can be left in the raised position to make a comfortable sitting area around a semi-permanent table. With the arrangement in A there is usually a folding table that fits between the bunks for eating purposes, but in most cases this table must be removed after meals because it blocks the passageway. With the dinette arrangement, however, the table is off center and, for the most part, out of the way. This is often a good arrangement when there are children aboard who need a convenient flat surface on which to put food and drinks, draw, or play games.

Arrangement C is really a compromise between A and B. There is only one quarter berth, and the galley is "L" shaped. This galley and the one shown in A have an advantage over B in that the sink may be located near the boat's centerline in order that there is gravity drainage when heeled on either tack. The sink in arrangement B might need its seacock or valve closed when the boat is heeled on the port tack. The most satisfactory sink is larger than the size of a large dinner plate. It is preferable that ice boxes open from the top in order to minimize the possibility of spillage and for maximum retention of cold air, because the cold air sinks to the bottom of an ice box.

Galley stoves should be gimballed so that they swing in the transverse direction. Pressurized alcohol types are quite popular, and they are very safe if properly used, in accordance with the instructions. Care must be taken not to spill when priming or filling the stove, and a fuel cut-off valve should

FIGURE 41: ACCOMMODATIONS VENTILATION

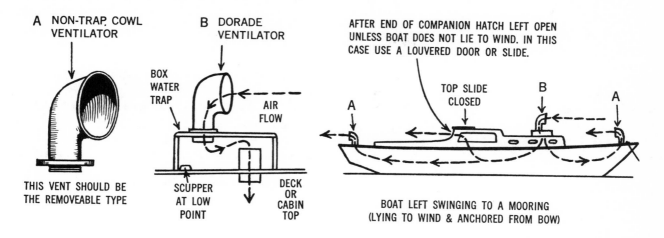

A NON-TRAP COWL VENTILATOR

THIS VENT SHOULD BE THE REMOVEABLE TYPE

B DORADE VENTILATOR

BOX WATER TRAP

AIR FLOW

SCUPPER AT LOW POINT

DECK OR CABIN TOP

AFTER END OF COMPANION HATCH LEFT OPEN UNLESS BOAT DOES NOT LIE TO WIND. IN THIS CASE USE A LOUVERED DOOR OR SLIDE.

TOP SLIDE CLOSED

A   B   A

BOAT LEFT SWINGING TO A MOORING (LYING TO WIND & ANCHORED FROM BOW)

FIGURE 42: COCKPIT COMFORT & CONVENIENCE DETAILS

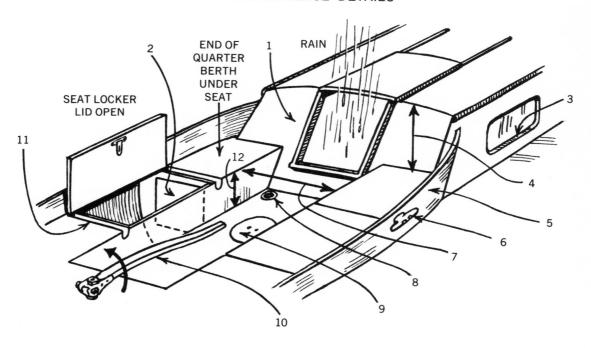

SEAT LOCKER LID OPEN

END OF QUARTER BERTH UNDER SEAT

RAIN

1—MINIMUM RAKE OF CABIN TRUNK'S AFTER END, 2—TRAP DOOR FOR QUARTER BERTH VENTILATION, 3—LIP OF OPENING PORT HORIZONTAL TO AVOID CATCHING WATER, 4—MINIMUM SEAT TO CABIN TOP HEIGHT FOR VISIBILITY, 5—COAMING HIGH FOR BACKREST & WASH PROTECTION, 6—COAMING SLANTED OUTWARD BUT NOT AT EXPENSE OF CLEAT ACCESSIBILITY, 7—COCKPIT CORRECT WIDTH FOR SEATING COMFORT AND LEG BRACING, 8—SCUPPERS FORWARD TO AVOID QUARTER WAVE, 9—WATERTIGHT ACCESS TO PROP & STUFFING BOX, 10— TILLER NOT EXCESSIVELY LONG & HINGED TO LIFT COMPLETELY UP, 11—DEEP, WIDE GUTTERS UNDER SEAT LOCKER LIDS, 12—COCKPIT DEPTH SUFFICIENT FOR SAFETY BUT ALLOWING ACCESSIBILITY TO ENGINE BENEATH.

be accessible away from the burners, in case they should happen to flare up. A fire extinguisher should always be located in the galley area. For very small boats, the one-burner, bulkhead-mounted, gimballed stove that burns a solid canned fuel such as Sterno, is a very satisfactory arrangement for cooking underway in rough weather.

All drawers, locker doors, and even sliding berths should have some simple means of locking or securing in the closed position to avoid their opening at extreme angles of heel. Also, shelves and the dining table should have *fiddles* or railings around them to prevent their contents from sliding off. It is important to have sufficient lockers to stow all clothing, stores, and gear. Lack of stowage space is a common fault on many modern, small cruisers.

Many stock racing-cruisers have optional ac-commodations arrangements, usually somewhat similar to those shown in Figure 40. In deciding how many bunks will be needed, an estimation should be made of the amount of time the boat will be used for such activities as distance racing, over-nighting, or family living. Distance racing requires more bunks than some people might think; because even though half the crew are on watch at night, the total number of crew is usually large, and bunks are occupied with sails or gear. Also some bunks on the windward side are difficult to use even with *bunk boards* (removable sides) and a dinette area is often used by the navigator. Quarter berths take away from stowage room under the cockpit seats, but they make good stowage areas themselves for sails and other soft gear. For family living, quarter berths are convenient for separating brothers and sisters. The girl can use the forward cabin, while the boy uses a quarter berth. The prospective boat buyer should check the dimen-sions of the dinette and berths especially when he or members of his family are unusually short or tall.

On medium to large size boats, variations of plan A are often used with *pilot berths* and *tran-som berth extensions*. The usual pilot berth is an elevated or raised berth near the side of the hull, while the transom is a settee or narrow seat be-neath and inboard of the pilot berth, which may be extended or slid out towards the boat's centerline to make a wide bunk (see plan C).

All cabins should be provided with ample venti-lation. In most cases there should be two side by side *Dorade vents* (named after the famous yacht *Dorade*) as shown in Figure 41, a stern cowl vent (aside from the engine room vents shown in Figure 38), and a cowl vent forward which can double as a hawse pipe for the anchor line. The cowl vents should be removable and their deck holes provided with screw plate covers. Ventilators should face as shown in Figure 41.

Figure 42 shows some desirable cockpit features for comfort and convenience. The dog house or cabin top should not be excessively high because it will block the helmsman's view when he is seated. It is also a help to visibility to have high cockpit seats, and of course, this gives good stowage space under the seats. As a general rule of thumb, the cockpit should be large enough to seat comfortably as many or more people than the number of berths below, cockpits should not be so narrow that knees knock when people sit opposite each other, but on the other hand, the cockpit should not be so wide that legs cannot span the cockpit's well in order that feet can be braced against the opposite seats when the boat is heeling. Leaking seat locker lids are a constant source of annoyance on some boats. There should be deep, wide gutters under the edges of the lids to carry off rain water or spray that finds its way through the cracks around the lids. These gutters usually drain into a self bailing cockpit. Cockpit scuppers should be large, fairly far inboard, and forward to prevent cockpit flood-ing from heeling and the quarter wave. They should be covered with a coarse screen to prevent clogging of the scupper pipes or hoses. Outboard cockpit scuppers, subject to flooding, should be provided with plugs.

Although the engine is usually serviced from below, in the cabin, by removal of the companion-way ladder, there nearly always should be some access opening in the bottom of the cockpit to inspect or service the propeller shaft and stuffing box. Flush hatch covers often leak, thus it is often preferable to have a large, threaded screw plate cover in the cockpit's bottom.

It is common practice with some designers to rake forward the after end of the cabin house as shown in Figure 42, but this rake can be a source of great annoyance when it is raining, because wa-ter can enter the cabin as illustrated, unless verti-cal slides are put into the companionway hatch. The after end of the cabin house should be almost vertical. Cabin house sides may rake inboard slightly but very little if there are opening ports in the sides, because if the rake is pronounced, water will lie in the lower lip of the porthole and will spill into the cabin when the port is opened. Cockpit coamings should be raked outboard slightly for backrest comfort but not to the extent of making cleats, mounted outboard on the coamings, awkward to reach.

Tillers should be hinged to the top of their rudder stock so that they may be lifted up to a height convenient for the helmsmen and also in order that they may be folded back out of the way when at anchor. A tiller should be no longer than is necessary for adequate steering leverage, because when unnecessarily long, it becomes a real obstruction to the crew in the cockpit. Furthermore, it is easy to *overhelm* (use excessive helm action) with too much tiller leverage.

Looks

As one who has been trained and has practiced in the field of visual arts, the author hates to put aesthetics in last place on the list of considerations for boat selection, however, with most new boat buyers the other considerations we have already discussed must come first. Price is a matter of necessity and safety a matter of survival. Most sailors prefer a comfortable, practical boat even if she is somewhat homely, and there are few racing skippers who will tolerate a *dog* (poor performer) no matter how beautiful she is. Fortunately though, beauty is not really incompatible with the other considerations, and appearance has a definite place on our list even if it is in last place.

Sailing yachts have often been thought of as being among man's most beautiful creations. The graceful flowing lines of a sleek racing hull have been favorably compared to works of sculpture, and even the shapes of the seagoing, sailing cruisers have traditionally had a functional kind of beauty. In recent years, however, there seems to have been a slight shift of emphasis away from the appearance of the small racing-cruisers, at least. This is partly due to the advent of new materials such as fiberglass which tends to give boats a cold, ascetic, non-luxurious look; and it is partly due to a new concept of ruthless practicality and functionalism prevalent especially in the area of small boat design. I am not against this concept, in fact I'm very much in favor of comfortable, low maintenance boats, but I do feel, very definitely, that

there are some unnecessarily ugly boats being produced today.

Designers of these boats argue that in the small boat field, designs should not be miniature replicas of handsome large boats, but that they should be conceived as separate and original entities. This might be considered the essence of the new concept, that custom and tradition is put aside, and the boat is designed in strict conformance to the theory that form follows function. There is an unarguable logic about this reasoning, but in the opinion of many, including myself, it is sometimes carried to an extreme.

It is true that it is difficult literally to scale down a big boat to a small size without the result being harmful to comfort or certain aspects of performance. But it is perfectly possible for small boats to have good proportions, harmonious lines, and visual unity at little if any sacrifice to room or speed. An example of a small boat which is not a literally scaled down big boat but which has the pleasing and harmonious proportions of a big boat is the "Shaw 24" class designed by William H. Shaw, the famous and successful yawl *Trina* being one of this class.

With many of the not so good looking classes, appearance is often hurt by excessively hogged or powder horn sheer lines, excessively high dog houses, overly large transoms, and needlessly chopped off overhangs. Moderation seems most suitable for the sheer especially if it is reversed. This kind of sheer can be visually deceptive. As drawn on the plans, it can often look quite graceful, but when the same sheer line appears on the actual boat it can make the boat look extremely hogged. One designer noted that a reverse sheer appearing conservative on the plans could make the boat herself look like a "beached whale." This may be due partly to highlights on the tumble home. Extreme concave sheers can be ugly too, especially on a small boat. This can make her look like a toy or rocker, and also the turning up of the stern can add to the size of the transom. A successful happy medium for small boats is the nearly straight sheer with bow higher than the stern whether the sheer is reversed or conventional.

There cannot be any hard and fast, axiomatic rules in the aesthetics of boat design (perhaps any aesthetics for that matter), because beauty is so much a matter of personal taste. However, I think that nearly anyone will agree that the "barn door"

FIGURE 43: HULL AESTHETICS

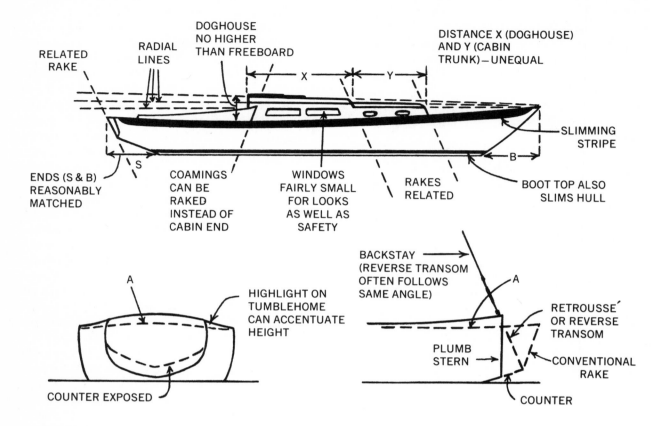

transoms found on some of today's racing-cruisers are ugly. Many of the owners will even agree to this. The question is whether these sterns are really necessary. In my opinion they usually are not, and in support of this, there are a number of all-around successful small racing-cruisers that have small, handsome sterns. One argument for an extremely wide stern is that it permits extra large overlapping jibs because lead points can be located far aft and yet can be a maximum distance out from the boat's centerline, but the measurement rules under which most boats race impose such penalties for oversized headsails that they are seldom worth extreme overlaps. Perhaps the most unattractive feature of the barn door transom is its height above the water at the boat's centerline. Many could be improved by trimming them down and flattening the sheerline aft as indicated by the dotted line A in Figure 43. If the transom is not excessively high, a generous width for after sheet leads or some other reason will not be too objectionable.

It is often helpful to appearance, especially with big boats, when the bottom of the transom is raised above the waterline exposing the counter. Raking the transom will visually decrease its top to bottom height when it is viewed from astern. With a reverse transom, sometimes called a *retroussé stern* (see Figure 43), the sailing length can be increased without adding a great deal to stern weight and without increasing the LWL or LOA as shown in the illustration. This type of stern was perhaps a little startling in appearance when it was first used, but we have become accustomed to seeing it on 12 and 5.5 meter boats and the reverse rake has seldom detracted from their good looks. The retroussé stern has also been used with visual success on certain small racing-cruisers when there is sufficient counter exposed. The Carl Alberg designed "Ensign" and its cruising version the "Electra" are good examples. Some of the One Ton Cup boats have also used this feature successfully.

A frequent eyesore in small racing-cruisers is the cabinhouse. There sometimes seems to be a determined attempt, beyond all reason, to get headroom in the very smallest of boats, and this results in doghouses of heights entirely out of proportion with the freeboards. Actually, all that is needed in boats under about twenty six feet LOA is sitting headroom. If it is considered essential to have standing headroom in the galley area, then an extra large companionway hatch with sliding cover or some kind of fold-up tent arrangement can be provided. Thus boats up to about twenty six feet LOA can have well proportioned and attractive looking cabinhouses. These can be seen on many small yachts, the Sparkman-Stephens "Dolphin" being a good example, or for a doghouse type cabin, the "Electra" is generally agreed to have good looks. For boats slightly larger, full headroom presents a problem, but this can usually be worked out satisfactorily with little sacrifice to looks. The proportionate amount of freeboard can be increased slightly, the cabin sole can be put deep in the bilge if the garboards are full, and a tasteful and harmonious doghouse can be used. It sometimes helps appearance if the doghouse slide and cabin tops follow radial lines from the stem head as shown in Figure 43. Attractive examples of high freeboard, low cabin types can be seen in some of the small Charles Morgan designs, while the Alberg designed "Triton" is a fairly successful example of the moderate freeboard, doghouse type.

There are many fine points and subtle details which can enhance or detract from the appearance of a design such as, the size and shape of the doghouse windows, *slimming* or use of a wide band of contrasting color painted below the rail to make the freeboard appear low (see Figure 43), the relation of raked cabin ends, size and style of port holes, the *crown* or camber given to the cabin top, harmonious rake of lifeline stanchions, the balance of overhangs, and more. Many of these things are brought up in the interesting book, *Sailing Yacht*

Design by Robert Henry and Richard Miller. It is encouraging to see that these authors and naval architects put considerable emphasis on a yacht's appearance. Most designers are quite artistic, but a few seem to feel that looks are a very minor consideration.

There are some who argue that beauty is a result of function and taste a result of exposure, that over a period of time we become so accustomed to certain practical features of design, we eventually find them pleasing to the eye. To some extent this is true. We have gradually grown accustomed to high freeboards, moderate reverse sheers, and the like, but there is much more to aesthetic evaluation than "handsome is as handsome does." If this weren't so, a garbage scow would be considered a thing of beauty. Down through the ages, handsome vessels of such contrasting types as the Viking long boats, clipper ships, and Gloucester fishermen have had the common denominator of harmonious lines, pleasing proportions, and balanced unity, even though these characteristics were not primarily for beautification. In all probability these vessels will forever be considered handsome. Let us hope the designers of the future will attempt to make each and every boat a joy to behold. If not, some of us may be forced to buy a cheap, fast, practical, but ugly boat; and this would be unfortunate, for every sailor should have a real satisfaction and pride in the looks of his boat.

As a last thought on choosing a racing-cruiser, it should be said that the perfect boat never exists. It is one of those elusive things we seek but can never quite find. The new boat may never satisfy all of the considerations we have mentioned in this chapter, but at least the attempt should be made to satisfy as many as possible and obviously the most important considerations should come first, depending on a realistic appraisal of how the boat will actually be used.

4
Hull Tuning and Equipping

Tuning might be defined as improving, adjusting, and refining the boat or her rig for the purpose of attaining the best performance. Tuning the hull includes such considerations as streamlining, smoothing and fairing underwater surfaces; stowage, ballasting and distribution of gear, tanks, and other weights in the hull; and planning, equipping and arranging the deck areas, especially the cockpit, for the greatest racing efficiency.

Underwater Surfaces

ANTIFOULING PAINTS. The greatest problem with the hull tuning is perhaps that of retaining the smoothest possible underwater surfaces. It is not difficult to get a smooth bottom to begin with. This is often simply a matter of sandpaper used liberally, but the real problem lies in keeping the bottom clean and smooth when haul-outs are difficult, expensive, or limited by local racing rules. As all experienced sailors know, in most boating areas, bottoms will soon foul with marine growth and barnacles. A slight amount of slime may not be harmful to speed and a very light coating of certain algae may actually be helpful, but coatings of moss, grasses, and barnacles are disastrous. The most harmful fouling occurs in warm salt or brackish water, but mild fouling takes place even in many fresh water areas.

Fortunately, there are some effective antifouling paints on the market that are a great help even if not a complete solution to the problem. These bottom paints come in two general forms, hard racing enamels and the soft *defoliating* types. The former kind gives an instant racing bottom which is hard and smooth immediately after the boat is painted, but most of these paints foul up relatively fast. On the other hand, the defoliating paints make a relatively rough surface immediately after application, but often they are more effective and last longer as antifoulants. These paints slough off and leach out the antifouling poisons gradually, over a long period of time. It may be possible to smooth up a defoliating paint slightly with very fine, wet sandpaper, but usually this will hurt the effectiveness of the paint, and also some of these paints should be immersed before the paint has thoroughly dried. Quite often this type of paint will become smoother several days or a week after the newly painted boat has been launched.

Enamel bottom paints are being improved all the time, and it often pays to use these when the boat can be hauled with reasonable frequency or in areas where marine growth is not a major problem. Some of the newer types use *TBTO,* tri-butyl tin oxide, sometimes called Bio Met antifoulant. In these paints, TBTO replaces the usual toxic ingredients copper oxide and mercuric oxide. TBTO permits a hard finish paint which can be made in a variety of colors, and it is very suitable for metal hulls, because it is said that electrolisis is avoided. Another occasional advantage with this paint is that the boat need not be launched immediately after painting. Nevertheless, in the opinion of many experienced skippers a soft, continually-leaching paint containing copper is the most effective antifoulant where haul-outs are limited and marine growth is a serious problem. A word of warning concerning some of the newer paints especially, is that they should be mixed thoroughly and applied exactly according to instructions. Failure to follow directions has produced some very unfortunate results.

When haul-outs are limited, the next best thing, but a poor substitute, is a bottom scrubbing while the boat is afloat. In some cases, small boats and/or centerboarders are gently grounded after which the crew jumps overboard and stands in the water. Then, with their feet braced against the ground for leverage, the crew scrubs off the boat's bottom with stiff scrub brushes or pieces of burlap bag. In some areas it might be possible to *careen* the boat, or roll her over on her beam ends by pulling on the halyards, but this puts a lot of unnatural strain on the moderately light mast and rigging of most racing-cruisers, and the boat's bottom may get scratched or scarred at the turn of the bilge. Of course, these cleaning methods are usually most feasible in areas of considerable tide.

Lacking a suitable place for careening or grounding, the best means of scrubbing the bottom is with a special long handled bilge brush such as the one illustrated in Figure 44. This can be used from a low floating dock or a dinghy. As can be seen in the illustration, the brush is equipped with a float that forces the bristles against the boat's bottom. The curved handle allows the brush to reach under the turn of the bilge. Soft defoliating paints are usually easier to clean than hard enamels, because the marine growth sloughs off with the soft paint, whereas the growth often sticks to the hard paints with dogged determination. With some soft types, care should be taken not to remove too much paint by over-scrubbing. A clean bottom is most important when running or reaching in light airs or when beating in almost any strength of wind.

SMOOTHING, FAIRING, AND STREAMLINING. Surface drag is not only caused by the rough surface of the paint itself, but by the irregularities, roughness, and unevenness of the hull surface under the paint. This hull roughness may be due to scars from ice, marks from resting on the cradle, raised flanges of through-hull fittings, fastenings and plugs, rudder straps, irregularities in the keel casting, keel corrosion or dents in a lead keel, and squeezed seams on a wooden hull. Molded hulls usually can be kept smoother than conventional wooden hulls because the latter often have problems with seams and fastenings especially when the wood hulls are stored out of water during the winter. If ice is not a serious problem, it is usually better to leave the wooden boat afloat all year round as this avoids the drying out and swelling of the wood which causes such problems with expanding and contracting seams. Wooden hulls having the strip planked, edge fastened, and glued seam construction, are generally easier to keep smooth than conventional plank-on-frame wooden hulls, and when a strip planked boat can be left afloat, there seldom are any serious difficulties with seams. Great care should be taken when wood, fiberglass, or aluminum boats are dry stored for lengthy periods, to see that the hulls are adequately supported. Light metal hulls can get dents and some fiberglass hulls can be distorted in extreme cases of improper cradling.

In sanding and smoothing a boat's bottom, particular care should be given to the forward half of the hull, because the boundary layer (discussed in Chapter 2) is much thinner forward than aft. Figure 45 shows the behavioral characteristics of a fluid flowing over a curved surface similar to that of a hull. Forward, the flow is smooth or *laminar*,

FIGURE 44: BILGE BRUSH

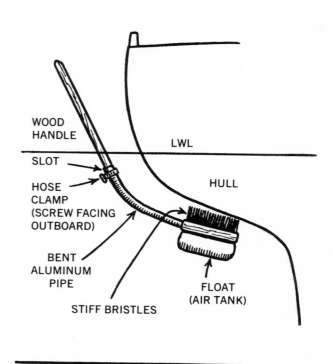

FIGURE 45: BEHAVIOR OF THE BOUNDARY LAYER

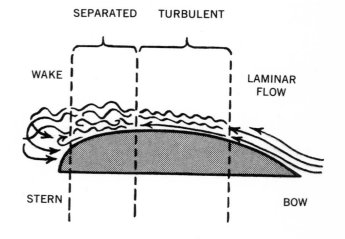

EXTENT OF FLOW REGIONS DEPENDS ON HULL SHAPE, SPEED & SMOOTHNESS OF SURFACE

but well before it reaches amidships, the boundary layer becomes turbulent with the outer molecules vibrating back and forth as they move aft. Still further aft, the flow separates and the inner as well as the outer boundary layer molecules begin to bounce off the hull and behave very erratically. Separation can be caused or aggravated by wide yaw angles or an abrupt turning of the hull form. In the wake region, all the way aft, there are low pressures that suck the molecules into back flows or reverse eddies.

There have been attempts to make laminar keels and centerboards where the flow was smooth over the entire surface, but so far these have not been entirely successful. However, the laminar flow region can be extended aft by smoothing fairing and proper streamlining. Any protrusion, bump or orifice on the forward part of the immersed hull breaks the laminar flow and causes turbulence. In the interest of minimizing frictional drag there should be a minimum of through-hull fittings with the smallest possible holes, especially in the forebody. Whenever possible, scupper drains, sinks, ice box drains, and so forth should use the same outlet. It was reported that one of Richard Carter's most successful One Ton Cup boats has but one through-hull orifice through which everything drains, even the head. It is doubtful that most yacht owners would want to go to this extreme, but the example illustrates the importance that a top designer puts on minimizing orifice drag. Centerboarders have an advantage in that some of the drains may empty into the centerboard well.

The flange lips of through-hull fittings should be flush with the hull surface. If the flanges protrude, the fittings might be replaced with flush-lip types, or perhaps the lips of the present fittings could be ground down to some extent or faired with a filler such as an epoxy cement. A few boats have been fitted with valve-type flaps to cover the holes.

Rough surfaces on the keel should also be filled and faired with cement or if these surfaces are continually peeling, blistering or rusting, perhaps the keel could be covered with fiberglass cloth using an epoxy resin. When blistering recurs in the same localized areas, check to see if the blisters are not caused by weeping plugs. Sometimes there are plugs in the keel for access to keel bolts or for some other reason, and water will often get behind the plugs and weep out, blistering the paint surface. If such is the trouble, the plugs should be removed, the holes thoroughly dried and filled with a permanently waterproof filler.

In Chapter 2 we briefly described what is generally agreed to be an ideal streamlined shape for a centerboard, keel or rudder. Authorities do not entirely agree in all details. Some favor a sharper leading edge than others. A slightly rounded leading edge tends to delay flow separation, which does not ordinarily occur at the usual sailing angles of yaw, but which does occur at certain times, for instance, when some rudders are greatly yawed to correct for excessive helm or when a boat loses speed just after tacking. Authorities usually do agree that the extreme forward end of the keel should be fine or parabolic, as shown in Figure 46, whether or not the actual edge is fairly sharp or rounded.

As for trailing edges, there seem to be two somewhat conflicting schools of thought: that these edges should be very sharp to reduce turbulence, or that they should be fine but cut off square to lessen wetted surface. Sharp-edge advocates sometimes grind down the after edges of their rudders or keels, but when this is not possible, those edges have been fined by extending them slightly further aft with strips of fiberglass cloth soaked in epoxy resin. Those sailors who advocate squaring off or blunting the trailing edge (see Figure 46) to reduce wetted area reason that this has little effect on form resistance, because the edge lies in the area of turbulent wake. This is the view held by the well-known Polish scientist-sailor, A.C. Marchaj. A blunted edge should be more beneficial in light airs rather than heavy breezes. Most experts agree that the trailing edge should never be rounded, as this would do little either to reduce turbulence or wetted surface. Those sailors who insist on sharp edges should bear in mind that it almost never pays to fine an edge to the point where it becomes fragile and subject to nicking or breaking.

Ideal centerboard or keel thickness is generally agreed to be about one-fifteenth to one twelfth of its fore-and-aft length, with the maximum thickness being between thirty and forty percent of the length abaft the leading edge. However, a keel this shape is not always possible or practical because of the usual placement of ballast at the forward end. A very thick centerboard will require a very wide slot which could cause excessive drag. When maximum thickness is in after locations, from thirty-five to fifty percent abaft the leading edge, there may be a slight extension of laminar flow, but with the more forward locations of maximum thickness, twenty-five to thirty percent abaft the leading edge, tests have indicated that the keel has greater lift at low yaw angles. Centerboard slots should be only as wide as necessary for proper board clearance.

When the rudder is attached to the keel it should be considered a part of the keel as far as streamlining is concerned. The keel's maximum thickness should not be compared with the length of the keel proper but with the keel plus rudder. The rudder's maximum thickness should be at its leading edge and this should be only slightly less than the keel's after edge. The rudder and keel should fit together snugly and be faired as smoothly as possible (see Figure 46). A spade rudder, on the other hand, should have an independent streamlined form, as indicated by the dotted lines showing the cross sectional shape in Figure 46. In the same illustration, an antifouling fin is shown just forward of the rudder. The addition of this fin is advisable in areas where there is even occasional floating seaweed that can lodge in between the top of the rudder and the hull. The small fin can be built of wood, metal or fiberglass.

Where propellers in apertures are concerned, there is again some disagreement among the designers, but all seem to agree that to minimize drag under sail, the propeller and aperture should be as small as possible. Most agree that excessively large apertures in rudders are particularly bad, because in addition to the aperture drag, there is the escape flow through the aperture which detracts from the rudder's effectiveness and makes it necessary that the rudder be held at an extra wide angle of yaw, and of course, this encourages flow separation (see Figure 47). A small keel aperture similar to Figure 25B, located a slight distance ahead of the rudder has an advantage in that it allows a two bladed propeller (turned so that its blades are vertical) to hide behind thicker deadwood, the escape flow is not as damaging to the rudder's effectiveness, and there is no need to cut away the rudder's area. When under power this propeller might cause some vibration, as both blades will strike the relatively dead water behind the keel simultaneously, but most racing skippers are willing to tolerate a slight vibration under power in the interest of minimizing drag under sail.

Solid propellers should be as small as possible

FIGURE 46: STREAMLINING

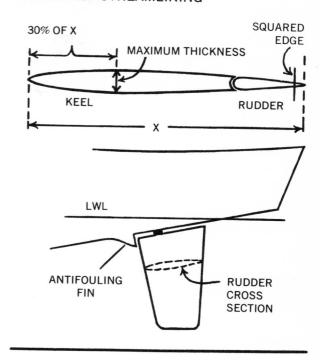

FIGURE 47: ESCAPE FLOW

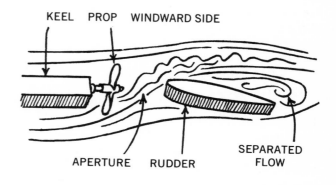

FIGURE 48: FOLDING PROP

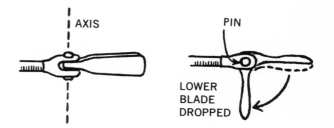

57

in diameter and blade width. A very general rule of thumb might be a diameter of a half inch to every foot of LWL and with a blade width of one quarter the diameter. High propeller pitch minimizes drag but may lead to the prop being rated as a feathering type. As said in Chapter 2, folding props cause by far the least drag, but they cost dearly in rating. Converting from a solid prop to a folding prop might increase the handicap rating by a foot of rated length under the CCA rule, but many skippers think that the reduction of drag is worth the price. With the folding prop, care must be taken to see that the axis of the blade hinges is vertical, because otherwise, the bottom blade might fall open as shown in Figure 48. Even a slight slant away from the vertical might make the blade fall open at a severe angle of heel. Some skippers have even gone to the trouble of wiring their prop blades closed immediately prior to starting a distance race to assure that the blade will not open.

To correctly position a folding prop so that its hinge axis is vertical, or a solid prop so that its blades are vertical and hidden behind the keel deadwood, the shaft should be marked so that the prop's position can be noted from inside the boat. Once the prop is in the correct position, it should be locked with the gear shift or a special shaft lock. Propellers tend to attract barnacles, and so they should be protected with antifouling paint. However, the metal in the paint should be compatible with the metal of the prop to avoid galvanic action.

As a final thought on reducing the friction of underwater surfaces, it should be remembered that the topsides are often submerged, and therefore these should be kept faired and smooth also. Usually, this is no particular problem because they may be painted with high gloss enamel paints. The topsides of new fiberglass boats need no attention except occasional cleaning or polishing, but old fiberglass hulls with chalky or scuffed up gel coats should be painted. Many of the new paints will last for two seasons with good care. Smearing the topsides with a liquid detergent may help reduce their friction, because the detergent increases wetting power and somewhat affects the boundary layer. However, only a small percentage of the topsides are submerged in light weather when wetted surface is the primary source of drag. Also of course, detergents soon wash away.

Recently, research has revealed that the presence of certain natural or synthetic polymers in the boundary layer can have a damping effect on the molecular oscillations within the layer's turbulent region, thereby extending the laminar flow. It has been suggested that these polymers could be introduced into the boundary layer with slow leaching paints or small holes at the stem or leading edge of the keel. The latest NAYRU Racing Rules (1969) prohibit releasing skin friction reducing substances such as polymers from containers, but these rules do not prevent leaching these substances from hull paint. The CCA Rules, however, prohibit any use of polymers or similar materials, which change water to a non-Newtonian fluid.

In a few sections of the country, antifouling protection is being provided by *boat baths,* portable boat receptacles into which toxic chemicals are poured to discourage bottom fouling growth. However, it is my own personal hope that this practice will not become wide-spread, and that it will be outlawed by many cruising boat racing associations because of complications, inconveniences, expense, and difficulties involved in the use of these devices, especially when boats use anchor moorings. Boat baths may have their place for certain small keel racers left moored in slips when fouling is a very serious problem; but please, let's not make life any more complicated by using chemical baths for large racing-cruisers left at anchor.

Stowage and Ballasting

As was said in Chapter 2, on most boats, pitching is minimized when major weights are concentrated amidship as much as possible. This applies to keel ballast, tanks, engine, and any ballast in the bilge not used for trimming the hull. The same thing holds true to a lesser extent for loose gear and equipment. If a boat has a tendency to hobbyhorse when beating into head seas, her ends should be kept light and free of gear. This is especially true with long overhanging ends. Heavy coils of line, chain, anchors, batteries, rubber life rafts, and so forth should be kept out of counter lazarettes or forepeaks, and of course crew weight should be kept amidships. If hobbyhorsing is a serious problem consideration should be given to moving tanks, batteries, exhaust blowers, or engine mufflers, when they are located far aft. Extreme forward and after spaces can be utilized for the stowage of light gear such as flags, light sails, light lines, aluminum swimming ladders, plastic pumps, plastic buckets, and so forth.

A small amount of inside ballast is often used for correcting the hull's fore-and-aft trim. It is important that the hull be trimmed so that it sits on or near its designed waterline, so that it is not excessively down by the bow or stern. Actually on many small and even medium size boats, it may be preferable to trim them very slightly down by the bow (provided this is allowed under the measurement rule) to offset crew weight in the cockpit. Occasionally, it may pay to trim some boats slightly down by the stern when they are reaching or running, in order to lengthen the waterlines of boats having long overhanging counters or to increase stability when the maximum beam is located somewhat abaft amidships. Any change in trim while racing, however, must be done with crew weight because after a boat is measured, her ballast and heavy gear cannot be shifted. The effect of trim on helm balance will be discussed in Chapter 5.

In stowing inside ballast, other considerations aside from hull trim should be given to its location. It should be placed as low as possible for the sake of stability and it should be placed so that it cannot possibly shift position during the most severe knockdown. *Boats have been lost because of shifting inside ballast.* If inside ballast is used for trimming purposes, of course, it cannot be placed amidships, but in most cases it is probably better not to place the ballast in the ends but to put it closer to amidships, and use more ballast as necessary.

Aside from ballast all weights should be placed with not only consideration for how they affect pitching, but also for stability. Of course the lower the weights are placed, the more effective they are in making the boat stiff. Some sailors believe that the more they load their boat with gear and supplies, the stiffer the boat becomes; but this theory is often erroneous because most modern racing-cruisers have their centers of gravity above their centers of buoyancy. Walter J. Bloemhard, who wrote a series of articles on sailing yacht design for *Motor Boating* magazine, tells us that if gear cannot be stowed very low, well below the vertical center of gravity, initial stability might actually be increased by taking gear off the boat. The center of gravity of most racing-cruisers is not very far from the LWL, so for the sake of stability, all

FIGURE 49: TANKS & STABILITY

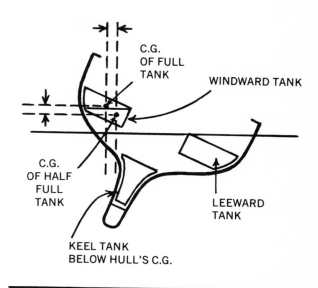

FIGURE 50: CREW WEIGHT

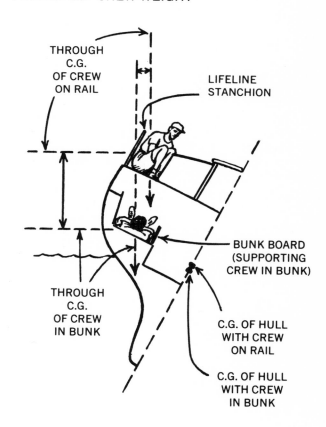

heavy stores should be stowed as far as possible below the waterline. This means that canned goods, tools, spare parts, heavy cooking utensils, and the like should be stowed in the lower drawers or lockers, under the lowest bunks or even in the bilge when there is no problem with bilge water.

Batteries and tanks should be placed as low as possible also. Some integral keel boats have water tanks deep down in the hollow of the keel and these can be very helpful to stability. Occasionally one hears arguments that side tanks, as illustrated in Figure 49, contribute to stiffness more than a keel tank (similar to the one illustrated) having a volume equal to both side tanks. It should be remembered, however, that the boat's CG remains on the centerline when the boat heels. Although the windward tank is helpful to stability, the leeward tank is detracting from stability. However, a keel tank lowers the hull's CG very slightly and there is no offsetting force. Tanks that are shallow and flat, the same type as the side tanks in Figure 49 have a disadvantage in that heeling causes the CG to shift quite far to leeward when such a tank is only partially filled, as illustrated in the diagram. To avoid this, such tanks may be kept full or empty. However, an NAYRU rule (Rule 22) forbids the filling of tanks after 9 p.m. on the day before a race. Unfortunately, violations of this rule are not unusual, because in all probability, some boat owners are not aware of the rule's existence. Also, under most measurement rules, certain tanks that are empty at the time of measurement must be kept empty while racing (See Chapter 7).

It is obvious that crew weight should be kept on the windward side for the sake of stability. Occasionally, one hears of some "gung ho" ocean-racing skipper rousing out the off-watch crew to man the windward rail when it breezes up in the middle of the night. However, a crew member might add just as much or even more to stability on a windward bunk down below where he is warm, dry, and getting needed rest. Figure 50 shows that the lower crew's weight is further outboard and because it is also lower, it slightly lowers the hull's CG. Most offshore or night racing regulations and the latest NAYRU rules state that the crew must be stationed at all times inside the life lines; so this prohibits any hiking out. Another advantage in keeping the crew below is the reduction of windage.

Over the sailing season, most racing-cruisers tend to grow heavy as a result of accumulating gear and supplies. It is a good idea periodically to give the boat a thorough cleaning and lightening provided she is kept close to her measured condition of trim and weight. It is my personal opinion, though some may not entirely agree, that overloading is harmful to the speed of most boats. This is especially so with light displacement boats.

Cockpit and Deck Layout

THE HELM. In the last chapter we discussed the cockpit from the standpoint of comfort, but now we shall discuss it from the standpoint of racing efficiency. A first consideration might be the type and location of the helm. In my opinion, it is always desirable to have a tiller on a small to medium sized boat that will be raced. If the boat has a heavy rudder, poor helm balance, or a helm that requires great physical strength to handle, then she needs a wheel for its greater mechanical advantage. However, when the boat is well balanced and does not have a heavy helm, a tiller will give quicker response and usually a more sensitive feel. Tillers are especially useful when a boat is running before following seas with the spinnaker set when there is a tendency to yaw. Under these conditions, a wheel usually requires a lot of tiring spoking or spinning for helm control.

If a wheel is used it should be of a gear ratio that requires a minimum turning for response. Captain J. H. Illingworth has suggested a general rule of three quarters of a turn from amidships to hard over for the wheel of a small yacht. Of course, this depends on the boat's balance, size and weight of rudder, and so forth, but it serves as a rough guide. Most sailors who have raced modern yachts in difficult downwind conditions prefer that the spokes be covered by an outside steering rim (see Figure 51). Exposed spokes may be romantic looking, but they tend to catch on everything and they often bark the helmsman's wrist or knuckles.

Opinions differ as to the location of the helm. The latest rage seems to be a forward location for the helm, placing the helmsman right up against the after end of the cabin house. Arguments for this arrangement are that the helmsman's vision is less hampered by the crew working the jib sheet winches in front of him; that the helmsman is closer to the companionway for communication with the navigator; that a measure of protection from spray or weather is afforded by the cabinhouse; that the helmsman gets a better view of the headsail; and that there is more room to extend the tiller for better steering leverage. However, there are a good number of arguments in favor of the helmsman being located further aft. Some of these are: that crew may be placed ahead of the helmsman to keep their weight out of the stern, that the skipper who is usually at the helm can see what his crew is doing; that if the dog house is high, the helmsman can see over it better when further aft; that when seated aft, he can better see to leeward of the jib; and in this location he does not have to crane his neck backwards to see the masthead wind indicator. Many of these advantages and disadvantages are shown in Figure 52.

Of course, the helm position will sometimes depend on the location of the rudder stock because the tiller is usually fastened to the head of the rudder stock. However, if the stock happens to put the tiller in a particularly awkward location, a wheel can be substituted, or a steering shaft with linkage to the rudder stock can be used as in E.G. Van de Stadt's "Excalibur" class. This is illustrated in Figure 51. On some boats with rudder stocks in the middle of the cockpit, the tiller can be folded back so that the helmsman sits abaft the stock. In this case, steering control is reversed with the bow turning in the direction the tiller is pushed. Steering in this manner requires a very strong tiller to rudder stock connection.

In general, I tend to favor the after location for the helmsman in small to medium size boats, primarily because it tends to keeps crew weight always closer to the boat's CG. Also, with the helmsman located forward, the jib sheet winches usually must be located behind him, and when he sits to windward, this means that after every tack or even change in jib sheet trim, some of the crew must climb around the helmsman to return to their usual heavy weather station, amidships on the weather rail. Of course, the crew sometimes interferes with the helmsman's view when he is in an after location, but he can sit to windward where his view is unobstructed for the brief time that the jib is being trimmed in just after tacking. Thereafter, the helmsman can sit to leeward if he so desires and there is no need for more than one jib trimming crew member to be in his way. In good breezes, the helmsman should usually be sitting to windward, because then he can watch approaching waves and puffs for the most effective steering, and

FIGURE 51: STEERING DETAILS

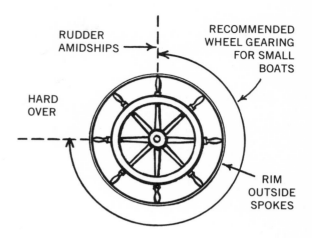

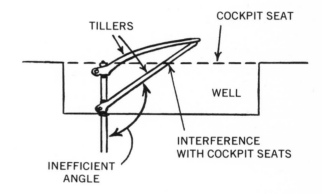

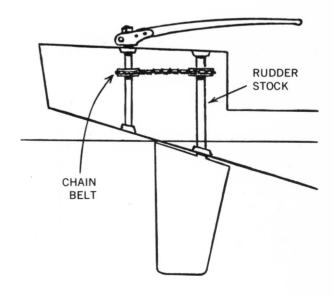

FIGURE 52: COCKPIT LAYOUTS

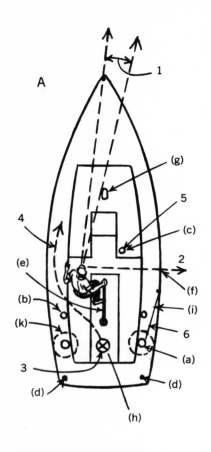

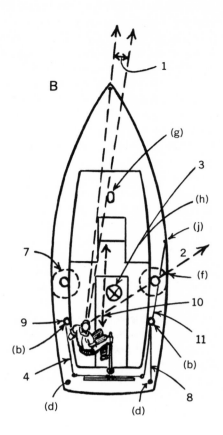

(a) primary jib sheet winch
(b) secondary winch
(c) mainsheet winch
(d) spinnaker leads
(e) tiller
(f) clew of genoa
(g) mainmast
(h) location of crew when primary winches are used
(i) genoa sheet
(j) secondary lead (for vang, staysail etc.)
(k) arc of winch handle

—ADVANTAGES—

1—WIDER VIEW OF JIB LUFF FOR HELMSMAN.

3—CREW WORKING WINCHES DON'T OBSTRUCT HELMSMAN'S VIEW.

6—THERE MAY NOT BE ANY NEED FOR A TURNING BLOCK (SEE TEXT) & PRIMARY WINCHES CAN BE USED FOR SPINNAKER.

—DISADVANTAGES—

2—GENOA BLOCKS HELMSMAN'S VIEW TO LEEWARD.

3—CREW WEIGHT TOO FAR AFT IN SMALL BOATS WHEN WINCHES ARE USED.

4—CREW MUST CLIMB AROUND HELMSMAN TO MAN WEATHER RAIL.

5—AN EXTRA WINCH IS NEEDED FOR MAINSHEET.

6—SPINNAKER AND GENOA SHEETS MUST BE TRANSFERRED OR CROSSED.

—ADVANTAGES—

3—CREW WEIGHT FARTHER ADMIDSHIPS.

2—HELMSMAN HAS BETTER VIEW TO LEEWARD, AND HE CAN MORE EASILY SEE MASTHEAD FLY.

4—MAY USE SECONDARY WINCHES FOR MAINSHEET.

8—SECONDARY WINCHES (OF AMPLE SIZE) MAY BE USED CONVENIENTLY FOR SPINNAKER.

7—WIDEST PART OF DECK FOR WINCH HANDLE CLEARANCE ON BOAT WITH NARROW STERN.

—DISADVANTAGES—

1—POOR JIB LUFF VIEW WHEN HELMSMAN SITS TO WEATHER.

9—SECONDARY WINCHES IN WAY OF HELMSMAN.

10—HELMSMAN SEPARATED FROM NAVIGATOR.

11—LINES FROM SECONDARY LEADS MAY HAVE TO CROSS PRIMARY WINCHES.

his weight there helps stability. Another advantage in being to windward is that the helmsman guards against fatigue by pulling against the tiller's customary weather helm rather than having to push against the weather helm, a much more tiring activity over a period of time. On the windward side, the helmsman will probably have his vision blocked less by the crew on the weather rail when he is sitting aft than when he is forward. I feel it is especially important for most small boats with overhanging sterns and cockpits extended almost to the transom to keep the crew forward. Some of these points are illustrated in Figure 52.

Some tillers that attach to nearly vertical rudder stocks on the floor of the cockpit can be most annoying. When these tillers are held low for efficient leverage they often strike the cockpit seats or worse, the legs of crew members seated in the cockpit when the helm is put hard over. This problem is avoided when the rudder stock lies abaft the after end of the cockpit's well and when the head of the stock is raised nearly to the level of the cockpit seats. When the rudder stock is so far forward that it must come through the cockpit floor, then perhaps a linked shaft arrangement similar to the "Excalibur's" could be used, or perhaps the head of the rudder stock could be raised off the cockpit floor as shown in Figure 51. This has been done on the new Sparkman and Stephens designed "Tartan 34." Such an arrangement minimizes tiller interference and allows the helmsman to stand up yet keep an efficient tiller-to-rudder stock angle as illustrated.

SHEETS AND WINCHES . Once the helm's position is determined, the next consideration is the location, size, and number of sheet winches. A typical top action sheet winch found on small and medium sized racing-cruisers is shown in Figure 53. Medium sized boats, perhaps thirty to forty feet LOA, usually have four headsail sheet winches, two on each side of the cockpit. However, if economy is a major consideration or if the boat is smaller than thirty feet LOA, two large winches may suffice. In some cases, it may be possible to install one large winch on the boat's centerline at the after end of the cockpit. Winch sizes are generally designated by numbering systems with the largest numbers being the largest sizes. The most common (but by no means the only) numbering system for ratchet sheet winches having handles is number 0 or number 1 being the smallest size, then

number 2 and number 3 being the next larger sizes. A number 5 size is generally a single-speed, geared winch. The next more powerful winches 'go to number 6 and number 7 single-speed, geared winches, or two-speed winches. Winches can be had with as much power as you'd probably ever want, but usually when power is increased, speed decreases, and price increases in not an arithmetic but a geometric progression.

The standard winches on many racing-cruisers are at least one size too small. The average new boat with basic equipment included in the boat's base price will have two undersize jib winches. The new owner should either substitute larger winches for the original base winches or keep the originals for secondary use, while adding larger new winches for primary use. The large primary winches are used for the Genoa jib, and smaller secondaries are generally used for the spinnaker or for interim spinnaker winches while the spinnaker sheets are shifted to the larger winches. In most cases when the original winches are used for secondaries, they are large enough to handle the spinnaker sheet or guy at all times and this makes transferring to the primary winches unnecessary.

As a general guide, the very smallest racing-cruisers should have at least number 2s for their primary winches, small boats under thirty feet LOA should have at least number 3s, larger boats with Genoas perhaps over 300 square feet should have number 5s; masthead rigged boats in the vicinity of thirty five feet LOA should have number 5s or number 6s, or the small two-speed geared winches, and forty foot boats should have at least number 7s or preferably two-speed winches similar to Barient number 28s (using a different numbering system). A small two-speed winch such as a Barient number 22 or a Barlow number 24, is an excellent substitute for a standard number 6, because it is smaller, fitting on the winch base of a number 3 or number 5, and lighter than most number 6s. In high gear, a small two-speed winch is as fast and powerful as a direct drive number 3, but in low gear, obtained by reversing the direction of the handle rotation, the two-speed winch is usually almost twice as powerful as a number 5.

Some sailors might think these recommendations for primary winch sizes are a little too high, and perhaps they are; but I think it is better to be slightly overpowered than underpowered. One hears warnings about pulling the clews out of jibs with winches that are too powerful, but modern synthetic sails of adequately heavy cloth are so strong that they can almost never be pulled apart by a slightly oversize winch unless the sail is very old and tired. Also it might be said that under-powered winches are not the best substitute for poor judgment by sail trimmers. Time and again, powerful crew members can be seen struggling to trim a large Genoa jib flat in a strong breeze. Sometimes the sheet must be led across the cockpit to the windward side so that two winches are utilized, and there are times when the jib is not trimmed in flat enough. Another argument for large winches is that racing can be a family sport, if the necessity for muscle is minimized.

The power of a winch is determined by the length of its handle, the radius of its drum, and when it is geared, by its gear ratio. The *power ratio* of a direct drive, non-geared winch is obtained by dividing the handle length by the drum radius. To figure the power of a geared winch, the ratio of the handle length to the drum radius is multiplied by the gear ratio, which is a comparison of the drive gear's rotation to that of the drum. A three to one gear ratio would mean that the gear turns three times to one turn of the drum. A winch with this gear ratio having a handle of ten inches and a drum with a radius of two inches would have a power ration of fifteen to one.

The advantage of a two-speed winch is that when the handle is turned in one direction to give high speed, the jib can be brought in very fast; but when power is really needed, usually when the jib's clew is a few feet from the point of proper trim, then the handle's direction or rotation can be reversed to operate the slow, but powerful low gear. Normal American one-speed winches turn clockwise to turn the drum, but when the handle is turned counterclockwise the drum is locked in place by ratchet pawls (see Figure 53). This ratcheting feature allows the winch cranker to make short, back-and-forth, turning motions with the handle instead of turning the handle entirely around in a circle. This enables the winch cranker to use his weight in the most effective manner for the greatest power during the last few inches of trim. Of course, two-speed winches do not have this kind of ratcheting, because when the handle's direction of rotation is reversed, the winch operates on high gear. However, a special ratcheting handle can be had for two-speed winches, and

this is highly recommended. This handle usually has a flip switch on top to change from ratcheting to non-ratcheting (see Figure 53).

The illustration of the ratcheting handle in Figure 53 shows an extra long hand grip. It is often a good idea to have this on one of the handles so that a cranker can use both hands or two men can grip the handle for extra power in strong winds. Some handles are made with an extended hand grip that is twice as long as the single standard hand grip, but for many small boats these are too long. Such extra long hand grips are clumsy, and they can catch on the life lines, interfering with complete rotation. It is often better to have an extended handle made perhaps slightly over one and a half times the length of a single grip.

All winches should be *free wheeling,* that is to say, when slack is taken in by pulling on the fall of the line, the winch drum should be able to turn without spinning the handle when it is not held. Non-freewheeling winches can be annoying and even dangerous, because if someone pulls on the fall of the sheet while the handle is inserted, it can spin around and knock a crew member (very often the one who does the pulling) on the arm or head.

Figure 53 shows a square spindle at the bottom of the winch handle that fits into a hole on the top of the winch. This is the best arrangement rather than having the spindle on the top of the winch and the hole in the handle, because sheets will often foul on a winch-top spindle, and every so often someone will accidentally sit on it, which can be a painful experience. The star-shaped spindle hole shown in the illustration is usually better than a square hole, because it is easier to insert the spindle into a star hole while the winch is turning.

A bottom action winch with its handle inserted at the bottom of the drum, as shown in Figure 53, has one slight advantage in that loops of the sheet can be put around the drum without removing the handle, but this advantage is more than offset by the fact that the handle cannot be turned entirely around in a 360-degree circle without the winch cranker's hand bumping into the sheet. Halyard winches will be discussed in Chapter 5, and the actual operation of winches will be discussed in Chapter 9.

The location of sheet winches should be very carefully thought out. Some factors that will influence their location are: the tiller location, the number of winches used, the mainsheet arrangement, width of the side deck, location of lifeline stanchions, the height of the cockpit coaming, beam at the stern, buoyancy aft, and the amount of jib overlap. Some sailors like to put their primary winches abaft the secondary winches as shown in arrangement A, Figure 52, while others like to put the primary winches forward of the secondaries as shown in B. In general, I tend to favor the latter arrangement whenever possible, but this depends on many of the factors we just listed.

Tiller location is a key factor because the winches must be placed so that the winch-working crew are not in the helmsman's way. This usually means that if the helmsman is forward, the primary winches should be aft, and if the helmsman is aft, the large winches should be forward. As said before, if a small boat's cockpit extends far aft or if the boat lacks buoyancy aft, the crew weight should be kept forward of the helmsman if possible. Width of the side deck and position of lifeline stanchions are important because the handle must be able to make a full 360-degree rotation, and without the winch cranker skinning his knuckles. The beam aft largely controls the location of the spinnaker sheet leads. If the beam is wide, those leads will usually be all the way aft at the corner of the transom, but if the stern is narrow the leads will be further forward on each quarter. The secondary winches should be where the spinnaker sheets can be led to them effectively and fairly, without chafe.

The same is true for the Genoa leads and the primary winches. There should be a carefully thought out relationship between the winch and lead point. This will largely depend on the Genoa's overlap, whether or not there is a *turning* or backup block as shown in Figure 54, and the

FIGURE 53: WINCHES

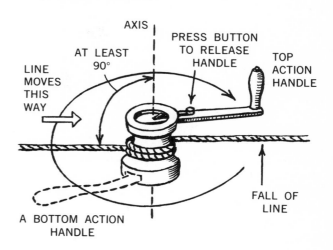

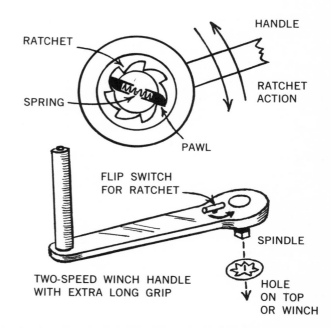

FIGURE 54: TURNING BLOCK

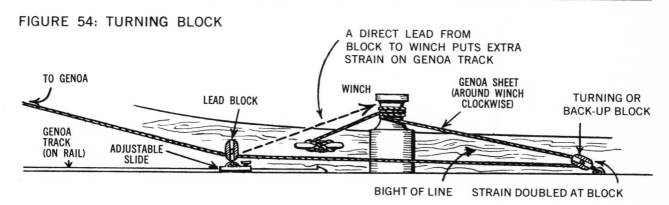

FIGURE 55: MAINSHEET ARRANGEMENTS

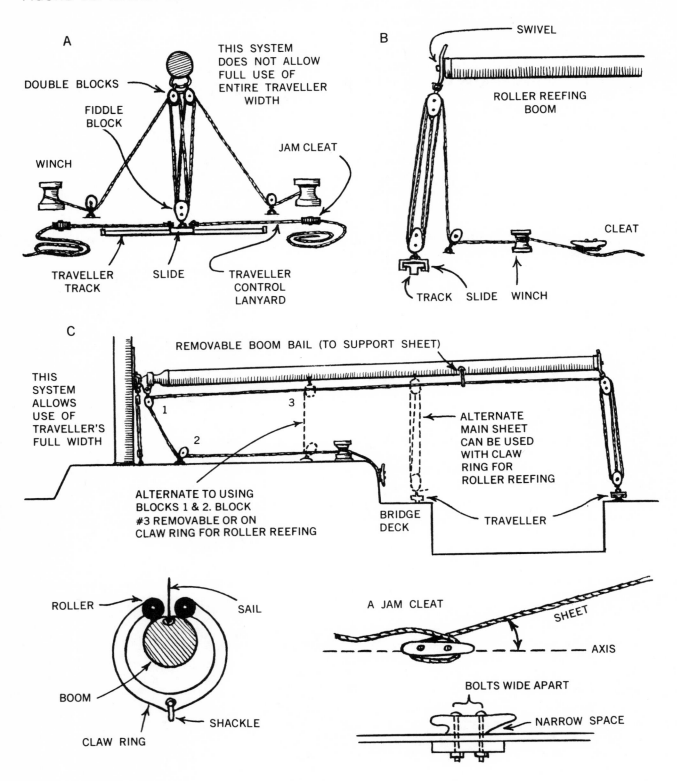

A

DOUBLE BLOCKS

THIS SYSTEM
DOES NOT ALLOW
FULL USE OF
ENTIRE TRAVELLER
WIDTH

FIDDLE
BLOCK

JAM CLEAT

WINCH

TRAVELLER
TRACK

SLIDE

TRAVELLER
CONTROL
LANYARD

B

SWIVEL

ROLLER REEFING
BOOM

CLEAT

TRACK   SLIDE   WINCH

C

REMOVABLE BOOM BAIL (TO SUPPORT SHEET)

THIS
SYSTEM
ALLOWS
USE OF
TRAVELLER'S
FULL WIDTH

1

2

3

ALTERNATE
MAIN SHEET
CAN BE USED
WITH CLAW
RING FOR
ROLLER REEFING

ALTERNATE TO USING
BLOCKS 1 & 2. BLOCK
#3 REMOVABLE OR ON
CLAW RING FOR ROLLER REEFING

BRIDGE
DECK

TRAVELLER

ROLLER

SAIL

BOOM

SHACKLE

CLAW RING

A JAM CLEAT

SHEET

AXIS

BOLTS WIDE APART

NARROW SPACE

66

height of the cockpit coaming. If the primary winches are aft as in Figure 52A, and the cockpit coaming is low, turning blocks may not be necessary, because the sheet's angle from the lead block to the winch will be nearly fore-and-aft to minimize side pull on the Genoa's lead track, and the sheet will be nearly parallel to the deck due to the winch being low. However, in many cases, even when the primary winches are aft, it is a good idea to use turning blocks to eliminate side pull and the extra upward strain illustrated in Figure 54. The average Genoa track often cannot be through-bolted, for it is mounted on the rail or very near the boat's side; and when a track is secured only by screws, it can be lifted or pulled loose.

Turning blocks should be extra strong (usually the foot block type) and through-bolted, because the jib sheet's pull is the same leading to the block as going away from it, and this doubles the strain on the block. In other words, if there is a 500-pound pull on the sheet before it turns through the block, there is also a 500-pound pull on the line after it turns and doubles back to the winch, and this puts 1000 pounds of strain on the block. For this reason, in the interest of safety, no one should ever stand or rest his arm within the *bight* or angle of the line running to and away from a turning block.

Another point to consider when leading a sheet to a winch is the angle of the sheet to the turning axis of the winch. Sheets generally cannot be led down to a winch, unless it is canted slightly, without the sheet turns *overriding* (one turn riding up over another and jamming). Usually, a sheet should be led slightly up to a winch or at right angles to the drum's axis as shown in Figure 53. Some winches are given a very slight outboard cant to improve the lead angle.

Some consideration should also be given to the crossing of sheets as in the infrequent case where a large jib and a spinnaker are being carried simultaneously. Crossed sheets are not always bad, but chafe and entanglement are apt to occur.

The main sheet arrangement has a bearing on the location of the headsail sheet winches because it may be possible to utilize the secondary winches for the main sheet. Figure 55 shows three common main sheet arrangements, and A illustrates how the secondary winches, which ordinarily would be used for the spinnaker, could double for use with the main sheet when beating to windward. Most

main sheets consist of a tackle with enough purchases to make a main sheet winch unnecessary except when the mainsail is strapped in while beating in a fresh breeze.

An important rule for the main sheet's location is that it be within easy reach of the helmsman. This is necessary because there are times when the helmsman might have to slack his main sheet instantly when there is no crew member near the cleat. Also there are times when the owner might want to sail shorthanded or even alone. It is possible to singlehand a fairly large boat as Francis Chichester has proved with his remarkable circumnavigation in the *Gypsy Moth IV*. With a helm that is located near the after end of the cockpit, sheeting arrangements A or B in Figure 55 might be suitable, but with a forward helm position perhaps arrangement C, with the main sheet winch and cleat on the cabin house, would be appropriate.

To some extent, the type of main sheet arrangement will depend on whether or not the boat has roller reefing. Since a roller reefing boom must be turned around to roll up the sail, the sheet must usually be attached to the extreme after end of the boom by a swivel or revolving ring as shown in Figure 55. Occasionally a *claw ring,* also illustrated in Figure 55, is used, but this arrangement is not always satisfactory because the ring can slip in a fore-and-aft direction and it can chafe the rolled up sail.

When roller reefing is not used and there is no need to rotate the boom, the mainsheet can be secured to the boom some distance forward of its after end as shown by the dotted lines in 55C. This arrangement has advantages, because it pulls the boom down in its middle, thereby counteracting the sail's upward pull which tends to bow upward an insufficiently rigid boom. If a boom's middle bends up, this can be harmful to the sail's shape especially in a strong wind. When it blows, we often want to bend the boom down, not up. For this reason some racing sailors prefer conventional reefing over roller reefing. When a boom-end sheet can be led to a block at the boom's middle (see block 3 in Figure 55C), strain on the boom can be more evenly distributed to avoid adverse bending.

Whenever possible mainsheets should be fitted with travellers. These are often through-bolted, transverse tracks with slides similar to those used for Genoa leads (see Figure 55 and 82), but it is preferable that the slides move on wheels with ball bearings. If the main sheet is attached near the boom's middle, the traveller might run across the bridge deck, when there is one. A boat with a short main boom and a boom-end sheet may have her traveller running across the middle of the cockpit. Most racing skippers feel that a traveller is an essential piece of equipment, but a makeshift substitute is a vang at the boom's after end, secured near the rail. However, this will mean that an extra adjustment will have to be made every time the sail's trim is changed. Vangs, travellers, and some fine points of trimming will be discussed in Chapter 6.

Careful thought should also be given to the type and location of cleats. The size of the cleat should be proportional to the size of the line it accommodates. This is especially true where jam cleats are concerned. As a rough guide for selecting the proper sheet size, we might say a 200 to 300 square foot Genoa might take a sheet three-eighths of an inch in diameter, a 300 to 400 square foot Genoa might take a one-half inch sheet, and a 400 to 700 square foot jib might require a five-eighths inch sheet. Pre-stretched Dacron is generally thought to be the best sheet material as it is very strong and has minimal stretch. Aside from strength requirements, sheets should be sufficiently thick to allow easy hand gripping. A jam cleat with a wide space at one end and a narrow space at the other (see Figure 55), very practical, but care should be taken to see that they are mounted facing the proper way so that the sheet goes around the wide end first and then wraps around to jam in the narrow end. Cleats are often out of the way when mounted on the outside of the cockpit coaming, but they are sometimes hard to reach, especially if the cockpit coaming rakes outboard, away from the vertical. If possible the primary winch cleat should be mounted horizontally on a block or pedestal near the winch. A cleat should usually not be placed in line with its sheet, but the cleat's axis (from one end to the other) should be slanted slightly away from the direction of the sheet as shown in Figure 55. Cleats on the boat's port side should not necessarily be placed in the same corresponding position as cleats on the starboard side, because most American yachts are equipped with clockwise turning winches on both sides. This means that a sheet will lead off the outboard side of the winch on the starboard side and the inboard

side of the winch on the port side. Needless to say, all cleats should be through-bolted.

Sheet stowage presents a problem on many small boats. If possible, sheets and other frequently used gear should not be kept in the seat locker on which the helmsman usually sits, for obvious reasons. Sheets might be kept in temporary handy locations, for instance on hooks just inside the companionway or on hooks accessible from the forward hatch. On medium to large size boats waterproof deck boxes, placed out of the helmsman's way in the cockpit or perhaps just forward of the doghouse are very convenient for stowing constantly used gear. Obviously, there should be consistency in the stowing of gear. Items should always be stowed in the same location so that they can be found quickly. It is often a good idea to mark sheets with colored tape or some other means for identification purposes. A simple means of differentiation might be to have some sheets of braided or woven line and others of laid or twisted line. Some braided lines might have a slight disadvantage in that they can slip on smooth winch drums a little more easily than laid lines, but braided lines are probably less apt to kink.

A winch handle should be stowed in a convenient location near the winch it operates. Some boats are provided with handle compartments in the winch bases, but if there are no such compartments, special winch handle holders can be obtained from a good yacht chandlery. Some holders made of rubber-like PVC are usually very satisfactory, but an extra large holder is required for a geared winch handle that has a spindle, because this can catch in the holder and make the handle's removal difficult. Very often, a simple solution for stowing winch handles is to fasten a holding strap across a corner of the cockpit or where the after end of the cabin joins the cockpit coamings.

All fittings should be kept properly lubricated, but this should not be overdone. Too much oil or grease can drip on teak decks, coamings, or rails and can stain the sails. In some cases, as with slides on tracks for example, wax or cake paraffin may be used effectively without any risk of staining.

KEEP THE DECKS CLEAR. When tuning for racing, unessential, lightweight deck gear that could be fouled by sheets and other lines or sails should be stowed out of the way. This is especially true on the foredeck. Most measurement rules specify that heavy deck gear such as anchors must be kept in the same location as when the boat was measured. (Of course, this only applies while the boat is racing.) It is usually a good idea to be measured with anchors off the foredeck, perhaps mounted on the cabin top or someplace where there is little or no chance of their being fouled. If there is a ventilator on the foredeck, this should be removed and replaced with a cap during a race. Even the engine room vents may be temporarily removed, for the Coast Guard has ruled that: "Sailboats used for pleasure purposes need not be ventilated when under sail alone, and may block off cowls and ducts leading to the engine and fuel compartments when under sail alone." In rough weather, racing offshore, sealing ventilators is a safety precaution for the watertight integrity of the hull, but the engine room should be provided with some ventilation from below, in the cabin. Also the engine compartment should be well ventilated and thoroughly sniffed for gas fumes before the engine is started.

A frequently encountered problem with a small boat's cockpit layout is the compass location. On large boats with steering wheels, the compass can be mounted in a binnacle on top of the steering pedestal, or in a separate binnacle on its own pedestal immediately forward of the wheel. On small boats, however, compasses must usually be mounted on the bridge deck bulkhead or on the after end of the cabin trunk. One difficulty with hanging the compass on the outside of a bulkhead is that sooner or later it will be fouled, stepped on, bumped into, or possibly hit with a winch handle. It is usually better to cut a small port or window through the cabin or bridge deck bulkhead and mount the compass where it is protected on the inside of the bulkhead, just below the window. Some boats have twin compasses, one mounted on each side of the cockpit for easy reading from either side of the boat. The trouble with this arrangement is that, aside from the double cost, the two compasses seldom exactly agree, and there must be adjustments and deviation cards made for each. Careful thought must be given to mounting the compass where it is as far as possible from magnetic influences, such as ferrous metals and electrical equipment, because these can cause serious compass errors. Deviation can be caused by the engine, instrument panel, engine controls,

fire extinguishers, steel winch handles, radios, fathometers, voltage regulators, and so forth. Even beer cans placed near the compass can affect it.

Safety Equipment

So far we have not talked about equipment that is intended entirely or primarily for safety. To begin with all boats must have the equipment required by Federal law such as, approved life preservers for every crew member, back-fire flame arresters for carburetors, bells, whistles, fire extinguishers, lights, and ventilators for engine rooms. Exact requirements should be obtained from your local Coast Guard, especially the rather complicated rules for engine ventilation. Basic ventilation regulations are set forth in the CG 395 pamphlet, but there are many variations in the engine arrangements of sailing auxiliaries and there may be several alternatives in meeting the Coast Guard requirements.

In addition to the above equipment and any extra items required by state laws for the waters sailed, local yacht racing organizations have minimum safety equipment requirements. A typical safety list for small racing-cruisers is the MORC requirements, which specify that in addition to lights and equipment required by Federal and State laws, boats must carry: compass, charts and navigation equipment and facilities adequate for the waters sailed; adequate grab rails, bilge pump, and ground tackle; safety belts and lanyards for watch on deck; a suitable life ring or buoy within reach of the helmsman, with, for night racing, an automatic water light attached; life preservers and whistle for each member of the crew; first aid equipment and instruction book; at least one waterproof flashlight; a stove capable of safe operation at sea; and a rigid, non-sinkable dinghy or life raft or inflatable raft with bottle inflation, unless the hull has positive floatation capable of supporting itself, its ballast, crew, stores and a 250-pound reserve. (As mentioned before, the MORC also requires additional accomodation equipment, namely two full-size berths at least six feet long and an adequate head or fitted bucket.) These are requirements of the MORC national organization, but there may be some more safety equipment items required by individual local stations.

For larger boats (and even small boats), many yacht racing organizations are using the newly prepared "NAYRU Recommended Minimum Equipment Lists" (first appearing in 1968) as a basis for racing safety requirements. In order to help establish adequate standards and uniformity in equipment lists, the NAYRU has divided offshore racing into classifications of four different categories. The NAYRU lists shown below (published 1-1-69) are subject to periodic minor changes. Up-to-date lists may be obtained from the NAYRU (address p. 132). Also it should be kept in mind that these lists are often modified by local racing associations.

Classification of Offshore Events

1. Long distance offshore races in open ocean where the vessel must be completely self-sufficient perhaps for extended periods and capable of withstanding heavy storms.
2. Distance races of extended duration along shoreline or in large, relatively unprotected bays or lakes which require a high degree of self-sufficiency of crew and yacht.
3. Medium distance races which extend overnight or across open water which is relatively protected.
4. Short day races close to shore or in protected waters.

Recommended Minimum Equipment and Accommodations Standards

	Race Category
Group A — Hull and Cabin	

1. Completely strong and watertight hull capable of withstanding solid water and knockdowns without significant leakage.....................................1, 2, 3
2. Hatches, companionways and ports essentially watertight and capable of being closed securely with strong hardware.....................................1, 2, 3
3. Structurally strong, essentially watertight, self-bailing cockpit permanently incorporated as a structural part of the hull................................ 1, 2, 3, 4
4. Cockpit companionways, if below main deck level, capable of being blocked off to deck level by solid, essentially leak proof and rigidly secured, if not permanent means...................1, 2, 3
5. Maximum cockpit volume over lowest coamings not to exceed six percent x LOA x Max Beam x Freeboard Aft. Cockpit floor at least 0.02 x LWL

above LWL....................................1, 2
6. Cockpit drains adequate to drain cockpit quickly and not less in combined area than the equivalent of two ¾-inch diameter drains. Yachts built after 1-1-71 must have combined area of drains not less than the equivalent of four ¾-inch drains.......................1, 2, 3
7. Rigid and strong coverings for all windows more than two square feet in area.1, 2, 3
8. Sea cocks or valves on all underwater openings except for integral deck scuppers. This does not apply to openings in the hull to accommodate the shaft, speed indicator, depth finder, etc. However, a satisfactory means of closing these openings shall be provided when it becomes necessary to do so........ 1, 2
9. Life lines and pulpits:
   a) Fixed bow pulpit (forward of headstay) and stern pulpit (unless life lines are arranged in such a way as to adequately substitute for a stern pulpit). Pulpits and stanchions must be through-bolted or welded. Taut double life lines with upper life line of wire to be secured to pulpits and stanchions. Pulpits and upper life line must not be less than twenty-four inches above the deck at any point. Stanchions shall not be spaced more than seven feet apart, except in the way of shrouds when life lines are permanently attached to shrouds. Lower life lines need not be extended through pulpits. Life lines need not be affixed to the bow pulpit if they terminate at or pass through adequately braced stanchions twenty-four inches high set inside of and overlapping the bow pulpit 1, 2
   b) Taut single wire life line securely attached with a minimum height of not less than eighteen inches................3
10. Approved running lights which will remain unobstructed by sails and when the yacht is heeled in heavy weather.... 1, 2, 3

Group B — Accommodations

1. Permanently installed toilet.............. 1, 2, 3

2. Permanently installed bunks.............. 1, 2, 3

3. Permanently installed stove having safely accessible remote fuel shutoff control... 1, 2

4. Stove... 3

5. Galley facilities including permanently installed sink............................... 1, 2, 3

6. Permanently installed water tanks which must be capable of dividing water supply into at least two separate containers... 1

7. Permanently installed water tank plus at least one additional container capable of holding five gallons................. 2, 3

8. Suitable water containers...................... 4

Group C — General Equipment

1. USCG approved (or equivalent) fire extinguishers as required by USCG (or country of registry) Rules, readily accessible in different parts of the yacht, but not fewer than three..................... 1, 2

2. USCG approved (or equivalent) fire extinguishers as required by USCG (or country of registry) Rules, readily accessible, but at least one.................... 3, 4

3. Two manually operated bilge pumps, one of which must be operable with all cockpit seats and hatches and all cabin hatches and companionways closed..... 1, 2, 3

4. One manual bilge pump operable with all cockpit seats and hatches closed........... 4

5. Two suitable anchors and cables........ 1, 2, 3

6. One suitable anchor and cable................. 4

7. Water resistant flashlights and signaling light.................................... 1, 2, 3

8. First aid kit and manual............... 1, 2, 3, 4

9. Manually operated foghorn........... 1, 2, 3, 4

10. Radar reflector 1, 2, 3

11. Set of international code flags and code book.. 1, 2

12. Shut off valves at all fuel tanks.
.... 1, 2, 3, 4

Group D — Navigation Equipment

1. Properly installed, adjusted marine compass............................... 1, 2, 3, 4

2. Spare compass.......................... 1, 2, 3

3. Suitable charts, light lists and equipment for piloting.......................... 1, 2, 3

4. Sextant, tables, and accurate time piece.. 1

5. Radio direction finder................... 1, 2

6. Radio receiver to receive 150-400 kc, broadcast, and 2-4 mc bands............. 1, 2, 3

7. Lead line................................... 1, 2, 3

8. Speedometer or log...................... 1, 2, 3

Group E — Emergency Equipment

1. Spare running lights and power source 1, 2

2. Storm trisail and storm jib.................. 1, 2

3. Heavy weather jib and reefing equipment for mainsail............................ 3, 4

4. Emergency steering equipment............. 1, 2

5. Bolt or rigging cutters.................... 1, 2, 3

6. Suitable tools and spare parts............. 1, 2, 3

7. Yacht's name on miscellaneous buoyant equipment such as life jackets, oars, cushions, etc........................... 1, 2

8. Radio transmitter, minimum power 35 watts AM, 20 watts FM, moisture proofed, with emergency antenna system, if regular system depends upon the mast..................................... 1, 2

Group F — Safety Equipment

1. USCG (or country of registry) approved life jackets for each member of crew................................... 1, 2, 3, 4

2. Whistles (referee or siren type) on life jackets................................... 1, 2, 3

3. Safety belts (harness type) for each member of crew.......................... 1, 2, 3

4. Covered life boat(s) or raft(s) rated to accommodate the entire crew and equipped with emergency provisions........... 1

5. Life boat(s) or raft(s) rated to accommodate the entire crew...................... 2, 3

6. Inflatable rafts must have automatic inflating device, at least two separate air chambers and must have been inspected, tested and approved within three years by the manufacturer or other competent authority.................. 1, 2, 3

7. Racing Rule 29.3 waived............. 1, 2, 3, 4

8. Horseshoe type life rings equipped with whistles (referee or siren type), dye markers and drogues:

a) two horseshoe life rings with high intensity automatic water lights each attached with twenty-five feet of floating line to a pole with a flag: the pole to be of a length and so ballasted that the flag will fly at least eight feet off the water in calm conditions 1

b) two horseshoe life rings, one equipped as in 8a 2

c) one horseshoe life ring with high intensity water light, or eighteen inches diameter USCG approved ring buoy with high intensity water light 3

d) one horseshoe life ring or eighteen inches diameter USCG approved ring buoy 4

9. Flare gun (Very pistol or equivalent) and flares, stowed in a waterproof container 1, 2, 3

a) twelve red and four white parachute flares 1

b) six red and two white parachute ... 2, 3

10. Heaving line (fifty-foot minimum and floating type) readily accessible to cockpit 1, 2, 3

Some of the required ocean racing equipment listed should have a few words of comment. The eight-foot (above the water) man overboard pole or *Dan-buoy* attached to a life ring is important at sea where the waves have deep troughs that can hide an ordinary life buoy. There is an excellent pole on the market that is fitted at its upper end with a very bright strob light. A less effective but simpler alternative to this pole light might be the placing of a small, shiny metal cooking funnel over the upper end of the pole (see Fig. 56). This can make a pole highly visible by flashing in the sun or reflecting a search light at night (of course this reflector is no substitute for the required water light attached to the horseshoe ring). The Dan-buoy and ring should not be lashed to the rigging, because they might become inaccessible in the event of a dismasting. They may be secured to the life lines or stern pulpit. The required drogue is a miniature sea anchor to lessen drift.

Safety belts are considered to be among the most valuable items of equipment for the ocean racing crew. The harness type required has a chest belt with shoulder straps. A short, stout lanyard is attached to the belt, and at the end of the lanyard, there is a large, strong snap hook suitable for snapping on the lifelines or some part of the rigging.

Bilge pumps should have a filter or heavy screen at their intakes to guard against clogging, and these filters should be accessible for easy cleaning when the pump is permanently mounted. Bilges must be kept clean, and all paper labels should be removed from canned goods stowed in the bilge to avoid pump clogging. One bilge pump should be near to or accessible from the cockpit, but it should not be mounted inside the cockpit seat locker or lazarette. It is always wise to carry spare parts for the pump as this is obviously an essential piece of equipment. A pump's outlet should be above the waterline and the discharge line should be looped and vented to assure against water siphoning back into the bilge. It is a good idea to have one of the bilge pumps portable so that it can be put in the deepest part of the bilge at any angle of heel and so that it can be moved to a new location if the usual pumping area is made inaccessible.

A radar reflector is a geometric shape made of folding, lightweight metal hung in the rigging to warn radar-equipped ships or boats of your presence (see Figure 56). This should be used at night or in foggy weather, especially near shipping lanes.

Some ocean racing sponsors do not require sea cocks on deck scuppers with outlets close to the waterline. However it is the safest policy to have a sea cock on every outlet, because the discharge lines could possibly rupture while the boat was heeled with the outlet deeply submerged. A valve should often be used on the engine exhaust to prevent water from entering in a following sea.

Although Race Category 4 does not require life lines and a bow pulpit, it is a good idea to install them. This is true not only for safety but for crew efficiency, especially on the foredeck. It can be very difficult handling or changing sails on the narrow, often slippery bow of a small boat without lifelines while she is heeled and pitching. Race category 3 allows life lines only eighteen inches high, but it is far safer to have them above knee level, at least twenty four inches high. Double lines are important at sea to prevent a man from slipping under the top life line when it is high off the deck. The top line must be wire, but the lower may be of rope. Stern pulpits are also important offshore, but most sailors would probably agree that neither stern pulpits nor double life lines are essential in the daytime, sailing in protected waters, unless there are very young children aboard.

Life rafts are considered much safer than dinghies for abandoning ship in an emergency. Inflatable rubber rafts designed especially for life saving are recommended. Most distance ocean-racing equipment lists require that the raft or rafts (capable of removing the whole crew) should be carried on deck or in a container opening on deck and used solely for life raft stowage. Rafts must inflate automatically, have two or more buoyancy compartments, and should be equipped with canopies to cover and protect the occupants. It is usually required that each raft be equipped with a sea anchor, an inflating pump, a waterproof signal light, three flares, two parachute flares, bailer, repair kit, two paddles, safety knife, rescue quoit and line, first aid kit, and emergency water. Careful thought should be given to stowing rafts where they are readily available, well secured, protected, and yet can be quickly released.

Suitable tools and spare parts (number 6 in Group E of the NAYRU list) for long distance ocean races should include such tools as: pliers, screw drivers, assorted wrenches, hatchet, hammer, hacksaw, wood saw, chisel, spike, drill, brace and bits, files, and a crow bar. Spares should include sails, line, an extra spreader, tiller, the longest stay, a coil of flexible wire, batteries, bulbs of every size, fuses, hoses, turnbuckles of every size, shackles, blocks, tangs, wire clamps, winch handles, stops, sail slides, hanks, and battens. Also there should be sewing and repair kits for sails, fiberglass, the head, life rafts, etc., and there should be an assortment of caulking materials, underwater epoxy, tape, glue, binding wire, small sheets of soft metal, nails, screws, pins, bolts, and soft wooden plugs tapered so that they can be driven into any through-hull orifice.

In addition to equipment required in the NAYRU lists, there is other safety related gear that many offshore sailors would deem essential or desirable. This equipment would include such items as a suitable bosun's chair for going aloft at sea, a face mask for underwater inspections, smoke signals for attracting attention in the daylight, Xenon strob lights that flash so brightly they can be seen in fog or daylight, a *whip radio antenna* (one independent of the rigging in case of a dismasting), deviation cards for all compasses, a barometer, *weather cloths* secured to the life lines to give protection to occupants of the cockpit, safety nets secured to the lifelines forward for the protection of the foredeck crew and to prevent headsails from washing overboard, a *collision mat* (a piece of canvas with lashings that can be hauled under a boat to help stop a leak or cover a hole), a sea anchor or some kind of drogue (even a small auto tire) to

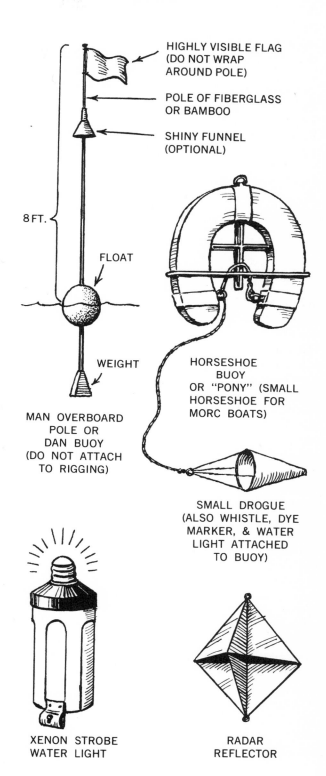

FIGURE 56: OFFSHORE SAFETY EQUIPMENT

HIGHLY VISIBLE FLAG (DO NOT WRAP AROUND POLE)

POLE OF FIBERGLASS OR BAMBOO

SHINY FUNNEL (OPTIONAL)

8 FT.

FLOAT

WEIGHT

MAN OVERBOARD POLE OR DAN BUOY (DO NOT ATTACH TO RIGGING)

HORSESHOE BUOY OR "PONY" (SMALL HORSESHOE FOR MORC BOATS)

SMALL DROGUE (ALSO WHISTLE, DYE MARKER, & WATER LIGHT ATTACHED TO BUOY)

XENON STROBE WATER LIGHT

RADAR REFLECTOR

lessen drift or slow a boat in extremely heavy weather, a storm mizzen or suitable riding sail set on the permanent backstay of a sloop, strong covers for large doghouse windows over approximately eight inches in height even if they have an area less than two square feet, adequate engine fuel in case of a dismasting, and an easily removable fuel line filter that can readily be cleared in rough weather.

Consideration might also be given to carrying a hand clamping tool (such as a Nico press) to install compression sleeve fittings on wire cables for the purpose of making rigging repairs. Optional masthead running lights allowed under the International Rules of the Road (Rule 5b) seem to be a very sound idea when normal lights are obscured by racing sails (Lighting has been covered in the author's earlier book, *Hand, Reef, and Steer.*) Another suggestion is the use of *jack wires* often found on British offshore racers but seldom seen on American yachts. A jack wire running along the rail or cabin trunk is for the purpose of accepting a safety belt lanyard's snap hook and allowing it to slide fore-and-aft so that a crew member can travel between the cockpit and foredeck in safety at night or in extremely rough weather.

All of this may appear to be a tremendous lot of gear, and such a list may seem out of keeping with advice given earlier about not overloading the racing boat. However, the equipment is actually not as much as it might seem to be. Robert Manry had much of this gear (and some more) in his thirteen and one-half foot *Tinkerbelle* when he sailed her across the Atlantic, and even she was not seriously overloaded. As said before, only light displacement boats will have their speed greatly affected by overloading. Of course, all the equipment listed is not needed for short day races, but for long races at night and in unprotected waters, safety must be the primary consideration.

Personal gear is not a part of hull safety, but it might be well to say here that for safety reasons, each crew member should wear non-skid deck shoes and each should carry a knife. Foul weather gear should be orange or yellow for best visibility, and most agree that the jacket ought to open in the front with snaps, because this is the easiest type to put on or take off.

Hull safety was discussed in the last chapter and rigging safety will be discussed in the next.

5
Selecting and Tuning the Rig

Choice of Rig

KINDS OF RIGS. The most common rigs for modern racing-cruisers are sloops, cutters, and yawls, with the former being the most popular. There is often confusion as to what distinguishes a sloop from a cutter. Of course, both are single-masted, but the cutter has her mast further aft, and she usually is *double head rigged* (with two headsails, a fore staysail and jib). One practical definition requires that a cutter have her mast located at least two fifths of her LWL length abaft the forward LWL ending. By this definition, most single-masted boats racing today are sloops, although some are very close to being cutters.

Until very recently, the trend has been towards efficient high aspect ratio mainsails with short booms, and if this trend continues, we could possibly see a greater use of the cutter rig. The reason for this possibility is that with a high aspect mainsail, the center of effort of the sails moves forward which upsets the helm balance, and the simplest way to correct for this is usually to position the mast further aft. Also, having the mast fairly far aft makes an efficient fore triangle for setting powerful jibs and spinnakers. In 1967, however, the CCA made a change in its measurement rule which substantially penalizes high aspect rigs and imposes a greater penalty on the fore triangle, and so this is somewhat discouraging to tall, narrow rigs or at least encourages greater use of seven-eighths or *fifteen-sixteenths* (between masthead and seven-eighths) rigs.

There are a few schooners that are raced successfully, the veteran *Nina* and the smaller *Ingenue* being two well-known examples. It is doubtful, however, that this rig will ever regain great popularity, because it requires a great number of tricky-to-handle sails and a large crew to handle them. Furthermore, single masted boats are usually more efficient for windward sailing. Conventional schooners have always been able to

"pick up their skirts" on a beam reach, but for the varied points of sailing over a modern closed course, the schooner usually needs a taller than normal foremast to support large jibs and spinnakers. Most schooners are not especially closewinded, but the *Nina* is certainly an exception to this rule, with her modern staysail rig.

The ketch rig is excellent for cruising, but it is not the most efficient rig for closed course racing. The large mizzen divides the sail area for ease of handling, easy reduction of sail, and helpfulness in balancing the helm for self-steering; but the rig allots too much sail area to the mizzen for optimum efficiency to windward, the fore triangle is smaller and less powerful than it could be, and the center of effort of the total sail area is lower than it should be for fast light air sailing. Furthermore, there is a rather large gap between the mizzen and a Marconi main that is difficult to fill with sail efficiently. One of the few successful small racing ketches, *Chanteyman*, owned by sailmaker Edgar Raymond, carries an unusual sail called a *mule* to fill this gap; but the sail has a very limited range of maximum effectiveness in terms of the points of sailing on which it will set efficiently without interfering with other sails. It certainly seems that after considering efficiency, rating, and all other factors, the most satisfactory rigs for racing are sloops and yawls.

YAWLS VS SLOOPS. The modern yawl rig is altogether different from the usual Marconi yawl rig of the twenties and thirties. The early boats had larger mizzens that served the purpose of dividing the rig for ease of shortening sail in heavy weather. The typical contemporary racing yawl, however, is more like a sloop with a small balancing sail at the stern. The mizzen itself adds very little drive, and in my opinion the mizzen staysail is a very much overrated sail (usually by sloop owners) when set from most of today's short, atrophied mizzen masts. The mizzen staysail has a very narrow point-of-sailing range when it can be carried effectively, and the extreme slant of its luff away from the vertical often makes the sail quite inefficient for its area. This sail, together with the mizzen, are inefficient in another respect also in that it can require an extra crew member to handle the sail combination.

The modern yawl rig has an advantage over the older rig, however, because it is generally more weatherly or closewinded. As a rule, cutters and especially sloops are considered as being more closewinded than yawls, partly because when sailing to windward, a mizzen is severely backwinded and thus is as much a detriment as an asset. To some extent this is true, but I believe that a mizzen can be a real help as a balancing sail especially when working to windward in light airs. Some sloops tend to be too perfectly balanced or slackheaded with no helm feel due to having insufficient weather helm in light airs, but a mizzen sheeted flat can give the rudder a little bite on the water, and this not only gives the helm a feel, but helps keel lift and the prevention of leeway when the rudder is hung on the keel.

In my sailing area, the Chesapeake Bay, there were a number of yawl-rigged sister boats competing against each other. Two of these boats tried racing a year or two without mizzens. No part of the rig was changed except that the mizzens were removed. This had the effect of lowering their rating slightly, but it moved the sails' total center of effort further forward, and of course, they lost the sail area of the mizzen and mizzen staysail. The conclusion I reached, after racing a yawl-rigged sister against these boats converted to sloops, was that there usually was not a great deal of difference downwind, but upwind the yawl was slightly superior in light to moderate winds. This may be surprising to some sailors, but it seems to bear out that the mizzen and mizzen staysail are overrated downwind and that the mizzen is underrated upwind. Of course in this particular example, the two converted boats might have been much more effective to windward and downwind as well, if they had added to their mainsails the sail area lost in the removal of the mizzens, but then, of course, their rating would have been higher.

For cruising, the yawl has several advantages over the sloop especially when sailing is done shorthanded. In heavy weather or in a sudden squall, the mainsail can be lowered and good balance is retained under jib and mizzen alone. Also, the mizzen alone is often useful for holding the boat's bow to the wind, as for example when the boat is anchored lying to a current and rolling to a beam swell. A disadvantage to the mizzen is that it adds to cost and upkeep. There are extra spars, rigging, and sails to buy, maintain, and replace.

Summing up the pros and cons of yawls vs. sloops, it would seem that in most cases yawls are somewhat more advantageous for cruising, especially when economy is not the prime consideration, but sloops are generally more advantageous for racing except in the larger boat sizes. The 1967 change in the CCA rules was somewhat favorable to yawls, but in my opinion (when considering cost, crew number, and all factors) the sloop is still the slightly more desirable rig for most small to medium sized boats when racing is the main consideration.

SIZE OF RIG. The amount of sail area in the rig will depend on a number of factors but primarily on stability of the hull, displacement, wetted area, and the lateral plane. The relationship of sail area to displacement and wetted surface has been mentioned in Chapters 2 and 3. As previously said, the CCA ideal sail area displacement ratio

$$\frac{SA}{d^{2/3}}$$

has been 15.4 for sloops, but many racing-cruisers have ratios higher than this. The lighter a boat, the less sail area she will need. The sail area wetted surface ratio (SA/WS) should be approximately 2.5 for good light weather performance.

Since the wind on the sails exerts a considerable side force against the hull, sail area should also be related to the lateral plane. As a general guide for a modern racing-cruiser, the sail area might be at least seven times the area of the lateral plane. The draft times the LWL times the lateral plane coefficient (described in Chapter 2) gives an estimate of the lateral plane area. Thus a normal, moderately heavy, keel ocean racer with a lateral plane coefficient of .60, drawing five feet, and with a waterline length of twenty five feet, would have a lateral plane area of seventy five square feet, and so her sail area should be perhaps 525 square feet or slightly more. This rough guide can be used to approximate the sail area when the lateral plane is known, or to approximate the lateral plane when sail area is known.

The side force exerted on the sails (and resisted by the keel) causes heeling, and of course, this is directly related to the size and shape of the sail area. A high aspect ratio rig has a relatively high center of effort and therefore exerts a greater heeling force than a low aspect rig. In this respect, it might seem that a yawl with its divided rig has a slight advantage over a sloop, but as previously said, the distribution of sail area in the yawl is fairly inefficient in the mizzen, at least.

One way of evaluating sail area with respect to stability is the Dellenbaugh coefficient method described in *Skene's Elements of Yacht Design* (revised by Francis S. Kinney). This gives a comparison with other boats for the angle of heel when the wind exerts a force of one pound per square foot on the sails (when the wind blows at about 16 m.p.h.). The formula is:

$$\text{Angle of heel} = \frac{57.3 \times \text{sail area} \times \text{heeling arm} \times 1 \text{ (lb. per sq. ft.)}}{\text{GM} \times \text{lbs. displacement}}$$

The heeling arm is the length from the sails' center of effort to the center of the lateral plane as shown in Figure 57. It will be remembered from Chapter 2, that the GM is the metacentric height (see Figure 34). This height can be obtained from an inclining test similar to that used when a boat is measured under the CCA rule (see Chapter 7). In fact, the GMs of many boats can be obtained from 1962 CCA rating certificates, as GMs were required at that time. The Dellenbaugh angles usually vary between ten degrees and twenty two degrees. Centerboard boats are generally about ten percent stiffer than keel boats, and large boats are generally stiffer than small ones. A moderately stiff, keel sloop of twenty two feet LWL might have an angle of about twenty one degrees, a twenty five-footer might have nineteen degrees, and a thirty-footer might have seventeen degrees.

To sum up very generally, sail area should be low in the interests of heavy weather performance and a favorable handicap rating, but the area should be high enough for good light-weather performance. A light displacement boat with low wetted surface and a fairly high rating, racing in areas where fresh winds are the norm, should have a low to moderate sail area; but stiff, heavy boats with low ratings and considerable wetted surface, racing in calm regions, obviously should have plenty of sail area.

Mast and Standing Rigging

It is almost universally agreed that the most practical standing rigging, the stays and shrouds, for today's racing-cruisers are composed of one by nineteen construction stainless steel wire (one strand made of nineteen wires). Unless the more expensive solid rod rigging is used, pre-stretched one by nineteen wire permits the least amount of

FIGURE 57: HEELING ARM

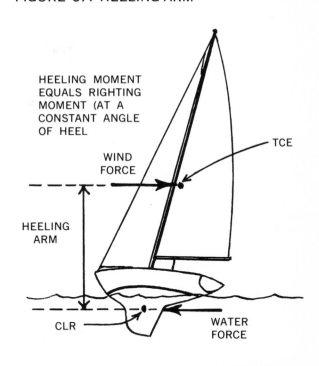

HEELING MOMENT EQUALS RIGHTING MOMENT (AT A CONSTANT ANGLE OF HEEL

TCE

WIND FORCE

HEELING ARM

CLR

WATER FORCE

FIGURE 58: STANDING RIGGING DETAILS

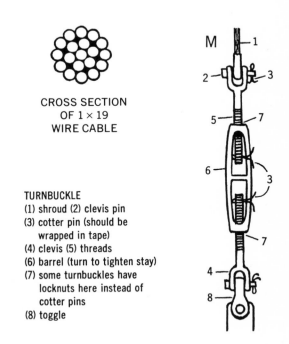

CROSS SECTION OF 1 × 19 WIRE CABLE

TURNBUCKLE
(1) shroud (2) clevis pin
(3) cotter pin (should be wrapped in tape)
(4) clevis (5) threads
(6) barrel (turn to tighten stay)
(7) some turnbuckles have locknuts here instead of cotter pins
(8) toggle

stretch, an extremely important factor, especially where a racing boat is concerned. This wire is very stiff and cannot be readily spliced, but it is customary to use swaged eyes or jaws at the wire endings that secure to *tangs* (mast straps for shrouds or stays) or turnbuckles (see Figure 58). Swaged terminal fittings are said to give up to 100 percent of the wire rope strength, whereas splicing gives only up to eighty percent strength. The greatest weakness with swaged terminals is that saltwater works its way into the top of the fitting and in time corrosion or possibly expansion from ice in freezing weather can cause tiny, hairline cracks in the terminal where it joins the wire. One supposedly effective solution to this problem is to oil or preferably to coat the terminal tops with "Rust-Oleum" 769 Damp Proof Red Primer; or removable terminals with swage inserts (such as "Norseman" brand) may be used.

The size of the standing rigging not only depends on the boat size and the amount of sail area but on stability. Stronger rigging is needed on a stiff boat than on one that is tender. A very rough rule of thumb is that the upper shrouds on a stiff boat should have a breaking strain equal to the boat's displacement. In some cases this might be a little heavier than necessary, but it allows an ample margin of safety for offshore sailing. Breaking strengths of a few of the common sizes of one by nineteen wire used on racing-cruisers are: one-eighth inch diameter — 2,100 pounds, three-sixteenth inch — 4,700 pounds, one-fourth inch — 8,200 pounds, nine-thirty-seconds inch — 10,300 pounds, five-sixteenths inch — 12,500 pounds, three-eighths inch — 17,500 pounds. Lower shrouds need not be this heavy when there are two of them at the same location on the mast. Headstays and permanent backstays are generally the same diameter as the upper shrouds, although some owners use slightly heavier jibstays in an attempt to lessen stretch and sag. A few years ago it was customary for some naval architects to specify extra heavy backstays for offshore racers. Presumably this was to cope with the jerking strains of alternately collapsing and filling heavy weather spinnakers in hard driving downwind conditions. But the practice of disproportionately "beefing up" the backstay has largely been abandoned at the present time, perhaps partly because the use of large-shouldered, heavy-weight spinnakers has been discouraged by the race committees of many long distance offshore races.

All shrouds and stays should be fitted with toggles as illustrated in Figure 58. These serve as a universal joint to prevent fatiguing of the wires and especially the turnbuckles. Some say that the jibstay or headstay should have a toggle at the top as well as the bottom of the stay. There is extra strain on the headstay because it is usually set up tight for windward work, the jib exerts a lateral force as well as a fore-and-aft force, and the spinnaker pole often lies against the stay. Furthermore, with an extra taut stay there is little mobility in the joint action of the toggle. For this reason, the headstay turnbuckle should be extra large and strong. Some yachtsmen go so far as to eliminate the headstay turnbuckle entirely, resorting to the backstay turnbuckle's pull aft on the head of the mast to tighten the headstay. I don't care for this practice, because of the fact that the masthead must be moved to change tension on the headstay, and this can alter the tune of the other stays and shrouds as well as give an unwanted mast rake. There is not any great danger of parting a headstay turnbuckle if it is amply strong, has toggles, and is continually inspected. Although some sailors have a fear of parting the headstay when beating and having the entire rig fall back into the cockpit, in most cases, if the stay breaks, the mast will be held temporarily by the wire in the luff of the jib. In such an accident, some helmsmen might instinctively luff into the wind, but the better action would be to bear off immediately so that the wind exerts its force forward. Then of course, the mainsail should be lowered, and the jib left hoisted until masthead halyards or other preventers can be made fast to the stemhead to hold the mast forward.

The safest fittings are forged, extruded, or machined from bar stock. Cast fittings are apt to have hidden flaws. A fitting of top quality stainless steel is harder and generally has greater tensile strength than a good bronze fitting of equivalent size. However, the stainless steel fitting is usually more expensive and perhaps more subject to fatigue or crystallization from constant bending pressures. Also stainless turnbuckles have occasionally been known to bind and peel their threads. An important point with turnbuckles is to be sure that there is ample length of the shanks screwed into the barrel, because there is great strain on the threads. Another point to remember is that when lock nuts are used instead of cotter pins to prevent the barrel

FIGURE 59: SPREADERS

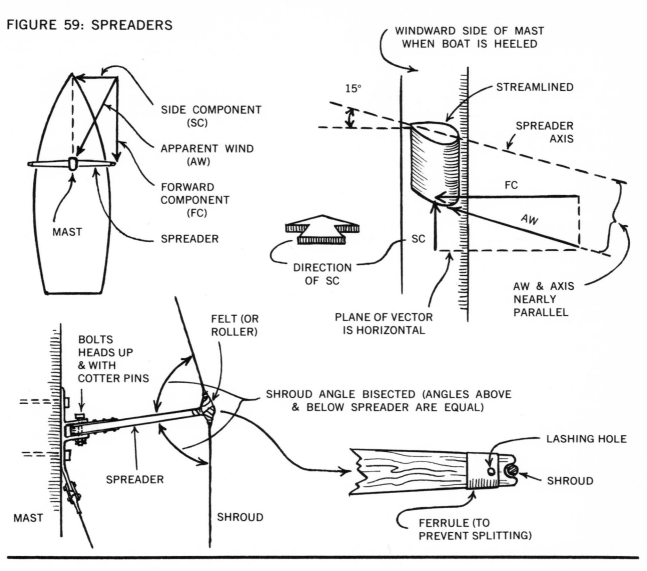

SIDE COMPONENT (SC)

APPARENT WIND (AW)

FORWARD COMPONENT (FC)

MAST

SPREADER

WINDWARD SIDE OF MAST WHEN BOAT IS HEELED

15°

STREAMLINED

SPREADER AXIS

FC

AW

SC

DIRECTION OF SC

PLANE OF VECTOR IS HORIZONTAL

AW & AXIS NEARLY PARALLEL

BOLTS HEADS UP & WITH COTTER PINS

FELT (OR ROLLER)

SHROUD ANGLE BISECTED (ANGLES ABOVE & BELOW SPREADER ARE EQUAL)

SPREADER

MAST

SHROUD

LASHING HOLE

SHROUD

FERRULE (TO PREVENT SPLITTING)

FIGURE 60: MAST SECTIONS

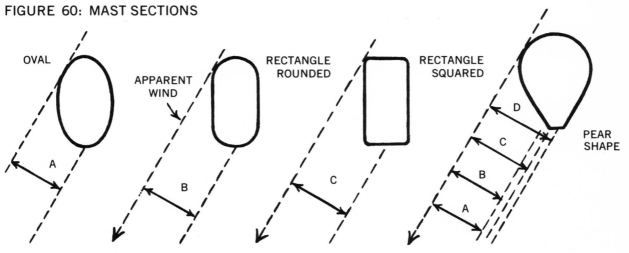

OVAL

A

APPARENT WIND

RECTANGLE ROUNDED

B

RECTANGLE SQUARED

C

D

C

B

A

PEAR SHAPE

from unscrewing, the nuts should be set up tight, and they should be constantly checked to see that they don't back off. Recommended sizes for forged bronze turnbuckles are: for one-eighth inch to five-thirty-seconds inch stainless steel one by nineteen wire–five-sixteenths inch turnbuckle, one-fourth inch or nine-thirty-seconds inch wire–one half inch turnbuckle, and five-sixteenths inch or three-eighths inch wire–five-eighths inch turnbuckle. The most thorough way to check for flaws or hidden cracks in a fitting is to have it x-rayed, but a simpler method of looking for hairline cracks is to paint the fitting with a mixture of Mercurichrome and liquid detergent. After application, the solution is wiped off, and any cracks should be clearly visible.

Spruce has not been entirely outmoded by aluminum as the material for spars, but light alloy masts have many advantages. Aluminum masts are generally lighter, stiffer, stronger, and easier to maintain than those of wood. In defense of spruce spars, however, they are quiet (halyards make an awful racket on aluminum masts), they may be tapered easily and uniformly to lower the center of gravity, and they are usually considered very handsome when varnished. Their bend is often better controlled when the rig is semiflexible (we shall discuss this later), they are usually cheaper, and there is not always as much difference in weight between a hollow spruce and an aluminum mast as many people might think. In my opinion, wood booms are generally more satisfactory than those of aluminum, because many metal booms are so light that they tend to ride up, and they require constant use of boom vangs to hold them down. In addition, a varnished wood boom will often help dress up the non-luxurious appearance of an aluminum-sparred, fiberglass boat.

Spruce spreaders can be both properly tapered and streamlined to reduce weight, windage, and interference with the air flow around the sails. Incidentally, a spreader's leading edge should be angled down perhaps seven degrees to fifteen degrees as shown in Figure 59, to reduce windage when the boat is heeled. If this is not done, the spreader exposes its wide underside to the wind even at normal heeling angles. This is explained in the diagram. Of course, it is very important that the spreader's length be angled upwards so that it bisects the shroud angle as illustrated. This is done to avoid any unnecessary bending moment or any

tendency for the spreader tip to slip on the wire. Naturally, the tip should be lashed or bound very securely to the shroud to prevent slippage. More than a few masts have been lost because of a spreader slipping. A wooden spreader tip should be fitted with a metal band or ferrule to prevent the shroud from splitting the wood (see Figure 59), and tips should be fitted with a roller or wrapped in felt to prevent chafe on Genoa jibs.

One of the main problems with any mast is windage and the fact that it interferes with the air flow around the sail it supports. To minimize this interference, a mast's diameter should be as small as possible without too much sacrifice to the mast's rigidity. Actually some compromise is nearly always involved between rigidity and small diameter. Fore and aft stiffness is especially important because lateral mast bend is usually easier to control with the shrouds and spreaders than is fore-and-aft bending.

In choosing the sectional shape for a mast, it should be kept in mind that when close hauled, the apparent wind blows against the mast at perhaps an angle of about thirty degrees from the fore-and-aft centerline; thus a streamlined section for a fore-and-aft flow is often a poor shape aerodynamically for non-rotating masts when actually sailing. Another consideration, sometimes overlooked, is that minimizing mast interference is of the greatest importance on the leeward side of the sail, because most of the sail's pull comes from this side. Square or square-ended rectangular mast sections are bad from the standpoint of interference, round sections cause minimal interference, but often lack fore-and-aft strength, and pear-shaped sections cause interference on the mainsail's important leeward side. Oval sections often seem a good compromise, because they have fore-and-aft strength, yet cause minimal interference to leeward. Testing has shown a rectangular section with round ends to be quite successful (see Figure 60).

On many small to medium sized racing-cruisers, the mast is stepped on top of the cabin house. There are pros and cons for this practice. Some of the advantages are that the mast does not take up space or block passageways below the deck; since the mast does not pass through the cabin top or deck, there is no problem with leaks around the *mast collar* (the canvas strip that fits around the mast at the mast partners to prevent water running down to the mast step); the mast is shorter which saves weight and size for convenience in winter storage; a *tabernacle* (pivot at the heel of the mast) may be used to lower the mast for low bridges or to raise the mast without a crane; and there is often less strain on the boat's garboards when compared with the mast that penetrates the deck and steps in a mast step on the floors.

One definite disadvantage of stepping the mast on the cabin top or deck is the difficulty in keeping the mast from developing compression bends, because its behavior is similar to a column with two pin ends, as an engineer might say, as opposed to a mast passing through the deck, which behaves like a column with a pin end at the top, but a fixed lower end. Another drawback to deck or cabin top stepping is the structural difficulty of supporting the tremendous downward thrust of the mast when stays are set up and the sails are strapped in while beating to windward. In some cases it is possible to transmit the load to the keel with a permanent pipe under the mast step, however, great care should be taken to see that there are adequate floors at the point under the mast to prevent straining the garboards. Without adequate strength in this region especially when pounding in a seaway, wood boats could begin to leak and fiberglass boats could develop cracks.

In most cases a pipe under the mast is not practical because the step is usually over a bulkhead doorway either into the head or forward cabin as shown in Figure 61. In case A, the head is enclosed, and its bulkheads extend out to the boat's centerline. There are heavy posts which can support the mast load on either side of the head doorway; but the mast step lies over the middle of the doorway, and the load must be supported by a fore-and-aft, horizontal beam across the top of the posts. With arrangement B, commonly seen on smaller boats, the load is supported in the same manner but the beam runs athwartship instead of fore-and-aft. Quite often, these beams are not adequate, and they sag in time. One solution to the problem is the addition of metal beams as shown in Figure 61. In case A, a channel beam has been added to span the posts above the deck. In case B, the transverse beam might hurt appearance above deck; so an inverted channel beam with concavely curved undersides for headroom or two right-angle beams fitted together for easier installation have been put under the deck.

As stated in Chapter 3, it is more convenient and probably better for the mast to leave one of anodized aluminum stepped the year around when the boat is left afloat, because the anodizing may become scratched with repeated spar removal and storage. However, the rigging should be slacked to allow for contraction in cold weather, and the wire ends of the halyards should be hauled aloft on *gantlines* (old or light pieces of line used for this purpose) in order that the rope ends of the halyards will be down and may be protected under the winter cover. The wire halyards and gantlines must be carefully tied away from the mast. Of course in the spring when the boat is commissioned, the owner or a reliable crew member should be hauled aloft to oil blocks and sheaves, seize and wrap the spreader tips, and carefully inspect all tangs and masthead fittings.

It is usually better for varnished spars to be removed from the boat during the winter for protection from the weather. They should be stored off the ground and *should be properly supported so that they lie straight*. A good spar can be permanently bent by being improperly stored.

Running Rigging

Running rigging consists of the movable lines and wires used to hoist, trim, or adjust the sails. Sheets were discussed in connection with sheet winches in the last chapter, so here we shall limit the discussion mainly to halyards.

On racing boats, wire halyards for jibs, mainsails, and mizzens are used to minimize windage and stretch. It is generally agreed that flexible wire rope of the seven by nineteen construction (seven strands, each made from nineteen wires) is the best wire for halyards. To minimize fatigue, sheaves of large diameter are recommended. This is one reason why sheaves installed in the masthead as shown in Figure 62, are preferable to small blocks hung at the *truck* (mast top). Mast sheaves should project slightly beyond the after side of the mast as shown in order that the halyard can be led fairly to the head of the mainsail for proper sail setting and the reduction of chafe. The main halyard should be on the starboard side of the mast and the jib halyard to port. This is done partly for safety because most crew expect this arrangement; and also it is done for efficiency, because the main halyard leads down the forward side of the mast, and its winch, located near the base of the mast, usually turns

FIGURE 61: MASTS STEPPED ON DECK OR CABIN TOP

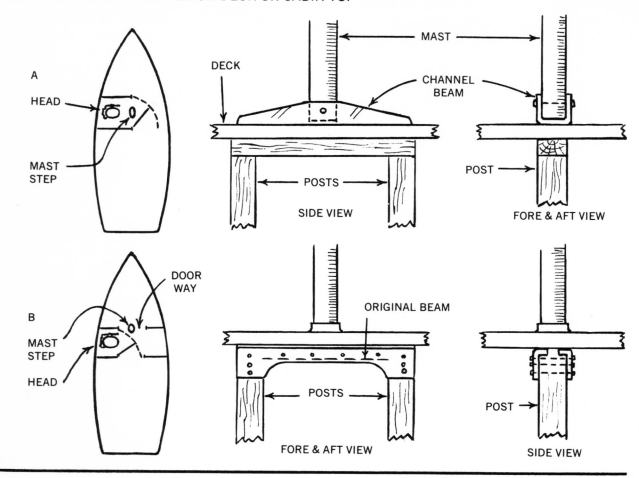

A

HEAD

MAST STEP

DECK

MAST

CHANNEL BEAM

POSTS

SIDE VIEW

POST

FORE & AFT VIEW

B

DOOR WAY

MAST STEP

HEAD

ORIGINAL BEAM

POSTS

FORE & AFT VIEW

POST

SIDE VIEW

FIGURE 62: MASTHEAD DETAILS

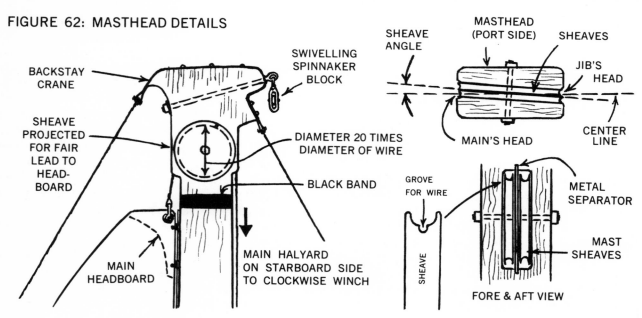

BACKSTAY CRANE

SWIVELLING SPINNAKER BLOCK

SHEAVE PROJECTED FOR FAIR LEAD TO HEAD-BOARD

DIAMETER 20 TIMES DIAMETER OF WIRE

BLACK BAND

MAIN HEADBOARD

MAIN HALYARD ON STARBOARD SIDE TO CLOCKWISE WINCH

SHEAVE ANGLE

MASTHEAD (PORT SIDE)

SHEAVES

JIB'S HEAD

MAIN'S HEAD

CENTER LINE

GROVE FOR WIRE

SHEAVE

METAL SEPARATOR

MAST SHEAVES

FORE & AFT VIEW

clockwise, and therefore the halyard must lead to its forward side (see Figure 62).

When there are two side-by-side mast sheaves, it is often a wise plan to have them installed on a slight slant away from the boat's centerline as illustrated, in order that the main halyard's after part is near the centerline. This will help fairleading, to prevent chafe on the lips of the sheaves, and also it will help prevent one halyard jumping over on top of the other and jamming. As a matter of fact, it is usually a wise policy to have a thin metal separator between the sheaves, as illustrated, to assure that each halyard remains where it belongs. Be sure that there is the very minimum of space between the sides of the sheaves and the mast or separator, because if the halyard jumps the sheave, it can jam with the sail hoisted, and such a jam sometimes cannot be cleared without unstepping the mast.

The same thing holds true with blocks. Be sure all blocks used for wire are intended for wire, and that a block is fitted with a swivel when the lead direction of its wire rope is expected to change. Be wary of using wire in a block with rubber cheeks, and of using wire in sheaves made of *Tuphnol* or other laminated cloth and plastic types that can be chewed by the wire. The minimum recommended sheave or winch drum size for a seven by nineteen wire halyard is twenty to one (sheave or drum diameter twenty times diameter of wire). Be sure that all non-metal blocks have metal straps connecting the sheave pins to the eyes by which the blocks are hung.

Halyard winches on small to medium sized boats are usually similar to the top-action racheting sheet winches discussed in the last chapter, but larger boats often use reel winches. This type is similar to a fishing line reel in that it winds the entire halyard up on its drum. Most of these are two speed and they have a frictional brake to stop drum rotation. Reel winches should be handled with caution, as some types can be dangerous. At times, with some types of reel winches, it may be necessary to relieve the load on the halyard with the inserted handle when the brake is first released, but this should not be done unless someone has a *firm grip* on the handle, because it can spin around and cause serious injury. Usually, a better way to relieve the halyard load is to slack the downhaul. Handles should be the kind that lock on the winch, and in some cases it may be advisable to use a *winch wheel* (a special wheel designed to take the

place of a handle) to avoid the risk of a runaway (spinning) handle in the event the winch operator loses his grip. Incidentally, never grease the brake band of a reel winch.

When standard ratchet winches are used, the halyards are wire but with rope tails, the rope part being spliced to the wire. When the sail is fully hoisted, the wire part is around the winch drum, but the rope tail is made fast to a cleat. The splice should lie between the drum and the cleat. A worn out rope tail is sometimes difficult to replace when it cannot be rove through the mast sheave designed to accomodate the wire only; thus it is often a good idea to use sheaves with double grooves, as shown in Figure 62. The small groove at the bottom of the large groove accomodates the wire. There are actually two ways by which the wire and rope may be joined: by eye splicing the rope to an eye that is spliced, swaged, or formed with compression sleeves in the end of the wire, or by a wire to rope splice. The latter method is sometimes difficult to do or have done completely satisfactorily, and wire snags sometimes work their way through the strands and serving, much to the discomfort of the crew. However, some riggers and yacht chandlers do a neat and strong job of this rather difficult splice. Wire to rope splices should not be left wrapped around the winch drum but the halyard should be adjusted so that the splice lies just below the drum and above the cleat, because bending the splice continually will break it apart and encourage wire snags.

When halyards are external (on the outside of the mast), there is usually no serious objection to joining the wire and rope with two eye splices, as mentioned, except that the eyes are liable to chafe the mast unless the halyards are tied off, and with this linkage also, the splices should lie between the drum and cleat when the sail is fully hoisted. As a matter of fact, all halyards should be tied away from the mast when at anchor to prevent them from rapping against the spar in a breeze in the interest of preventing chafe and wear. This is especially important with aluminum masts because of the problem with noise.

The rope parts of halyards should usually be of dacron since this is highly resistant to rot, strong, easy to handle, and resistant to stretch. Braided dacron line is sometimes used for spinnaker halyards because it is not likely to become twisted or kinked.

FIGURE 63: WEATHER HELM WHEN REACHING

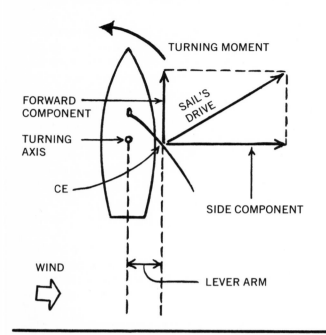

TURNING MOMENT

SAIL'S DRIVE

FORWARD COMPONENT

TURNING AXIS

CE

SIDE COMPONENT

WIND

LEVER ARM

Helm Balance and the Rig

Good helm balance is essential to top sailing performance, and yet its attainment is one of the most perplexing problems for the yacht designer; since there is no entirely scientific way of properly balancing all boats for varying speeds and weather conditions. Once the hull is designed, it becomes a question of where to place the rig so that the center of effort of the sails (the geometric center of the sails' lateral plane) properly relates to the center of lateral resistance (the geometric center of the hull's underwater lateral plane). The wind's side force, theoretically concentrated at the sails' center of effort (CE), exerts its pressure laterally in one direction, while the water's side force, concentrated at the center of lateral resistance (CLR), exerts it pressure on the other side of the boat in the opposite direction. This is the simple, basic (not entirely correct but convenient) assumption we start with, that the CE and CLR are two opposing forces on opposite sides of the boat. It would seem that if the two forces were directly opposed, working in the

FIGURE 64: WATER FORCES PRODUCING UNBALANCED HELM

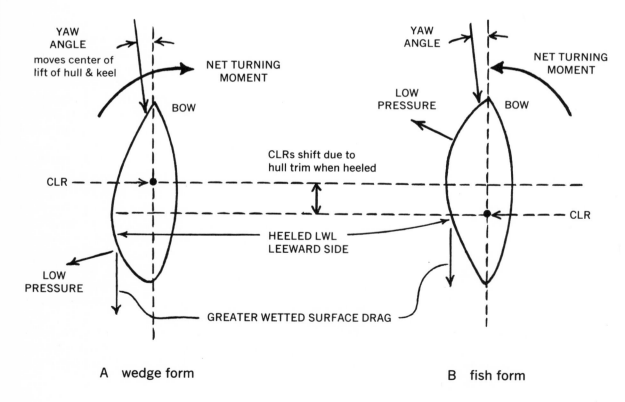

YAW ANGLE
moves center of lift of hull & keel

NET TURNING MOMENT

BOW

CLRs shift due to hull trim when heeled

CLR

HEELED LWL LEEWARD SIDE

LOW PRESSURE

GREATER WETTED SURFACE DRAG

A   wedge form

YAW ANGLE

NET TURNING MOMENT

LOW PRESSURE

BOW

CLR

B   fish form

same vertical transverse plane, that the hull would be in balance; however, this is not true for several reasons.

In the first place, neither the sails nor the hull's underbody are flat planes. They are, of course, curved surfaces. A sail usually has its greatest curvature forward; thus its after, flatter portion presents a broader angle to the wind, and this tends to produce a turning movement into the wind. Then also there is the thrust, or forward component, of the wind's force on the sail which acts to leeward of the boat's turning axis, and so this also tends to turn her into the wind or give her weather helm. When the sheets are started and the main boom is broad off on a beam reach the thrust is especially far to leeward which increases the turning moment, and this helps explain why so many boats have severe weather helms when reaching (see Figure 63).

It is convenient to consider balance as a problem of hydrostatics, but of course in actuality, hull movement is very much involved, and the CLR shifts its position when the boat is underway. This center will often wander considerably, but its exact position will depend on hull shape, yaw angle, speed, and angle of heel. It will be recalled that hull shape in respect to balance was discussed in Chapter 2. The fish form often tends to develop lee helm whereas the wedge form develops weather helm when heeled. This phenomenon may be explained by the fact that the fish form trims down by the stern moving the CLR aft when heeled, while the wedge form does the opposite. Also, there is greater curvature forward on the leeward side of the fish-shaped hull which lowers the pressure (according to Bernoulli's principle) forward of the CLR, but on the wedge form this pressure is abaft the CLR. This is shown in Figure 64. Notice that the greater friction on the leeward side also has a slight influence. Of course, the yaw angle has a considerable influence. Hull A should have its keel well aft to improve balance while B should have its keel extended well forward.

If the helm is extremely unbalanced because of the hull's shape, correction may not be possible by simply changing the position of the CE of the sail plan. In many such cases the keel must be extended or shortened or sometimes a fin or skeg may be added. Balance is often easy to control with tandem centerboards, but these are seldom used on racing boats because of rating, increased drag, ex-

tra maintenance, or some other reason. The famous British ocean racer *Outlaw* has a retractable daggerboard aft which moves her CLR aft and gives her greater directional control downwind without the need of resorting to a spade rudder. A very few American yachts have lifting rudders (see Figure 32) which may be used to alter the position of the CLR, and the well-known, Halsey Herreshoff designed, *Alerion* originally had a retractable skeg, although it was later changed to a fixed skeg. Two boats of my acquaintance had small fins added forward of the keel (one was movable like a bow rudder) in an attempt to help correct for slight lee helms, although in these particular cases, balance probably could have been improved with rig changes.

Lee helms (counteracting the tendency for the boat to fall away from the wind) are usually more harmful than weather helms (counteracting the tendency to round up into the wind). The reason for this is that with lee helm, a rudder attached to the keel no longer contributes to the keel's hydrodynamic lift (explained in Chapter 2 and Figure 36), and as a result, leeway and forward resistance increases. Furthermore it is difficult to feel a boat and work her to windward when she has a lee helm. A boat that turns to leeward when she heels over in a breeze will not only suffer in performance, but she can be positively dangerous, because she will not round up into the wind during a knockdown. Fortunately there are few boats with extreme lee helms. Most of today's hulls are not of the extreme cod's head and mackerel-tail form, but are modifications of symmetrical or moderate wedge forms. These forms are usually fairly well balanced and have some weather helm when heeled.

A mild weather helm is usually desirable on boats with keel attached rudders in order to attain hydrodynamic lift from the keel rudder combination when beating to windward. Optimum rudder angles vary from about three degrees to five degrees for most racing-cruisers. In other words, at a moderate angle of heel when beating, a tight tiller (with no play between it and the rudder stock) should be held about three degrees to five degrees to windward of the boat's centerline to hold the boat on a straight course.

The next consideration after hull form in the attainment of proper balance, is obviously the location of the sail plans' CE. Figure 65 shows how the

FIGURE 65: CENTERS OF EFFORT & LATERAL RESISTANCE

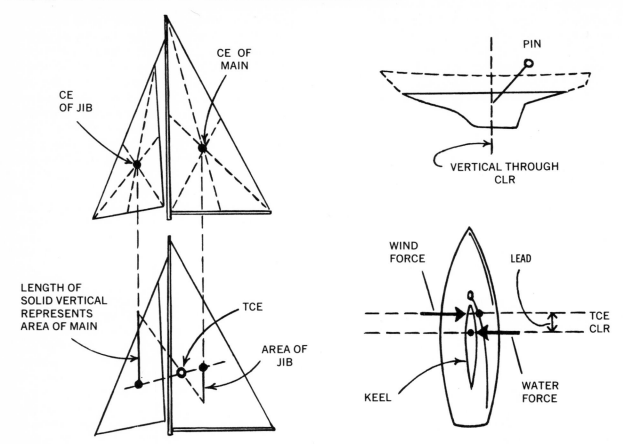

CE of a triangular sail is found. Each side is bisected by a straight line drawn from the side's opposite angle and these lines intersect at the triangle's geometric center, the sail's CE. If the boat is sloop rigged, the CE's of the jib and mainsail are found and their combined or total center of effort (TCE) must be located. This can be done by drawing a line between the two CE's and locating the TCE on this connecting line at a position that is in accord with the comparative areas of the sails. A simple method of finding the position of the TCE is illustrated in Figure 65. As shown, if the main's area is double the jib's, the TCE on the connecting line would be twice as far from the jib's CE as from the main's CE. This is based on the incorrect but convenient assumption that the sails are flat and there is no mast interference.

The CLR can be found by simply balancing the underwater profile on a ruler or hanging it from a pin, as illustrated. Once these two centers are lo-cated, it is a question of where the TCE should be located relative to the CLR. Some yacht designers will tell you that the TCE's designed position is the result of an educated guess based on knowledge of some fundamentals and the observation of various boats. One thing is nearly always certain, that the TCE should be forward of or *lead* the CLR. The lead may vary from two to twenty percent of the waterline length, but as a rough estimate, a fairly flat-bilged, beamy, fin keel or centerboard racing-cruiser might have a lead in the neighborhood of fifteen percent of the LWL, whereas a narrow, fairly symmetrical hull with a longer keel might have a lead of only five percent or so.

Since the exact optimum lead of the TCE is very difficult if not impossible to pinpoint, many boats suffer from minor balance faults that must be corrected through tuning. The TCE and CLR may be moved slightly to alter the lead by: (1) changing the mast rake, (2) raising or lowering a pivoting centerboard, (3) altering sheet trim, (4) altering the mainsail's leech tension, (5) changing the fore-and-aft trim of the hull, (6) lowering the mizzen on a yawl, (7) setting higher or lower jibs, (8) increasing or decreasing the ballast, (9) changing the rig or the position of the mast step, or (10) changing the lateral plane profile. Of course, the first methods should be tried first because they are more easily done. The latter methods should only be tried in cases of extreme imbalance.

Raking the mast aft will move the CE aft and therefore increase weather helm, whereas a forward rake will have the opposite effect. Raising the centerboard slightly will move the CLR aft thereby decreasing weather helm, however, I think most boats should be tuned so that they balance well with the board fully lowered for maximum draft and to lessen the effects of harmful board bending, when beating in all but the lightest and heaviest winds. In a strong breeze, it often pays to ease the mainsheet to relieve a weather helm. This not only moves the CE forward, but it helps reduce heeling which often causes weather helm due to the asymmetrical shape of the hull when heeled. Leech tension can be adjusted with the boom vang or with a special adjustable *leech line* sewn into the leech tabling (edging), or tension can be altered by a sailmaker; however, any permanent alteration should be done with caution, because it can be harmful to the efficiency of the sail's shape. More will be said on this subject in the next chapter. A tight mainsail leech will increase weather helm and a loose leech will ease weather helm.

Trimming the hull slightly down by the bow will move the CLR forward thereby increasing weather helm, whereas trimming the hull down by the stern will have the opposite effect. At the same time, however, mast rake will be changed by the hull trim; and so the change of CE due to the altered rake will partially counteract the relocation of the CLR due to the altered hull trim. Moving the crew slightly aft on a moderately wedge-shaped hull may relieve weather helm not only by moving the CLR aft, but by improving stability through extra bearing and weight leverage at the hull's beamiest part. Of course, the addition of ballast will also help relieve weather helm caused by excessive heeling.

Setting small or large sails forward or aft obviously moves the TCE, with a larger area forward tending to produce lee helm or reduce weather helm, while the larger area aft has the opposite

effect. With this method or any method of changing balance, care should be taken to see that the improvement in balance is not made at the expense of over-all performance. Setting a small jib in light weather, for example, may produce a better feel to the helm, but the boat will lose power and speed.

If it becomes necessary to change the rig or the underwater lateral plane for an extreme case of poor balance (and this is seldom the case with a boat designed by a reputable naval architect), the simplest, least expensive method should probably be tried first. It may be simpler to reshape the rudder or add a skeg or balancing fin than to relocate the mainmast, for this might entail moving chain plates, changing major structural supports under the mast, and buying new sails. Of course, changing the sail plan may greatly change the rating, too.

Tuning the Standing Rigging

Most modern racing-cruisers have either of two basic rigging plans, the masthead or the seven-eighths rig, illustrated in Figure 66. Small or large boats may be rigged using either plan, but usually no matter which plan is used, the larger the boat, the more rigging she needs to hold and control the mast. Boats above the medium size often need *intermediate shrouds* (between the upper and lower shrouds as illustrated) with an extra pair of spreaders. One thing seems certain, however; the rig should be the simplest possible version that will do the job for which it is intended. Extra rigging causes windage and adds unnecessary weight aloft. Windage reduces speed far more than many people realize, and it has been said that a two-and-a-half-pound weight at forty feet above the water will be approximately equivalent to subtracting 100 pounds of keel ballast.

It seems that most of today's small to medium sized racing-cruisers use the masthead rig shown in Figure 66A. This is a simple, effective arrangement with the headstay being directly opposed by the permanent backstay. Some of the modern fiberglass boats have only single lower shrouds, and this gives the advantage of allowing the main boom to go further forward when running. However, I prefer the lower shroud's chain plate to be somewhat abaft the upper shroud's for better control of mast bend. The upper shroud chain plates should be exactly abeam of the mast's lateral centerline on a racing-cruiser having a non-flexible rig and non-hinging spreaders, because otherwise the downward pull of the upper shrouds will tend to bend the mast and spreaders. Another reason why chain plates are often put in the same fore-and-aft location is that they may be fastened to a transverse bulkhead as illustrated. This is an effective construction method for a fiberglass boat, and it allows the chain plates to be moved inboard (instead of being located at the rail) which allows flatter trimming of overlapping headsails. This is advantageous, but is sometimes overdone. One class even has its chain plates secured to the sides of the cabin trunk. However, in most cases, a large Genoa should never be trimmed very far inboard of the rail because it loses forward drive and backwinds the mainsail as well. Another point is that when the chain plates are set inboard, the shrouds often have a less effective angle with the mast. It is preferable that the angle between the mast and shroud be fifteen degrees but seldom less than twelve degrees, otherwise there is too much of a compression load on the mast. Long spreaders often present a problem because they are apt to chafe an overlapping jib, but as a general rule, they should have at least sufficient length to give their shrouds a twelve degree angle at the masthead (see Figure 66).

Seven-eighths and fifteen-sixteenths rigs, with their smaller fore triangles, were given a break under the 1967 change in the CCA rule, but they have several serious disadvantages for small to medium sized racing-cruisers. With this rig large, powerful jibs and spinnakers cannot be carried, and it is often difficult to keep the head of the mast from bending aft when the jibstay is set up taut unless running backstays (runners) are used. These backstays are often necessary on large boats with tall masts, especially those having seven-eighths rigs, in order to assure taut jibstays, but on small boats where runners are not really necessary, they are a nuisance. This is obviously because of the need to slack off the leeward runner and set up the one on the windward side every time the boat is tacked.

Many large boats with very tall masts need not only runners, but a forestay directly opposing the backstay's after pull (see Figure 66), in order to keep the mast straight. Of course, a forestay is obviously needed for a double head rig, when a forestay sail is carried with a jib or jib topsail in fresh winds, or when a forestay sail is the only headsail carried in heavy winds. It is customary that the forestay be attached to the deck with a quick-release lever, in order that the stay can be released from the deck and brought back where it can be secured out of the way at the mast or shrouds when a large Genoa jib is carried in light airs. When the wind is light and there is no problem keeping the mast straight, a forestay set up tight at its deck position will only interfere with the handling of a large jib when tacking.

Adjusting the standing rigging for proper tune is a somewhat controversial subject, because some boats respond well to one kind of treatment and others respond to another kind. Some sailors advocate loose rigging and others insist on tight rigging. Generally speaking, small boats with bendy or *semiflexible* rigs (having masts that can be bent aft to alter sail curvature) usually seem to sail better with their shrouds quite loose, but larger racing-cruisers, especially those with masthead rigs, seem to perform best with their rigging set up at least moderately taut.

To begin with, let us consider the adjustment of the shrouds as we view the mast from the bow or stern. A basic uncontroversial premise is that the mast should be vertical when the boat is unheeled. In other words, the mast should be at right angles to the plane or chord of the deck as shown by the horizontal dotted line in Figure 66A. Of course, when the boat heels, the force from mast and sail weight and wind pressure pulls against the windward shrouds stretching them taut and causing the leeward shrouds to go slack. This is perfectly normal; however, the shroud adjustment should be tight enough to prevent excessive leaning of the mast to leeward when the boat is heeled. The ninety degree angle of the mast with the deck plane cannot be preserved, but the angle should not be allowed to change a great deal for the sake of minimizing loss of sail efficiency due to heeling. Beyond small angles of heel, a sail begins to lose projected area, and the sail's drive, the resultant of the wind's side force and the forward thrust, begins to be directed downward instead of straight ahead.

From this same fore-and-aft view, the mast should be kept approximately straight. This means that the upper shrouds should be kept more taut than the lowers, provided all shrouds are the same diameter, because the uppers are longer, pass over spreaders, and consequently have more stretch. If there are intermediates, they should be slightly

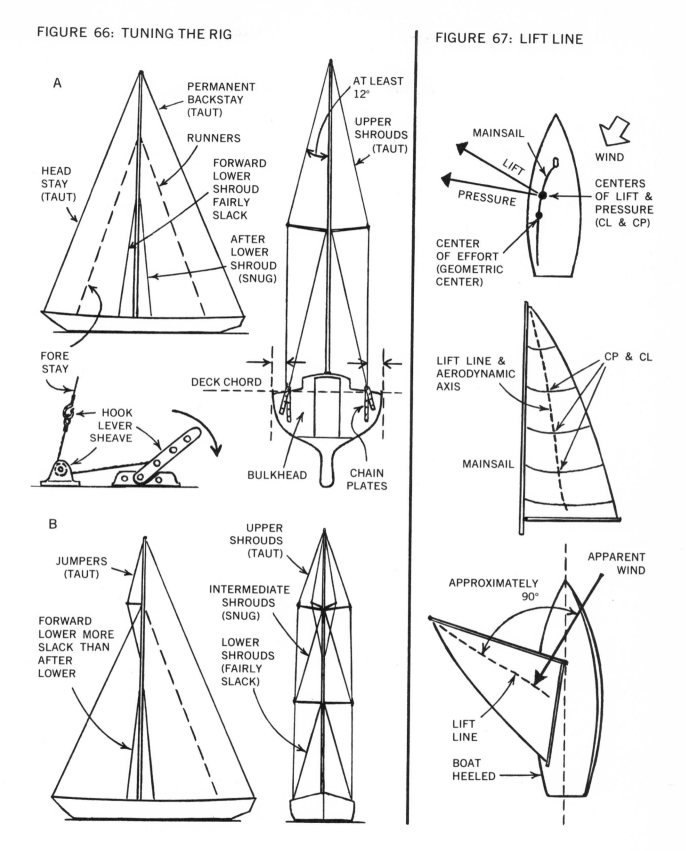

FIGURE 66: TUNING THE RIG

A

PERMANENT BACKSTAY (TAUT)

RUNNERS

FORWARD LOWER SHROUD FAIRLY SLACK

AFTER LOWER SHROUD (SNUG)

HEAD STAY (TAUT)

FORE STAY

HOOK LEVER SHEAVE

AT LEAST 12°

UPPER SHROUDS (TAUT)

DECK CHORD

BULKHEAD

CHAIN PLATES

B

JUMPERS (TAUT)

FORWARD LOWER MORE SLACK THAN AFTER LOWER

UPPER SHROUDS (TAUT)

INTERMEDIATE SHROUDS (SNUG)

LOWER SHROUDS (FAIRLY SLACK)

FIGURE 67: LIFT LINE

MAINSAIL

LIFT

PRESSURE

WIND

CENTERS OF LIFT & PRESSURE (CL & CP)

CENTER OF EFFORT (GEOMETRIC CENTER)

LIFT LINE & AERODYNAMIC AXIS

CP & CL

MAINSAIL

APPROXIMATELY 90°

APPARENT WIND

LIFT LINE

BOAT HEELED

89

more slack than the uppers but more taut than the lowers. This is a general basic rule; however, there are some small boat sailors who think it advantageous to let the head of the mast bend slightly to leeward in a fresh breeze in order to minimize heeling and open up the jib slot. On a racing-cruiser I think it is desirable that the mast be approximately straight when viewed from the bow or stern, but if it becomes necessary to tighten the after lower shrouds to control fore-and-aft mast bend (when viewed from the side), a very small amount of lateral bend to leeward might be tolerated if this has no adverse affect on the shape of the mainsail. However, the mast should rarely be allowed to bend so that its top hooks to windward, and any "S" curves in the mast are nearly always harmful.

Viewing the mast from the side, we are concerned with rake and fore-and-aft mast bend. Both of these are rather controversial subjects. There is a fair amount of talk now about raking the mast according to the so-called *lift line theory*. According to some sailors' interpretations, this calls for a considerable amount of rake (inclination from the vertical) aft. The *lift line*, a line drawn through the centers of lift (where we can consider the lift is concentrated) at all heights up the sail, and the *aerodynamic axis*, a line drawn through the centers of pressure (where we can consider the pressure concentrated) at all heights up the sail, are essentially at the same location on the sail, although the forces act in different directions. The lift line drawn through these centers of lift and pressure will lie about twenty-five to forty percent of the sail's width (from luff to leech) abaft the luff when sailing close hauled (see Figure 67) depending on the exact boom angle and the draft or camber (curvature) of the sail. As can be seen in the illustration, the mainsail's lift line rakes forward considerably. Proponents of the lift line theory advocate considerable rake aft when beating, especially for *una-rigs* (catboats, with single sails) in order that the line be vertical, because maximum drive which acts almost horizontally will be most efficient acting at right angles to the lift line.

This theory may hold true for una-rigs, but for boats with jibs, the lift line rakes aft on the headsail, and also boats with low booms and bendy rigs usually have their masts bowed aft when beating; therefore, except with some una-rigs and possibly a sloop with a fairly high boom and very small jib,

I don't think that rake aft should be any more than moderate. There is also another factor to consider with this theory. When a boat heels moderately, as she usually does when beating, a forward raking lift line almost meets the apparent wind at right angles. This is shown in Figure 67. Thus a racing-cruiser that is not sailed upright need not carry a lot of rake aft to satisfy the lift line theory.

Mast rake affects the tune of a boat in many ways, but perhaps the most significant effect is on balance. As has been mentioned a rake aft will increase weather helm, and so in my opinion raking the mast for optimum balance should be the first consideration. An important benefit of some after rake is that it helps tighten the jibstay or headstay for effective windward work. However, a pronounced rake aft is detrimental to downwind performance for three main reasons: gravity adversely affects the mainsail, the wind doesn't meet the vertical plane of the sail at right angles, and the center of effort is further aft than it would be if the mast were plumb or raked forward. For steering control downwind, it is advantageous to have the CE forward. Also with rake, area is lost in the fore-triangle, an important consideration for racing-cruisers, and the mainsail loses area if it becomes necessary to raise the end of the boom for clearance.

A few relatively minor benefits of rake aft are that the masthead is slightly further amidships to lessen hobbyhorsing; there may be very slightly less windage due to the rigging being inclined further away from the vertical; gravity lets the mainsail hang more effectively when sailing on the wind (but less effectively off the wind unless the backstay can be eased to let the mast go forward a small amount); the CE is lowered somewhat which is beneficial in heavy winds (but not in light winds); and the foots and clews of sails will be lower, a benefit at times (but of course, this should be accomplished by the original cut of the sails based on estimated rake); and mast rake will raise the outboard end of a boom when it is broad off to lessen the possibility of tripping in a seaway.

The major considerations should be the effect of rake on balance, sail area, and on the tautness of the headstay. Most racing-cruisers are designed to carry a slight rake aft, and of course the designed rake should be tried first. Then if it is found that this doesn't work, the mast should be moderately inclined further aft or forward. It is very seldom that a mast should be raked more than slightly forward of the vertical. The average well-balanced racing-cruiser with a mainsail luff of thirty-five feet may carry a rake aft of about one foot (measured at the base of the mast from a plumb line attached to the hoisted halyard to the after side of the mast).

Another somewhat controversial subject is mast bend. Bowing the mast so that the head of the mast bends aft and middle part bows forward is a common practice with dinghies and small racing boats. Rigs intended for bowing are called *bendy,* or *flexible.* The purpose of such a rig is to increase the versatility of the mainsail. A full main with a lot of draft can be used on straight spars in light airs, and when it blows the spars can be bent to flatten the sail. The mast bowing forward in its middle will take up slack in the sail's material along the luff to leech dimension, while the masthead bending aft will ease tension on the leech. This often works very well in small boats and many small boat sailors moving up to big boats want to flex the rig of their racing-cruiser. Several well-known sailmakers and designers, such as Peter Barrett, Ted Hood, and Robert Derecktor have advocated or tried bendy rigs on big boats (some people have lost masts trying this too).

Perhaps some day, flexible rigs will be commonplace on ocean racers. However, the newcomer to racing-cruisers should have a few words of warning about the practice. First of all, spars must be designed to be bent and sails must be specially cut to fit the bent spars. Otherwise, the spar can be strained or broken and the sails badly distorted. Second, bending the mast on a boat that is masthead rigged (the most common rig for small to medium sized racing-cruisers) can lead to detrimental complications. Some of the effects from bending a masthead rig are: that the masthead will be lowered thereby slacking off the rigging, area is lost in the fore triangle, a region of special importance in the masthead plan, and the headstay and other rigging cannot be kept as taut because a column bent in compression is not as stiff as a straight one. Furthermore, many experienced sailors feel that bending a long mast when offshore in heavy winds puts serious if not dangerous stresses on the rig. Sailmaker Owen C. Torrey has said, "When masts are longer than, say, thirty-five feet, the stresses on the rig make it difficult to control any bend large enough to have a significant effect on the sail."

The CCA, under whose rule the vast majority of U.S. distance races are presently sailed, has ruled against bendy rigs under the following miscellaneous restrictions: "Double luffed sails (other than spinnakers or squaresails), rotating masts, *mechanically or permanently bent spars* or other similar contrivances are excluded for yachts measured under this Rule" (italics are mine). Of course, a "sea lawyer" might take you to court over what constitutes mechanical bending, and an exact interpretation would have to be given by the CCA measurement rules committee, and the final decision on whether or not mast bending is allowed would lie with the local yacht racing organization. However, it seems clear to me that the CCA means to discourage deliberately bending masts with special stays or mechanisms intended for that purpose.

The mast bend we have been discussing involves the hooking aft of the masthead. The opposite bend, with the masthead hooking forward, should almost never be tolerated. If such a bend develops, the forward lower shrouds or a seven-eighths forestay should be set up tight to counteract. On a seven-eighths rigged boat, slacking the jumper stays and setting up on the permanent backstay may correct this bend.

Everyone agrees that the jibstay or headstay should be kept taut for the most effective sailing to windward, but in my opinion this has become almost a fetish with many racing skippers. Complete elimination of headstay sag is an impossibility even with rod rigging. If there were no sag, the stay loading would approach infinity when beating in a strong breeze. Sailmakers realize this and allow for some sag when cutting a jib; thus a slight sag will not be harmful to the actual set of the sail. An extremely tight headstay can put harmful compression bends in the mast, strain the hull and stem, introduce extra stress at the mast step, and pull the rig forward.

Some sailors use headstays of extra large diameter in order to minimize wire stretch. This sounds logical, and I tried this for one season of racing but came to the conclusion that it doesn't work unless of course, the wire is too small to begin with. The extra large wire only adds to weight and windage aloft, and adds to the difficulties in keeping the mast straight as a result of the increased compression load.

In my opinion, it is advantageous to slightly

tighten the headstay and/or backstay prior to the race, being sure that no compression bends are put in the mast. Then after the race the stays should be slacked off again to their former tension in order to let the boat relax and keep the strain off her most of the time. Hulls under constant strain can and do change shape.

Halyards can contribute a certain amount to mast compression. Sometimes, on a seven-eighths rigged boat, the main halyard can cause the mast to bend to starboard because it leads down the starboard side of the mast. Halyard locks at the head of the mast can reduce the halyard compression load by one half. Locks are frequently used on small boats sailing in sheltered waters, but be careful with their use on a large boat offshore, in case of the possibility of a jam. There are some good locks on the market that are based on the principle of a ball or cylinder, swaged to the halyard, sliding under a slot on the metal fitting. But be sure the lock is foolproof.

When adjusting the rigging, sight up the mast track at the after side of the mast to see that the mast is not being adversely bent. The track should be viewed from the side and also looking forward. After the rigging is adjusted, the mast should be examined while underway. Sight up the track while the boat is heeled when beating to see if it remains reasonably straight. Also watch the mast move-

ment when the boat pounds into head seas. The mast should not be absolutely rigid, but excessive mast movement should not be allowed. When the shrouds are too loose mast movement may strain the hull or rig and shake some wind from the sails; but on the other hand, if the rig is too tight the mast cannot give to the boat's motion, and the wind may be bounced or jolted from the sails. In my opinion, it is seldom wise to make rigging adjustments while underway, because when sailing, strains on the rigging are unevenly distributed, and it is difficult to estimate the amount of adjustment needed and to exactly duplicate shroud adjustment on each side of the boat.

It is often difficult to keep the upper part of the mast on a seven-eighths (or even a fifteen-sixteenths) rigged boat from bending aft when there is considerable tension on the jib stay. To avoid this bend, the jumper stays must be kept taut. Usually they must be taut enough to give the masthead a very slight bow forward when the boat is not under sail. Jumper stays are usually fairly light, and of course they pass over struts; thus they frequently need periodic adjustments. Shrouds also need periodic adjustment, because rigging stretches somewhat, especially new rigging, and the hull may change shape slightly during the course of a long hard sailing season.

6
Sail Selection, Shaping, and Trimming

Today the universally accepted materials for racing sails are Dacron (called Terylene in England) and nylon. Both these materials are synthetics which are highly resistant to rot, mildew, and water absorbtion. Furthermore, they are strong, smooth, and relatively non-porous, and new sails of these cloths need little if any "breaking-in," as is necessary when sails are made of cotton. However, there is a great difference between Dacron and nylon in that the former is quite *stable,* or resistant to stretch, while the latter is somewhat elastic, stretching out of shape in a strong wind, but recovering to its original shape. With mainsails, Genoa jibs, working jibs, fore staysails, mizzens, and other sails carried to windward in fresh breezes, stability of the sailcloth is extremely important. But with certain sails carried downwind or upwind in very light airs, such as spinnakers, spinnaker staysails, and drifters or *ghosters* (light-weight reaching jibs), a certain amount of stretch can be tolerated, and nylon of great strength is made in very light weights.

Although Dacron cloth is highly resistant to stretch compared with other materials, every woven cloth is subject to *bias elongation.* This occurs when the cloth is pulled diagonally to the directions of the weave. A simple demonstration of this can be given with an ordinary pocket handkerchief. If a square handkerchief is held with both hands, each grasping the middle of two opposite sides, and then the hands are pulled apart in an attempt to stretch the handkerchief, it will be found that there is very little noticeable stretch in the cloth. This is due to the fact that the pull is in the direction of the weave which runs parallel and at right angles to the edges. However, if we hold the handkerchief at two diagonally opposed corners and pull our hands apart, there will be very noticeable elongation of the cloth (see Figure 68). Only a small part of this elongation is actually due to fiber

stretch. Most of it is caused by slippage or realignment of the fibers when the cloth is pulled at a forty-five degree angle to the direction of the weave. Essentially the same kind of elongation can take place even with highly non-stretch Dacron cloth. Diagonal tension will distort the square configuration of the weave, causing the cloth to become longer in one direction and shorter in the other. As a matter of fact, Dacron may yield to bias tension more easily than some other fabrics because of the smooth, hard, and slippery nature of the synthetic material.

Excessive bias elongation is harmful to a sail, because as the wind increases, the sail will lose its proper, designed shape. In a fresh breeze, the draft or curvature tends to move from the sail's forward area to its after area. This not only causes loss in drive, but increases weather helm and adds to the heeling moment.

One of the greatest problems for the sailmaker is how to minimize and cope with this bias elongation. There are several methods of combating the problem: (1) increasing the weight of the cloth, (2) arranging the cloth panels of the sail in such a way that bias tensions occur in the least harmful locations, (3) cutting the sail to allow for a predicted change in shape, (4) weaving the cloth as tight as possible, and (5) using a plastic *filler* between the woven fibers to lock the threads in place. Most of these methods are used in every sail, but some sailmakers favor a tight weave with little if any filler, while others favor liberal use of filler.

The pioneer of extra tightly woven sailcloth was sailmaker Ted Hood of Marblehead, Massachusetts. He began weaving cloth especially for his own sails as early as 1951 and has developed a cloth that is highly resistant to bias elongation. Now however, other sailmakers weave their own cloth or buy fabric milled specifically as sailcloth and not intended for other use. At present, nearly all sailcloth is reasonably tight or closely woven, though in varying degrees.

There is some disagreement among sailmakers as to the use of fillers. Some claim that fillers break down in time and permit stretch, while others say they remain effective even after the sails have been exposed to years of hard use. Fillers give sails a hard, stiff, slippery, and parchment-like finish, whereas unfilled sails are relatively soft and easy to furl and handle. For this reason, many owners of racing-cruisers prefer the unfilled softer finish, but in a strong wind they may have to accept a little more stretch. There is also disagreement as to what size sail is most suitable for fillers. At least one prominent sailmaker reasons that large sails are subject to the greatest stresses and therefore they should be made of the firmest, filled cloth; but other leading sailmakers maintain that fillers break down under great stress, and thus should not be used in large sails. This latter school of thought seems to feel that fillers are more suited to smaller size sails or large sails used in winds of moderate strength only.

Despite these conflicting thoughts, the following points seem reasonably clear: good racing sails have been made filled and unfilled in almost every size; with the small to medium sizes or larger sails not carried in extremely strong winds, the firm, filled sails are more resistant to stretch with weight, weave, and all other cloth characteristics being equal; more allowance for stretch should be given when cutting an unfilled sail as compared with one that is filled; and as a result of improved weaving and new finishing processes, the stability of Dacron sailcloth is improving all the time.

It is generally agreed that the most stable cloth is the so called "yarn tempered" cloth that is filled and has seams that are both glued and sewn. However, handling such a sail of a large size could be quite a problem. Such a sail should probably be left bent to the boom, *faked down* (accordian folded on top of the boom) or furled, and protected with a sail cover, or if the sail is removed, it should be folded in such a way that the fold creases run fore-and-aft. The other alternative for a large mainsail, perhaps over thirty-five feet on the luff, would be to use a softer finish cloth of the tightest practical weave, *heat set* (finishing process which tightens the weave), with fairly narrow panels, and of ample weight.

Dacron weight is figured in ounces per yard for the American standard width of twenty-eight and one-half inches, and weights vary between two and twelve ounces. There is a general rule of thumb for selecting the proper weight of cloth for the mainsail. This consists of adding the LOA in feet to the main's luff length in feet and dividing by ten to obtain the weight in ounces per yard. This gives a rough idea of mainsail weight. Actually it might be slightly heavier or lighter depending on the expected average strength of sailing wind in areas where the wind is fairly steady or consistent, and

also depending on the weave and finish of the cloth. I tend to favor the heavier weight in most cases unless the vast majority of races will be sailed in light airs, because weight gives the sail a little more body to hold its shape especially when it is exposed to backwind from a large Genoa. Furthermore, racing-cruisers are usually restricted to one mainsail which must be carried over a wide range of wind velocities. A special light or heavy weather main may not be used.

Although much smaller than mainsails, mizzens should usually be almost as heavy if not the same weight as the mainsail, because they are often needed for balancing sails in the heaviest weather. For this reason, their rigging should be amply strong despite the additional windage.

The weight of Genoas depends on how many Genoas are carried. If there is a choice between three or four Genoas then naturally the largest can be quite light, but if only one Genoa is carried it should be a versatile sail capable of performing well over a wide range of conditions. Such a sail might be about seventy-five percent of the mainsail's weight, or slightly lighter. With the working jib it also depends on how many are carried. If there is a small storm jib this should be the same or nearly the same weight as the mainsail and a large working jib could be perhaps twenty percent lighter than the main, but if only one medium sized working jib is carried, it should be the same weight or only slightly lighter than the main. A storm trysail should be about the same weight as the mainsail, but slightly heavier in a very large boat (perhaps over fifty feet LOA).

Thus far we have only talked about Dacron sails. We shall consider nylon weights in the next section when we discuss what sails are needed especially for racing.

Sails Needed

The selection of sails will primarily depend on two factors: how much money one has to spend on them and the kind of sailing that will be done. If a great deal of distance racing will be done offshore, then a good many sails will be needed, but for round-the-buoy racing in protected waters, a large sail inventory is not necessary. Surprisingly enough, it is sometimes an advantage to have a limited number of versatile sails rather than a great variety of sails on short distance races, because there is less chance of carrying the wrong sail and

FIGURE 68: BIAS ELONGATION

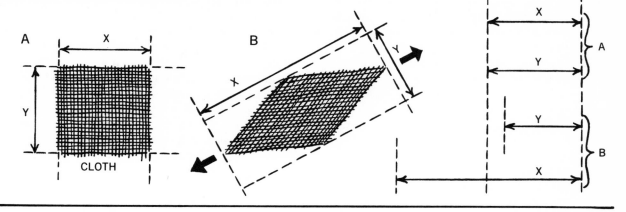

FIGURE 69:   PRINCIPLE SAILS

A
LIGHT
WEATHER
UPWIND
SAILS

B
LIGHT
WEATHER
DOWNWIND
SAILS

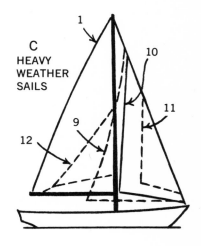

C
HEAVY
WEATHER
SAILS

1 — MAINSAIL
2 — NO. 1 GENOA
3 — DRIFTER OR REACHER (sheeted to main boom or deck)
4 — MIZZEN
5 — MIZZEN STAYSAIL
6 — SPINNAKER
7 — SPINNAKER STAYSAIL
8 — BALD HEADED SPINNAKER STAYSAIL (top cut off & sail hoisted with 2 halyards to avoid blanketing spinnaker)
9 — NO. 2 GENOA
10 — WORKING JIB
11 — STORM JIB OR SPITFIRE
12 — STORM TRYSAIL (sheeted to main boom or deck)

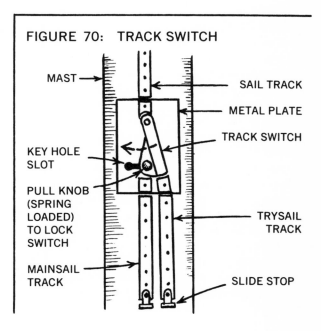

FIGURE 70:   TRACK SWITCH

95

of wasting time changing to the correct sail when conditions of wind or sea change in the middle of the race as so often happens. The principle sails are shown in Figure 69.

The very minimum sail inventory needed to begin racing a small to medium sized sloop is: (1) a large, general-purpose mainsail, (2) a number one (largest size) general-purpose Genoa jib, (3) a large, non-overlapping working jib or a number two (next smaller size) Genoa or number three (still smaller) Genoa, and (4) a large, general-purpose parachute spinnaker. You cannot race successfully with fewer sails than this, but many sailors start off with this combination and then may gradually add other sails in following years. When choosing between the working jib and number two or three Genoa, consideration should be given to how much cruising will be done when short handed. The working jib will undoubtedly be easier to handle for family cruising, but the small Genoas will probably be more effective for most heavy wind racing conditions except in the very heaviest weather. If the boat is yawl rigged, of course, a mizzen and mizzen staysail should be carried, and obviously, if she is double head rigged, she will have a fore staysail.

If one spinnaker is carried it should be very versatile, one that can be used effectively in all breezes for reaching and running. Such a spinnaker should probably be of 1.2 ounce or .75 ounce (in areas of predominantly light airs) nylon cut moderately flat (without a deep belly) for effective reaching. If two spinnakers are in the inventory there should be one of .75 ounce (or .5 ounce) nylon cut fairly full for running and another heavier spinnaker of perhaps 1.5 ounce nylon cut flatter for reaching and for heavier winds.

For offshore, distance racing or any sailing away from sheltered waters, a few more sails are necessary, principally a storm jib or small, heavy working jib and a storm trysail. Some storm trysails are rigged with a double track and *switch* as illustrated in Figure 70 in order that this sail can be set in the quickest, most convenient way. The trysail may trim to the side deck (to a through bolted fitting, often the base of a stanchion) or its clew can be secured to the main boom. In the latter case, the trysail can frequently be used as a substitute for a triple reefed (reefed to a third row of reef points or a very deeply reefed) mainsail. Using the trysail in this manner, it becomes more than a mere storm

sail; in combination with a small Genoa, it can often drive the boat to windward quite effectively when racing in heavy weather. It is usually wise to give the main boom some support with the topping lift when the trysail is carried in this way. Also, the sail track on the mainmast should be bolted to the mast opposite the head of the trysail.

It is advisable to have a number two or three Genoa for racing at sea. However, a headsail of this kind should be raised a foot or slightly less off the deck with a *tack pendant* (a short wire strap) in order that seas and/or the bow wave will not break against its foot. Any headsail that is short on the luff (a working jib, small Genoa, or storm jib) should be fitted with a *head pendant* that extends the length of the jib halyard so that only wire goes around the winch when the halyard is composed of part wire and part rope. In other words, the head pendant should make up for the lower position of the head of a smaller jib so that the weight of the sail will not be supported by a wire to rope splice.

The next most important sails to have after the basic sails already mentioned are special purpose headsails. The spinnaker staysail, sometimes called the *cheater* is usually most effective in medium to fresh winds when the wind is near the quarter. This sail is usually made of spinnaker cloth and fills in the gap under a well-lifted spinnaker. The cheater should have a fairly short luff or be bald-headed (as shown in Figure 69) to avoid blanketing the 'chute when broad reaching. A tall, narrow spinnaker staysail, called a *tallboy* or *ribbon staysail,* tacked to the weather rail seems to work best for running. A *reacher* is generally a large sail, cut fuller than a Genoa, of lightweight Dacron and designed, as its name implies, especially for reaching. A drifter or ghoster is also a large jib of the lightest nylon for extremely light airs. Both the reacher and drifter are often cut high in the foot to trim from the end of the main boom to get the maximum outboard lead. In the drifter's case, the high foot is also customary, because it concentrates the area aloft where the breeze is frequently stronger, and there is a minimum of weight at the foot to keep the sail from lifting and filling out. Drifters are usually *set flying* (without being hanked to the jib stay or with one hank only at the head) on their own luff wire to allow rapid sail changing. This causes considerable sag at the luff but this is really not a serious problem in very light airs because a little sag gives extra fullness to the sail. These sails are often effective against the increasingly difficult problem of motor boat swells in light airs.

A recent fad is the *light air double head rig* that consists of a lightweight *Genoa staysail* (an overlapping fore staysail with low foot) and a jib topsail or yankee jib cut similarly to a drifter (see Figure 75). This rig is designed to give maximum headsail area for a given handicap rating. On some boats the rig has proven quite effective when beating in light airs and close reaching in all but very strong winds, but there are times when it will be difficult to trim the two headsails so that they will not interfere with each other, and of course, the rig requires greater crew effort and coordination, especially when tacking. It may be well worth while, in the interest of economy and versatility, to investigate the possibility of having a drifter that can double as a light air jib topsail and a cheater for beam reaching that can double as a Genoa staysail for sailing on the wind. In this case, both the staysail and jib should probably be made of the lightest Dacron so that they will hold their shape when beating in light to moderate breezes. The jib topsail will normally be cut to trim from the spinnaker lead position near the quarter, while the staysail will be cut to trim from a position slightly inboard of the Genoa track. Usually the staysail will have a wire luff to prevent sag, and unless the boat has her shrouds set inboard of the rail, the staysail will probably be cut so that its leech fits under the lower spreader with the foot passing through the slot between the upper and lower shrouds. More will be said about the size of these sails when we discuss the "LP" measurement later in the chapter, and more will be said about cheaters when we discuss spinnakers in Chapter 9.

Draft and Cut

Draft or camber is the luff-to-leech curvature that gives a sail an efficient airfoil shape. This curvature should correctly bend or change the direction of a maximum amount of air flowing around the sail. On most points of sailing the flow moves from forward to aft, and it moves faster on the leeward than on the windward side of the sail; thus in accordance with Bernullis's principle, the pressure to leeward is lower, and it exerts a leeward pull acting approximately at right angles to the sail's surface. The efficiency of a sail depends to a very large extent on the amount and character of its draft.

If the draft is such that it bends the wind too abruptly the flow to leeward will separate, break away, and the sail will *stall* as shown in Figure 71. On the other hand, however, if the wind is bent only slightly, stalling is avoided, but the sail may lack maximum effectiveness as an airfoil. A deep draft that fails to bend the wind at a close *angle of incidence* (angle of trim or inclination to the wind) will often result in the sail luffing as illustrated in Figure 71. Both luffing and stalling are caused by the depth and location of draft and the wind's angle of incidence, often called *angle of attack,* as in airplane terminology. Excessive draft near the luff will encourage luffing, but excessive draft near the leech will encourage stalling. A very deep draft near the sail's middle may cause luffing at the luff and stalling at the leech simultaneously (See Figure 71 C).

In Chapter 2, we discussed the keel acting as a hydrofoil and mentioned that the yaw angle created lift and drag forces (refer to Figures 28 and 36). Essentially, the same forces act on the sails but on the opposite side of the boat. These are illustrated in Figure 72. When sailing upwind or somewhere higher than a broad reach, the principal force giving drive to the sail is lift, while before the wind, the primary forward drive is caused by drag. In other words, when running we want a sail shape that will give maximum drag, but for sailing higher, and especially to windward, we want a high lift sail. In the fore triangle we can change sails for optimum shape on various points of sailing, but the mainsail must be an extremely versatile sail able to perform reasonably well both to windward and downwind.

Such a mainsail might have draft curves approximating those in Figure 73. These curves are shown at approximately a third of the luff measurement up from the boom and at another position about two-thirds up. The maximum draft may be slightly less than ten percent of the chord length at the top position illustrated but slightly greater at the lower position, and it will lie between a third and half the chord length abaft the luff. On the mainsails of many modern racing-cruisers, the deepest draft is closer to half the chord length. Notice that the chords are angled progressively further away from the boat's centerline the higher they are located. This is caused by sail twist, or the falling off of the leech. A certain amount of this is important to allow for the fairing of the apparent wind at greater heights above the water. There are conflicting opinions concerning the optimum angle of twist. C. A. Marchaj has written that the twist allowance should be only about seven degrees (this would be added to the boom's angle), but the expert sailmaker-sailor Lowell North has suggested a greater leech curve of about six percent of the leech length (the distance between the arrows shown at A, top chord, Figure 73) when close hauled. This would give a slightly wider angle than the one illustrated for a sail of medium aspect ratio.

Optimum sail twist and draft actually depends on a number of factors. If the boat is large and fast her sails should not have a great deal of draft. If the average winds are strong but the waters are fairly protected in the sailing locale, draft should be moderate; but for rough seas or light airs, draft should be considerable. For distance racing or when it is expected that downwind sailing will predominate, the sails should have ample draft located nearly midway between luff and leech. When it is desirable to emphasize upwind ability, the mainsail should be cut fairly flat when carried behind a large Genoa. Twist should generally be greater at the top of the main on a seven-eighths rigged boat than on one with a masthead rig. Tender boats in fresh breezes might need sails with moderate draft located low and forward. Then too, the stability of the cloth and the sail's cut has a very important effect on adjusting the draft for changing conditions. Some variations of draft curves (used on sails made of soft cloth) illustrating these points can be seen in Figure 73. Notice that the curves are at least slightly parabolic, with the curves flattening near the leech, even when the maximum draft is near the sail's middle. This is necessary because too much curvature in the area just forward of the leech will cause lee-side suction, acting nearly at right angles to the sail's surface, to pull the boat backwards instead of ahead when the sail is trimmed in for beating. In addition, this draft near the after part of the sail will cause extra heeling.

Draft is built into a sail by using one or a combination of two methods: by cutting *rounds* (slight roaches) at the luff and foot or by tapering and/or slightly overlapping the seams. Both these methods are illustrated in Figure 74. With the round method

(74 A), the draft forms in the sail abaft the luff when this rounded edge is set on a straight mast, while draft forms above the foot when it is bent to a straight boom. The roach at the leech has nothing to do with adding draft. It simply adds area which is unpenalized in most measurement rules.

With the tapered construction (Figure 74 B), the individual *cloths* (cloth panels) are cut wider in their middles than at their ends. When the spaces, shown in the illustration, are sewn together more material and therefore draft is put into the sail's middle. Quite often the width of the seams is varied also to help shape the draft. For sails carried upwind, the very stable Dacron sailcloth is suitable for the tapered construction, whereas a slightly softer, springy cloth is often used for the round construction, because this lends itself to draft adjustment through altering edge tension.

The principle methods of arranging the cloths are shown in Figure 74. The cross cut sail is the most usual arrangement for large mainsails, but the miter cut seems to be growing in popularity. With both cuts, bias elongation at the leech is minimized. This is highly desirable, as leech control is vital to sail efficiency, and it is an area under great strain especially when the sail is strapped in when beating. Notice that on the cross cut sail, the luff and foot seams are at angles less than ninety degrees which allows some bias stretch along the mast and boom. This permits some draft alteration through the adjustment of the sail's outhaul and downhaul or halyard. With the miter cut, however, the foot and luff below the miter seam are not subject to bias stretch which may be beneficial in some ways, but it does not allow effective, evenly distributed draft alteration through alteration of edge tension. A miter cut mainsail bent to the boom (not loose footed) often relies on a zipper or some other device to alter draft which we shall discuss presently. With this kind of mainsail, occasionally there is a problem with the miter seam forming a ridge. This is usually due to bias stretch on either side of the seam. Despite this problem, however, a good sailmaker experienced in making miter mains can make the proper allowances for stretch. Certainly some beautiful racing-cruiser mainsails have been made to this cut.

For maximum area, all mainsails and mizzens should have a tack angle, the angle between the chord of the luff and foot, of exactly ninety degrees as shown in Figure 74. Some sailors insist on a

FIGURE 71: LUFFING VS STALLING

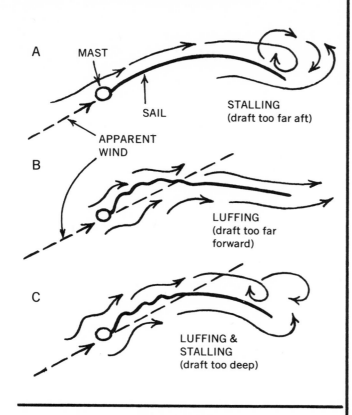

A

MAST

SAIL

APPARENT WIND

STALLING
(draft too far aft)

B

LUFFING
(draft too far forward)

C

LUFFING & STALLING
(draft too deep)

FIGURE 72: SAIL LIFT & DRAG

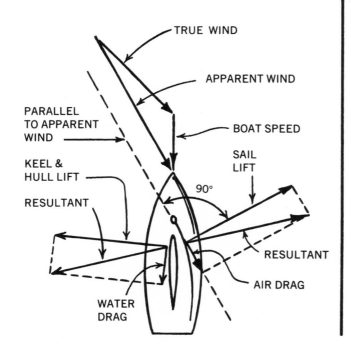

TRUE WIND

APPARENT WIND

PARALLEL TO APPARENT WIND

BOAT SPEED

KEEL & HULL LIFT

SAIL LIFT

RESULTANT

90°

RESULTANT

AIR DRAG

WATER DRAG

FIGURE 73: DRAFT & TWIST

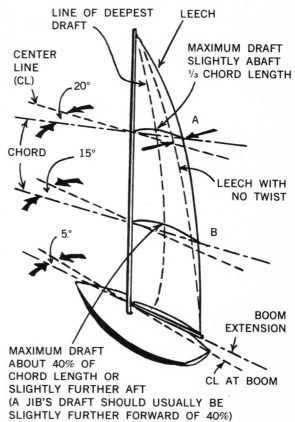

LINE OF DEEPEST DRAFT

LEECH

CENTER LINE (CL)

MAXIMUM DRAFT SLIGHTLY ABAFT ⅓ CHORD LENGTH

20°

CHORD

15°

A

LEECH WITH NO TWIST

B

5°

BOOM EXTENSION

CL AT BOOM

MAXIMUM DRAFT ABOUT 40% OF CHORD LENGTH OR SLIGHTLY FURTHER AFT
(A JIB'S DRAFT SHOULD USUALLY BE SLIGHTLY FURTHER FORWARD OF 40%)

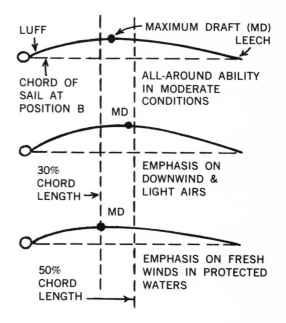

LUFF

MAXIMUM DRAFT (MD)

LEECH

CHORD OF SAIL AT POSITION B

ALL-AROUND ABILITY IN MODERATE CONDITIONS

MD

30% CHORD LENGTH

EMPHASIS ON DOWNWIND & LIGHT AIRS

MD

50% CHORD LENGTH

EMPHASIS ON FRESH WINDS IN PROTECTED WATERS

tack angle greater than ninety degrees (giving a droopy boom appearance) in the belief that the obtuse tack angle gives the greatest untaxed area, but this notion is erroneous as can be proven by simple geometry.

Genoa jibs are usually miter cut, although a few are either cross cut or "spider web cut" (with two or more miter seams) and others have quite unorthodox arrangements of paneling at the foot. Some sailmakers use a very sophisticated, scientific approach, even utilizing computers for sail designs, and this sometimes results in unusual cuts. The computer approach is not just an advertising gimmick; it can be very effective. However, it should be kept in mind that results are only as good as the information fed into the computer, and much of this information is based on assumptions and estimations. The computer does the complicated arithmetic based on the sailmaker's even more complicated judgment. One prominent sailmaker recommends that a jib's maximum draft should be located thirty-five to forty percent of its chord length abaft its luff for effective windward work. Maximum draft is generally slightly closer to the luff on a jib than on a mainsail. The exact location and amount of draft however, will depend on the sailcloth and other factors. If a very stable cloth is used, maximum draft can be located slightly further aft as compared with the draft location on a sail made of less stable cloth. A sail made of stable cloth can also have a little deeper draft than one having greater stretch. Draft will also depend on whether the jib is intended for light or heavy weather. Number two or three Genoas are usually cut a little flatter than number ones. Headsail draft should be designed with consideration for the mainsail. Too much draft, draft located too far aft, or a tight leech on a Genoa can hurt the efficiency of the slot between the jib and main causing the latter to be backwinded.

Most authorities agree that a Genoa should have some *reverse roach* (concave "round" on the leech). Speaking from personal experience, I noticed great improvement in the performance of a Genoa that suffered from a badly curling leech after it was given a greater reverse roach. The loss of area from recutting resulted in little if any noticeable reduction of speed when reaching; and the leech area, so often a problem on Genoas, was greatly improved to increase speed on the wind.

The area of a Genoa is controlled by the LP measurement shown in Figure 75. This is a perpendicular from the luff to clew and is the altitude in the formula used to obtain the area of a triangle: area = ½ (base X altitude), the base being the luff dimension. The CCA measurement rule charges a small graduating penalty after 150 percent overlap (an overlap one and a half times the base of the fore triangle as shown in Figure 75). Most racing Genoas vary between 150 and 180 percent, as shown in the illustration. Any jib greater than 180 percent seldom pays, because there is too much penalty for what little benefit (if any) is gained by the extra overlap. Notice in Figure 75 that the same LP dimension will allow a variety of jib shapes. They may be low to the deck as with jib (a) or have the foot off the deck and have more overlap as with jib (b). The latter jib has an advantage in that, it may have additional, unpenalized area by having a comparatively large foot roach (shown by the dotted line). However there is a practical limit to this foot roach concept, because if the curve is too great, the sail cannot be trimmed and set efficiently. If the sail is cut high enough, a small staysail might be set beneath it to add area. This is the principle of the light air double head rig we discussed earlier. The rig can create an area over thirty percent larger than a 180 percent Genoa, but without penalty for exceeding 150 percent overlap. It should be pointed out, however, that two headsails may not always operate with the same efficiency as a single jib, and, as mentioned, there are certain handling difficulties with the double head rig.

The low jib (a) does not have as much overlap, but it is low to the deck, and this is an advantage in that it helps prevent the escape of air from the sail's high to its low pressure side. Some jibs, called *decksweepers,* are so low that they touch or almost touch the rail, but this has some practical disadvantages on racing-cruisers that we shall discuss later. Furthermore, when the boat heels, the wind is deflected slightly upward instead of down, and the windward side of the heeled hull causes turbulence at the foot of most sails especially under the mainsail. Captain Illingworth actually prefers that the main boom be high (according to D. Phillips-Birt), in order that the mainsail is working in clear air. However, Illingworth usually keeps his Genoas low.

Some mainsails are made with a so called *foot shelf* which is a flat area (nearly horizontal) in the

FIGURE 74: COMMON SAIL CUTS

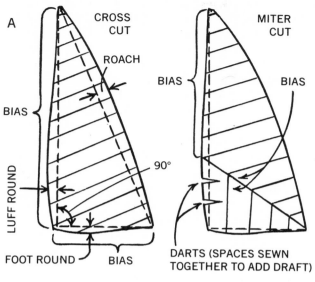

A — CROSS CUT — ROACH — BIAS — LUFF ROUND — FOOT ROUND — BIAS — MITER CUT — BIAS — BIAS — 90° — DARTS (SPACES SEWN TOGETHER TO ADD DRAFT)

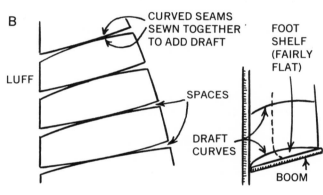

B — CURVED SEAMS SEWN TOGETHER TO ADD DRAFT — LUFF — SPACES — DRAFT CURVES — FOOT SHELF (FAIRLY FLAT) — BOOM

FIGURE 76: GENOA OVERLAP

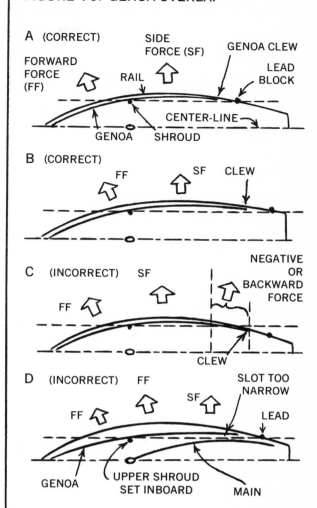

A (CORRECT) — FORWARD FORCE (FF) — SIDE FORCE (SF) — GENOA CLEW — LEAD BLOCK — RAIL — CENTER-LINE — GENOA — SHROUD

B (CORRECT) — FF — SF — CLEW

C (INCORRECT) — SF — FF — NEGATIVE OR BACKWARD FORCE — CLEW

D (INCORRECT) — FF — FF — SF — SLOT TOO NARROW — LEAD — GENOA — UPPER SHROUD SET INBOARD — MAIN

FIGURE 75: JIB AREA

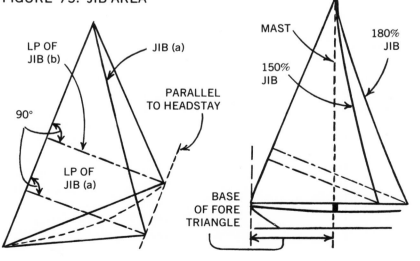

LP OF JIB (b) — JIB (a) — PARALLEL TO HEADSTAY — 90° — LP OF JIB (a) — MAST — 180% JIB — 150% JIB — BASE OF FORE TRIANGLE

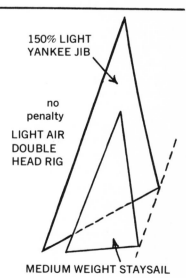

150% LIGHT YANKEE JIB — no penalty — LIGHT AIR DOUBLE HEAD RIG — MEDIUM WEIGHT STAYSAIL

sail just above the boom (see Figure 74). This allows a proper, sufficiently-deep draft curve to be located at the very foot of the sail. It may also have the effect of helping to prevent the down draft under the boom. In this case, the foot shelf may act as an end plate or "fence" similar to that on the keel shown in Figure 31.

Determining the proper size for the number one Genoa, between 150 and 180 percent, is often a difficult decision. This depends on several factors: the average wind velocity in the sailing locale, the character of the race courses (the amount and length of windward and reaching legs), and the ease with which the hull can be driven; but perhaps the most important and easily estimated considerations are the shape of the mainsail and the shape of the hull above the waterline. Results of a wind tunnel test at Southhampton University in England (according to C. A. Marchaj) indicated that the headsail leech should come abaft the point of maximum draft on the main for greatest advantage. Thus, the location of the mainsail's draft would have an important bearing on the Genoa's overlap.

A common sense rule for headsail overlap has been given by Wallace C. Ross, president of Hard Sails. Under this rule overlap is determined by the beam, half-breadth shape at the rail, and shroud location. Since the Genoa passes outside the shrouds and leads to the rail in nearly all cases, Ross suggests that the lead position should be located no further aft than a point where the rail is intersected by a line drawn from the outboard shroud parallel with the boat's centerline. This is illustrated in Figure 76. Of course, the Genoa's clew would be some distance forward of the lead position depending on the height of the clew, but most low cut Genoas would have their clews only slightly forward of the lead block when beating. The illustration shows two correct size Genoas and two incorrect, oversized jibs. Notice that in the correct examples the suction force to leeward of the sail does not pull in a backward direction, but in case C, the force near the leech pulls backwards. This is not only due to the tremendous overlap, but also to the fact that boat C has such a narrow stern. Boat B, on the other hand, has a wide stern, so she may carry a fairly large overlap without developing negative forces at the leech. Boat D has her shrouds set inboard with the chain plates mounted on a transverse bulkhead or on the cabin sides. This allows the jib to be trimmed in so that the leeward force components are forward; but the jib is trimmed so flat that it closes the slot, blocks the flow between the sails, and severely backwinds the main.

Draft Control

Since the mainsail especially, must be a very versatile sail, good upwind and down in a variety of weather conditions, there should be some means of controlling or adjusting draft. The usual means of draft control are spar bending, edge tension, and zippers or luff and foot *roach reefs*. We discussed mast bending in the last chapter, and it was pointed out that there were certain difficulties, impracticalities, and even rules against this practice for racing-cruisers. Almost the same thing holds true for booms. First of all, the boom would have to be bent a great deal for this to have any significant effect on flattening the sail; and second, if the boom were limber the boom vang would tend to bend it when reaching, just when we want a straight boom and maximum draft in the sail. Furthermore, in using a limber boom, there might be difficulties with sidewise bend, unless the boom were wide and flat, but this type would make roller reefing very difficult.

This leaves us with the other two alternatives, edge tension and roach reefing. Edge adjusting is an ancient but effective means of changing draft that is surprisingly neglected by some skippers of racing-cruisers. As pointed out earlier, the cut of the sail and the kind of sailcloth have a direct bearing on this method. Cross cut sails with luff and foot rounds, having little if any foot shelf and made of material having slightly more spring than the most stable material respond well to edge adjustment. Sails intended for edge adjustment should be fastened (preferably hand sewn) to moderately stretchy bolt ropes or heavy cloth tapes at the luff and foot edges while under uneven tension (with less tension near the tack) for best control of the draft.

When beating in a breeze, if the seas are not too large, the sail is flattened by tightening the luff with the boom downhaul or halyard, and the foot is tightened with the outhaul. Running and reaching or beating in light airs or choppy seas the luff and foot should be slacked for maximum draft. Tightening the luff and foot pulls the draft forward towards the mast and down towards the boom and

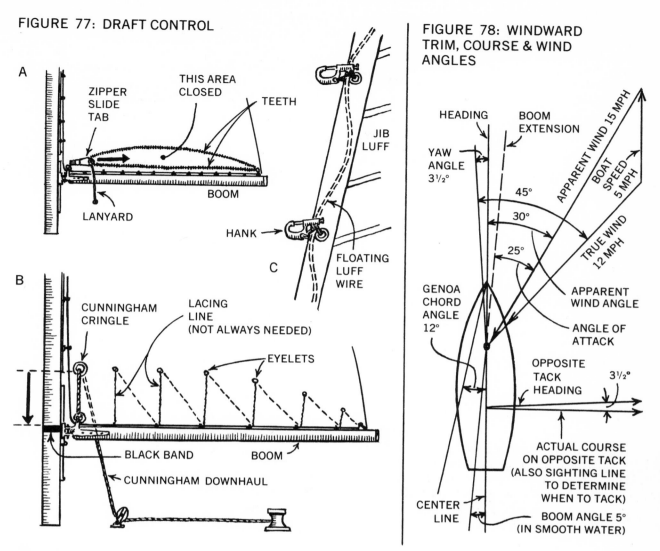

FIGURE 77: DRAFT CONTROL

A

ZIPPER SLIDE TAB

THIS AREA CLOSED

TEETH

BOOM

LANYARD

B

CUNNINGHAM CRINGLE

LACING LINE (NOT ALWAYS NEEDED)

EYELETS

BLACK BAND

BOOM

CUNNINGHAM DOWNHAUL

C

JIB LUFF

HANK

FLOATING LUFF WIRE

FIGURE 78: WINDWARD TRIM, COURSE & WIND ANGLES

HEADING

BOOM EXTENSION

YAW ANGLE 3½°

APPARENT WIND 15 MPH

BOAT SPEED 5 MPH

45°

30°

TRUE WIND 12 MPH

25°

APPARENT WIND ANGLE

ANGLE OF ATTACK

GENOA CHORD ANGLE 12°

OPPOSITE TACK HEADING

3½°

CENTER LINE

ACTUAL COURSE ON OPPOSITE TACK (ALSO SIGHTING LINE TO DETERMINE WHEN TO TACK)

BOOM ANGLE 5° (IN SMOOTH WATER)

generally flattens the sail in its middle. It is especially important to tighten the luff in a fresh breeze as the draft begins to move aft due to stretch or bias elongation.

Miter cut and/or foot shelf type mainsails that don't respond as well to alteration through edge tension are often fitted with a foot zipper or roach reef to change the draft. Figure 77A shows a sail zipper in the open, full draft position. To zip closed, to reduce draft, the sliding tab is pulled aft and the teeth come together similarly to any ordinary zipper. Early sail zippers were sometimes prone to jamming, but the modern type made of nylon are not as apt to jam. However, any zipper is difficult if not almost impossible to close when the mainsail is strapped in while beating in a breeze. Another disadvantage with zippers is that draft

alteration is not variable unless there are several zippers. Also, the amount of draft that can be reduced by this device is a rather insignificant area just above the boom that needs little alteration if the cloth is highly stable.

A more effective roach reefing arrangement, in my opinion, is illustrated in 77B. This features a *Cunningham cringle* (named after the famous helmsman Briggs Cunningham according to one well-known yacht racing author, although there was a *Cunningham reef* system used long ago on square riggers). This cringle located above the tack is pulled down and lashed to the tack, thereby folding the material beneath the eyelets running from the cringle to the clew. The lacing line which is one continual light line rove through the eyelets, is then tightened to gather in and secure the loose

103

FIGURE 79: BASIC BOOM POSITIONS—boom angle equals apparent wind angle minus angle of attack

A) CLOSE HAULED

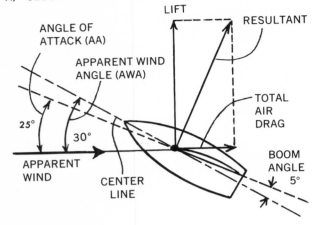

ANGLE OF ATTACK (AA)
APPARENT WIND ANGLE (AWA)
25°
30°
APPARENT WIND
CENTER LINE
LIFT
RESULTANT
TOTAL AIR DRAG
BOOM ANGLE 5°

B) CLOSE REACHING

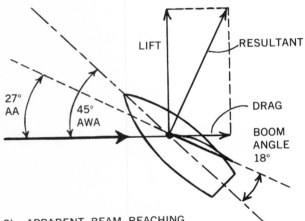

LIFT
RESULTANT
DRAG
27° AA
45° AWA
BOOM ANGLE 18°

C) APPARENT BEAM REACHING

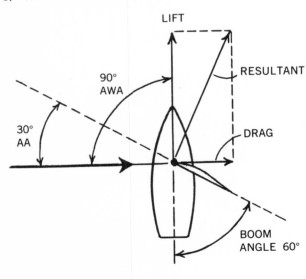

LIFT
90° AWA
RESULTANT
DRAG
30° AA
BOOM ANGLE 60°

D) BROAD REACHING

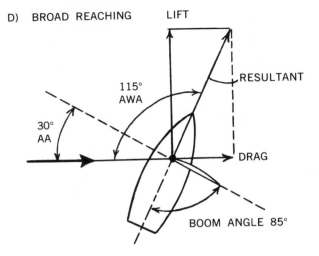

LIFT
RESULTANT
115° AWA
30° AA
DRAG
BOOM ANGLE 85°

E) NEAR QUARTER REACHING

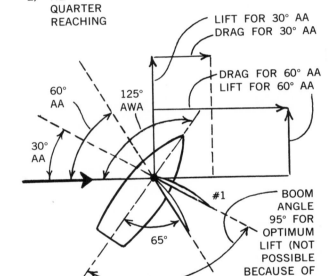

LIFT FOR 30° AA
DRAG FOR 30° AA
DRAG FOR 60° AA
LIFT FOR 60° AA
60° AA
125° AWA
30° AA
#1
65°
#2
BOOM ANGLE 95° FOR OPTIMUM LIFT (NOT POSSIBLE BECAUSE OF SHROUDS)

F) RUNNING

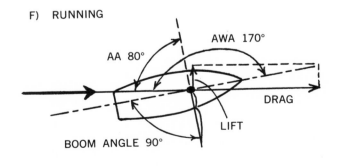

AWA 170°
AA 80°
DRAG
LIFT
BOOM ANGLE 90°

excess material at the foot. This has the effect of removing material from the bottom of the sail, of flattening the draft, and pulling it forward. For Cunningham reefing the luff should be cut with some round, and the cloth should have a little give for the most effectiveness. One feature of this system that doesn't appeal to me is all the string hanging in the foot area, but many sailors feel that this does little if any harm to the air flow. A similar system could be used to reef excess area on the luff. This has been used effectively, but luff reefing is outlawed by the CCA.

Also illustrated in Figure 77 is a means of controlling draft in a jib. This features a "floating," or loose, luff wire in a sleeve. Essentially this is the same as the so called *stretchy luff jib* which has no luff wire but, in its place, a luff tape or rope. However, there is a difference with the type of draft control illustrated, because in this case the loose wire imposes a definite limit on stretch. Without a luff wire in a breeze, it may seem that the luff could almost be stretched forever without getting it sufficiently tight, but a loose floating wire in a sleeve gradually gives up slack as the luff is tightened, through hoisting with the halyard (or with a tack downhaul in some cases), until the luff wire is stretched taut. When this happens, draft is pulled forward and sag is minimized. When first sailing with this type of jib, the tendency is not to slack the luff sufficiently in light airs. The outline of the luff wire can be seen through the semi-transparent cloth, and it should bend like a snake as illustrated. It doesn't matter if there are a few horizontal wrinkles along the luff so long as it is sufficiently slack in light winds.

One minor consideration with regard to stretchy sails is the fact that they must be made slightly smaller in projected area than those made of stable cloth with tailored panels (sometimes called "mold-cut" sails). This is because sails cannot exceed their measured area under the measurement rules. Thus in light airs, when maximum area is needed, luff and foot lengths are short; but in a fresh breeze when there should be less projected area, it becomes necessary to increase the luff and foot lengths by stretching them to reduce draft.

Sail Trim

The successful racing sailor must develop an instinct for sail trim. The approach to proper trim may be somewhat intuitive, but it should be based

on, or developed from, an understanding of the basic aerodynamic principles involved. This does not mean that one should try to trim his sails at precise angles derived from scientific theory. The approach should primarily be empirical and experimental, based on trial and error. However, a knowledge of the wind forces and sail reactions should be helpful in establishing basic trim positions from which deviations and fine adjustments can be made.

Figure 78 illustrates the basic wind, course, and trim angles when beating to windward in a medium sized racing-cruiser in moderate conditions of wind and sea. Actually these angle estimates are based on the performance of a boat I sail, an Ohlson 35 yawl of average windward ability. Obviously, the boat's forward speed brings the apparent wind considerably forward of the true wind; and of course, the apparent wind direction is shown by the telltales (ribbons or threads on the shrouds) or the masthead indicator, although the latter might show the wind to be a little more fair (further aft) because the wind velocity is often slightly greater at the higher altitude. The apparent wind angle, shown at thirty degrees, is the angle between the boat's heading and the apparent wind. The angle of attack is the angle between a forward extension of the sail's bottom chord (or the boom) and the apparent wind. The boom angle (in this case five degrees) subtracted from the apparent wind angle gives the angle of attack. The angle between the boat's heading close-hauled on the starboard tack and her close-hauled heading on the port tack will be about eighty-six and one-half degrees but due to an assumed three and one-half degree angle of leeway or yaw, the angle between the actual courses on the two tacks is about ninety-three and one-half degrees. Notice that although the main boom is trimmed in to within five degrees of the boat's centerline the Genoa's chord is at approximately twelve degrees. As a general rule, when one sail lies behind another, the after sail must be trimmed flatter especially when there is an overlap. The airfoil shape of the Genoa deflects the wind so that its luff is sailing in a lift (favorable change of wind direction), while the deflection causes the mainsail to sail in a header (unfavorable change of direction).

Figure 79 illustrates the basic boom positions for the various points of sailing when considering the mainsail without jib interaction. Exact boom positions will vary with the boat size, wind and sea conditions, sail draft, aspect ratio, and especially with the addition of a headsail. Actually, the close-hauled point of sailing shows the main to be trimmed about correctly for when a Genoa is carried; but with the successive points of sailing, the further the boom is away from the centerline, the more the jib will turn the air flow against the mainsail's lee side until the jib is blanketed by the mainsail when the wind is quite far aft. The lift-drag forces illustrated are rough estimates that will vary, of course, with different hull forms and sail plans. Lift acts at right angles to the apparent wind, while drag acts in the same direction as the apparent wind. The optimum angle of attack, in most cases, might lie between twenty-five degrees and thirty degrees, closer to twenty-five degrees when closehauled but closer to thirty degrees when the wind draws aft. It can be seen that the lift force is principally utilized until the wind is slightly forward of the quarter. When broad reaching or sailing somewhat further off the wind, some sailors trim the main so that it is almost square to the wind, but it can be seen that this is usually not correct. The sail should be eased considerably more to utilize optimum lift-drag and to better align the direction of the sail's pull with the boat's heading.

When the boat bears off beyond the near quarter reaching point of sailing (Figure 79E), interesting things begin to happen. This point of sailing was discussed in a fascinating article by Eugene M. Reardon in *One Design and Offshore Yachtsman* magazine (March, 1967). When the apparent wind is approximately 127 degrees off the bow, there are theoretically two optimum boom angles, one with the boom far off (position number 1 in the diagram) which continues to principally utilize lift at about a thirty degree angle of attack, and the other boom angle much more narrow (position number 2) which utilizes the drag force at an angle of attack of about sixty degrees. These positions are based on a lift-drag polar diagram (curve) similar to the one shown in Figure 80. The curve is made up of points at the end of an infinite number of lift-drag vector resultants as illustrated. The dashed lines show examples of lift and drag forces with their resultants shown as arrows. The numbers indicate angles of attack.

The curve illustrated is for a modern, light-displacement boat with one Marconi sail, but it shows

FIGURE 80: CHARACTER OF A LIFT-DRAG POLAR

(FOR ABOVE WATER PORTION OF A UNA-RIGGED, LIGHT DISPLACEMENT BOAT)

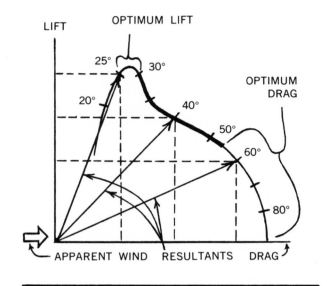

FIGURE 81: SPINNAKER INFLUENCE ON MAINSAIL TRIM

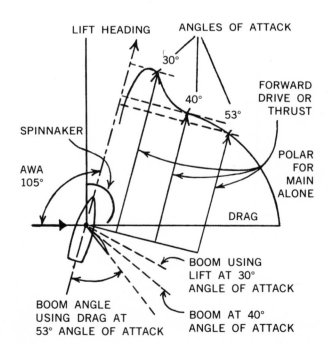

the character of most sail polars in that lift increases to its optimum point (around twenty-seven degrees in Figure 80), then drops sharply when stalling occurs, and then the curve gradually rounds out (although there may be an additional slight hump in the curve) as lift decreases more slowly and the drag increases rapidly. The hollow part of the curve, shown extra heavy in the diagram, should be avoided because at these angles of attack (between thirty degrees and fifty-three degrees for this polar), we are not getting properly directed optimum lift or drag.

As Mr. Reardon points out, this study does not take into consideration the considerable effects of a jib or spinnaker. In applying this information to a racing-cruiser, we would have to eliminate optimum position number 1 (Figure 79E) because of the interference of shrouds with the boom. This would mean that on this point of sailing, we should shift from using optimum lift to optimum drag, and surprisingly, this could mean that, as we bear off (at the time of shifting), we *might* slightly *trim in* the main rather than slacking it off as is customary. To generalize and perhaps oversimplify, we might suggest keeping the main well eased out to the verge of luffing until it is interfered with by the shrouds or especially headsail backwind, and then if we need to bear off more, we might trim in slightly (or slack off no more) when shifting to utilize mainly drag. After this point of trim, we slack the mainsheet progressively the further we bear away until the boom touches the shrouds.

When carrying the spinnaker, we will probably have to shift from using optimum lift to optimum drag much sooner. If the spinnaker is carried on or just below a beam reach, the main must be trimmed in closer than indicated in 79C to prevent excessive backwind, but the main should be out as far as possible to make the most of lift, because this acts in nearly the same direction as the boat's heading. At broader angles to the wind, it will probably pay to use optimum drag forces in order to open up the slot between the main and the spinnaker to avoid backwind. An example is shown in Figure 81, where the boat is headed 105 degrees from the apparent wind. Obviously, if the boom were slacked off to about seventy-five degrees, the main would give the greatest forward drive by utilizing optimum lift, but at the same time the boom might be too close to the clew of the spinnaker. Notice that if the angle of attack were

increased to forty degrees, there would be considerable loss of forward drive component and the slot would not be opened a great deal. However, if the angle of attack is increased to fifty-three degrees, there is little additional loss in forward component, and the slot is opened up considerably. Of course, we cannot be sure of the polar's exact shape when the spinnaker is set, but the example illustrates that we probably shift from lift to drag much sooner when the spinnaker is set and that the main boom angle may be little if any greater on this point of sailing than when beam reaching. There is also an indication that if a racing-cruiser's main, at optimum trim is badly backed by the spinnaker, a good reaching jib might be more effective than the spinnaker when beam reaching. Spinnaker trim will be discussed later in Chapter 9.

Considering the points of sailing above a beam reach, when the Genoa is carried instead of a spinnaker, we might say that the old rule of keeping the sails eased out until they are on the verge of luffing holds quite true; because if we decrease the angle of attack by slacking sheets, this causes luffing, and if we increase the angle of attack by over trimming, the sails tend to stall. Mainsail stalling is delayed by the venturi effect of any overlapping jib, but a Genoa especially, will often throw backward against the main and cause premature luffing. There are some indications that, at times, more of this backwind can be tolerated than some of us realize particularly when the main is heavy and stable, with some "body." The principle consideration is to keep the proper width slot between the main and jib. If the slot is too wide it will lose its venturi effect of speeding up the flow to leeward of the main; but if the slot is too narrow, the flow will be constricted and blocked. The slot should generally be wider in fresh winds than in light airs; and since sheets should be eased in light weather, the main should perhaps be eased a little more than the jib, even if the main is very slightly backwinded. The jib should be kept on the verge of luffing, and the helmsman should use the jib luff as a guide to optimum pointing rather than the partially backwinded mainsail luff.

An occasionally maladjusted slot is the one between the mizzen and mizzen staysail. Some sailors tend to trim these sails in such a way that the slot is too constricted. If the mizzen is badly backwinded, the staysail sheet should be eased; but if this results in undue luffing, the mizzen or staysail should be lowered. Generally speaking, all light downwind sails should be eased off and allowed to flow and lift as much as possible. More will be said of this later when we talk about spinnakers.

Optimum sail trim must change constantly with every wind shift, change in boat speed, or wind velocity. Thus sheets should continually be adjusted or "played." Sheet playing will be less if the helmsman changes course for wind changes, but the sheets will require more tending when the helmsman holds a comparatively steady course. During lulls, the sheets should be eased, but in puffs they should be trimmed back in. When the boat picks up speed, sheets should be trimmed in, but when she loses speed, as after tacking, sheets should be eased out. To reiterate, theory merely gives us a point of departure for proper trim. The real test is how the boat performs when sailing alongside of her competition. A fine instinct for sail trim is developed from an awareness of the problems involved, astute observation, experience, and a penchant for experimentation.

Vangs and Travellers

The principal value of boom vangs and travellers is that they control sail twist and to some extent the draft curvature. When a sail is twisted, its head has a broader angle to the boat's centerline than its foot (see Figure 73). Sail twist becomes progressively larger as the boom is slacked off until the sail begins to lie against the spreaders and shrouds. Twist is a result of the sheet pulling the sail mostly inward, towards the boat's centerline, rather than downward. This allows the boom to ride up and twist the sail. A boom vang supplies downward pull when reaching and running, while a traveller performs the same function when beating. As said in Chapter 4, a vang led to the leeward side deck when beating has somewhat the same effect as a traveller, but the latter is much more convenient because a side deck vang needs continual adjustment at every change in sheet trim.

On small boats, boom vangs can usually be secured at the boat's centerline near the base of the mast, and of course this eliminates the need for adjustment when the sheet's trim is changed. On racing-cruisers, however, this on-center vang often cannot be used (unless the main boom is quite high) because of interference with the cabin house or too little space between the gooseneck and cabin top or deck; thus an off-center vang, some-

times called a *go fast*, must usually be rigged to the sidedeck. These are illustrated in Figure 82. Notice that the on-center vang tends to thrust the boom forward against the mast when the sail is trimmed in, but when the sail is slacked off for reaching or running the thrust is lateral against the gooseneck track. On these off-the-wind points of sailing, there is a tremendous sidewise strain at the gooseneck, and so if an on-center vang is used, the gooseneck should be extra strong and its slide track should often be bolted to the mast.

The off-center vang (A in the diagram) pulls directly downward on the boom, but with this arrangement the vang must be relocated and readjusted as the boom is pulled in or slacked off. Usually three or four location points on the side deck are necessary with the points being either directly under the vang's point of attachment to the boom or somewhat further forward. When the vang is rigged in this manner, there is no need for a preventer being rigged to guard against an accidental jibe, *unless* the boat is rolling or heeling and apt to dip the end of her boom in a sea. In such a case, there is a possibility of breaking the boom, so a preventer, running from the outer end of the boom to the foredeck (as illustrated), should be rigged. Some offshore racers have *anti-tripping reef points* (also illustrated) to raise up the end of the boom and help prevent such an accident. Some boats carry their off-center vangs attached to a slide on the Genoa track, but this should not be done unless the track is bolted or very securely fastened because the vang exerts a tremendous upward and sometimes slightly lateral pull. Some life line stanchions have strong securing straps at their base (see Figure 39), and these are often convenient for the vang's attachment when the stanchions are through bolted to the deck as they should be.

Mainsheet travellers were described and illustrated in Chapter 4 (Figure 55). The mainsheet lead should be kept on the boat's centerline or perhaps even slightly to weather of the centerline in light airs; but the lead, which slides on the traveller track, should be eased to leeward slightly as the wind increases. The traveller acts similarly to the vang in removing excess twist and somewhat flattening the draft. Both the vang and traveller also tighten the leech. Care should be taken that it is not over tightened when beating; however tightening the leech is nearly always beneficial in downwind sailing especially when the luff is well

FIGURE 82: VANG & TRAVELLER

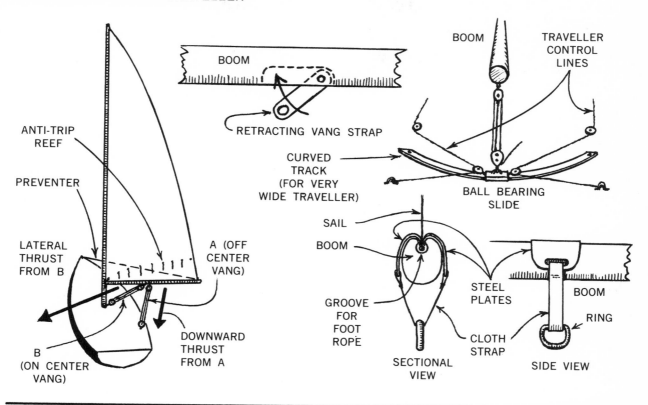

ANTI-TRIP REEF

PREVENTER

LATERAL THRUST FROM B

A (OFF CENTER VANG)

B (ON CENTER VANG)

DOWNWARD THRUST FROM A

BOOM

RETRACTING VANG STRAP

BOOM

TRAVELLER CONTROL LINES

CURVED TRACK (FOR VERY WIDE TRAVELLER)

BALL BEARING SLIDE

SAIL

BOOM

GROOVE FOR FOOT ROPE

STEEL PLATES

CLOTH STRAP

SECTIONAL VIEW

BOOM

RING

SIDE VIEW

---

slacked to increase and move aft the sail's draft. In my opinion, very wide travellers should be slightly curved to follow the arc of the boom so that the traveller may be adjusted for wind changes without adjusting the main sheet when sailing close-hauled (see Figure 82).

There is sometimes a slight problem in attaching the vang to a roller reefing boom. If the sail's foot is attached to the boom with slides on a track, a strap may be inserted between the sail and the boom; but if the foot is attached to the boom by a bolt rope fitting into a boom groove, the problem becomes more difficult. Some boats often have a swaged ball on the vang which fits into a keyhole slot on the underside of an aluminum boom, but this is usually insufficiently strong when used on a large, offshore racer. Alternatives are a vang with a claw ring (see Figure 55) or a slit cut in the sail's foot just above the boom for a strap when the vang is the off-center type. When the vang is rigged on center a pivoting strap that retracts into a boom slot is sometimes used (Figure 82). Obviously, the metal strap is retracted when the boom is turned

FIGURE 83: SAIL TWIST WHEN RUNNING

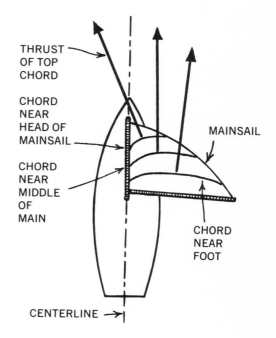

THRUST OF TOP CHORD

CHORD NEAR HEAD OF MAINSAIL

CHORD NEAR MIDDLE OF MAIN

MAINSAIL

CHORD NEAR FOOT

CENTERLINE

while roller reefing. A simple alternative for a wooden boom is a small hole drilled through the boom near its top. A copper tube can be driven through the hole to prevent water leaking into the boom, and then a removable nylon rope for securing the vang is passed through the tube. Another innovation is the use of two curved steel plates that fit into a grooved boom as shown in Figure 82.

Most top racing sailors realize the importance of proper vang and traveller adjustments, but in some cases I think there is a tendency for some former skippers of small boats with bendy rigs when sailing racing-cruisers with nonflexible rigs to overdo on these adjustments because pulling the boom down will often overly tighten the leech when the top of the mast will not bend aft. In light airs when sailing close-hauled, the vang should be used sparingly. Also vang tension should be moderate when the boom is heavy except in a fresh breeze. With a large overlapping headsail, the vang should not be so tight nor the traveller setting so wide that the bottom of the jib slot is closed or seriously constricted. The larger the mainsail is in relation to the jib area, the greater the importance of proper vang adjustment. Vang tension becomes increasingly important as the wind increases and swings aft. When quarter reaching and running, the vang tension can help prevent yawing and rolling because without the vang, the sail's head twists so far forward that its pulling force can work to windward of the boat's centerline even though the foot pulls to leeward (see Figure 83).

Ordering Sails

When ordering new sails, it is best to give the sailmaker all possible information even remotely related to the shape, size, and cut of each sail. With mainsails, the most vital measurements are, of course, the mast and boom lengths. If the boat does not have a rating certificate showing luff and foot lengths, it is preferable that the sailmaker make these measurements, but quite often this is impossible when the boat and sail loft are a long distance apart. Luff and foot measurements are nearly always marked by *black bands* one inch wide, of paint or tape, circling the spars at the upper, lower, and outer limits of head, tack, and clew, when the luff and foot are stretched taut (see Figure 62). In handicap racing, black-banding spars is done to obtain the best possible sail area rating for a sail of given size. Spar measurements

for sailmaking purposes should be made between the inside edges of the black bands (between the top of the bottom band and bottom of the top band on the mast, and between the after side of the mast and the forward edge of the after band on the boom). If the spars are not banded before the sail is made, the boat owner must decide what luff and foot measurements will give him the most speed for the least rating. He may prefer, as most owners do, that the sailmaker use the boat's standard sail plan as drawn by the boat's designer. However, if the winds are generally light in the racing area, the owner may wish slightly longer luff and foot lengths with the bands placed at the very ends of the spars. On the other hand, if the racing area winds are generally heavy or the boat is somewhat tender, the owner may decide to decrease the rating with a slightly smaller mainsail. At any rate, if the spars are not banded before the sail is made, they should be banded after the sail is made for maximum rating benefit. More will be said of this in the next chapter when we talk about measurement rules.

When making luff and foot measurements for the sailmaker, use a steel tape stretched taut, and give the full, maximum measurement. Do not try to allow for sail stretch. This is the sailmaker's job, and of course, stretch allowance will depend on the cloth finish, weight, edging material, and the sail's cut. It is very important that the sailmaker know the exact locations of the tack and clew fittings. If possible, these should be positioned so that the luff and foot make straight lines when those edges are stretched taut. In other words, the outhaul and gooseneck fitting pins that pass through the clew and tack grommets should not be excessively low or high off the boom nor should the tack pin be excessively close or far away from the mast. If the pins are located so that the luff and foot cannot be stretched to make straight lines from head to tack and from tack to clew, the fittings should be moved or changed; but if this is impossible, the sailmaker should know the exact pin locations. When boats have roller reefing it is usually necessary that the tack pin is set excessively far abaft the mast's sail track. In this case, the sailmaker must cut the sail in such a way as to compensate or secure the sail slides with a *jackline* (a short line running along the lower luff that holds the lower slides a short distance away from the luff).

Other information that will be helpful to the

sailmaker is: how you tune your boat's rig, whether or not the mast will be absolutely straight, how taut the jib stay will be carried, and the amount of mast rake; hull form, beam, displacement and stiffness; jib overlap; description of other sails that will be carried simultaneously with the new sail; traveller length and lead positions; typical racing weather conditions; wave conditions; whether emphasis should be placed on upwind or downwind sailing; a description of the existing sail inventory; how much the new sail will be used for racing or cruising; whether the sail will be unbent or left bent to its boom; any unusual sailing habits or characteristics of the skipper, crew, or boat; and so forth. Obviously, if the boat has been measured, a copy of her rating certificate should be sent to the sailmaker. Also, he should have a copy of her hull plans as well as her sail plan if these are available. Most sailmakers will have standard sail plans of stock boats. Of course, there should be ample communication by letters, telephone, or preferably visits between the sailmaker and buyer. Sails are expensive, and so it is well worthwhile being careful and thorough in supplying the sailmaker with pertinent information.

Some Practical Considerations

The following is a list of miscellaneous suggestions concerning sails, that have not already been mentioned.

(1) Lower battens should be stiff but slightly flexible at the inner end, while the upper batten should be quite flexible, especially at the inner end.

(2) When roller reefing is provided, the bottom batten should be horizontal so that it can be rolled around the boom without bending. It is sometimes desirable to have two or three grommets put in the leech of the sail at the most probable reefed clew locations in order that a line may be rove through to facilitate pulling back on the leech and thereby preventing wrinkles at the foot.

(3) Some sailmakers use small, light-weight shackles to secure the sail slides to the sail. These are strong, dependable, and if the proper type, do not chafe the sail.

(4) When mainsails are small, it is generally desirable that they be unbent from their booms when not in use. If possible, try to fold them so that the creases run fore-and-aft. When mainsails are too large to fold, it is often best to leave them bent and furled or faked down (accordian folded) on top of the boom. Be sure to cover the sail with a loose fitting (for ventilation) sail cover to protect against sun rot, bird droppings, and industrial smog.

(5) Jibs or other sails that must be stuffed into bags should be hoisted at least fifteen minutes or more before the start of a race in order that the wrinkles and creases have a chance to smooth out.

(6) Use a strong main topping lift, adjustable at the mast. It should be capable of supporting the mainsail (in case the main halyard parts) or, on a seven-eighths rigged boat, supporting a man in a bosun's chair. If the sail's leech is chafed, the lift may be held away from the sail with a piece of shock cord (elastic cord) attached to the permanent backstay. It is often simpler to temporarily disconnect the lift, when it is not needed, from the boom's end.

(7) An excessive roach on the mainsail (or mizzen) is unpenalized sail area, but it is hard to control. Large roaches often cause the leech area to fall forward causing a hard ridge just forward of the battens. Extra tension on the vang to tighten the leech can help correct this fault.

(8) It is usually a good idea, for more versatile sail control, to have leech lines in the main as well as the Genoa and a *foot line* in the drifter. These lines are sewn into the tabling (edging), and they can be adjusted to tighten or slack the leech or foot. These lines should generally be tightened when sailing downwind especially in light airs. On a battenless jib, the leech line can help prevent the frequently experienced *leech flutter* (rapid, machine-gun flapping). However, when close hauled, the leech line should seldom be tightened to such an extent that it causes the leech to curl inboard, because this will block the airflow through the jib slot and turn it against the lee side of the mainsail. A mild leech flutter is not considered very harmful.

(9) Goosenecks should be the sliding type so that luff tension can be regulated with a downhaul. The luff can be adjusted with the halyard but this influences draft mostly at the top of the sail, whereas downhaul adjustment influences draft closer to the more important middle and bottom of the sail. Also, slacking the halyard lowers the sail's head which is undesirable in light weather, at the very time when the luff should be slack but the sail should be high.

(10) An efficient outhaul adjustment is a must for racing. The worm screw type with a handle at the end of the boom is very powerful and satisfac-

tory, but this type has one drawback in that it cannot be adjusted while the boom is broad off. The outhaul that uses blocks and cleats mounted near the middle of the boom should not be used with roller reefing, because in this case, the boom should be smooth so it will be harmless to the sail when a reef is rolled in. An effective outhaul is the type that has a wire running through the boom which winds up on an internal reel and is operated by a removable crank handle at the forward end of the boom.

(11) A difficult problem with low cut Genoas on racing-cruisers is the interference of life lines with the foot of the sail. Several solutions to the problem are suggested in Figure 84. The simplest solution would be to rig the life lines with *pelican hooks* (hinged hooks held closed with sliding rings) permitting removal of the life lines from the pulpit when the Genoa is carried, but this would sacrifice safety, and such a practice would not be permitted by many race sponsoring organizations. Method A, shown in Figure 84, is satisfactory to some organizations, but there is still some sacrifice of safety because there is a gap between the most forward stanchion and the pulpit. However, there is little life line interference because the Genoa is always outside of the life lines. In this case it is usually best that the forward stanchions be bent slightly inboard to permit efficient, flat trimming of the jib when beating.

With method B, the life lines are tied down at the shrouds. This does not sacrifice safety and allows the forward part of the jib to be inside the life lines, but there is a slight drawback in that the jib foot will ride up over the life line when the sheet is slacked when reaching.

Method C is perhaps the most satisfactory solution. Here the forward stanchion is set close but slightly inboard of the pulpit leaving a narrow gateway through which the sail can pass. The jib is then outboard of the life lines and there is little if any sacrifice of safety.

(12) Most Genoas are very sensitive to lead adjustments. A change of a few inches can make a significant difference in performance. The usual Genoa lead is a slide on a track mounted on the rail, and thus there is no transverse adjustment (except that due to hull curvature at the rail) but only fore-and-aft adjustment. Sliding the lead forward will tighten the leech and slack the foot, and sliding it aft will slack the leech and tighten the foot. The lead should be adjusted so that when the

FIGURE 84: LIFE LINES & THE GENOA

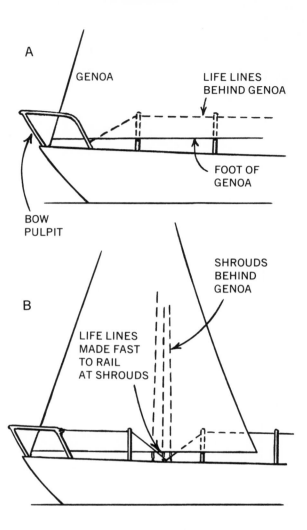

A

GENOA

LIFE LINES BEHIND GENOA

FOOT OF GENOA

BOW PULPIT

B

SHROUDS BEHIND GENOA

LIFE LINES MADE FAST TO RAIL AT SHROUDS

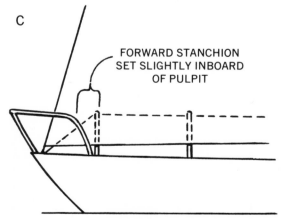

C

FORWARD STANCHION SET SLIGHTLY INBOARD OF PULPIT

boat is turned towards the wind, the jib will luff more or less evenly from foot to head, first beginning to break (luff) somewhere around a third of the luff distance up from the foot. Many Genoas seem to perform best when beating if the foot lies tight against the shrouds (when these are set outboard) and when the upper leech area is several inches away from the end of the spreaders. Of course this will vary with individual boats, rigs, and sails. Generally, the lead should be slightly farther forward in light airs than in a fresh breeze. There should be ample experimentation when racing near competition and once optimum lead points are found, these should be marked, perhaps with waterproof adhesive tape that is labeled to indicate the sail, weather conditions, and point of sailing. Quite often the stopper holes for the sliding leads do not correspond on each side of the boat. Measure these carefully, and either move the track, or have new holes drilled so that the positions on each side correspond exactly.

(13) One-design boats with inboard jib sheet leads often use a device called a *Barber-haul* which is essentially an extra, secondary sheet led to a point near the rail or outboard of the primary sheet lead in order to control the athwartship position of the jib lead. Of course, the usual racing-cruiser's Genoa leads to a track on the rail, but if the shrouds are set inboard, and the Genoa's overlap is moderate, it may pay at times, when beating, to move the lead position slightly inboard of the rail. This might be done by rigging a Barber-haul from the Genoa's clew to a winch mounted on the cockpit coaming.

7
Rules, Measurement, and Racing

Common Measurement Rules

Some of the most commonly used handicap measurement rules are very complex and often confusing to many owners of newly acquired racing-cruisers, especially to racing novices or former skippers of one-design classes. The purpose of the rules discussion in this chapter is not a detailed study but an attempt to explain, in the simplest way, the main points and basic principles.

The two principal handicap rules for racing-cruisers presently used in America have already been mentioned. These are the CCA (Cruising Club of America) and the MORC (Midget Ocean Racing Club) rules. Other rules of some popularity that will be described very briefly are the *Storm Trysail Club* (STC) and the *Off Soundings Club* (OSC) rules. The MORC was formerly for boats under twenty-four feet LOA, but the size limit was extended and now includes boats up to thirty feet LOA. Yachts racing under this rule are customarily divided into two classes: division A, for boats twenty-four feet but under thirty feet LOA and division B, for those under twenty-four feet LOA. The CCA rule is generally for boats between thirty and seventy-three feet LOA. In some racing areas, however, boats slightly under thirty feet (with a rated length of perhaps over twenty-two feet) are allowed to race under the CCA rule; and so in this case these small boats may have an option to race under CCA or MORC. Of course, it is up to the race sponsoring organization to choose the handicap rule, but as said, the great majority of important races in the United States presently use the MORC for small boats and the CCA for larger boats. The new *International Offshore Rating Rule* (IOR), not yet in use, has been published recently. This will be discussed after the OSC, STC, MORC, and CCA rules.

In Chapters 2 and 3 we discussed a yacht's vari-

ous speed affecting dimensions and characteristics. Some of the most important and readily measurable of these are the sailing length or "L" (the effective LWL when the boat is underway and heeled), sail area, displacement (or hull depth), beam, draft, stability, freeboard, rig, and propeller (size, type, and location). The more complex rules, CCA, IOR and MORC, take into consideration most of these speed factors, but the simpler rules, Off Soundings and the 1963 STC consider merely the vital sailing length, sail area, propeller, and displacement (in the STC), beam, and rig allowance (an allowance for the efficiency of the rig). As said previously, the most fundamental measure of a boat's speed is her sailing length, because the square root of this measurement approximates her easily attained top speed (at a speed-length ratio of 1.0) when sailing full and by in moderate winds. Sail area is equally important, because this is the driving or motivating force, and displacement or hull depth with beam, considered as resistance, can be thought of as the bulk or weight to be moved. In the various measurement formulas, sail area (SA) is expressed as a square root because this is a surface or square measurement; while displacement (disp. or D or P), expressed as volume or cubic measurement, is shown in the formulas as a cube root. In other words, the rated lengths of racing-cruisers of different sizes vary with the square root of their sail area and the cube root of their displacement.

The rating formulas give a rated length in feet which is then applied to time allowance tables to obtain the actual handicap time for a particular race. This will be discussed later. Yachts assigned a rating under the rules mentioned in this chapter must be measured by official measurers approved by the race or rule sponsoring organization or club.

NOTE: As we go to press, it is becoming increasingly apparent that the new IOR rule will soon replace the CCA and perhaps even the MORC rules for important, formal races. However, some yacht clubs may cling to the older rules for some time to come if (as we suspect) there will be some rating inequities or problems involved in measuring large numbers of boats of all sizes and designs to the new rule. Even if the new rule proves entirely successful and completely replaces the CCA rule, a familiarization with the latter is well worthwhile, partly because such a large portion of the cruising club rule is used in the IOR such as: similar sail area measurements , the stability test, and the concept of "base" measurements (to be explained later). As for the OSC and STC (1963) rules, these are relatively simple rules, and there may always be a need for these (or similar rules) for the numerous informal races such as those held on yacht club squadron cruises.

The common designations for sail area measurements are illustrated in Figure 85. These are essentially the same for all the rules we have mentioned, but there are slight variations in the definitions of some measurement limits; thus the exact wording should be taken from the particular rule in use. The P designation is the mainsail (or P miz is mizzen) luff length, B is the mainsail (or B miz for mizzen) foot length, P_2 or I is the height of the fore triangle, J is the base of the fore triangle, and LL is the jib luff length. An LP measurement, as explained in the last chapter, is a perpendicular from the jib luff to the clew, and this is illustrated in Figure 75. Black-banding spars was also described in the last chapter. The rules state that these bands must have accompanying stoppers (to prevent pulling the sails beyond the bands) or halyard markers (to show when the head of the sail has reached the bottom of the upper black band).

When a halyard is marked (painted bands are usually required) to indicate hoist limit, be sure the top of the sail's headboard is no lower than the bottom of the black band, so that the sail may be hoisted to the greatest height for light air sailing and in order that maximum distance is allowed for luff adjustment. If judging the headboard and band alignment from the deck, remember that perspective will often make it appear that the headboard is properly aligned when it is really several inches lower than the band. Try to check the alignment from aloft, at the same level as the band, or else from a location some distance away from your boat when the halyard is marked to indicate full hoist.

Off Soundings Club Rule

Although relatively informal and used less often than the other rules we shall discuss, the OSC is a good rule to look at first, because it is quite simple, and it incorporates only a few handicapping fundamentals. Measurements for this rule are quite easily made, because neither displacement nor a direct calculation of stability is involved. The formula (1968) for a yacht's rating is as follows:

$$\left(\frac{L + \left(2 \times \sqrt{\dfrac{MSA}{}} \times \text{Rig Allow.}\right)}{2.5}\right) \times \text{Prop. Allow.} = \text{Rating (in feet)}$$

L represents sailing length with a consideration for beam, MSA is the measured sail area, Rig Allow.

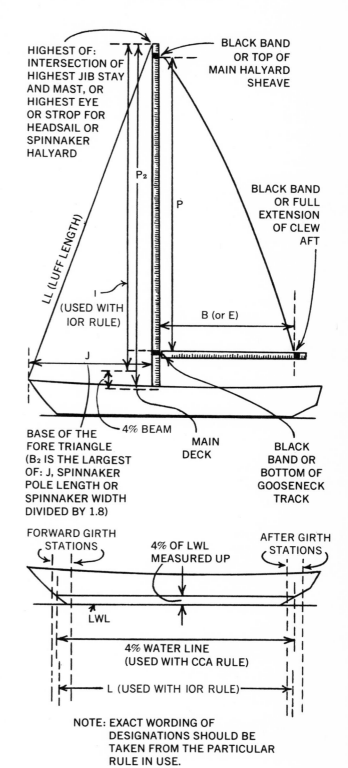

FIGURE 85: MEASUREMENT DESIGNATIONS

HIGHEST OF: INTERSECTION OF HIGHEST JIB STAY AND MAST, OR HIGHEST EYE OR STROP FOR HEADSAIL OR SPINNAKER HALYARD

BLACK BAND OR TOP OF MAIN HALYARD SHEAVE

BLACK BAND OR FULL EXTENSION OF CLEW AFT

P_2

P

LL (LUFF LENGTH)

I (USED WITH IOR RULE)

B (or E)

J

4% BEAM

BASE OF THE FORE TRIANGLE (B_2 IS THE LARGEST OF: J, SPINNAKER POLE LENGTH OR SPINNAKER WIDTH DIVIDED BY 1.8)

MAIN DECK

BLACK BAND OR BOTTOM OF GOOSENECK TRACK

FORWARD GIRTH STATIONS

4% OF LWL MEASURED UP

AFTER GIRTH STATIONS

LWL

4% WATER LINE (USED WITH CCA RULE)

L (USED WITH IOR RULE)

NOTE: EXACT WORDING OF DESIGNATIONS SHOULD BE TAKEN FROM THE PARTICULAR RULE IN USE.

is an allowance given for estimated efficiency of the rig (gaff or jib-headed catboat, sloop, yawl, schooner, or ketch), and Prop. Allow. is the allowance given for a feathering or solid two or three bladed propeller.

L in the OSC formula is obtained in the following manner: Length over-all (LOA) is measured. Then plumb lines are dropped from the stem and stern, and a ruler is floated on the water to measure the distance from the plumb lines to the boat at the points where her hull meets the water at the bow and stern. This gives the overhang forward (OHF) and overhang aft (OHA). These two overhangs are subtracted from the LOA to give the load water line (LWL). A preliminary length (PL) is obtained by adding LOA and LWL and dividing by 2. Greatest beam ("excluding rub rails, flanges etc.") is then measured, and a beam correction (BC) is applied to the PL. The BC is four times the difference in the greatest beam and 0.25 LOA. Excess is subtracted from and deficiency added to PL. In other words, if the beam is greater than one-fourth LOA, BC is subtracted from PL, but BC is added to PL when beam is less than one-fourth LOA. Thus beam is here considered as resistance, and L is PL + or − BC.

The mainsail's sail area is figured at .45 PB (see Figure 85). The fore triangle, however, is not simply a measurement of its actual area, but considerations for the overlap of the largest jib and for the aspect ratios are given also. The formula for this area is: Fore Triangle = $0.5 \ (P_2 \times J) + 0.6 \ [ALH - 0.5 \ (P_2 \times J)] + 0.2J \ (P_2 - 2J)$. ALH stands for the area of the largest headsail, and this is equal to 0.5 (luff length) × (clew to luff). The clew to luff measurement is the shortest distance between the after end of the clew cringle and the forward side of the luff, and this is really equivalent to an LP measurement. Details and the areas for other sails can be obtained from the actual measurement certificates published by the Off Soundings Club.

Examples of the rig allowances are one hundred percent for jib headed sloops, ninety-seven percent for jib headed yawls, seventy percent for jib headed schooners. Prop allowances are ninety-seven percent for feathering, ninety-four percent for two blade solid, and ninety-two percent for three blade solid.

The OSC rule gives great credit for beam, and it often favors some light displacement types to such an extent that many times these are relegated to a special class. The rule works best for boats of similar type. The usual OSC rating may be slightly higher than a 1967 CCA rating and much higher than a STC rating.

OSC rules state that the hull measurements are "to be made with yacht afloat, completely rigged and with all sails to be used when racing on board stowed in the normal racing stowage position. Working jib and main to be rigged or stowed in working position. Water and fuel tanks wholly below the lowest cabin sole must be full and pressed up. Tanks wholly or partially above the lowest cabin sole must be empty. Bilges or sump tanks shall be empty. All equipment necessary to support a weekend cruise (other than optional consumable supplies) shall be onboard. All equipment which will be aboard while racing must be aboard and in the place occupied while racing."

The Storm Trysail Club Rule

Another simple but quite commonly used rule is the 1963 STC. Since its inception in 1948, the rule has been steadily growing in popularity especially in the northeastern United States. The Storm Trysail Club has put into effect a new, more complicated handicap rule in the spring of 1968. However, the club has announced that it will continue to publish its simple 1963 rule, because undoubtedly, many yacht clubs will prefer to continue using the older, simpler rule which usually has proven to be quite successful and suitable in the past. The 1968 version attempts to assess wetted area in a rough way with a lateral plane measurement. However, accurate measurement of the wetted surface would also require a number of girth measurements. It may take a few years of racing under the new rule to determine the new STC rule's accuracy and fairness. In the meantime, the more proven old rule will hopefully continue in use, and this version is given here.

The 1963 STC formula is as follows:

$$.15 \times \frac{L \times \sqrt{SA}}{\sqrt[3]{D}} \times PA = \text{rating (in feet)}$$

In this formula L equals

$$\frac{2 \ LWL + LOA}{3}$$

116

SA is the sail area; D is the displacement in cubic feet, obtained from a recent displacement certificate, designer's certification, or an actual weighing of boat (using sixty-four pounds per cubic foot); and PA is propeller allowance. As can be seen, this rule is as simple or more so than the OSC rule, but measuring for the STC rule is more complicated because of the displacement requirement. The 1963 STC formula does not consider beam, draft, freeboard, or direct stability, and yet the rule has worked surprisingly well.

Sail area is rated as follows: The mainsail is $0.5 \ B \times P$, but the fore triangle is $0.9 \ J \times P_2$ which means that this area is rated at 180 percent, or to put it another way, a square foot of fore triangle costs 180 percent of a square foot of mainsail (Since one hundred percent of a triangle area is .5 of the base (J) times the altitude (P_2), then $0.9 \ J \times P_2$ is 180 percent of the area). Headsail overlap is considered by the addition of $0.5 \ (LP - 1.7J) \ P_2$ to $0.9 \ J \times P_2$. The overlap up to 170 percent (see Figure 75) is free, and there is no penalty for high aspect ratio.

Propeller allowances in this STC rule consider off-center and centerline installations. Some examples of commonly used types are: 98.1 percent for a two bladed, solid, on-center wheel, 99.4 percent for a two bladed feathering on-center, and 98.8 percent for a two bladed folding off-center propeller.

The Midget Ocean Racing Club Rule

The MORC, founded in 1954, was inspired by the *Junior Offshore Group* (JOG), a British club devoted to racing small boats offshore. Like the British group, the MORC incorporates safety regulations into their measurement rule. These safety measures have been listed and discussed in Chapter 3.

The handicap part of the MORC rule was based on the CCA rule in use in 1954. Actually, when the MORC rule was first developed by designer William Shaw with the help of Olin Stephens, the CCA rule was tried on a number of boats below twenty-four feet LOA, and it was found that this rule favored abnormally heavy boats with very large sail areas, and of course, small boats are relatively deeper and beamier than large boats. Thus the CCA rule, then extant, was modified (by adjusting the rule constants) to suit the smaller boats.

Both the MORC and CCA rules use the *base boat* concept for handicapping. Through careful study and observation of various racing-cruiser types, a base boat or imaginary ideal boat is conceived. The base boat is theoretically a fast, seaworthy, and generally wholesome type, and its dimensions serve as a standard of comparison with the dimensions of the actual boat being measured. When the measured dimensions (or other measured characteristics) tending to increase speed are greater than those of the base boat, the differences (after being multiplied by a constant) are added to the L, measured length (effective sailing length), but when the dimensions tending to increase speed are less than those of the base boat, the differences (after being multiplied by the constant) are subtracted from the L. Of course the reverse is done when the dimensions tend to decrease speed. In this case, the L is increased when a measured dimension is less than its base dimension, but the L is decreased when a measured dimension is greater than its base.

The MORC and CCA rules consider, in addition to the speed affecting fundamentals used in the OSC and STC rules, additional factors such as draft, stability, freeboard (for the MORC), and both beam and displacement. The net effect of draft is considered as being helpful to speed; stability, helpful to speed; high freeboard, harmful to speed; beam, harmful to speed but helpful to stability; light displacement, helpful to speed; and of course; sail area, helpful to speed.

The MORC formula (1965 with corrections for 1968) is:

$$0.85 \ (L \pm B \pm D \pm P \pm F \pm S - I) \times R \times Prop = Rating \ (in \ feet)$$

In the formula, L is a length which normally lies between LOA and sailing length, B relates to beam, D relates to draft, P relates to displacement, F relates to freeboard, S relates to sail area, I is an iron keel credit, R is a ballast ratio, and Prop is the propeller drag correction (prop allowance). The plus and minus signs in the formula are credits or debits depending on whether the measured dimensions (or other measured characteristics) are greater or less than the base dimensions.

In this rule, L is the sum of 0.3 LWL and 0.7 LOA. Although the Ls in the STC and the CCA rules approximate a boat's normal sailing length, the L in the MORC rule is usually much greater, and the emphasis put on the LOA tends to favor short ended boats.

Entire details of the rule will not be covered here, but an example of a base measurement with its multipliers (constants) is as follows: "Base draft shall be $.147L + 0.8$ for yachts without centerboards and $.113 L + 0.6$ for yachts with centerboards. (a) If the yacht's measured draft exceeds the Base Draft, multiply the excess by .85 and insert in the formula as a plus quantity. (b) If the yacht's measured draft is less than Base Draft, multiply the difference by .75 and insert in the formula as a minus quantity."

Iron keel credit is a credit (a minus in the formula) for the use of iron instead of lead as keel ballast. This is done to compensate for the relatively higher center of gravity of iron. Displacement is obtained by weighing the boat, or calculation from the lines based on measured freeboards and overhangs, or precalculated tables of displacement vs freeboards and overhangs obtained from designers of stock boats. The cube root of the boat's displacement (in cubic feet) is compared with the cube root of the base displacement and a credit is given when the boat is heavier than her base but a penalty given when she is lighter than her base.

Stability is an important consideration, because obviously, this gives a boat power to carry sail in a breeze. In the MORC rule, the ballast's contribution to stability is estimated with a ballast-displacement ratio, and also the great effect of beam on stability is taken into consideration in the following way:
(a) When Measured Beam is less than Base Beam, Base Bal./Disp. equals

$$.44 + .5 \left(\frac{\text{Base Beam} - \text{Measured Beam}}{\text{Base Beam}} \right)$$

(b) When Measured Beam exceeds Base Beam, Base Bal./Disp. equals

$$.44 - .5 \left(\frac{\text{Measured Beam} - \text{Base Beam}}{\text{Base Beam}} \right)$$

When actual ballast-displacement exceeds its base, Bal. R (R in the formula) equals $1 + .35$ (Bal./Disp. minus Base Bal./Disp.), but when ballast-displacement is less than its base, Bal. R equals $1 - .175$ (Base Bal./Displ. minus Bal./Disp.)

As compared with the CCA and IOR rules, the MORC puts a larger penalty on high ballast/displacement ratios.

Freeboard has an effect on stability and also windage. If the measured freeboard is less than its base of $.0566L + .9$, the difference is multiplied by two and inserted in the formula as a plus quantity. If freeboard is above its base but less than $.069L + 1.0$, the difference is multiplied by 1.5 and inserted in the formula as a minus quantity; but when freeboard exceeds $.069 L + 1.0$, three-fourths of the excess is added to 1.5 times the difference between $.069L + 1.0$ and the base, and this is inserted as a minus quantity.

Prop allowance =

$$1 - \frac{\text{Prop Factor} \times \sqrt{\text{Depth} \times \text{Diameter}}}{14 \times \sqrt{\text{Base Draft}} \times \sqrt[3]{\text{Meas. Disp.}}}$$

Examples of prop factors are: 3.0 – solid two blade on center in aperture, 2.0 – folding off center, 1.0 – feathering two blade on center in aperture.

S (in the MORC formula) is the difference between the square root of the base sail area $(.716 L + .7)$ and the square root of the rated sail area (RSA), but the difference is multiplied by 1.15 when rated area exceeds base. Measured area for a jib headed main is $.5B \times P$, but there is a penalty, the addition of $.25B (P-2.4B)$, for an aspect ratio above 2.4, and mainsail rated area is $0.90 \times MA$ (measured area). The fore triangle is rated at

$$1.50 \frac{P_2 \times B_2}{2} \text{ (150 percent area) where } B_2 \text{ is the largest of:}$$

(a) J, the actual fore triangle base,
(b) the spinnaker pole length,
(c) $\frac{\text{spinnaker girth,}}{1.8}$
(d) $\frac{\text{LP of the largest jib}}{1.7}$

There is no penalty on a jib overlap up to 170 percent of J.

Cruising Club of America Rule

Except for having different multiplier constants, the CCA rule prior to 1962 was very similar to the MORC rule; but after that date, the CCA substituted for the ballast to displacement ratio, a procedure of physically inclining yachts to measure their stability. It was felt the ballast ratio should be abandoned because some of the new boats, especially some of those made of fiberglass, were legitimately designed with heavier than normal structural weight below the waterline. Although this extra weight was for the primary purpose of accepting greater strains permitted by synthetic sails and new hull and rigging materials, the weight actually amounted to "free" or unpenalized ballast. This particular problem was eliminated, however, when inclining was put into effect.

In 1967 a CCA rule change eliminated the consideration for freeboard, because inclining makes the effect of freeboard on stability redundant, and it was felt that certain inequities had resulted from relating freeboard to windage. The 1967 CCA rating formula is:

$$(L \pm Bm \pm Dra. \pm Disp. \pm S) \times Stab. \ F \times Prop. = rated \ length.$$

Bm stands for Beam correction; Dra., draft correction, and Stab. F, Stability factor (determined by inclining the boat). L in the formula is .3 LWL + .7 (four percent WL) + TC. The four percent WL is the measurement of a waterline four percent of the LWL above the LWL (See Figure 85), and the TC is a transom correction used only if the four percent WL plane intersects the stern transom.

The four percent WL is also used in the beam measurement. Measured beam equals:

$$\frac{Max \ LWL \ beam + four \ percent \ WL \ beam}{2}$$

and base beam is .187 L + 3.2. The difference between measured and base beam is multiplied by a figure designated as K to give the beam correction (Bm in the formula). If measured beam is less than its base, K = .5, and beam is inserted in the formula as a plus correction; but when beam is more than its base, K = .25, and beam is inserted as a minus.

Base draft = .147 L + 1.5 and there is a centerboard factor (CBF) of maximum exposed centerboard area (in square feet) divided by .167L. Draft correction (Dra. in the formula) for keel yachts is .85 times the difference in base and rated draft (measured draft for keel yachts but measured draft + CBF for centerboarders) when rated draft exceeds base draft, and this is inserted as a plus quantity. On the other hand, when base exceeds

rated draft, the difference is multiplied by .75 and it is inserted as a minus.

Draft correction for centerboarders and many other details of the rule will not be given here. The complete rule details are given in two booklets published by the CCA. One small booklet contains instructions for inclining yachts, and the other contains about forty pages of details of the measurement rule. These booklets should be studied prior to measuring, especially the sections that explain the owner's preparation of the hull and rig for measurement and the owner's responsibility after measurement.

Some of the more important requirements of preparations for measurement are: that the boat be completely rigged and ready to sail; that all working sails are furled in place with booms secured; that all sails used when racing are aboard, stowed below in usual racing stowage locations; that all working equipment and stores are in places occupied while racing including two anchors with warps or chain, dinghy, and/or life rafts, etc.; that also in place should be the normal navigating, galley, electrical and engine equipment; that all water and fuel tanks used while racing are full or empty depending on which condition maximizes the rating, and tanks not used while racing are empty; that all sump tanks and bilges are dry; and that consumable stores aboard shall not exceed twenty pounds per man of crew; the crew number being determined by

$$3 + \frac{Rated \ Sail \ Area}{250}$$

(any excess over a whole number is taken as a whole number). The preceding is *not* the *exact* wording of the rule. Details and exact wording should be taken from the latest measurement rule booklet.

The CCA requires that displacement is obtained by actually weighing the boat. Many yards throughout the country can do this for a very reasonable charge, but be sure that the scales are approved by the CCA or the yacht racing association under which you race. The cube root of the base displacement is .179 L + .8. The penalty for being lighter than base was slightly increased in 1967 by changing the multiplier from 4 to 4.5

Details of inclining will not be given here, but Figure 86 may help explain the basic principles involved. A pendulum of light line with a weight or bob at its end, is hung, usually from the forward end of the companionway hatch on the boat's centerline, with the bob in a bucket of water placed directly under the pendulum's point of suspension to record the angles of heel. Until recently (1968), the customary means of inclining a boat was to use the weight of men or dead weights positioned at the rail and then half way from the rail to the boat's centerline in order to give her small angles of heel. Now, however, the CCA rule requires the use of an *inclining boom* (or booms), a pole rigged horizontally abeam from which weights are suspended as illustrated in Figure 86. There are variations of this procedure allowed. Using two opposite poles, the weight can be hung successively at one pole's extreme end, at a point on this pole half way to the boat's centerline, on centerline, with the weights being hung on the other pole at the same distances from the centerline as in the case of the first pole; or alternatively, half weights instead of half distances may be used to give righting moments (weights times distances).

On the Pacific coast, a recommended "comparable procedure" is used whereby a jerry can (a portable container for gasoline or other liquids) is suspended from the end of one boom and this can is filled with water until it produces approximately one degree angle of heel. Then two cans (or sets of cans) are secured to the end of the boom with lanyards in such a way that the lanyards can be tightened or slacked from the pole's inboard end (see Figure 86) to float the cans, hoist one, or hoist both. With both cans hoisted, the angle of heel should be at least two degrees. When the boat is inclined with both cans hoisted, one can hoisted, and when both cans are floated, the pendulum deflection is noted on a ruler taped to the top of the bucket in which the plumb bob is suspended. Angles of heel may be calculated with the formula:

$$\frac{\text{pendulum reading}}{\text{pendulum length}} \times 57.3 = \text{angle of heel.}$$

Knowing what angles of heel are produced by the righting moments of one and then two cans (the can weights times their distance from the boat's centerline), an accurate righting moment (inclined RM) can be determined for a one degree angle of heel.

The inclined RM is multiplied by two factors,

FIGURE 86: INCLINING

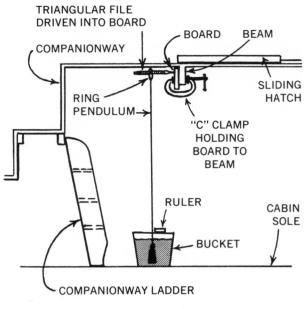

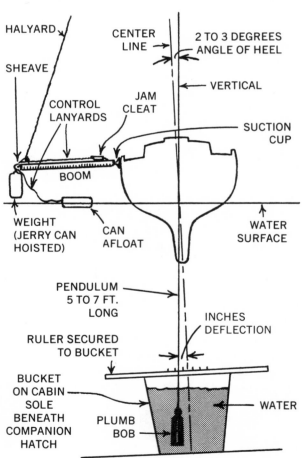

120

one that considers the effect of beam (arm factor) and the other of topsides flare (flare factor) on the righting moment, to give the Adjusted RM. The stability factor (Stab. F) is derived from a comparison of the Adjusted RM with a Base RM. Then of course, Stab. F (as well as the Prop.) is multiplied by the corrected L (L after additions or subtractions for beam, draft, displacement and sail area) to give the rated length in feet. This rating under the CCA rule is normally a little lower than sailing length.

The propeller Drag Correction (Prop. in the rating formula) is equal to

$$1 - \frac{\text{Prop. Factor} \times \sqrt{\text{depth in feet}} \times \text{Diameter in feet.}}{14 \sqrt{\text{Base Draft}} \times \sqrt[3]{\text{Mes. Disp.}}}$$

Prop Factor depends on type (solid, feathering or folding), number of blades, whether the propeller is in or out of an aperture, and whether or not there is a strut. Examples of the Prop. Factor are: Folding, any number of blades, out of aperture, without strut 0.50, but with strut 2.50; feathering, two blades, out of aperture, with strut 3.00; and solid, two blades, in aperture 5.00.

Sail area correction (S in the rating formula) is derived from a comparison of RSA (rated sail area) and a base. The square root of the sail area base is equal to 4.3 times the cube root of the base displacement. The mainsail's RSA amounts to 70 percent of its measured sail area (the actual square footage using the P and B measurements) RSA = .35 P X B + .3B(P – 2B). This permits a "free" or unpenalized aspect ratio up to 2:1 but there is an increasing penalty above this figure. The fore triangle is rated at 110 percent plus a consideration for headsail overlap and aspect ratio. As said in the last chapter, overlap is free up to 150 percent of the fore triangle base, but there is a graduating penalty above 150 percent. Aspect ratio charge is the same as for the mainsail.

Mizzen RSA is P Miz × B Miz multiplied by a factor that ranges from 0.1, where mizzens are ten percent or less than the combination of main and fore triangle, to 0.2, where mizzens are fifty percent of the combination. When the mizzen is larger than this, the yacht is measured as a schooner. The charge for mizzen staysails is twenty percent of the area in excess of 2.8 times the mizzen Measured Sail Area. The rating of spinnakers under the vari-

ous rules will be discussed in Chapter 9 when we talk about spinnakers.

International Offshore Rating Rule

The latest handicap rule, the *International Offshore Rating Rule* (IOR) has been developed to enable racing-cruisers from different countries to compete on an equitable basis. At the time of this writing (May, 1969), the rule has been drafted and released (it will soon be published and obtainable from the NAYRU), but the rule is untried, unproven, and may be modified at a later date if it proves inequitable in any way. If it proves successful, the rule may be ideal for major ocean races and many international events such as the "Ton" cup races. It is even possible that this rule will eventually completely replace the CCA rule, but whether or not this comes about will depend, to a large extent, on how favorably current U.S. designs will rate under the IOR rule. Of course, it is up to the individual yacht racing organization to choose the handicap rule under which its races will be sailed. In the unlikely event that the new rule will not be favorable to certain types of American designs, especially those numerous smaller boats that will not compete internationally, certain yacht racing associations might elect to keep the CCA rule or use some other handicap system.

The IOR rule is, for the most part, a compromise between the rules of the CCA and RORC (Royal Ocean Racing Club). Sail rating and measurements are quite similar to those of the CCA, but hull measurements are more closely related to those of the RORC. Determination of L is quite similar to the RORC method of measuring distance between points established fore-and-aft by girth measurements related to beam. Also similar to RORC practice, is the new rule's use of hull depth measurements together with beam instead of displacement as an assessment of hull resistance. Stability is measured by an inclining test similar to that of the CCA. An attempt was made to introduce a hull strength (scantlings) factor, but this proved too complicated and so the factor was dropped, at least temporarily, from the rule. Hull measurements for the IOR rule will be quite complicated, but re-measurement should not be required unless the hull is altered. Since displacement is not considered, weighing is obviously not required.

The basic IOR formula is as follows:

Measured Rating, MR =

$$\frac{0.13L\sqrt{S}}{\sqrt{BD}} + 0.25\,L + 0.20\sqrt{S} + DC + FC$$

L is rated length, B is rated beam, D is rated depth, S is rated sail area, DC is draft correction, and FC is freeboard correction. The concept of this formula is similar to the STC rule in that L times the square root of the sail area is divided by what we might call the under water bulk. In modern STC rules bulk is the cube root of the displacement (plus a lateral plane consideration in the latest STC rule); but in the original STC, the RORC, and the IOR rules, the substitute for displacement as a measure of bulk is the square root of the beam times the hull depth.

The final rating in the new offshore rule is $R = MR \times EPF \times CGF$ where EPF is an engine and propeller factor and CGF is a center of gravity factor, derived from the inclining test.

The rated length (L) is length between the forward and after girth stations (LBG) minus a forward and after overhang component (FOC and AOCC). Girths (distances measured around the hull with the upper and lower parts of the girth lying in the same vertical athwartships plane) are taken at four stations: the forward girth station (FGS) where the girth is equal to one-half of B, the forward inner girth station (FIGS) where the girth is equal to three-quarters of B, the after girth station (AGS) where the girth is equal to three-quarters of B, and the after inner girth station (AIGS) where the girth is equal to seven-eighths of B. See Figure 85 for the approximate location of these stations on a typical hull.

The formula for the forward overhang component is:

$$FOC = GSDF\ \frac{(FF - 0.3B + 0.15BF)}{(0.125B + FSFD - 0.15FSBD)}$$

GSDF is girth station difference forward; FF is freeboard forward; BF is beam forward; FSFD is forward stations freeboard difference; and FSBD is forward stations beam difference.

The formula for AOC is long and complicated, and so it will not be given here. For our rating rule discussion, it should be sufficient to say that the formula attempts to position the after end of L in such a way that it is fair to all boats with every type of stern. Under the RORC rule, the AOC had somewhat encouraged the development of boats with narrow, "pinched-in" sterns in order to reduce the rated length while maintaining a long, actual sailing length. Many yachtsmen, Americans particularly, feel that narrow beam aft in the smaller boats detracts from comfort in the cockpit area and lessens buoyancy where it is needed. Thus the new International Rule's AOC formula attempts to encourage sterns that are considerably broader than those seen on many existing recent British designs.

D considers the immersed depth of the hull proper, and the formula is

$$D = 1.15\,MDI + 0.9FDI + 0.055\,(3\ FOC\text{-}AOCC) + \frac{L + 10}{30}\ ft.$$

AOCC is the AOC corrected. MDI and FDI are the midship and forward immersed depths. MD (midship depth) is taken at one-half of LBG abaft FGS and is measured vertically from a horizontal straight line joining the top of the deck at the sides of the yacht to a point on the outside of the hull one-quarter of B out from the centerline. FD (forward depth) is taken at one-quarter of LBG abaft FGS and is measured vertically from a horizontal straight line joining the top of the deck at the sides of a yacht to a point on the outside of the hull one-tenth of B out from the centerline. MDI and FDI are obtained by deducting from MD and FD the freeboard at those stations respectively.

Base draft for keel boats (DB) is $0.145\,L + 2.0$ feet. The difference between DB and measured draft (DM), called hull draft in this rule, is designated as draft difference (DD), and this may be either positive or negative. Where DD is negative keel boat draft correction is

$$0.10\,DB\left(\frac{3}{3\text{-}DD}\right) - 1.0\ ft.$$

Where DD is positive and not more than 1.0 feet, the correction is 0.85DD, and where DD is more than 1.0 feet. the correction is DD−0.15 foot.

Base draft for centerboarders (DCB) is $0.120L + 2.0$ feet. Draft difference is DM plus a centerboard factor (the square of the centerboard's vertical extension divided by 0.425L in the case of a single centerboard) minus the DCB. When DDC (draft difference for centerboarders) is negative, the correction is

$$0.10DCB \left(\frac{3}{3 - DDC} \right) - 1.0 \text{ ft.}$$

When DDC is positive and not more than 1.0 foot the correction is 0.85 DDC, and when DDC is more than 1.0 foot the correction is DDC – 0.15 foot.

Freeboard correction is derived by taking a mean of the freeboards at the forward and after girth stations and comparing this to a base freeboard for a penalty or credit. Base freeboard (FB) is 0.057L + 1.20 feet. Measured freeboard (FM) is

$$\frac{1.2 \text{ FF} + 0.8 \text{ FA}}{2}$$

If the measured freeboard exceeds the base, then FC = 0.15 (FM – FB) and will be subtracted from the measured rating, but if the measured freeboard is less than the base then FC = 0.25 (FB – FM) and will be added to the measured rating.

All the details of the engine and propeller allowance will not be given here, but the engine propeller factor (EPF) results from the formula

$$EPF = 1 - \frac{EMF + DF}{100}$$

EMF is an engine moment factor which considers the engine's weight and its distance from the midpoint of LBG. DF is the propeller drag factor. Examples of propeller drag which enter into a DF formula are: a folding, out-of-aperture propeller is given a factor of 0.50; a two-bladed, solid propeller in aperture, 2.25; and a two-bladed feathering propeller out of aperture, 0.75. There is also a condition that the EPF shall apply only when the yacht can attain with the racing propeller a calm water speed in knots equal to .75$\sqrt{L}$ feet.

The center of gravity factor is found by inclining the boat (similarly to the CCA method) to find the righting moment at one degree of heel (RM). This is entered in the formula

$$\frac{0.97L \times (BWL)^3}{RM}$$

to give a tenderness ratio (TR). Then the center of gravity factor

$$(CGF) = \frac{1.4}{TR-6.1} + 0.9350$$

Until all existing boats of every type are measured and raced under this new rule, it is difficult to speculate on what particular type of boat, if any, the rule will encourage. A special effort has been made to draft a rule that will not be overly exploited and will not lead to designs of an extreme type. Boats that will rate best under the rule will probably be those that both lack the narrow ends of the extremely "pinched-in" RORC types and the wide sterns of the extremely full, flat American designs. Perhaps we will be seeing a greater use of integral skegs in small boats, not only to improve wave resistance and directional stability, but to supply buoyancy aft at minimum cost in rating. The IOR rule does not assess wetted area, and thus we are likely to see a continuance of the trend towards short keels and separated rudders. Not a great deal of emphasis is put on stability, so we shall probably continue to see the ballast-displacement ratios creep upwards, especially since there is presently no scantlings factor in the IOR rule. The rule may encourage more centerboard designs in Europe, but perhaps the trend towards centerboarders will be somewhat retarded in America. There could be some difficulties with using this rule for very small boats racing against large ones, because of the usual differences in proportions and distribution of buoyancy in boats of extremely different sizes. Only time will tell how successful the IOR rule will be, but such a rule is certainly needed for international competition at least.

Time Allowance Tables

When a yacht's rated length (in feet) has been calculated, it is applied to time allowance tables to obtain the handicap for a particular race. The commonly used tables are the NAYRU (North American Yacht Racing Union) Time Allowance Tables. These tables, which have been used since 1908, are based on the assumption that, considering the average summer winds experienced while racing over a triangular course, the rate at which boats draw apart approximates 0.6 of the time differences between the boats when their speeds are equal to the square roots of their ratings. As stated in the preface of Time Allowance Tables, the allowance per mile between yachts of different ratings is:

$$\frac{2160}{\sqrt{r}} - \frac{2160}{\sqrt{R}}$$

(R being the larger yacht's rating and r the smaller yacht's rating). The figure 2160 is the number of seconds in one hour multiplied by 0.6.

To illustrate how the allowance tables work, let us suppose a boat rating sixteen feet races a boat rating twenty-five feet over a one mile course. At a speed to rated length ratio of 1.0, the sixteen-foot boat makes four knots (the square root of sixteen) and the twenty-five foot boat makes five knots (the square root of twenty-five). It takes the sixteen-footer 900 seconds to cover the mile and the twenty-five footer 720 seconds. Subtracting the difference of seconds per mile and multiplying by .6 we arrive at the figure 108. The Time Allowance Tables give the allowance for one nautical mile in seconds and decimals. If we look up in the tables the allowance for a sixteen-foot rating and a twenty-five foot rating, and then subtract the two allowances, we also arrive at the 108 figure which is the seconds per mile that the twenty-five foot boat gives to the sixteen-footer. The usual race, of course, is much further than one mile; and so the allowance must be multiplied by the number of miles in the race course.

In the standard NAYRU Time Allowance Tables (1 and 3) the figures show in seconds or decimal hours the allowances yachts ranging between the ratings of 10.0 and 99.9 receive from a yacht rating one hundred feet (formerly 150 feet) sailing over one nautical mile. The Fishing Bay Yacht Club of Virginia, however, has devised a handy set of tables (derived from the standard NAYRU tables) which assume that the scratch boat (having zero time allowance) is always a hypothetical entry with a rating of thirty feet. Pages from these tables

are reproduced in the appendix. With a standard time allowance table, a yacht's allowance is subtracted from her elapsed time (actual time over the course) to obtain the corrected time (the yacht with the best corrected time wins the race). With the Fishing Bay Yacht Club (FBYC) tables, this procedure is the same for yachts rating under thirty feet, but for ratings *over* thirty feet the time allowances are *added* to their elapsed times. In the FBYC tables, time allowances for ratings from 15 to 44.9 feet are calculated for races ranging from ten to thirty-two miles long; thus for races within this distance range, the allowance of each entry may be read directly from the tables. These tables can not only simplify time allowance calculations for the race committee, but they enable the skipper to learn quickly how much time he gives or receives from another yacht. By timing his own and a competitor's rounding of a mark of known distance from the start, the skipper or navigator can make one simple subtraction (or addition if one of the yachts rates above thirty feet) to determine his boat's corrected time position during the race or at the finish. This should help eliminate the complaints occasionally heard from one-design sailors that they object to handicap racing because they have to "wait for Monday's morning newspaper to read the results of Sunday's race."

The latest NAYRU time allowance publications not only give allowances in seconds per mile (Tables 1 and 2), but they give allowances in decimal hours (Tables 3 and 4). These latter tables are time saving for the race committee, but they require the use of a decimal clock. When a committee uses the decimal system, it is often confusing to us sailors who think of time in terms of hours, minutes, and seconds. However, the NAYRU booklets contain handy tables which convert decimal hours to minutes and seconds.

When the course is upwind, the time allowances favor the large, high-rated boats; but when the course is downwind, the smaller boats are favored. To compensate for this, the race committee may use an assumed course length greater or less than the actual length of the course, when the wind direction or some other factor favors boats of one size range. An assumed course length shorter than actual reduces handicaps and hence favors the larger boats, while an assumed course length longer than actual would tend to favor the smaller boats.

If an assumed course length is used, the distance is often stated in the race circular in areas of prevailing winds, but in areas of unpredictable winds, contestants might be notified at the start by signals explained in the circular and given by the committee boat.

Some General Thoughts on Handicap Rules

From time to time, especially when one boat or type of boat seems to win most of the races, there is a good deal of discussion about the "spirit of the rule." There can be no hard and fast definition of a handicap rule's spirit. Moral implications are subject to individual interpretations. The preamble to the CCA measurement rule contains a succinct discussion of the subject which is expressed as follows:

"It is the intent of this Measurement Rule to make it possible for yachtsmen to race seaworthy cruising boats of various designs, types and construction *on a fair and equitable basis*. The rules are not, and can never be, perfect. In order that the rules may serve this purpose, yachtsmen themselves must interpret them in keeping with the Spirit of the Rule.

"No infringement of the Spirit of this Rule nor any method of reducing the rating of any yacht by utilizing questionable, unreasonable, or unsafe methods will be acceptable; and the Cruising Club will not issue a rating certificate to any yacht owner who in any manner attempts to defeat the purpose for which this rule is intended.

"All Race Committees conducting races under this measurement rule are strongly urged to require that any unusual practice in rig, hull, ballast, or other factors not covered specifically within these rules, be reported to the Race Committee for a ruling, and in any case, be subject to protest. The test of said ruling shall be whether or not, in the opinion of the Race Committee, the practice would give unfair advantage or in any way violate or circumvent the intent of the rule."

In my opinion, it seems unreasonable to assume that naval architects will not design fast, seaworthy boats with the lowest possible rating, and it also seems unreasonable to think that owners will not take all the measures they are legitimately allowed in the interest of obtaining a low rating. To quote again from the CCA Rule booklet (1963), the Introduction says, "It is, however, a fact that most racing-cruising boats in American waters are cur-

rently designed to the CCA Rule rather than to any of the many simpler rules. Consequently naval architects are legitimately concerned with taking every permissible advantage of the rule's provisions and it is therefore necessary to keep closing loopholes as individual designing ingenuity finds them, in order to maintain the greatest degree of equity possible in the resulting ratings." For this reason, measurement rules, especially the CCA rules, are periodically changed as loopholes are exploited. However, rule changes often do not require remeasurement. In fact, most rating certificates are valid for at least three years.

The simpler rules, the OSC and 1963 STC rules, are most suitable for boats of similar type that are not specifically "designed to" the rule, or designed to take advantage of any rule loopholes. The OSC rule especially seems best for the more informal races such as those held during club cruises where some boats may not have up-to-date, valid rating certificates and/or their exact displacement is not known. The more complex rules, MORC, CCA, and IOR are generally best suited for the more formal races and when there are considerable variations in the designs of the competing boats. The CCA especially has been frequently modified to close loopholes as they are discovered, but it must be expected as soon as one loophole is closed "designing ingenuity" will find another.

The present weaknesses of the CCA and perhaps the IOR rules, in my opinion, are that they do not consider the full effect of wetted surface, that the current inclining test doesn't predict with accuracy very much more than static, initial stability, and there are some problems with tank legislation and hull trim in the CCA's case. As a result, there are an increasing number of short fin keel boats with separated rudders that take advantage of the lack of penalty on low wetted surface. Also, ballast-displacement ratios are creeping upwards, because heavy ballast, which contributes so much to sail carrying power at moderate angles of heel in fresh winds, and the effects on stability of a boat's movement are not entirely taken into account by the present inclining method of determining stability.

Until fairly recently, the rules governing the placement of tanks and their condition of being filled or empty allowed some opportunity to improve on the rating with a tank arrangement that could affect hull trim and stability. The present

FIGURE 87: EFFECT OF TRIM ON STABILITY & LWL

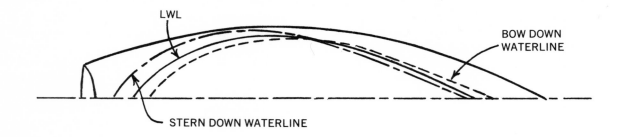

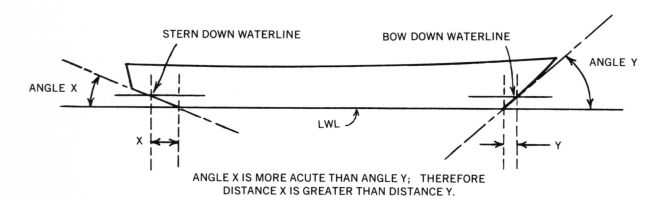

ANGLE X IS MORE ACUTE THAN ANGLE Y; THEREFORE
DISTANCE X IS GREATER THAN DISTANCE Y.

rules deal with the problem fairly successfully, but there is still the problem of free surface, requiring that tanks must be completely full or empty at the time of measurement. However, the rules cannot require that tanks must be kept in their measured full condition if the engine is used going to the start or if water is used for washing or drinking; thus many owners elect to race with their tanks more empty than full when they deem this beneficial to speed. The IOR rule requires that water tanks are empty at time of measurement, but this might possibly overly encourage ballast tanks in keels and give a special advantage to boats with deep, hollow, integral keels. Other ramifications of the hull trim problem will be discussed briefly a little later. On the whole, the CCA rule has proven remarkably satisfactory when boats are carefully and correctly measured, because as advantages are taken of weaknesses, the rule is modified to compensate.

There might be considered two general courses for handicapping in the future: a turning back to simpler or more empirical rules, or a more complex and scientific approach. There are good arguments on both sides. A relatively simple method of handicapping might be accomplished, as has been sug-

gested, by requiring that boats be rated under several simple rules and that the competing skippers be informed of the rule under which they are to race only immediately prior to the start. In this way boats could not be advantageously designed to a particular rule. Another approach to handicapping is the empirical or arbitrary rule used on the west coast called the *Pacific Handicap Racing Fleet* (PHRF) rule. In this case, a boat is given an arbitrary rating by a handicapper, an experienced sailor or designer qualified to judge boat speed and performance. This rating is later adjusted to reflect actual performance after the boat begins racing. One drawback of the rule is perhaps that it reflects the vicissitudes of skipper performance, nevertheless the rule is said to work well.

A more scientific approach to handicapping would theoretically improve the accuracy of the ratings, but it might also cause more complicated, arduous, and expensive measurements. Actual wetted area could be obtained from the designer or designer's plans or could be physically measured when the boat is hauled. The latter might be accomplished with a number of half girth measurements (perhaps eight or ten) applied to Simpson's

Rule (as described by Kinney in "Skene's Elements of Yacht Design" for example). Stability might be calculated at higher angles of heel than is presently done under the CCA; or if this proves too laborious or expensive, the present CCA inclining test might be combined with a ballast factor or a rolling test (timing the period of roll). It also seems possible that future handicap measurements might include a simple towing test to estimate hull drag.

In selecting a cruising boat to race or preparing a boat for measurement, most owners are quite naturally interested in obtaining the lowest possible rating. However, it should be fully realized that if the rating ruling under which the new boat will race is at all accurate (and most rating rules are quite accurate), *the lower the rating, the slower the speed.* In other words, drastic reductions in rating will almost surely make the boat slower. Some owners spend a great deal of time and money in an effort to materially lower their rating; but in most cases when the rating is lowered the boat performance suffers, and the time and money would have been better spent on tuning and practice. Of course, minor rating improvements or at least the best possible rating for a given speed potential, can be had by utilizing such legitimate measurement preparations as black-banding the spars and advantageously loading, ballasting, and trimming the hull.

Most rating calculations are carried out to four decimal places, but the actual assigned rating is usually resolved to the nearest tenth of a foot; thus .05 of a foot will resolve to .1 but .049 will be .0. The entire range from .95 through 1.049 will be counted as 1 foot of rating, yet there is almost a tenth of a foot between the extremes of the range. This near tenth of a foot amounts to a free means of making the boat go faster. As an actual example of this, a Cal 28 of my acquaintance with a rating of 24.9530 could have as much as 11.37 square feet of area added to her mainsail which would increase her rating to 25.0485, but with or without the added sail area, her actual resolved rating would be 25.0. Of course it will nearly always pay to get the most sail area for a given rating, and this is one reason why some of the leading sailmakers offer computer programing services. These services are usually available at low cost whether or not sails are ordered.

For optimum rated sail area be sure: that the LPs of light headsails are no longer than the number one Genoa's LP, that there is no penalty for excessive batten length, and that the spinnaker pole is no longer than J.

Under the CCA and IOR rules it may pay to add some inside ballast in locales where strong winds prevail, since it seems evident to me that the inclining procedure in current use does not completely reflect the advantages of ballast at moderate to high angles of heel. However, in these rules as well as in the MORC, stability factors (in the basic formulae) should not be above 1.0, because these factors are multipliers rather than additions to the corrected sailing lengths. In loading boats for measurement, it often pays to put on as much gear and supplies as legally allowed, and in general, to keep this weight fairly far forward, but the present CCA rule requires that the boat be trimmed "level." Until quite recently it was common practice to trim a boat down by the bow to offset the weight of crew in the cockpit and to obtain in most cases, the most favorable plane of flotation for measurement. This bow down condition often produced an optimal LWL for rating purposes, and the flotation plane often minimized stability in the wedge-shaped hull. This is illustrated by the exaggerated example in Figure 87. It also shows how on this type of hull, waterline beam and hence stability might be increased when sailing by moving crew members somewhat further aft.

Allowable hull trim under the CCA rule is now determined by freeboard differences at the LWL ends. Measurers are given a list of differences for various stock classes of boats (for example, a Cal 40 has a 1.16 foot differential). In the case of an individual, custom, or new class boat, freeboard differential for designed or optimum trim must be obtained from the designer. However, if this data is not available, the measurers have been instructed to measure the freeboard while the regular crew is aboard, "stationed as they would be when racing." Then with the crew ashore, gear is rearranged, if necessary, to reproduce the same freeboard differential for actual flotation measurements.

Although it is necessary to prevent excessive down by the bow trim for measurement, it is my opinion that there are certain weaknesses in the present method of determining trim. Many owners want a *very slight* bow down trim in order to offset crew weight that can hardly help but accumulate in the cockpit at most times. Furthermore, it seems to me there is little point in measuring freeboard while the crew is aboard at fixed stations, because during a race they are usually moving about or stationed at different positions according to: the strength of wind, point of sailing, condition of seas, and various job or occupational locations. In my opinion, it might be better not to make any hard and fast rules, but to leave the question of trim up to the educated judgement of a well-qualified measurer. Of course, the new IOR rule attempts to circumvent this problem of determining the L from flotation measurements by basing the L on length between girth stations.

It could be considered that there are three possible types of potentially competitive boats for handicap racing: (1) the very fast boat with a high rating, (2) the smart, fairly fast boat with a moderate rating, and (3) the slow boat with low rating. It is possible to have a slow boat with a fairly high rating, but it is rarely, if ever, possible to have a fast boat with a very low rating for any length of time (without the rule being changed or the boat being barred from racing under the rule). In my opinion, the most desirable type is either (1) or (2). The most important consideration for racing should be boat performance and speed no matter what the handicap rule. The second consideration (again, in my opinion) should be the general wholesomeness of the type. Some extreme designs may enjoy temporary advantages before rule loopholes are closed; but for long range racing enjoyment, the boat should be wholesome, fast but thoroughly seaworthy, comfortable, and soundly designed and constructed.

NAYRU Racing Rules

Nearly all formal races in this country use the NAYRU racing rules (see Chapter 1) or to be technically correct, The Racing Rules of the International Yacht Racing Union (IYRU) as adopted by the North American Yacht Racing Union (NAYRU). These are not rating measurement rules, but rules for race conduct, management, and right of way. Certain parts of these rules concerning signals, starting lines, and other aspects of race conduct were discussed in Chapter 1, but what has not been discussed yet, is the extremely important matter concerning right of way. Details will not be presented here but only the basic principles. As said in Chapter 1, a copy of the current

FIGURE 88: MAST ABEAM

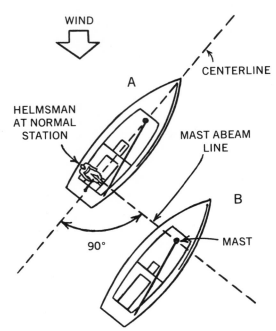

BOAT A, PASSING TO WINDWARD OF B, HAS JUST REACHED THE MAST ABEAM POSITION. PRIOR TO REACHING THIS POSITION, A COULD HAVE BEEN LUFFED BY B, BUT NOW B HAS LOST HER LUFFING RIGHTS.

NAYRU rules should be carried on every racing boat, and these rules (especially the parts dealing with right of way) should be learned and studied periodically to refresh the memory. Obviously, there is real danger of collisions and accidents when a large group of racing boats congregate at the starting line or a turning mark if even one skipper does not know the right of way rules. Furthermore, damage can be extensive when large, heavy racing-cruisers collide. Part I, "Definitions" and Part IV, "Sailing Rules When Yachts Meet, Helmsman's Rights and Obligations Concerning Right of Way" of the 1969 NAYRU rules are printed verbatim in the appendix.

At this point, it should be said that *currently* the rules of the road expressed under the Inland Rules for U. S. waters do not entirely agree with the NAYRU racing rules (or the International Rules of the Road). However, it is expected that a new uniform rule, which essentially brings the rules of the road for U.S. waters into agreement with the International and NAYRU rules, will become effective in the near future.

The novice racing skipper should first of all familiarize himself with the racing terms definitions given in Part I of the NAYRU rules, and then he should learn Rules 31 through 46 given in Part IV (see the appendix).

Essentially, in a very simplified form, the rules are as follows: When boats on opposite tacks converge, the one on the starboard tack has the right of way (with three exceptions: when a premature starter returns to the starting line on the starboard tack to restart, when a mark toucher (see Rule 52) returns to reround the mark on the starboard tack, and at a downwind mark when the inside boat on the port tack with a proper overlap has the right of way over an outside starboard tack boat).

When boats on the same tack converge, the windward boat keeps clear.

The boat clear astern shall keep clear of the boat clear ahead; "A yacht is *clear astern* of another when her hull and equipment, in normal position, are abaft an imaginary line projected abeam from the aftermost point of the other's hull and equipment, in normal position. The other yacht is *clear ahead.*" Two yachts overlap if neither is clear astern.

"A yacht which establishes an overlap to leeward from clear astern shall allow the windward yacht ample room and opportunity to keep clear and during the existence of that overlap the leeward yacht shall not sail above her proper course."

"When one yacht is required to keep clear of another, the right of way yacht shall not (except to the extent permitted by Rule 38.1, Right of Way Yacht Luffing after Starting), so alter course as to prevent the other yacht from keeping clear; or to obstruct her while so doing."

When on a free leg (not a windward leg) after starting, the windward yacht may not bear off below her proper course when she is within three lengths of either a leeward boat or one clear astern which is steering a course to pass to leeward. However, after starting, the leeward boat or one clear ahead may luff (alter course towards the wind until head to wind) as she pleases, except that: the leeward boat shall not sail above her proper course while the overlap exists if the helmsman of the windward yacht has been abreast or forward of the mainmast of the leeward yacht. This is referred to

as the "Mast Abeam" position and it is illustrated in Figure 88. Before the start, boats are allowed to luff, but they must do so slowly. Actually, there are some fine distinctions between luffing before the starting signal has been made, luffing after the starting signal but before the boat has crossed the starting line, and luffing after the starting signal after the starting line has been crossed. These distinctions might seem minor, but they should be carefully studied in the NAYRU rules (see the appendix). Some important aspects of luffing will be discussed in Chapter 8.

When tacking or jibing a boat must keep clear of a yacht "on a tack". (a boat that is not tacking or jibing).

When boats are overlapped rounding or passing a turning mark, the outside boat must give the inside boat room to round or pass it except in several cases, such as an outside starboard tack boat converging on the mark with an inside port tacker at the end of a beat or when boats are *barging* at the start (barging situations often develop at the start, and these will be discussed in the next chapter when we talk about starting techniques). A boat clear astern shall not establish an overlap and be entitled to room when the boat clear ahead is within two of her own lengths of the mark. However, a boat may tack between the mark and another boat within two lengths of the mark and thereafter claim room.

When safe pilotage requires one of two close-hauled boats on the same tack to make a substantial alteration in course to clear an obstruction (defined in Part I of the NAYRU rules), and if she intends to tack, but cannot tack without colliding with the other boat, she shall hail the other boat for room to tack.

The preceding is a condensed and simplified version of the right of way principles. Exact wording should be taken from the NAYRU rules themselves.

A yacht can protest another for racing rule infringements. The protesting yacht should fly a red flag (mentioned in Chapter 1); an attempt should be made to inform the yacht protested that a protest will be lodged; and usually the protest should be delivered to the race committee as soon as possible after the finish. Exact protest procedure can be obtained from the NAYRU rules or the race circular or instructions. A hearing is held by the Race Committee or a Protest Committee, and one (or both) of the parties involved in the protest may be disqualified. Decisions of the Race or Protest Committee may be appealed for final determination to the NAYRU Appeals Committee when there is a question involving solely the interpretation of the rules. Results of appeals are published by the NAYRU in a book entitled *Decisions of the Appeals Committee,* and it is highly recommended that the serious racing skipper acquire and study this book.

NAYRU Rules and Appeals may be obtained from NAYRU, 37 West 44th Street, New York, New York, 10036. Measurement rules may be obtained by writing to the following addresses: CCA and IOR rules—the NAYRU, same address as above; MORC—Secretary MORC, P.O. Box 4092, Grand Central Station, New York, New York, 10017; STC—Storm Trysail Club Secretary, c/o Ivy Hill, 18 E. 48 Street, New York, New York; and OCS—Off Soundings Club Measurer, 9 Gravel Street, Mystic, Connecticut. Additional information or more up-to-date addresses might be obtained from your local yacht racing organization.

8
Starting Technique

Thoughts on Starting

This section on starting is intended chiefly for sailors who are beginning to race, but it is also intended for small boat racing skippers beginning to race large boats. There is a definite difference between starting in a lightweight dinghy and a large, relatively heavy, slower turning, and more elaborately rigged racing-cruiser. Chapter 1 presented the basic mechanics of starting: the signals, time, setting and slanting the line, etc., but here we will talk about how we attempt to maneuver our boat at optimum starting speed into one of the best positions as the starting signal is made.

The time immediately prior to the start is often the most nerve-racking part of the race. Even the most casual-appearing skipper usually has "butterflies in his stomach"; if not, the chances are he is not one of the best starters. The reason for tensions and keyed-up emotions at the start is that many boats are all fighting for a few top starting positions, and every competent skipper realizes that he is at a disadvantage unless he starts at one of those positions. Races are sometimes won or lost at the start of a short race for small, one-design boats. The start is not quite that crucial for a variety of racing-cruiser types sailing a long course, but the skipper of a handicap racer might find that the difference between a good and bad start would be the equivalent of a change in his rating by almost a foot in an average 'round-the-buoys race.

In the opinion of many experts, the main considerations for obtaining good starts, listed in order of importance, are:

(1) acquiring freedom to go where you want immediately after the start (in order to follow the best course strategy).

(2) obtaining clear wind immediately after the start.

(3) being positioned, with right of way, at the *favored end* of the starting line at the starting signal.

(4) being close to or at the line with full way as the starting signal is made.

The first listed consideration will depend, of course, on the over-all race plan or strategy, and this will result from observation and prediction of wind, current, wave conditions, and other factors. We shall discuss these in Chapter 10.

Clear wind, listed as No. 2, is freedom from disturbed air in the form of wind shadow and especially backwind. In large racing fleets, the "dirty" or disturbed wind in the starting area can have a devastating effect on boat performance. Sails not only make turbulence, but they cause a partial absence of wind in their blanketing zone (wind shadow), and they bend or deflect the wind at the region ahead of the luff and especially behind the leech. This is shown by the boats beating to windward in Figure 89. Boat B's wind shadow is the shaded region directly to leeward of the apparent wind. Notice how the wind flow is deflected by B so that A is sailing in a lift or favoring wind slant while boat C is sailing in a header or heading deflection. Successful starts very much depend on the skipper's awareness and understanding of the behavior of disturbed wind.

The third listed starting consideration suggests that the boat making a good start has the right of way. With a windward start, this means starting on the starboard tack and being clear to leeward (not converging with right of way boats to leeward). Occasionally there are times when it might pay to make a port tack start, when for example you are making a port tack approach and find the rest of the fleet is late getting to the line or there is a gap in the group of starboard tackers through which you can pass to cross the starting line; but usually in large fleets, a port tack start is too risky. A general rule of thumb is that if you can easily fetch the mark (or committee boat) while on the starboard tack, a starboard tack start should be made.

The third consideration also suggests being at the favored end of the line. This means being at the end that is the shortest "sailing distance" to the first turning mark of the course. If the start is downwind, the shortest sailing distance is usually the shortest actual distance, but if the start is to windward (the usual closed course start), the shortest sailing distance includes tacking and this is *not*

FIGURE 89: BACKWIND & WINDSHADOW

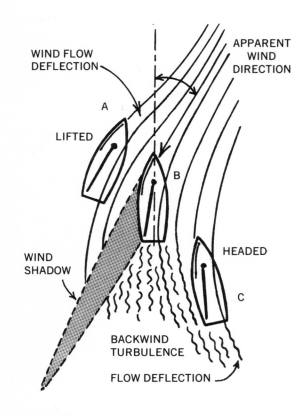

WIND FLOW DEFLECTION

APPARENT WIND DIRECTION

A

LIFTED

B

WIND SHADOW

HEADED

C

BACKWIND TURBULENCE

FLOW DEFLECTION

always the shortest actual distance. One end of the line is favored when the line is slanted away from being perpendicular to the *rhumb line* course (direct, straight line course) to the first mark when starting downwind, or when the line is slanted away from the perpendicular to the wind direction with a windward start (this was discussed in Chapter 1).

Figure 90 illustrates how a windward starting line's slant or angle to the wind makes one end favored. Before boats A and B cross the line, the leeward end of the line is favored; but after they cross the line, the wind shifts causing the windward end to be favored. A simple test to determine the favored end just prior to the start is shown by boat C in the illustration. She is luffing head to wind near the middle of the line, and her bow is pointing closer to the leeward than to the windward end of the line, indicating the leeward end is favored at that time. If her bow were pointing nearer to the windward end while she lay head-to-wind, the windward end would be favored. Figure 90 shows that a start at the favored end can put a boat far ahead of a competitor starting at the line's opposite end when the wind holds steady, but it also shows that a shift can quickly change the situation.

FIGURE 90: FAVORED END OF THE STARTING LINE

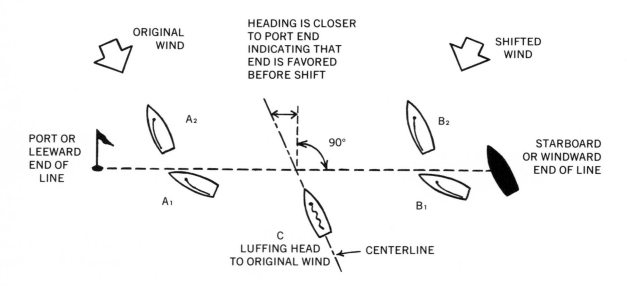

ORIGINAL WIND

HEADING IS CLOSER TO PORT END INDICATING THAT END IS FAVORED BEFORE SHIFT

SHIFTED WIND

PORT OR LEEWARD END OF LINE

A_2

A_1

90°

B_2

B_1

STARBOARD OR WINDWARD END OF LINE

C
LUFFING HEAD TO ORIGINAL WIND

CENTERLINE

The fourth consideration for good starting is quite obvious. The closer the starting boat is to the line and the faster she is moving, the sooner she will cross the line. However, this is less important than the other considerations already mentioned. In the interest of reaching the proper side of the course in the quickest time, or in getting clean air, it may well pay to make a slow or late start. Generally speaking, boat speed at the start will often depend on the size and weight of the boat. Large, heavy boats should have ample headway at all times, because they are relatively slow to accelerate, and they usually need greater speed for best maneuverability and steering control as compared with light displacement, dagger board dinghies that can "turn on a dime."

The Windward Start

Windward starts are the ones most frequently encountered when racing over a closed course, and as said in Chapter 1, the race committee nearly always trys to set the line approximately square to the wind. Of course, the committee attempts to position the line with respect to the wind so that neither end is favored, and all starting points anywhere along the line are equally attractive. This is the perfect starting line, but unfortunately, it is an ideal that is seldom achieved, because the wind rarely holds absolutely steady. A last minute shift usually favors, if only slightly, one end or the other.

All starts are either one or some combination of five types: (1) *the timed start,* (2) *running the line,* (3) *sitting on the line,* (4) *dipping,* and (5) *barging.* These are illustrated in Figure 91 which shows how the basic types are commonly used when the windward or starboard end of the line is favored and also when the port or leeward end is favored. Actually, many starting situations may require a combination of two or more types, as for example, when a timed start is combined with a sitting or no headway start as shown by C + B when the leeward end is favored.

There are several variations of timing a start. In Figure 91, situation 2 (leeward end favored), boat B "runs the line" or actually reaches along the line while the time is taken with a stop watch as she sails from one end to the other or from one end to the line's middle. It is then known how long it will take for her to get from the middle back to the favored end, after allowance is made for the time it

takes to turn, or in the case of C + B, after allowance is made for the boat to pick up speed after way has been lost.

A commonly used timing method is known as the Vanderbilt system, and this is illustrated in Figure 91, situation 1. Boat A crosses the starting line headed away from the first turning mark, two minutes and twenty seconds before the starting signal near the location on the line where the actual start will be made. It is estimated that the boat can be jibed around in fourteen seconds; and so this is added to the 2:20 time remaining (until the start) which makes 2:34. This figure is divided in half to give 1:17. The helmsman then steers the boat on a steady course away from the line until there is one minute seventeen seconds remaining and then he jibes around to head back for the selected starting spot. After taking fourteen seconds to jibe, the boat is allowed one minute three seconds to return to the line. She should reach it as the starting signal is made provided there is no current, the wind is steady, and there is no interference from other boats. The boat does not have to cross the starting headed the wrong way (away from the first mark) at exactly 2:20 before the start. She can cross any time around two or three minutes (or a greater or lesser time) before the starting signal. It is only necessary that the time remaining be added to the time allowed for jibing or tacking, and then this figure is divided by two which gives the proper time remaining at which the turn should be made. The courses for this kind of start should be, as nearly as possible, beam reaches in order that boat speed be the same leaving as approaching the line.

The Vanderbilt system often works well when there are only a few boats racing, but alas, today's starts are usually crowded and the interference of other boats (or if not the boats themselves, their disturbed air) nearly always upsets any starting method that relies on precise timing. For all practical purposes, most effective timed starts in crowded fleets must result from practice in judging and controlling the boat's speed and from close observation of competitors and the anticipation of their maneuvers. In a crowded fleet it is often wise to begin following a tentative Vanderbilt plan, but if a crowd begins to form in your selected starting area, make your turn early in order to allow for interference. If that interference never materializes, then your boat's speed can be killed by slack-

FIGURE 91: WINDWARD STARTING METHODS

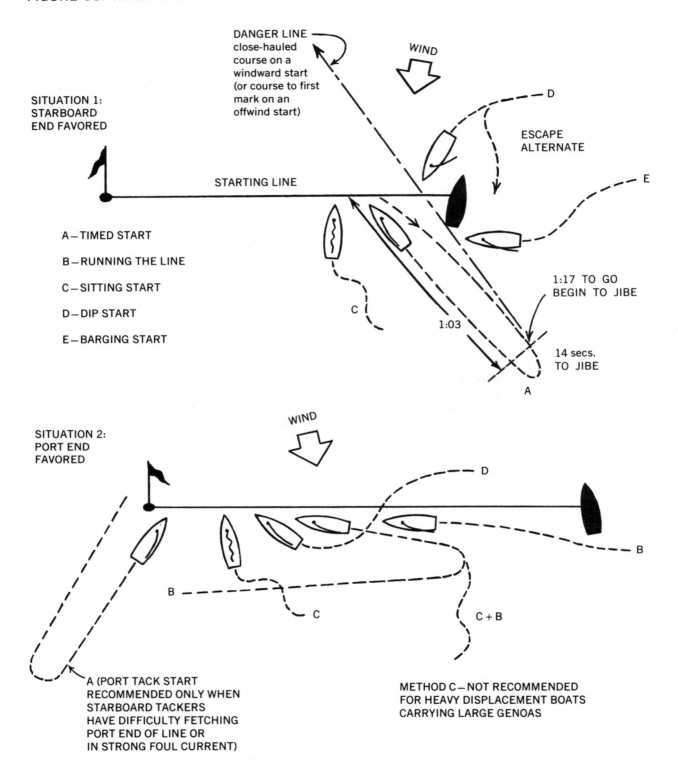

DANGER LINE
close-hauled
course on a
windward start
(or course to first
mark on an
offwind start)

WIND

SITUATION 1:
STARBOARD
END FAVORED

D

ESCAPE
ALTERNATE

STARTING LINE

E

A — TIMED START

B — RUNNING THE LINE

C — SITTING START

D — DIP START

E — BARGING START

1:17 TO GO
BEGIN TO JIBE

C

1:03

14 secs.
TO JIBE

A

WIND

SITUATION 2:
PORT END
FAVORED

D

B

B

C

C + B

A (PORT TACK START
RECOMMENDED ONLY WHEN
STARBOARD TACKERS
HAVE DIFFICULTY FETCHING
PORT END OF LINE OR
IN STRONG FOUL CURRENT)

METHOD C — NOT RECOMMENDED
FOR HEAVY DISPLACEMENT BOATS
CARRYING LARGE GENOAS

ing sheets or sailing a crooked or slightly weaving course.

Running the line, as shown by boat B in Figure 91, is probably the most commonly used start for large racing-cruisers when the leeward end of the line is favored. Although we shall not consider this a true timing method, with most starting methods a certain amount of timing is almost always involved. The skipper or helmsman should constantly be informed of the time remaining especially just prior to the starting signal. In the case of boat B running the line, it should be known how long it takes her to reach along the line from one end to the other, then her skipper can best judge when to begin running the line in order to arrive at the selected starting spot at gunfire (as the starting signal is made). When the line is crowded, it is often wise to begin running the line early to allow for course alterations, and if it is found that you are arriving at the starting spot too early, sheets can be slacked to reduce speed. The danger in this starting method is that boats to leeward have the right of way, and the line runner could be forced over the line prematurely. For this reason the run should be made a safe distance to leeward of the line and a careful lookout should be kept for converging boats to leeward.

A commonly used method in small dinghies is the sitting start (boat C in Figure 91). Since small, light displacement boats can usually pick up speed or accelerate very rapidly, it is common practice among some small boat skippers to stay very close to the selected starting spot keeping very little way on their boats by luffing or slacking sheets. Then a few seconds before gunfire they bear off, trim in, and are off with the starting signal. This seldom works with large racing-cruisers because they are relatively slow to pick up speed. When a heavy displacement boat tries a sitting start she will more than likely end up a "sitting duck." She is also in a very vulnerable position with boats to leeward, because before starting a leeward boat, even if she is behind the mast abeam position (see Fig. 88), may luff a windward boat provided the latter is given opportunity to keep clear and the luffing is done slowly. However, before her starting signal, the leeward boat behind the mast abeam position cannot luff above a close-hauled course. (See Rule 40.) Although Rule 38.1 (luffing *after* starting) does not allow an overlapped boat to leeward to sail above her proper course while the overlap exists *if*

at any time during its existence the windward boat was ahead of the mast abeam position, there is no proper course before the starting signal, and the leeward boat forward of "mast abeam" can luff slowly, higher than close-hauled even if she had been abaft the mast line (mast abeam position) when the overlap began. Thus it can be seen that the heavy line sitter is particularly vulnerable to leeward boats.

Another consideration with line sitting and being dependent on quick maneuvering and acceleration, is the size of headsails carried on many racing-cruisers. A large masthead Genoa cannot be tacked or trimmed in as quickly as the jib on a small one-design boat, and furthermore the Genoa with great overlap can get caught aback when the boat is killing way by luffing head to wind. However, when there is plenty of open water around the boat, usually several minutes before the start, a large boat can use a modified sitting method (provided some headway is retained) when this method is combined with line running or a timed start as shown by C + B in Figure 91.

An early, cautious port tack approach as illustrated in situation 2 by B or C + B (or further up the line when the windward end is favored) is often an effective means of maneuvering into the desired position for the final starboard tack charge for the starting line. The early approach on the port tack usually allows maximum room to maneuver in relatively clear air. If the starboard tackers are late in arriving at the line, the port tack boat can come about ahead of them, but if they are early, the port tacker can often find a hole or gap astern of the first group of starboard tack boats through which she can pass to tack. A port tacker doesn't have the course altering restrictions of a starboard tacker (see Rule 34).

The dip start (shown by boats D in the illustration) can be very dangerous, but there are one or two occasions when the method can be effective. As can be seen in the illustration, the dip starter stays on the wrong side of the line until just prior to the start at which time she dips back across to the correct side of the line at or near the desired starting location. The principle danger in this kind of start is in not being able to find a space or hole into which to dip. Obviously, the dipper has no rights over boats to leeward. The time when this kind of start might be effective is when there is a strong current with the wind that causes most conventional starters to be late in reaching the line.

A commonly used dip start for small boats is shown in situation 1 where the windward end is favored and the committee boat is at that end. In this case, there is often a small, semi-protected area into which a small boat can dip, but this is not always true where a big boat is concerned. The large boat cannot maneuver as quickly and needs more space than a small one. The large boat might attempt a dip method if she leaves an escape opening, however, as shown by D (alternate) in situation 1. In this case, D maneuvers some distance to weather of the committee boat and when it appears that the starting fleet will be late, she dips, but if there is no room, she jibes over while still to weather of the committee boat and makes a barging start similar to the start of boat E.

One of the most commonly used and over-used starts is the barging start (boat E). Before beginning to race and especially before attempting a barging start, the novice skipper should thoroughly acquaint himself with the Anti-barging Rule (NAYRU Rule 42.1,e). This is an important exception to the rule that requires an outside overlapped boat to give room to an inside boat at a mark of the course (see Rule 42). When the windward end of the line is favored, and a boat approaches the mark at that end to windward of the starboard tack, close-hauled course (or course to the first mark on an off wind start), as illustrated by the dot-dash line in Figure 91, she is said to be barging, and she cannot claim room from an overlapped leeward boat. Before the starting signal, the leeward boat may slowly luff above her close-hauled course if she is forward of the mast line, but after the starting signal before crossing the line, the leeward boat may not deprive the windward boat of room by sailing above her close-hauled course (or by heading above the first mark on an off wind start). However, if she is near enough to the starting line mark, she may be able, while holding a proper close-hauled course (or a course to the first mark on an off wind start), to prevent an overlapped windward boat from squeezing in on the correct side of the mark. Of course, after crossing the line, normal luffing rights after starting (Rule 38) become effective.

Barging is perfectly legal if there is room to leeward of the barger, but when there is not room, the barger must kill way or circle to wait for an opening or gap between the mark and boats to leeward of the mark. Barging starts are risky when the windward end of the line is crowded, but the method can be effective when (1) there are not many boats, (2) in light airs when it is wise to stay near the line and approach it on a fast reach, and (3) when it is desired for strategy purposes, to get to the right-hand side of the course in the quickest time. It is common practice to barge on leeward (off wind) starts also. In this case, the danger line (shown in Figure 91) is the course from the windward end of the line to the first mark.

On a crowded, well-set, windward starting line (set nearly square to the wind), boats will be fairly evenly distributed along the line from one end to the other. Leeward boats, especially the one furthest to leeward, will be at a disadvantage if the correct course lies to the right-hand side of the race course. However, if the correct course is to port, the leeward boats (especially the one furthest to leeward) will benefit in two ways: by being closer to the correct side of the course, and by having clear wind yet the capability of backwinding windward competitors. A commonly used technique for obtaining clear wind is illustrated by boat A in the line's middle in Figure 92. A slowly luffs boat B, to windward of her, in order to widen her starting space and to move further to windward of C. Before losing too much headway, A bears off onto her proper course, and hopefully she is mostly clear of C's backwind. Boat D has an ideal start *if* a lifting shift is expected or if she is especially close winded and can work to weather of B's backwind. However, D would be hurt by a header and would have to tack at the first opportunity.

The boats furthest to windward have an advantage in that they are not boxed in or trapped by windward boats, and thus they can soon tack to clear their wind. If the correct strategic course lies to starboard, they can come about and hold on the port tack; but if the correct course lies to port, a windward boat can take a short *hitch (board or tack)* for wind clearing purposes but then return immediately to the starboard tack as shown by boat E in Figure 92. Boat F, furthest to leeward, should have the theoretical advantage over all boats to windward when clear wind is the only consideration; but a heading shift could prevent her from fetching the leeward end of the line; while a lifting shift would cause her to lose sailing distance on her windward competitors.

It is generally the safest policy not to aim for the

FIGURE 92: OBTAINING CLEAR AIR ON WINDWARD STARTS

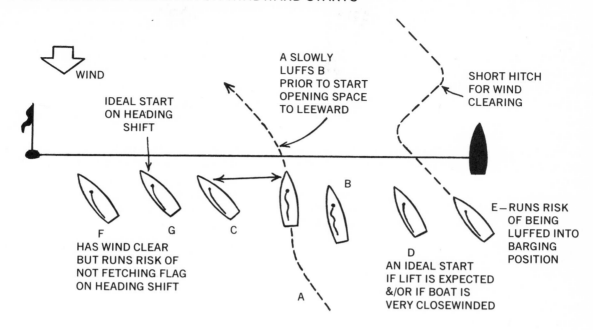

WIND

IDEAL START
ON HEADING
SHIFT

A SLOWLY
LUFFS B
PRIOR TO START
OPENING SPACE
TO LEEWARD

SHORT HITCH
FOR WIND
CLEARING

F

G

C

B

A

D

E—RUNS RISK
OF BEING
LUFFED INTO
BARGING
POSITION

HAS WIND CLEAR
BUT RUNS RISK OF
NOT FETCHING FLAG
ON HEADING SHIFT

AN IDEAL START
IF LIFT IS EXPECTED
&/OR IF BOAT IS
VERY CLOSEWINDED

FIGURE 93: SPEED CURVES & WIND SHADOWS

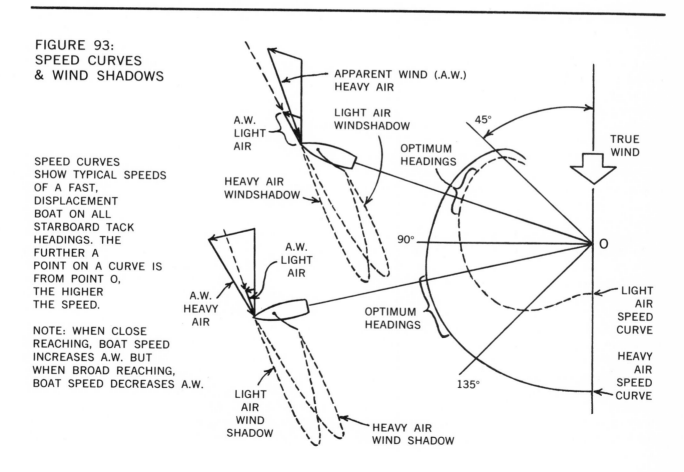

SPEED CURVES
SHOW TYPICAL SPEEDS
OF A FAST,
DISPLACEMENT
BOAT ON ALL
STARBOARD TACK
HEADINGS. THE
FURTHER A
POINT ON A CURVE IS
FROM POINT O,
THE HIGHER
THE SPEED.

NOTE: WHEN CLOSE
REACHING, BOAT SPEED
INCREASES A.W. BUT
WHEN BROAD REACHING,
BOAT SPEED DECREASES A.W.

APPARENT WIND (.A.W.)
HEAVY AIR

LIGHT AIR
WINDSHADOW

A.W.
LIGHT
AIR

OPTIMUM
HEADINGS

45°

TRUE
WIND

HEAVY AIR
WINDSHADOW

A.W.
LIGHT
AIR

90°

O

A.W.
HEAVY
AIR

OPTIMUM
HEADINGS

LIGHT
AIR
SPEED
CURVE

HEAVY
AIR
SPEED
CURVE

135°

LIGHT
AIR
WIND
SHADOW

HEAVY AIR
WIND SHADOW

starting spot furthest to leeward or windward, because of this wind shift risk in the former case, and because, at the most windward spot, there is danger that a wind shift or a competitor's luff will put you in a barging position. If the committee boat happens to be at the leeward end, there is the added danger for the most leeward boat of being trapped in the "coffin corner" as described in Chapter 1 (Figure 7). It is usually the best policy for a leeward starter sailing into this trap to jibe around and attempt a port tack start behind or through a gap in the starboard tackers. On crowded lines, safe yet advantageous starting spots are often found in the vicinity of a sixth of the line's distance or slightly less from either end, depending on which side is correct for the course strategy and which end is the most favored when considering minimum sailing distance to the first mark.

Leeward Starts

Most race committees will always try to set a windward starting line, but on a point-to-point course it is often not possible to start dead to windward. Thus the skipper of a racing-cruiser who will compete in distance races can expect more than a few leeward or off-wind starts.

The most serious wind disturbance is caused by backwind on the windward start, but on downwind starts the effects of blanketing gain in relative importance. As said in Chapter 1, the Race Committee usually gives the reaching starting line a considerable slant away from the perpendicular to the rhumb line course with the leeward end being set closer than the windward end to its first mark. This is done in an attempt to spread boats evenly along the line. If the line were set square to the rhumb line course, boats would jam at the windward end in order to avoid wind shadows and at the same time to blanket their leeward competitors. However, if the line is sufficiently slanted, the leeward boats will be slightly ahead of the wind shadows of competitors getting equally good starts to windward. An important point to keep in mind concerning wind shadows is that they lie directly to leeward of the *apparent* wind. Since boats move slowly in light air, the wind shadows often lie further forward in light than in heavy winds *but not always*.

Figure 93 shows examples of two boats reaching, one sailing above and one below the beam reach. Approximate but typical speed curves for the boats (high performance, displacement racing-cruisers) are shown on the right-hand side of the diagram for all points of sailing in light and heavy winds (no stronger than needed for optimum speeds). Notice under the low sailing boat, the light air wind shadow lies slightly forward of the heavy air wind shadow as might often be expected, but the opposite is true with the close reaching boat. This is true because optimum speeds lie above the beam reach in light winds but below the beam reach in heavy winds, and also because the apparent wind results from the relativity of boat speed to true wind speed. Some dinghy sailors new to racing-cruisers might fail to fully appreciate that, unlike a boat that easily planes, a displacement boat often has her heavy air wind shadow ahead of her light air shadow. Of course, a close scrutiny of wind indicators will be most helpful in this matter.

When starting at the leeward end of the line on a reaching start, one should be sure he is ahead of the wind shadows of boats to windward, and that his course will be one of optimum speed or at least in a further off the wind and divergent direction to avoid being blanketed. Of course, windward starters should try to blanket boats to leeward provided they don't become engaged in costly luffing matches.

The speed curves in Figure 93 suggest that on a near beam reaching start, a course slightly higher than a beam reach should be favored in light airs, but one slightly lower than the beam reach should be favored in heavy winds. Light and heavy wind reaching starts are shown in Figure 94. In light winds, when the line is adequately slanted toward the first mark, boat A starting at the line's leeward end will probably pull ahead of B starting at the other end, provided wind and current are the same for both and that boat speeds are the same on identical points of sailing. In heavy winds, however, the opposite is the case. The odds are that boat B at the windward end will take the start and soon put A in her wind shadow, especially if the line is not adequately slanted. Also B will have a slightly better chance to set her spinnaker than will A. Before the start wind conditions at both ends of the line should be carefully observed. If the windward end is near a shore, there might be a partial lee or disturbed area near that end. When the wind is light and particularly if the current is foul (against you), *stay close to the line*. However, if the wind is light but the current fair, keep a good distance directly up current of the line so as not to take a chance on being swept by or over the line in case the breeze dies. Under such conditions the anchor should be rigged and available for instant use.

An important consideration for handicap racers on any kind of start is relative boat performance due to variations in size and design. This will be talked about in more detail when we discuss tactics, but it should be sufficient at this point to say that before the start, the competition should be looked over and "sized up." Obviously, it would be unwise to start slightly to windward and behind an extremely close winded competitor that could work across your bow on a windward start, and it would also be unwise to start just ahead and to leeward of a larger, faster boat that would soon pass to windward giving you a devastating dose of bad air. This risk must be carefully weighed before making a leeward end reaching start in a small boat.

On near beam reaching starts, the Vanderbilt start often works well, because speed sailing away from the line should be nearly equal to the speed sailing back to the line. However, on downwind as well as upwind starts, some allowance in timing must be made for maneuvering to avoid other boats when the line is crowded.

Broad reaching and running starts obviously involve carrying the spinnaker, and so the time of setting and manner of carrying this sail will be the critical factors. More often than not on reaching starts it will pay, in my opinion, to delay setting the spinnaker until immediately after the start.

This is especially true for the less experienced skippers. The delay will allow maximum freedom to maneuver and the ability to luff competitors carrying spinnakers. Often a well-timed, leeward-end start, when the wind is not too far aft, will allow the boat carrying a large jib to luff and completely collapse the 'chutes of her rivals to windward. Of course, the boat carrying her jib should have her spinnaker rigged and ready to break out or set at a moment's notice.

Consideration of course strategy is important with downwind starting even though the first turning mark can be fetched. It is seldom that a straight rhumb line course is the fastest one, because a boat should be sailed, whenever possible, on her fastest points of sailing in the regions of most favorable current and wind. Thus it is also important

FIGURE 94: REACHING STARTS

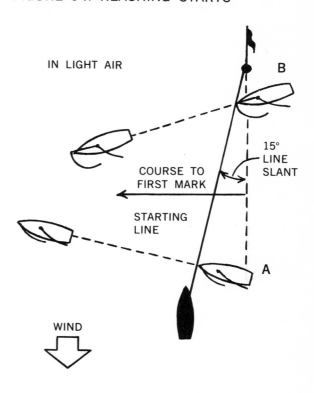

IN LIGHT AIR

B

15° LINE SLANT

COURSE TO FIRST MARK

STARTING LINE

A

WIND

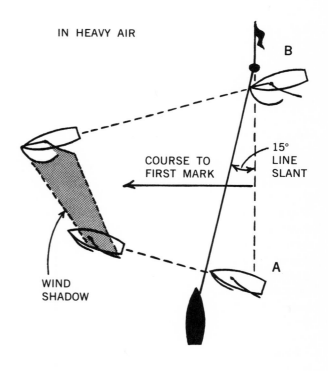

IN HEAVY AIR

B

15° LINE SLANT

COURSE TO FIRST MARK

A

WIND SHADOW

139

on a leeward start to avoid getting "boxed in" at the wrong end of the line and to think in terms of having freedom to go where you want to immediately after starting. If the first leg of the course is a long, close reach, it will probably pay to start to leeward, bear off slightly, and foot rather than pinch up. The footing boat to leeward will profit by a lifting shift which will enable her to ease sheets for more speed, and she will profit by a significant heading shift because this will put the windward boats further behind her. More will be said of this when we discuss strategy in Chapter 10.

The following is a list of preparations and suggestions for starting that might be helpful for the beginner:

(1) Arrive at the starting area at least a half hour before the start of your class.

(2) Observe the wind, weather, current, and the starts of classes ahead of yours.

(3) Study the race circular and current tables, lay out the course on the chart, and write down the compass direction of each rhumb line course.

(4) Size up the competition. Determine your most dangerous competitors, consider the performance characteristics of rival boats, try to estimate where they will start, and observe what sails they are carrying.

(5) Set your own sails early, to smooth out wrinkles and make the proper adjustments. Rig telltales and wind indicators. Locate and lay out all gear that will be needed.

(6) Plan the over-all course strategy and let this be the first consideration in planning the start.

(7) Try to determine where there will be the cleanest air. Observe where boats seem to be bunching or making trial runs.

(8) Luff head-to-wind to determine the favored end. Note your heading on the compass. Then luff up five minutes or so later and note compass heading to determine whether the wind has shifted. Keep track of the shifts.

(9) Run the line and take your time from one end to the other.

(10) Be informed of the time continually. Especially just prior to the starting signal, a timer should call out time remaining to the helmsman, and another crew member should watch the signals.

(11) Start on the starboard tack unless there is an obvious advantage in a port tack start.

(12) Be very cautious with a barging or dip start and always look for boats to leeward. Check the race circular to see that there is no *five-minute rule* or some variation of it. This is an occasionally used special rule that forbids crossing the line or its extensions after the preparatory signal.

(13) In most cases, during a windward start, don't try for the extreme end of the line but aim for spots a few boat lengths closer to line's middle.

(14) With large heavy boats, especially, keep ample headway for best maneuverability and starting speed.

(15) If you are late for the start, bear off and crack sheets for maximum speed.

(16) If you are a little early, pinch *slightly,* let the sails luff, or sail a crooked, weaving course. In small boats, the jib is sometimes backed to kill way, but this can be risky for a large boat with a large Genoa. In this case, it is often better to slack the main to kill way. Try to trim in and pick up speed again well before the starting signal.

(17) Favor the timed or modified timed start with a large, heavy boat especially when the line is not overly crowded or with reaching starts.

(18) Consider an early port tack approach when there is bunching at the windward end during a windward start.

(19) If using the Vanderbilt system, turn slightly sooner than you normally would when the starting area is congested.

(20) Never get far away from the starting area, and in light airs stay close to the line.

(21) Be very cautious of current in light air. Stay up current of the line and have the anchor ready for instant use.

(22) In most cases avoid the middle of a line on a windward start, because one end is usually favored, and there is a chance of becoming trapped or boxed-in at the middle.

(23) When starting to windward on a crowded line, try to open up space by slowly luffing the boat to windward and working away from the boat to leeward.

(24) If a boat to leeward luffs up a great deal, consider trying to slow down and reaching under her stern at top speed.

(25) Auxilliary engines must be shut off before the preparatory signal, but in light airs, be sure to fully utilize your legally allowed engine time to maneuver into the most advantageous position.

(26) On downwind starts try to blanket competitors, but avoid luffing matches. Have the spinnaker ready to set, but when reaching, delay setting it until immediately after the start.

9
Sailing Technique

As mentioned, it is assumed that the reader is familiar with the fundamentals of sailing and boat handling; therefore, this chapter will merely try to emphasize some of the finer and most important points pertaining to racing helmsmanship and sail handling. Although some sailors feel that seamanship must occasionally be sacrificed to win a race, and it is true that there is sometimes a fine line between risky sailing and optimum performance, this book will support the theory that sound, safe, and efficient sailing techniques are not only the most prudent but nearly always produce the most speed.

Helmsmanship

To begin with, let's consider the helm itself. There is little doubt that a well balanced boat with a light, sensitive, and responsive helm encourages good helmsmanship. On the other hand, a poorly balanced boat with a heavy helm that lacks "feel" can seldom be sailed up to her optimum to windward or downwind. A boat that "steers like a truck" may be sailed like one.

Helm response and feel will depend on such matters as helm balance; size, type, and location of the rudder; hull size, weight, and shape; mechanical advantage of the wheel, or length of the tiller, and so forth. We have already talked about balance, certain aspects of wheel vs. tiller steering, and rudder design. It should be sufficient to say here that the following conditions should be met to encourage the best helmsmanship:

(1) Most boats should have a *slight* weather helm when beating in moderate breezes at optimum angles of heel. As a general rule, boats having rudders attached to their keels should carry more weather helm than boats with rudders separated from their keels. However, the helm should never be so unbalanced as to stall the rudder on a beat, and of course, this should be avoided whenever possible on any point of sailing. Semibalanced spade rudders should have almost no weather helm, but a lee helm should rarely, if ever, be tolerated. In most cases, it should only be necessary for the helmsman to push *or* pull the helm (depending on which side of the boat he is occupying) but not to *both* push *and* pull the helm when beating in smooth waters. Corrections for imperfect balance have been discussed.

(2) Small rudders and long tillers make the helm light and easy to handle, but when this is overdone the rudder tends to stall easily and steering control and quick response are sacrificed. Conversely, large rudders and short tillers make a heavy but effective helm. Obviously, there should be a happy medium. Instant helm response is needed when sailing downwind in heavy seas with a spinnaker set. For this reason the rudder should be well aft, the tiller should be located where it will not be obstructed, and a wheel should not have too much mechanical advantage (perhaps three quarters of a turn from rudder on-center to hard over for a small yacht as shown in Figure 51).

(3) Helm mechanisms (gears, cable sheaves, etc.) should be well lubricated for smooth operation, and "play" or looseness in the tiller should not be tolerated. Figure 95 illustrates an effective tiller-rudder stock connection. A square hole through the tiller fits over the square end of the rudder stock, and there is a short threaded section with a nut (A in the diagram) just above the squared part of the stock. Notice that the squared section is tapered so that when looseness develops in the connection, nut A may be tightened to force the tiller further down on the stock to eliminate the play. Care should be taken, however, to see that the assembly is such that tightening the nut will not draw the entire rudder upwards so that it binds or rubs against the hull or fairing piece between the rudder's head and the hull. Many tillers of the type illustrated are fitted with a bolt and nut shown at location B to tighten or control the vertical motion of the tiller handle. This should be kept tight also. It is always wise to inspect the rudder carefully each time the boat is hauled or slipped to see that the rudder has not warped, that there is no binding of the rudder stock, jamming in the hard-over position, or excessive play at the gudgeons. A loose tiller or a binding rudder may not only be

FIGURE 95: TILLER-RUDDER STOCK CONNECTION

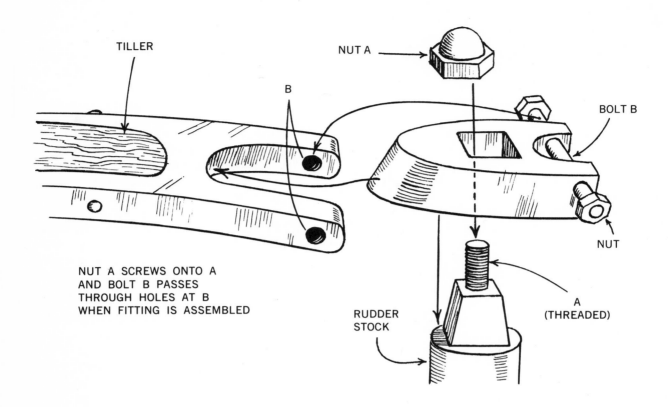

TILLER

B

NUT A

BOLT B

NUT

A
(THREADED)

NUT A SCREWS ONTO A
AND BOLT B PASSES
THROUGH HOLES AT B
WHEN FITTING IS ASSEMBLED

RUDDER
STOCK

unsafe, but also these can be quite damaging to optimum helmsmanship.

Different kinds of boats require slightly different helm techniques when beating to windward. The most effective technique can only be determined after complete familiarity with one's boat and considerable practice and experience racing in various conditions of wind and sea. With some boats it pays to foot off slightly or sail full and by, to gain speed and lessen leeway but with other boats it may pay to pinch up slightly to gain distance to windward if the cost in leeway and speed is not too great. The important consideration when beating, regardless of the amount of leeway, is the boat's actual course and her speed which shows her *speed made good* (Vmg) or her actual progress dead to windward. Certain boats respond well to the feathering technique (pinching up sharply in the puffs to reduce heel and gain distance to windward) but others do not. A slow, easy action on the helm is most suitable for some boats, but others respond well to a quicker, instant response to

headers and lifts. One must get to know his own boat.

To be very general, when the fore foot is deep and sharp and there is ample draft and lateral plane, the boat might be sailed very close to the wind provided she has an efficient sail plan. On the other hand, a boat with a full entrance and soft (shallow) forefoot with below normal draft should generally be sailed full and by. Heavy keel boats with deep narrow hulls that make large waves at high speeds should often be pointed high in good winds. Beamy centerboarders should usually not be pinched, at least to the extent that they make considerable leeway, as this causes great forward resistance especially in a seaway. In smooth water, however, some centerboarders with deep, high aspect ratio, dagger-type boards can point exceedingly high when they have sufficient speed. Heavy boats with long keels and large rudders should usually be sailed with a gentle, easy helm action, whereas light, fin-keelers might be turned much more quickly. The former type should be

142

tacked slowly and allowed to fore reach a good distance in some cases, but comparatively speaking, the latter might almost be slammed about in a moderate wind with smooth water.

Regardless of boat type, beating nearly always involves some sort of a weaving, up and down helm action as a result of attempting to avoid the rougher waves and conforming to changes of wind velocities and brief shifts and also as a result of alternately prodding the wind to gain distance upwind and then bearing away to pick up speed when the boat begins to slow. When the wind is fresh, puffy, and shifting rapidly, the helmsman who anticipates and responds instantly to each fluctuation in the wind can gain considerable distance to windward over the relatively steady helmsman who turns the boat slowly to meet only the more definite fluctuations, *provided* the boat can tolerate the quick helm treatment.

The best windward helmsmen, whether or not they are fully aware of it, make use of nearly all their senses. They *watch* the luff of the sails (especially the jib) for lifting or fluttering, *watch* the fluctuations of wind indicators (especially the telltales), *watch* the waves and puffs on the water, *watch* for changes in jib stay sag, *feel* the liveliness of the boat, *feel* the changes in pressure on the helm, *feel* the changes of wind direction and velocity on the face and neck, *feel and see* any changes in angle of heel, *listen* to leech flutters and the rattle of sail slides indicating a fluttering luff, *listen* to the sound of breaking seas, *listen* to the splash of the bow wave, and even *listen* to the rush of water along the rail and the hiss of the quarter wave. It is especially important that the racing-cruiser helmsman develop use of all his senses and not merely rely on vision alone, because distance racing often involves sailing at night or occasionally in fog.

In this age of scientific gadgetry, the sailor has not been neglected. There are many mechanical aids available for the helmsman. In the interest of simplicity and economy, I am not in favor of overloading a boat with expensive gadgets, but there is no doubt that certain instruments can be helpful at times. Some of these aids for the racing sailor are: speedometers, to show speed differences as a result of changes in sailing angles, sail trim, and sail changes; wind sensors, electrically powered sensors to measure wind pressure on the sails; electrically operated dial wind indicators, to give exact,

easily-read, angular changes in apparent wind; inclinometers, inexpensive devices to measure angle of heel and hull trim; and the tackmaster repeating compass, to help the helmsman determine the most favorable tack. Although some may argue that wealthy skippers have the advantage over those who cannot afford such gadgetry, we sailors belonging to the latter group should not despair. By using ordinary compasses and landmarks, we can keep track of true wind shifts; shroud telltales and masthead feathers or wind socks can show us the variations in the apparent wind; close scrutiny of nearby competitors can tell us, with reasonable accuracy, the change in speed that results from a change in sailing angle or sheet adjustment; of course, the quiver of the sail luff can tell us when we are sailing too high; and bits of yarn taped to a sail near its leeward luff can tell us (by the erratic up and down movements of the yarn) when the sail is stalled as a result of sailing too low with the sheet trimmed too flat.

Instruments are perhaps of most value at night when ordinary aids to helmsmanship such as telltales and sail luffs cannot be seen. Of particular value, in my opinion, is the dial wind indicator which damps wild oscillations often caused by the boat rolling or pitching and gives a clear reading of the apparent wind in degrees. This device is not only helpful to the helmsman but to the sheet trimmer for figuring correct boom or chord angles when reaching.

When sailing at night there is a common tendency to pinch because heavy night air can cause the helmsman to misjudge wind strength and the sound and feel of boat speed. Some skippers station a man forward to *"call the jib"* (watch the jib luff and inform the helmsman when he is sailing too high). This can be a help when sailing at night, but personally, I deplore this practice for daytime sailing, because the helmsman can usually watch the jib himself, and furthermore he is using many other sights, sounds, and feelings to aid in steering; thus a competent helmsman in the daytime is best able to judge for himself whether he is sailing too high or too low.

A relatively recent consideration for the racing helmsman in some parts of this country, is the technique of sailing in motorboat swells. Previously, he only had to be concerned with an occasional passing motorboat, but in the future, on any coastal or inland body of water, he will be sailing

FIGURE 96: DOWNWIND STEERING

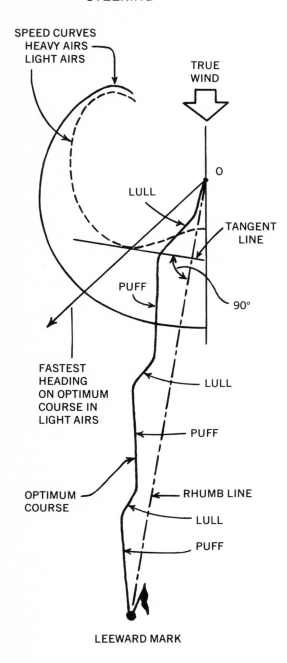

SPEED CURVES
HEAVY AIRS
LIGHT AIRS

TRUE WIND

O

LULL

TANGENT LINE

PUFF

90°

FASTEST HEADING ON OPTIMUM COURSE IN LIGHT AIRS

LULL

PUFF

OPTIMUM COURSE

RHUMB LINE

LULL

PUFF

LEEWARD MARK

NOTE: THE FASTEST LIGHT AIR HEADING FOR THE RHUMB LINE COURSE IS FOUND BY DRAWING A LINE FROM POINT O (THE COURSE BEGINNING) THROUGH THE POINT WHERE THE TANGENT LINE TOUCHES THE LIGHT AIR SPEED CURVE.

144

FIGURE 97: TACKING TECHNIQUE

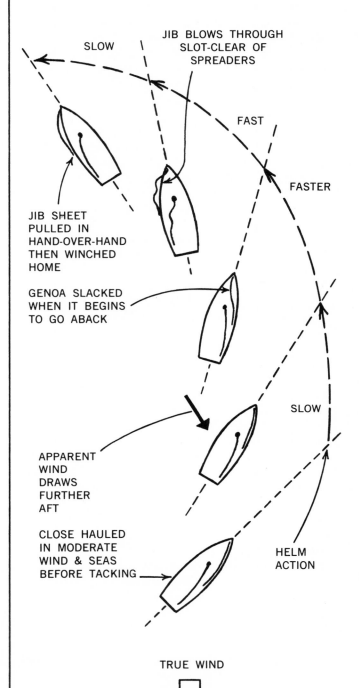

SLOW

JIB BLOWS THROUGH SLOT-CLEAR OF SPREADERS

FAST

FASTER

JIB SHEET PULLED IN HAND-OVER-HAND THEN WINCHED HOME

GENOA SLACKED WHEN IT BEGINS TO GO ABACK

SLOW

APPARENT WIND DRAWS FURTHER AFT

CLOSE HAULED IN MODERATE WIND & SEAS BEFORE TACKING

HELM ACTION

TRUE WIND

almost continually in a confused sea caused by boats under power. Today, a definite strategy consideration is planning a course that will avoid frequently travelled power boat tracks. It would be helpful if there were an educational program to inform power boat owners of the harm they can do to a racing fleet through disturbance of not only the water, but the wind. Of course sailboat skippers cannot expect complete absence of interference, but they have the right to expect a motor boat nearby to slow down and pass astern. For some time, I have thought it would be a good idea for U. S. racing yachts to fly a special, easily identifiable and publicized, uniform racing flag in order that the skippers of boats under power could recognize boats engaged in a formal race.

Sailing in a seaway, especially a confused sea, is a technique that can only be learned through practice. In general, it might be said that the boat must be sailed full and by and that she should be worked to weather only in the relatively smooth spots. In good breezes, however, it often pays to luff into a steep sea to gain distance to windward and then to bear off quickly to gain speed as the wave passes under the hull. Sails should be cut full and held securely against slatting. Sheets must be alternately eased in and out when pitching in power boat swells in order to damp the waves' jolting effect and to allow for the sudden changes in apparent wind caused by the pitching. Light weight drifter type jibs are often good in light airs, because they fill out quickly after collapsing in confused seas. Non-electronic masthead wind indicators that are often a great aid when sailing downwind in smooth waters are usually useless in a seaway because of their oscillating back and forth with the rolling and pitching of the boat. It is often a help to remove the counterbalance weight from the indicator under such conditions. Before crossing a particularly sizable powerboat wake, it is sometimes a good idea (when it fits in with the strategy) to tack just before reaching the disturbed wind and water. The slap of the waves under the counter can sometimes actually be helpful. Of course, in light airs and confused seas, the boat should be heeled slightly to leeward and allowed to foot with eased sheets. Heavy displacement boats with large sail areas often have the advantage in these conditions, because they have the momentum to carry through a rough patch of water if they are kept moving.

When sailing downwind, it seldom pays to run off dead before the wind except in heavy winds. The skipper should try to determine and utilize those points of sailing that give optimum speeds at various velocities of wind. Optimum points of sailing can be used by "working" the boat to leeward, or in other words, using the technique of bearing away in puffs and heading up in the lulls. This is illustrated in Figure 96 which uses the same light and heavy wind speed curves as shown in Figure 93. These curves represent the speeds for all points of sailing, and the further any point on a curve is from the central point 0, the faster the speed.

It can be seen that optimum speeds are on considerably higher points of sailing in light airs as compared with heavy winds, especially when the wind is well aft, thus the weaving course illustrated is faster than the rhumb line course, because advantage is being taken of variations in wind velocity. If the wind is gradually freshening, it may pay initially to stay high of the rhumb line course, and conversely if the wind is growing lighter it may pay to stay low initially so that later you can sail higher as the wind lightens. When the wind is shifty, it may pay, in addition to working to leeward, to "tack downwind" a method of broad reaching on an optimum point of sailing on one tack, then jibing over and broad reaching on the other tack. We shall discuss this in the next chapter when we talk about strategy. Spinnaker helmsmanship will be discussed later when we deal with spinnakers.

Tacking Technique

On American racing-cruisers, the large Genoa jib is still the most commonly used headsail for beating in all but the lightest and heaviest winds; thus proper handling of the Genoa is a must in developing an efficient tacking technique. The difference between good and poor handling of this sail when coming about can mean a difference of many boat lengths in distance gained to windward.

The crew should be organized so that one man is stationed forward just prior to tacking in order to help the Genoa around the mast when the boat is head to wind. Two men are stationed at the large sheet winch that will be taking in the Genoa on the new tack. One of these men will be the *cranker* (one who turns the winch handle) and the other will be a *tailer* (one who pulls and keeps tension on the tail of the sheet while it is being cranked in). Another crew member, perhaps the helmsman on a small racing-cruiser, slacks off the Genoa sheet on the boat's opposite side just before she is turned into the wind.

It is important that the man slacking the sheet not do it too fast or too suddenly as this can kill the boat's momentum. In most cases the sheet should be eased when the boat is head to wind or nearly so. At this point, the man stationed forward quickly gathers in the foot of the sail, pulling it forward so that it will clear the shrouds and mast. As the boat turns through the eye of the wind, the jib blows through the space between the mast and jib stay. The tailer at the leeward winch has perhaps two or three turns on the winch with the sheet and he begins pulling in the sheet, hand over hand, as quickly as possible while the man forward comes aft to help by pulling aft on the clew of the Genoa. This is a very critical point in the tacking maneuver, because if the tailer can gather in the sheet fast enough before the sail begins to fill, he can save a great deal of time that would have to be spent slowly cranking the sail in. When the jib fills, the tailer quickly flips another turn or two around the winch and the cranker inserts the handle and begins to crank by turning the handle all the way around in circles until he no longer has the strength for this. Then he ratchets with a back and forth motion on the handle. Incidentally, when a sheet or guy goes from a turning block to a winch, there is a trick in pulling in the line while it is under strain before the winch handle is used. The sheet tender can greatly increase his power by pulling on that part of the sheet that is between the sail and the block with one hand while he pulls on the sheet's tail with the other hand.

The helmsman can be a great help to the jib trimmers by bearing away fast after passing through the wind's eye in order that the jib blow through the slot *with its leech clear of the spreaders*. Then the helmsman can momentary reverse the helm to slow the turning speed and thereafter turn slowly in order to facilitate rapid trimming. This is illustrated in Figure 97. Of course, exact helm technique will vary with individual boats. As said, large heavy boats should be allowed to fore-reach by turning slowly in order to gain distance to windward, but small light displacement boats should generally be turned more quickly because they lose speed faster. Regardless of boat type, however, the basic principle illustrated in Figure 97 should nearly always be used. Notice that as

the boat is turned toward the wind the apparent wind draws further aft (relative to the true wind) as a result of the speed decreasing and the side wind created by the boat turning. This is one reason why it is important not to cast off the jib sheet until nearly head-to-wind. When tacking a light air double head rig, it often pays to cast off the staysail sheet when beyond head-to-wind. The backed staysail will help turn the boat and allow the jib topsail to quickly slide around the staysail.

The apparent wind is also quite far aft just after the boat completes the tack but before she picks up speed. For this reason it is important not to sheet the jib in as flat as it is normally carried to windward until the boat gains full headway. Also the mainsheet should be temporarily eased at this time. If there is a crew member assigned to slacking the jib sheet at the beginning of the tacking operation, he may then switch over to slacking the main after completing his first job. Surprisingly, mainsheet slacking is often neglected on racing-cruisers, but the practice can be effective on small boats, and in one respect this should be even more effective on a large boat because she takes longer to accelerate. The man who slacks the jib, however, should see that the jib sheet is entirely clear before he leaves it. There is nothing that can ruin a good tack quicker than having the windward sheet foul or jam in its lead block.

Good, free-turning shroud rollers (*thin* tubes of wood, metal or plastic, which fit over the lower part of the outboard shrouds) can not only prevent chafe but also help speed up tacking, because they reduce the friction caused by the Genoa and its sheet dragging across the shrouds. Be sure that the jibsheet shackle is not a kind that will foul on the shrouds and be sure it cannot come open when the sail is flapping violently. Some sailors prefer to tie their jibsheets to the sail with bowlines mainly to eliminate the risk of a foredeck crew member getting hit with a flogging shackle. This is a wise precaution where a working jib is concerned, but in my opinion, it should not be necessary to discard the sheet shackle on an overlapping Genoa. If the Genoa's clew is very close to the lead block, it might be possible to trim the jib a little closer by using a shackle rather than a knot. With drifters or other light weather sails it is nearly always advisable to tie the sheets and thereby eliminate the weight of a shackle.

Shortening Down and Changing Sails

For optimum racing performance boats should have their sail plan and area matched to the strength of wind. Obviously, in light airs the greatest possible area and the lightest weight headsails will be carried. In moderate winds, large but heavier jibs are carried; and when it really breezes up, sail should be reduced to prevent excessive heeling or broaching to when running. If weather helm becomes excessive, or the lee rail becomes buried, it is definitely time to shorten sail. Of course, on a short leg during a race, this might be too costly if the sail reducing operation is slow; thus it might pay to temporarily slack off the main and let it luff temporarily until rounding the turning mark if the next leg provides a better opportunity to alter the sail plan.

The shift from a drifter to Number 1 Genoa or vice versa is not usually much of a problem, because most drifters are set flying, with only one hank near the head of the sail. Quite often the change can be made while tacking so that very little way is lost, but of course this takes practice. When shifting from Genoa to drifter on a beat, the drifter is tacked to the stem head and the sail is laid out along the windward side of the foredeck with its sheet attached. Then the boat is tacked, and while she is head-to-wind, the Genoa is quickly dropped. This operation is most efficient with at least two men forward. One crew member (the bow man) stands near the stem head, pulls the Genoa down the stay, and quickly removes its halyard shackle from the head. The other man (the mast man) having cast off the fall of the halyard at the mast goes forward and receives from the bow man the halyard shackle, which he immediately snaps into the head of the drifter, while the bow man snaps the drifter's top hank to the jib stay above the lowered Genoa. In the meantime, the mast man has returned to his station near the mast and hoists the drifter as the boat fills away on her new tack.

When switching back to the Genoa again, the drifter is dropped while head-to-wind during a tack. The bow man unsnaps the halyard shackle and hands it to the mast man who snaps it onto the Genoa head while the bow man unsnaps the drifter hank and clears away that part of the drifter that is lying on top of the Genoa. In the meanwhile, the mast man has gone back to the fall of the halyard and is already hoisting. In some cases, the operation might be expedited with a third man who is permanently stationed at the mast to handle the fall of the halyard.

It may be possible to hoist the drifter on another halyard, the spinnaker's for example, and without the top hank being snapped to the stay, in order that the drifter can be hoisted before the Genoa is lowered or vice versa. Of course, this minimizes loss of headway during the sail change, however, most drifters will not set well on a spinnaker halyard without the head being hanked to the jib stay. The head of the sail may even develop a twist, thus in my opinion it usually pays to take a few seconds longer and to lose slightly more headway in order to set the drifter properly. The time lost will soon be compensated by the more efficient sail shape.

The same basic principles of shifting from Genoa to drifter are also involved when shifting from Number 1 Genoa to a Number 2 or a working jib, except that the operation takes longer due to the fact that the heavy weather jibs have hanks along their entire luffs. It is often easier to make this shift while tacking, and the new jib being bent on should be laid out along the weather rail of the foredeck. The bottom hank of the hoisted jib usually should be unsnapped from the stay, and the jib to be hoisted should be hanked on under the hoisted jib. It will save time if the new jib is supplied with its own sheet to eliminate the need of transferring the sheet from one jib to the other. When the boat is tacked, the hoisted jib is lowered when head-to-wind and the bow man hurriedly unsnaps all hanks as the sail comes down. The halyard shackle is transferred by another crew member, the lowered sail is cleared from the top of the one to be hoisted, and the new jib can then be raised. Unless the boat is quite small, it is usually most expeditious to have three men forward, a bow man, halyard man, and an intermediate, when changing Genoas.

There is a new device available for the purpose of speeding up jib changes. This is a preloaded hank magazine called the "Kwick Switch" that holds the jib hanks open so that they run onto the stay when the new jib is hoisted. The device eliminates the need to attach the new jib and to detach the old jib until after its replacement is hoisted. Information and instructions may be obtained from the Dungan Kwick Switch Co., Palmetto, Florida.

Obviously, for greatest speed and efficiency, every part of the sail changing operation should be carefully planned and everything that can be done before the jib is lowered should be done. Hanks should be kept well lubricated to help speed the operation and lessen the time spent when there is no headsail set. Large boats or cutters having a double head rig will usually set a fore-staysail as an interim sail while the jibs are being changed. Even boats without foresails may carry a spinnaker stay-sail as an interim headsail, but in my opinion, on most small boats, this seldom pays and only adds to the confusion on the foredeck.

Distance races usually require frequent headsail changes with the Number 2 or Number 3 Genoa or a double head rig used when it begins to blow. At sea or in rough waters, a high cut jib should be used in order that its foot will not scoop up the leeward bow wave. However, in short, round-the-buoys races it is often too costly to take the time to change jibs when it breezes up in the middle of the race; thus many skippers prefer to leave up the Number 1 Genoa and roll a reef in the main if the boat is equipped with roller reefing. Such a method of shortening sail can be very effective, because the boat will lose little if any speed during the reefing operation, and the sail's TCE will be moved forward to help correct for extra weather helm caused by excessive heeling. The drawbacks of the method are that the large Genoa might scoop up seas, and the sail is difficult to handle in a blow, especially if the winches are under-size and when frequent tacking is antici-pated. Also, it should be kept in mind that when the main halyard has a rope tail, the reefed sail is supported by the strength of the wire-to-rope link-age, and when the halyard is internal (inside the mast), the sail must be supported by the relatively weak linkage of a wire-to-rope splice (as opposed to eye splices). If frequent reefing is anticipated, and especially if the halyard is internal, it is usually wise to use an all wire halyard on a reel winch.

Roller reefing normally requires two crew mem-bers stationed near the mast, where one turns the crank handle which rotates the boom, and the other eases off the halyard and sees that the lower sail slides come off their track as the mainsail is rolled around the boom. Certain types of reel hal-yard winches, however, may require that an extra man be stationed at the mast in the interest of safety, to see that winch handle is securely held during the entire operation (see discussion of reel winches in Chapter 5). Another crew member is

FIGURE 98: SHOCK CORD REEFING

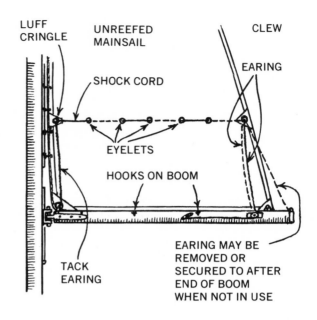

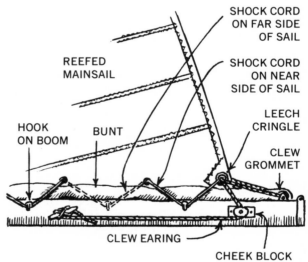

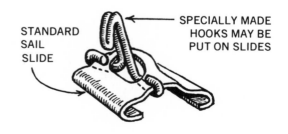

usually needed at the after end of the boom to pull aft on the leech in order to get the smoothest possible roll.

The chief advantages of roller reefing are that the operation is quick, can be done with minimum loss of headway, and the reef is variable (sail can be reduced any amount). The disadvantages are that no cleats, winches, blocks, etc., can be permanently attached to the center of the main boom; the sheet must be attached to the boom's end thereby encouraging the boom to bend in the wrong direction; the tack fitting must usually be set back a fair distance from the mast in order to accommodate the roller reefing gears; the after end of the usual roller reefing boom tends to droop down when a reef is rolled in; and the main will often not roll smoothly because of the sail's draft near its middle. Some of these difficulties can be minimized, however, by using gear of proper size and design.

The roller gear should be large (even oversize) and strong, and the boom must be round or rounded (an oval or rectangular section with corners well rounded). Captain John Illingworth suggests a slight boom taper with the greatest diameter aft in order to keep the after end of the boom from drooping and to improve the set of the sail. The *Finisterre* is equipped with a number of "shims", three foot long wedges tapering from one inch at one end to almost no thickness at the other end. These wedges are inserted at the leech as the sail is rolled around the boom. This gives the same effect as a tapered boom, but care must be taken to keep the sail fairly full to prevent the shims from flying out of the leech when the sail is unrolled. Some skippers prefer to place padding, perhaps soft coils of line, into the pocket between the sail and the boom to fill in the draft curve and to take up slack in the leech when the sail is being rolled if there is a real problem in obtaining a smooth roll. Before rolling in the reef, be sure to slack the boom downhaul, and after the sail is reefed, be sure that the boom's gooseneck slide is at its highest position on the mast track. This will alleviate some of the droopy boom problem. It may be helpful to install an extra Cunningham hole above the primary hole (see Figure 77) in order to avoid using the downhaul to tighten the luff after the sail is reefed.

Care must be taken to see that the sailmaker allows for the exact amount of tack fitting setback.

There has recently been some experimentation with a new type of roller gear that houses the mechanism in the mast to eliminate tack setback. Most standard roller fittings have a hollow area under the tack to accommodate the accumulation of luff rope. It has been suggested that when the main has a taped luff, a towel can be stuffed in at the tack as the sail is being rolled to fill in the space normally occupied by the luff rope. If the main halyard winch is a reel type, it is preferable that it have an adjustable (toggle and screw pin) brake in order that the halyard can be eased gradually. It often helps to have a series of cringles or grommets in the lower leech to facilitate pulling the leech aft with a clew earing to help pull wrinkles out of the sail's foot.

Sailors who feel that there are too many disadvantages with roller reefing usually employ some quick variation of conventional (reef point) reefing. One such variation is the *shock cord reefing* shown in Figure 98. The shock cord (heavy elastic cord) can be rove through conventional reef point eyelets, and it can be stretched down and inserted under hooks on the side of the boom as shown in the illustration. Normal, conventional reefing requires that reef points are tied between the sail and the boom in order that the sail's bolt rope at the foot will equalize the strain on all reef points. But with shock cord reefing, the cord has enough elasticity to allow its being secured directly to the boom. The earings shown in the diagram need not be attached until just prior to reefing. If the leech cringle is too difficult to reach, the earing may be left rigged, but its lower parts may be made fast to the end of the boom so that it will lie abaft the leech and not interfere with the sail when the earing is not in use (see Figure 98).

When reefing is done by this method, the topping lift is set up just enough to take the full weight of the boom off the sail. Then the main is lowered slightly while the tack earing is hauled taut to pull the luff cringle down close to the tack shackle. The luff cringle is secured to the shackle or tack grommet, and then the leech cringle is pulled aft and down and secured to the boom. Notice in the illustration that the cheek block is slightly abaft the clew cringle so that the cringle is pulled aft as well as down. However, it may be advisable to rig another lashing as shown, between the cringle and clew grommet to assure that the leech does not move forward. Most boats with this kind of reefing have a winch mounted on the boom to facilitate tightening the clew earing. After both cringles are secured, the bunt or loose cloth at the foot should be rolled up, placed on top of the boom, and the shock cord hooked to hold the bunt in place. Then the topping lift can be eased. With practice, the operation can be remarkably fast.

A relatively modern innovation is *zipper reefing*. This is essentially the same as any conventional reefing except that the closed zipper holds the area above the bunt down to the boom. The sail is lowered until the two halves of the zipper meet; and after the tack and clew earings are secured, the pin at the end of the zipper teeth is inserted into its slide fastener, and this is pulled aft with a strong lanyard attached to the slide tab to close the zipper. This kind of reefing is said to be simple and very strong, but it might be wise to have an alternate reefing method in case the zipper should jam.

A common method of reducing headsail area on cruising boats is with the use of *roller furling* jibs. Sail is reduced by pulling on a furling line wound around a drum near the jib's tack which rotates the jib's luff wire and thus winds the sail around its luff. Conventional roller furling has not been popular on racing boats primarily because of the unavoidable excessive sag in the jib's luff which is harmful to windward performance. However, a recently improved variation called *Rodluff* has been devised by the Nautical Development Company of Port Washington, N.Y. In this case the usual luff wire is replaced by a solid rod stay which eliminates luff wire twist caused by the winding rotation and reduces luff sag. This makes roller furling practical for some racing-cruisers. Advantages of the method are obviously that headsail area can be reduced quickly and with minimum effort. However, there are several minor and major disadvantages. The sail usually must be left hoisted but entirely wound up on its luff rod when at anchor, and this means that the sail is susceptible to sun rot unless it can be covered. Special light air jibs usually cannot be carried unless they are entirely hankless, and such sails would not perform well to windward. When a roller jib's area is reduced, the vertical position of the CE is changed very little, whereas normally when reducing sail, it is desirable to lower the CE. Also, there is always the unlikely possibility that a roller jib will jam; thus it is not recommended for offshore sailing. Roller furling seems best suited for round the buoy races with short windward legs and when sailing short handed. Whether or not roller furling is used, a rod luff or headstay will often reduce sag, but it will probably be necessary to add a rod backstay to help prevent this stay from stretching. Also, it should be kept in mind that rod stays set up extremely taut put great stresses on the hull and mast.

When your boat is badly overpowered but lacks roller reefing, or roller furling and no time can be spared to reef by a slower means, you might try lowering the main completely. Some boats sail surprisingly well under a Genoa jib alone, especially if the jib has considerable overlap.

Spinnaker Technique

It is assumed that the reader is familiar with the modern parachute spinnaker, that he knows its nomenclature, and that he understands the rudiments of handling the sail. These topics were dealt with by the author in a previous book, *Hand, Reef, and Steer*. What will be discussed here are some of the finer points involved in racing with the spinnaker and handling the sail on a racing-cruiser.

As was said in Chapter 6, the choice of spinnaker cut and weight depend on the number of spinnakers in the sail inventory. If you carry only one 'chute (parachute spinnaker), it should be a versatile sail capable of running or reaching. This should probably be a moderately flat sail of .75 or 1.2 ounce nylon with moderately broad *shoulders* (ample girth near a third or less of the luff distance below the head). When two spinnakers are carried, one might be a light air sail for running, .75 or .5 ounce, with a slightly deeper belly and the other a flatter sail of heavier weight, 1.2 or 1.5 ounce, for reaching in heavier winds. If a third 'chute is carried, this might be smaller and heavier, perhaps 2.2 ounces for a fairly large boat, with narrow shoulders for running in strong winds. For maximum strength, spinnakers should be made of *ripstop* material (cloth with a weave containing a heavier thread every quarter or eighth inch making a pattern of small squares over the whole sail for the purpose of tear resistance).

At present nearly all modern spinnakers are basically cross cut, because this gives maximum projected area, minimizes bias stretch and seam friction on reaches (when the air flows from luff to leech), and gives a leech that can be made more resistant to curling. However, the cloth panels at the head are often arranged in a different, more intricate way such as the radical arrangement shown in Figure 99. It is generally agreed that a fairly spherical spinnaker (looking roundish when viewed from the front or back) is the most successful shape when considering the combination of projected area, maximum drag, versatility in reaching and running, and *spinnaker stability* (freedom from oscillations). The leading handicap measurement rules, however, put a limit of 180 percent of J on spinnaker girth, and this gives a cylindrical shaped, banana-topped sail when viewed from the side (see Figure 99), a sail that is about the same girth from its foot to about a third of its luff length below the head. Although any parachute spinnaker is a poor shape for close reaching, it may pay to carry a spherical 'chute in light winds on a one-design boat when the apparent wind is quite far forward of the beam, because the area of this sail is far greater than that of the usual one-design's jib. On a racing-cruiser, however, it seldom pays to carry the smaller handicap spinnaker much above a beam reach, when a large jib shaped for close reaching efficiency can be carried. Sometimes a flat, heavy weather spinnaker with narrow shoulders can be carried on a fairly close reach with the outboard end of the pole dropped as low as it will go to tighten the luff (rules forbid securing the tack to the stemhead). Such a sail is often called a *spanker*. The sail is sometimes fitted with a Cunningham hole just above the tack cringle to help tighten the luff for close reaching. The spanker is actually a symmetrical spinnaker that can be converted to a large reaching jib.

There are several fundamental rules for trimming the spinnaker. For the sake of speed, simplicity, and efficiency, it is a good plan to set the sail initially in accordance with these rules and then vary the trim to suit specific conditions. In other words, the fundamentals should be used, not as an inflexible dictum, but as a point of departure for subsequent fine adjustments. The rules are as follows: (1) The chord of the spinnaker should be about parallel with the chord of the correctly trimmed mainsail (sailing between a beam reach and dead run), (2) the pole should be more or less squared (at a ninety degree angle) to the apparent wind, (3) the pole should be level or cocked up slightly, and its inboard end should be at the highest position on the mast except in light airs, (4) the clew should be level with or only slightly lower

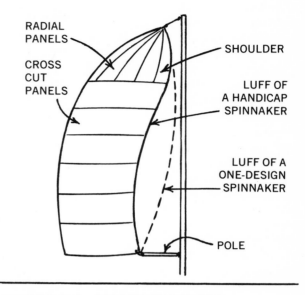

FIGURE 99: HANDICAP SPINNAKER

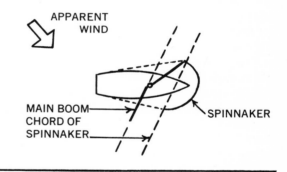

FIGURE 100: SPINNAKER CHORD POSITION

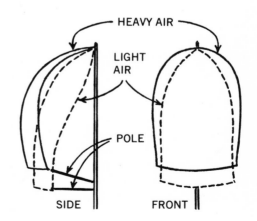

FIGURE 101: SPINNAKER DRAFT

than the tack, and (5) the halyard should be eased slightly in fresh winds.

The first rule is explained in Figure 100. In my opinion, this is probably the most basic preliminary consideration, although it should not be taken absolutely literally. When sailing lower than a beam reach and higher than a dead run, the spinnaker's chord should be aligned so that it is nearly parallel to the main boom when the mainsail is trimmed to utilize optimum drag (as discussed in Chapter 6). Reciprocally, of course, the main boom can be adjusted to agree with a correctly positioned spinnaker chord. However, when sailing near a beam reach care must be taken to see that the spinnaker doesn't significantly backwind the mainsail.

The rule of keeping the pole squared to the apparent wind is a very good one, but it should not be absolutely hard and fast. At least a few experts advocate carrying the pole slightly further forward in moderate winds for the reason that this allows maximum easing of the sheet and moves the chute forward away from the mainsail. Certainly it is true that when the wind and the pole are well aft, the chord of the spinnaker cannot be kept parallel to the mainsail's chord, and a narrow handicap 'chute may not be able to produce maximum drag acting in the direction in which the boat is moving. Of course, we want to use maximum drag rather than lift when running (see "Sail Trim" in Chapter 6). If the pole is angled a little forward of being squared to the apparent wind, however, care must be taken to see that the spinnaker is not blanketed by the main. This is especially true in light airs. For this reason and the fact that the upper area of the 'chute may sag forward of being squared to the wind in light airs, some successful sailors prefer to slightly over-square the pole (bring it a little further aft), but only when the wind is light. In heavy winds it may pay to under-square the pole (ease it further forward) for better steering control especially if the boat is tending to heel or take knockdowns to windward.

The spinnaker should be encouraged to lift in all but the lightest airs or very strong winds when steering control becomes a problem. In order that the sail be allowed maximum upward lift, the inboard end of the pole should be at its highest position on the pole track (attached to the fore side of the mast) when the strength of wind is sufficient to support the weight of the sail or keep it well lifted. In light airs, however, the wind will not have

the strength to lift the sail, and thus the inboard end of the pole should be lowered. The pole should be kept level (horizontal when the boat is unheeled) to take advantage of the pole's full length thereby keeping the spinnaker tack the maximum distance away from the mast. There are several exceptions to the rule, however. In fresh winds, the pole's outboard end might be cocked up slightly to give the sail extra upward lift when the inboard end is at the top of its track, and in order that the pole follow the same angle the guy makes with the deck to help equalize strains on the pole lift and downhaul (foreguy). In very strong winds, however, when the spinnaker has excessive lift, it may pay to lower the outboard end of the pole below the level of the inboard end in order to flatten the sail and so that the angle of the guy exerts a downward pull to help equalize the extra upward pull of the lifting spinnaker. It might even pay to rig a forward lead block, perhaps near the shrouds, for the guy to increase its downward pull.

The modern spinnaker's draft is largely controlled by the up and down position of the pole. Raising the pole and thus raising the sail's foot slacks the leeches, widens the shoulders, and flattens the draft; while lowering the sail tightens the leeches and especially the luff, narrows the shoulders, and increases the cross sectional curvature or luff to leech draft. This is one reason why it often pays to keep the pole low in light airs, to increase the spinnaker's draft. Generally speaking, the foot should be raised when reaching in moderate winds, but lowered when running in light airs. The effect on spinnaker shape of raising and lowering the foot is illustrated in Figure 101.

The pole should never be raised to such an extent that the tack is considerably higher (perhaps no more than seven percent of the luff length higher) than the clew because this will create a lopsided and thus less effective spinnaker shape. Using a lightweight sail and light sheets without shackles will permit the maximum amount of clew lift. Raising the main boom on its gooseneck track will not only increase the mainsail draft, which is desirable when running, but it will allow the spinnaker sheet passing under the boom to rise up which in turn will let the 'chute's clew fly higher. When the 'chute's clew and leech are badly hooking inboard and backwinding the mainsail, it will often pay to lead the spinnaker sheet through a block at the end of the main boom, similarly to the way a high cut reaching jib is usually led.

The spinnaker halyard should be eased a foot or more in fresh breezes to move the sail's head away from the mainsail. The amount of easing will primarily depend on the strength of wind. Usually the halyard should not be eased when this lowers the head. There should be sufficient wind to make the head move almost horizontally away from the spinnaker halyard block. The head should be only slightly lower than the level of the block. Easing the sheet, guy, and halyard will move the entire spinnaker forward which will help the sail avoid the main's blanket and move the CE of the sail plan forward. This can be helpful to steering control while running, but if the spinnaker begins to oscillate, the halyard at least should be *two-blocked,* (the sail should be hoisted all the way up). Furthermore, in a strong wind, the 'chute should be flattened with its sheet and by lowering the pole for better control.

If the halyard can be sufficiently eased on a reach, a large jib might be carried effectively simultaneously with the spinnaker. This is sometimes referred to as the *double slot,* where there is a slot between the spinnaker and jib and also between the jib and main. It requires a good breeze so that the halyard can be eased generously, perhaps two or three feet, the pole must be well lifted to flatten the 'chute and get its luff and leech to leeward, and the sheet's lead should be far aft. This sail combination is most effective on or just below a beam reach. When the wind is further aft, a jib will often interfere with the spinnaker, but when the breeze is sufficient to lift the 'chute, a spinnaker staysail, especially the bald-headed type (see Figure 69), can fill in the lower space efficiently. Usually however, even this staysail will not draw effectively when the wind is on the stern. Lately, some success has been had with tall narrow staysails *(tallboys* or *ribbon staysails)* tacked to the weather rail near the mid foredeck, thus avoiding the mainsail's blanket while running. Such a sail might also be used effectively to damp rolling when the leech is brought in close proximity to the mainmast with the chord of the staysail aimed slightly forward at an angle of about sixty degrees to the boat's centerline.

When sailing in unsteady, shifty winds, the spinnaker's trim or the boat's heading must be constantly changed to meet the changes of wind direction and velocity. Most successful racers use a combination of changing course and trim. The helmsman bears off in the puffs and heads up in the lulls, and of course, he bears off when headed and heads up slightly when the shift is lifting (coming from further astern). He must be careful not to sail so high that the spinnaker luff begins to break, nor should he sail so low that the spinnaker becomes blanketed by the main. Either of these extremes of sailing too high or too low can cause the sail to collapse completely. At the same time, while the helmsman is making moderate course alterations, a competent crew member should be playing the sheet. This man, the sheet trimmer, is as important as the helmsman. He should keep the spinnaker luff *on edge* (on the verge of luffing), and he is primarily responsible for preventing the 'chute from collapsing. The sheet should be kept eased until the luff begins to roll inward. A quick tug on the sheet can prevent the luff from breaking. The sheet trimmer should be stationed forward, perhaps near the main shrouds, when reaching so that he can see the spinnaker and watch a wind indicator at the same time. In light to moderate winds, he can put a turn or two of the sheet around its winch and then lead it forward. In heavy winds, a secondary trimmer can be stationed aft near the winch, while the primary trimmer stands forward, calls instructions to the secondary man, and pulls down on the sheet when the luff begins to curl. If the sheet is too far outboard for the primary trimmer to reach with his hand, he can use a *snatch line* or *tweaker* (a short line attached to the sheet for the purpose of pulling it in or down to prevent the luff from breaking).

It is important that the helmsman constantly refer to his wind indicators (telltales or especially the masthead indicator) in order that he change course to keep the pole nearly square with the apparent wind. Of course, this is also accomplished by adjusting the guy. Perhaps the greatest difference between cruising and racing with the spinnaker is the amount of pole and guy adjustment. On a cruiser, the guy is usually anchored or rarely adjusted; but on a racer, especially when the helmsman alters course only slightly, the guy is more constantly adjusted in order to keep the 'chute properly positioned to the apparent wind. Another adjustment that should be made frequently is the pole height. Generally speaking, the pole should go up on a reach and in puffs, but it should be lower when running and during lulls in accordance with the draft alterations mentioned earlier. It almost never pays, by the way, to run dead before the wind except in fresh winds.

It might be considered that there are two basic means of setting the spinnaker: by stopping it, or by setting it from a turtle or bag. The first method consists of rolling or bunching the leeches together and binding them at about two or three foot intervals from head to foot with weak cotton thread so that the entire sail resembles a long, thin sausage usually with two thin legs (representing the stopped clews) at the bottom. The stopped sail is then hoisted, and the sail is broken out (the stops broken) by hauling aft on the sheet. Formerly, this was the commonly accepted manner of setting a spinnaker, but the method is very rarely used today except on large boats in heavy weather. It is usually far quicker and simpler to set the sail from a turtle or bag.

There is little if any difference between setting from a turtle or a sail bag because the bag is actually a kind of turtle. About the only difference is that the turtle (a spinnaker setting container in the form of a specially designed bag, box, or bucket) is often secured forward of the jib stay, but when an ordinary sail bag is used in lieu of a turtle, the bag is generally secured abaft the jib stay on the foredeck just forward of the mast. This method of using the ordinary sail bag on the foredeck is very popular, and it is shown in Figure 102.

Before preparing the spinnaker for setting, it first must be determined which tack the boat will be on after rounding the windward turning mark when the boat is on the desired downwind heading. This may be figured mentally, or by watching boats that have rounded ahead of you, or by laying out the next course on the chart and drawing in the direction of the true wind. Figure 102 shows a boat approaching the turning mark on the starboard tack. It illustrates how the spinnaker is prepared for hoisting when the boat is to remain on the starboard tack after rounding, with the pole rigged to be carried on the starboard side (drawing A), and it also shows how the 'chute is prepared when the boat will jibe onto the port tack after rounding, with her pole rigged to be carried on the port side (drawing B). The preparation shown in B would also be correct if the turning mark were to be left to starboard, requiring a tack at the mark with the downwind course to be sailed on the port tack.

The first step in preparing the 'chute for hoisting is to see that it is properly bagged or turtled. This requires that the leeches be folded together uncrossed before bagging in order to prevent the sail from becoming twisted when it is hoisted. A recommended procedure is to dump the loose sail on a bunk down below where it is out of the way and protected from the wind, and then have a crew member or two pull the two leeches together, starting at the head and working towards the foot. The two side-by-side leeches are neatly accordian folded until a short distance from the foot. Then the two clews are pulled apart, and the loose bulk of the sail is stuffed into the bag followed by the folded leeches, but the three corners of the sail (the head and clews) are left hanging out of the bag's top. Next, the draw string at the mouth of the bag is pulled taut and tied with a slip knot, and the bagged sail is taken to the foredeck where it is secured to a deck eye or cleat with a lanyard made fast to the bag's bottom. After this, the three corners are shackled or tied to their respective lines as shown in Figure 102.

Notice in the diagram that the guy is led around the jib stay and that the outboard end of the pole is hooked onto the guy. This is the way it is usually done. After the 'chute is hoisted, the guy is pulled aft and this hauls the tack of the sail close to the pole and then pulls the pole aft to its desired position. However, if it is desired to snap the pole onto the ring of the guy's swivel shackle (see Figure 103) in the interest of minimizing chafe on the guy (or for some other reason), the bag must be moved closer to the jib stay and the tack of the 'chute should then be carried around the stay where it is secured to the guy shackle to which the pole is attached. Of course, the guy and sheet should be led aft outboard of the shrouds. These lines together with the halyard should be led over (not under or through) the life lines up forward, but the sheet and guy usually must lead under the life lines aft to reach their lead blocks.

Although the spinnaker is occasionally hoisted to windward of the jib on small racing boats, this is rarely done on a larger racing-cruiser, except perhaps in very light airs when the wind is well aft. The accepted practice is to hoist the 'chute to leeward of the jib, as illustrated. This prevents the sail from fouling on the jib stay, and it provides a lee for the 'chute behind the jib. Of course, it usually pays to drop the jib quickly after the spinnaker is hoisted, unless the wind is well forward

FIGURE 102: PREPARING THE 'CHUTE FOR HOISTING

A—POLE SET TO STARBOARD

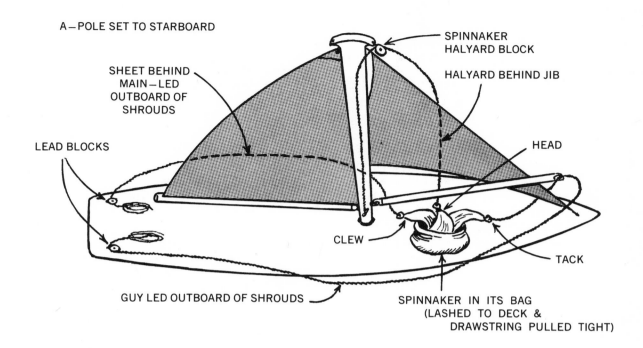

SPINNAKER HALYARD BLOCK

HALYARD BEHIND JIB

SHEET BEHIND MAIN—LED OUTBOARD OF SHROUDS

HEAD

LEAD BLOCKS

CLEW

TACK

GUY LED OUTBOARD OF SHROUDS

SPINNAKER IN ITS BAG (LASHED TO DECK & DRAWSTRING PULLED TIGHT)

B—POLE TO BE SET TO PORT

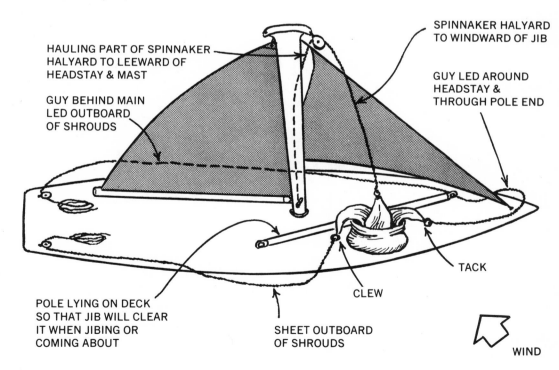

SPINNAKER HALYARD TO WINDWARD OF JIB

HAULING PART OF SPINNAKER HALYARD TO LEEWARD OF HEADSTAY & MAST

GUY LED AROUND HEADSTAY & THROUGH POLE END

GUY BEHIND MAIN LED OUTBOARD OF SHROUDS

TACK

POLE LYING ON DECK SO THAT JIB WILL CLEAR IT WHEN JIBING OR COMING ABOUT

CLEW

SHEET OUTBOARD OF SHROUDS

WIND

155

and strong enough to allow a double slot sail combination. Notice in Figure 102 A that the halyard runs behind the jib. B's halyard will also be to leeward of the jib after she has jibed or tacked.

The pole lift and downhaul (foreguy), are not shown in Figure 102 for the sake of simplifying and clarifying the drawing, but obviously these lines must be attached to the pole. Two popular ways of rigging the pole are shown in Figure 103. Arrangement A, with the lift and downhaul attached to the pole's middle, is the simplest and often the most satisfactory method for small and even medium-sized boats, but arrangement B, with a bridle and downhaul attached near the pole's end, is often preferable on larger boats and when there is a great deal of strain on the pole. Incidentally, the pole lift should not be rigged in Figure 102 B until after the jibe or tack has been completed so that the jib will not foul the lift.

On racing-cruisers, there are really two different basic methods used to jibe the 'chute: *end-for-ending the pole* and the *dip-pole jibe* (sometimes called the *free-wheeling jibe*). The first method is illustrated in Figure 104. Of course this requires a pole with similar fittings at each end, and matters are simplified when the lift and downhaul are rigged from the pole's middle as shown in the illustration. As can be seen, the inboard end of the pole is unhooked from the mast and is hooked onto the sheet (or shackle ring). At the mid-point of the jibe, the pole is not attached to the mast at all, but to each clew of the 'chute or to the guy and sheet. The pole end that is attached to the former guy (the new sheet after jibing) or its shackle ring is then detached from the corner of the sail, and it is hooked onto the mast. Thus where one end of the pole was connected to the mast on one tack, the other end is connected on the opposite tack.

Although the illustration shows only one man on the foredeck, larger boats may require another crew member or more up forward to help handle the pole. Generally speaking, however, it is a good policy to use the least number of men forward who can do the job efficiently, in the interest of keeping excess weight off the foredeck. Furthermore, there should be ample crew in the cockpit for jibing the main and for the all important jobs of handling the sheet and guy. The lines should be adjusted so as to keep the chord of the 'chute more or less square to the wind during the jibing operation, and the sheet should be trimmed promptly after jibing.

Figure 105 illustrates the principle of the dip-pole jibe. As can be seen, this method differs from end-for-ending in that the pole remains connected to the mast during the entire operation and the spinnaker clews are attached to the same pole end fitting on each tack. Dip-poling usually requires that the inboard end of the pole be raised to its highest position on the mast in order that the pole can be swung from one side of the boat to the other, with the outboard end having clearance to swing under the jib stay. Figure 105 shows two men on the foredeck, but another man will be needed to control the pole lift. Of course, he would be stationed at the mast if the lift is cleated on the mast, or stationed at the fore end of the cockpit if the lift is controlled from the cockpit area. This man has an important duty to see that the pole is lowered at the right moment to pass under the jib stay but without "beaning" a crew member on the foredeck.

In step A of Figure 105, the pole is eased forward where crew member number 1, the bow man, can reach the tripping lanyard (see Figure 103) and release the outboard pole end from the guy. Meanwhile crew member number 2 grabs the sheet and pulls it slightly forward and inboard. In step B, crew number 1 has helped the pole under the jib stay and has received the sheet (which will become the new guy) from crew number 2 who then crosses over to the opposite side of the boat where he grabs the new sheet (former guy). It may be necessary for crew number 2 to help crew number 1 attach the pole to the new guy before crossing over to the boat's other side. In fresh winds it is a good idea to use a jibing line as illustrated to get sufficient slack in the guy for easy attachment. Whether or not number 1 will need help may depend on several factors, an important one being the design of the pole end fitting. The trigger fitting shown in Figure 103 can greatly simplify the pole to guy attachment. Most agree that the spring loaded pin on a pole end fitting should be facing upward, as shown in Figure 103 B, for quick release and connection of the guy, but many sailors prefer that the pin face down on the end-for-end jibe to facilitate hooking the pole to the mast. In step C of Figure 105, crew number 1 has hooked the pole to the guy, and number 2 pulls aft on the sheet helping to keep the chord of the 'chute nearly square to the wind. The main should be slacked off slowly to prevent it from blanketing the 'chute

FIGURE 103: DETAILS OF SPINNAKER POLES & FITTINGS

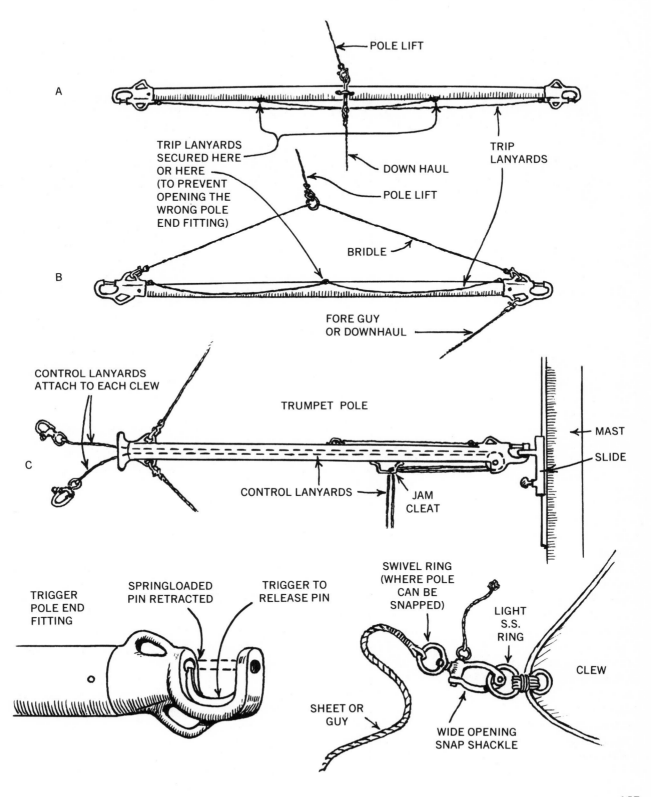

POLE LIFT

A

TRIP LANYARDS
SECURED HERE
OR HERE
(TO PREVENT
OPENING THE
WRONG POLE
END FITTING)

DOWN HAUL

POLE LIFT

TRIP
LANYARDS

BRIDLE

B

FORE GUY
OR DOWNHAUL

CONTROL LANYARDS
ATTACH TO EACH CLEW

TRUMPET POLE

MAST

SLIDE

C

CONTROL LANYARDS

JAM
CLEAT

TRIGGER
POLE END
FITTING

SPRINGLOADED
PIN RETRACTED

TRIGGER TO
RELEASE PIN

SWIVEL RING
(WHERE POLE
CAN BE
SNAPPED)

LIGHT
S.S.
RING

CLEW

SHEET OR
GUY

WIDE OPENING
SNAP SHACKLE

157

FIGURE 104: THE END-FOR-END JIBE

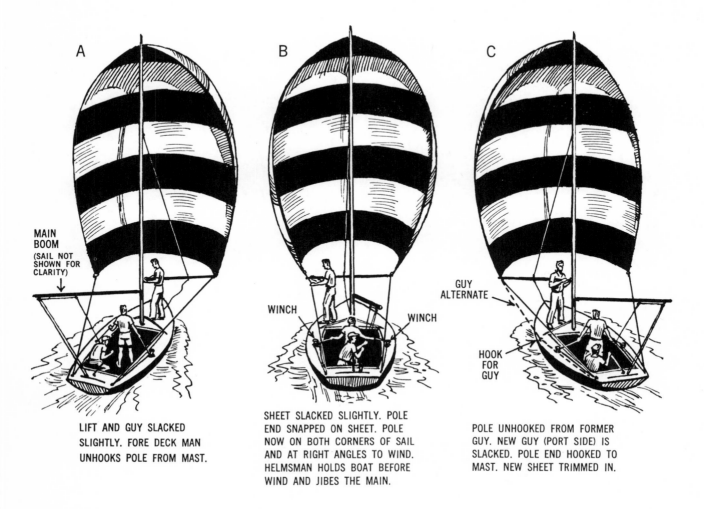

A

MAIN BOOM
(SAIL NOT SHOWN FOR CLARITY)

LIFT AND GUY SLACKED
SLIGHTLY. FORE DECK MAN
UNHOOKS POLE FROM MAST.

B

WINCH   WINCH

SHEET SLACKED SLIGHTLY. POLE
END SNAPPED ON SHEET. POLE
NOW ON BOTH CORNERS OF SAIL
AND AT RIGHT ANGLES TO WIND.
HELMSMAN HOLDS BOAT BEFORE
WIND AND JIBES THE MAIN.

C

GUY ALTERNATE

HOOK FOR GUY

POLE UNHOOKED FROM FORMER
GUY. NEW GUY (PORT SIDE) IS
SLACKED. POLE END HOOKED TO
MAST. NEW SHEET TRIMMED IN.

before the pole has been guyed aft and the boat turned onto her new course.

On big boats in heavy weather it is common practice to rig double sheets and guys (two lines from each clew) to facilitate dip-pole jibing. This method has several variations, but these are similar in basic principle. One variation is shown in Figure 106, method 1, which shows a jibe from starboard to port tack. In step 1, the sheet, A, is taut while the extra sheet, C, is slack. When the pole is swung under the jib stay in step 2, the bight of the slack sheet C is carried forward (outside the shrouds) and attached to the pole end, and this line becomes the new guy in step 3. In the meanwhile, old guy B (formerly carried slack while extra guy D took the strain) is now pulled taut and becomes the new sheet while D is carried slack. With this method, the line with the aftermost lead block is used for the sheet, but the line with the lead block located further forward becomes the guy.

There is another variation sometimes referred to as the *lazy guy* or *interim guy* method where the sheet and guy both use the aftermost leads and the extra guy is only used as an interim line to hold the spinnaker's clew that will become the tack on completing the jibe. By this method, line C takes the strain in step 1 (Figure 106, method 1) while A is slacked off and its bight carried forward where it is hooked to the pole end (the same way C is rigged in step 2). After the jibe, A takes the strain again and C is slacked off.

Still another method of dip-poling is shown in Figure 106. This makes use of a *trumpet pole* (illustrated in Figure 103) or a similar type pole

FIGURE 105: DIP-POLE JIBE FOR MEDIUM SIZE RACING-CRUISERS

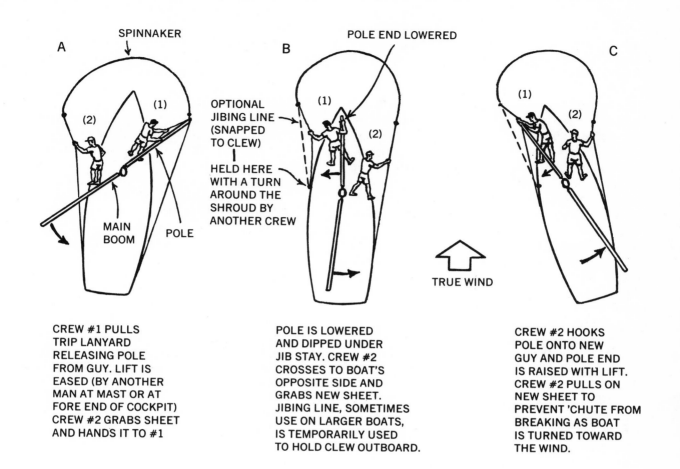

CREW #1 PULLS
TRIP LANYARD
RELEASING POLE
FROM GUY. LIFT IS
EASED (BY ANOTHER
MAN AT MAST OR AT
FORE END OF COCKPIT)
CREW #2 GRABS SHEET
AND HANDS IT TO #1

POLE IS LOWERED
AND DIPPED UNDER
JIB STAY. CREW #2
CROSSES TO BOAT'S
OPPOSITE SIDE AND
GRABS NEW SHEET.
JIBING LINE, SOMETIMES
USE ON LARGER BOATS,
IS TEMPORARILY USED
TO HOLD CLEW OUTBOARD.

CREW #2 HOOKS
POLE ONTO NEW
GUY AND POLE END
IS RAISED WITH LIFT.
CREW #2 PULLS ON
NEW SHEET TO
PREVENT 'CHUTE FROM
BREAKING AS BOAT
IS TURNED TOWARD
THE WIND.

FIGURE 106: DOUBLE LINE METHODS OF DIP-POLING

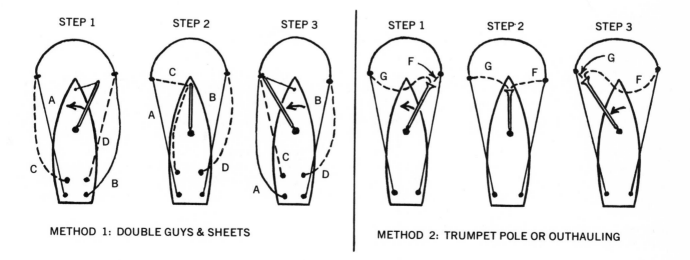

METHOD 1: DOUBLE GUYS & SHEETS

METHOD 2: TRUMPET POLE OR OUTHAULING

with internal (or external) *controlling lanyards* or *outhaulers*. In step 1 (Figure 106, method 2) controlling lanyard F is slacked while G is hauled taut at the inboard end of the pole (these lines run through the pole as shown in Figure 103). The pole is then dipped and moved over to the 'chute's other clew.

Experienced sailors do not always agree on which basic jibing method is the most effective, but generally speaking, end-for-ending seems most appropriate for small or perhaps medium-sized boats, when the lift and downhaul are rigged from the pole's middle, when jibing from one running course to another, and when the wind is not very strong. Dip-poling seems more suitable on large boats, when the downhaul and pole lift is rigged to the pole's outboard end, when the pole end fittings differ, when making a wide-turning jibe (jibing from a run to a reach or reach to a reach), and when it is blowing hard.

The generally accepted means of handing or lowering the 'chute is to first hoist the jib (if it is not already up), then to guy the pole all the way forward, release the tack shackle, and let the tack fly off to leeward. The helmsman holds the boat on a somewhat downwind course, if possible, to help blanket the sail, and it is hauled down under the main by the leech and stuffed down the companionway. As the leech is hauled down, the foot is gathered in to keep the sail out of the water. The luff must be allowed to fly off to leeward so the sail cannot fill. In a very light breeze when on a dead run or nearly so, it may pay to lower the spinnaker on the windward side by detaching the pole from the mast, sliding it aft, and hauling the 'chute in by its tack instead of its clew. If there is any strength in the wind, however, the sail should be handed in the lee of the jib. The man who lowers should always keep a turn of the halyard around a winch or cleat if the wind is fresh. When approaching a downwind turning mark beginners often wait until the last minute to lower the 'chute, and sometimes they are carried beyond the mark. Try to approach the mark on a broad reach so that the spinnaker can be lowered early. If the mark is approached with the wind slightly forward of the quarter, the jib can be made to draw effectively, and this will permit an earlier handing of the 'chute.

The following is an abbreviated list of frequently encountered spinnaker difficulties with a few suggestions on avoidance and/or rectifications. Of course, it goes without saying that these troubles can be minimized with careful planning and much practice.

(1) PREMATURE FILLING (the 'chute filling before it is fully hoisted and cleated): *Cause*– Failure to keep the 'chute completely blanketed while hoisting or the twine breaking too soon when the sail is stopped. *Avoidance*– Keep the jib up while hoisting and steer off the wind. A *"Zip-R-Turtle"* can be a help. This is a substitute for stopping, and it consists of a zipper whose two halves are stitched about a foot apart up the sail's centerline from the head to a point just above the foot. That part of the sail between the zipper's halves forms a tube which holds the "gathered" or bundled body of the sail after the two zipper halves have been closed. The zipper is opened by trimming the sheet. Most sailmakers can install the device, and they supply complete operational instructions. If the 'chute is stopped, consider using fairly heavy twine with a special breaking line rigged under the stops to break them. In strong winds hoist the 'chute with a turn of its halyard around a winch. *Rectification*– If the 'chute should fill prematurely while you are hoisting it, quickly put a turn of the halyard around the nearest cleat or winch, and tell the helmsman to bear off and blanket the sail at once.

(2) FOULED HALYARD (spinnaker halyard wrapped around the headstay aloft): *Cause*– Many boats carry shackles at both ends of the halyard so that the 'chute can be hoisted with either end. When the halyard straddles the headstay (as in Figure 102A) the leeward end is sometimes carried forward to get it behind the jib when preparing the 'chute for hoisting. This will make the halyard wrap the stay, and it is perhaps the most usual cause of fouling. *Avoidance*– Carry the leeward end of the halyard around behind the leech of the jib) before attaching it to the head of the 'chute or carry the windward end of the halyard around the headstay being sure that the spinnaker block swivels. It is often a good plan to hook the halyard to the bow pulpit just before hoisting, but don't carry it there permanently, because it causes harmful

160

windage when beating. Always look aloft to see that everything is clear before hoisting.

Rectification– jibe onto the tack that mitigates the halyard's wrap, and haul the 'chute down in the lee of the main. Normally, this would mean that if the 'chute were set on the starboard tack it should be handed on the port tack.

(3) CHAFED HALYARD:

Cause– When on the same tack for lengthy periods, especially at sea in rough waters or ground swell, the hauling part of the halyard to windward of the headstay is apt to chafe on the stay.

Avoidance– Take the hauling part of the halyard to leeward of the stay. See that the spinnaker block is on a crane or bolt (see Figure 62) that holds it well clear of the headstay. Be sure to check the legal limits allowed by your handicap rule, however (for instance, MORC does not allow a spinnaker halyard block to be mounted ahead of a point $.012 \times P_2$ forward of the foreside of the mast).

Rectification– If the halyard is badly chafed, it should be replaced. This can often be done without going aloft by *marrying* the new halyard to the old one. The two halyards are sewn together, end-to-end. Then the old halyard is pulled through its block, and this automatically reeves through the new halyard.

(4) HOUR-GLASSED SPINNAKER (a twist more or less halfway up the 'chute that prevents the sail's middle from filling. Above and below the twist, however, the sail fills out or balloons, and this makes it look like an hour glass):

Cause– Improper turtling or bagging or improper hoisting.

Avoidance– Be sure the leeches lie together when the sail is bagged, and be sure there is a swivel at the head of the sail. Have a crew member help the sail out of its bag during the hoisting, and keep tension on the sheet. "Zip-R-Turtles" can help with this problem also.

Rectification– If the twist is not too far down from the head it can very often be cleared by slacking the halyard slightly and giving it several quick jerks. This will often cause the swivel to turn and the sail to untwist. A twist near the bottom might be cleared in light airs by slightly slacking the halyard and interchanging the tack and clew under the lee of the jib, but don't try this in a strong wind. If neither of these methods work the sail must be lowered to be cleared.

(5) HEADSTAY WRAP. (This occurs when the middle part or belly of the sail wraps around the headstay):

Cause– The spinnaker is particularly vulnerable to wrapping in rough water and damp air when the sail collapses and lies against the headstay.

Avoidance– Try to keep the chute full by paying close attention to helmsmanship (especially avoid sailing by the lee in light winds) and sheet trim. Also, be extra careful when jibing in a seaway. Be sure the jib is hoisted while handing or hoisting the 'chute. A fool proof way of preventing a wrap is to set a *spinnaker net* (a network of lines or cloth tapes hoisted in the fore triangle as shown in Figure 107). Of course a spinnaker net can be troublesome on a short race; thus many boats carry two or three *anti-wrap lines* (also illustrated in the Figure 107). These are lines, usually of shock cord, permanently rigged from the mast to rings or slides on the headstay. When the jib is hoisted, its top hank carries the rings or slides aloft, thereby hoisting the lines out of the jib's way.

Rectification– There is not always a sure way to recover from a bad wrap. A few spinnakers have had to be cut away with a knife, but these were extreme cases. When the wrap first occurs, try jibing at once to get the wind that caused the wrap on the boat's other side, but hold a course before the wind. The sail may unwrap itself. If this doesn't work, it may be possible to detach the tack and clew, bring them together, and bodily unwind the sail. The jib halyard should always be detached from the lowered jib when the 'chute is hoisted, because the halyard could also get wrapped, and the sail could become pinched between the halyard and stay. Also, the halyard might have to be used to send a man aloft in a bosun's chair to clear the wrap.

(6) BREAKING THE POLE:

Cause-(a) Improper rigging of the pole lift and downhaul (foreguy), (b) allowing the pole to strike or bear too hard against the headstay, (c) compression on the pole when beam reaching.

Avoidance-The lift and guy should be rigged from the same position on the pole as shown in Figure 103 A or B. It is safer to use rig B in strong winds when there is great upward pressure from the lifting spinnaker. Try to equalize upward and downward pressures by raising or lowering the outboard end of the pole or changing the guy lead. Keep the pole from bearing hard against the headstay by keeping sufficient tension on the guy. Use prestretched dacron or in some cases wire for guys. Keeping the outboard end of the pole low will give the pole more resistance to breaking against the headstay. Pole compression results from the guy pulling aft when the pole is guyed all the way forward. This problem can be solved by using a *reaching strut* illustrated in Figure 108. The strut holds the guy away from the windward shrouds thus preventing chafe, reducing the pole's pressure against the headstay, and reducing compression by increasing the angle between the pole and the guy.

Rectification-A broken pole must be replaced, but if the pole is only slightly damaged or cracked, a temporary repair might be made by tightly binding wood splints to each side of the pole at the damaged area.

(7) SPINNAKER KNOCKDOWNS (these can occur to leeward or windward):

Cause- A windward knockdown occurring in a strong wind can be caused by guying the spinnaker too far aft while running, by slackening the sheet too much, and even by insufficient use of the main boom vang which allows a bad twist at the head of the mainsail. Leeward knockdowns occurring in strong winds can be caused by trimming the sheet too flat while the pole is guyed forward and the boat is steered too high.

Avoidance and Rectification-To avoid windward knockdowns, flatten the 'chute by trimming the sheet, guy the pole further forward, and head up. To avoid leeward knockdowns ease the sheet when the boat begins

FIGURE 107: SPINNAKER NETS

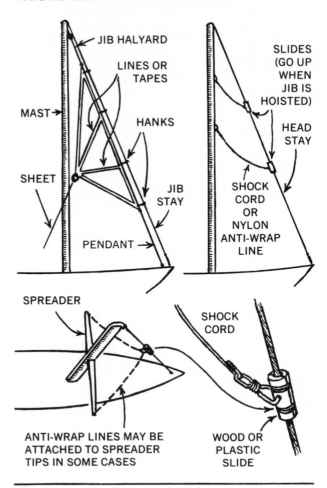

FIGURE 108: REACHING STRUT

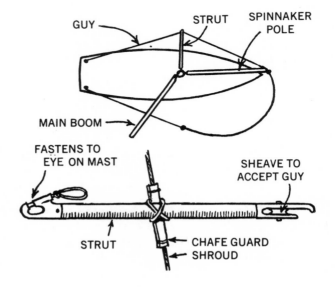

162

to heel and bear off to gain stability. If the boat begins to heel severely and broach to, slack the spinnaker sheet all the way. Have a man standing by to slack the vang to prevent tripping on the main boom. If the spinnaker sheet becomes submerged so that it cannot be reached in a severe knockdown, ease the guy until the pole is against the headstay, and then release it so the line will run through the pole end fitting and allow the chute to spill its wind.

(8) STEERING AND CONTROL PROBLEMS:
Cause-(a) Carrying the chute in too much wind and/or in heavy seas, (b) poor spinnaker design, (c) rudder too far forward on a hull having a short keel.
Avoidance-Flatten the 'chute by lowering pole, overtrimming the sheet, and two-blocking the halyard. Use a small, flat spinnaker with narrow shoulders. Be sure the main boom is well vanged. Tillers give a quicker helm response than wheels, skegs help directional stability, and spade or after-mounted rudders are beneficial to steering control. When there is a tendency to roll rhythmically or yaw, try to avoid violent rudder changes as this only aggravates the tendency. Don't fight the helm but use an easy, minimal helm action.
Rectification-According to C. A. Marchaj, recent wind tunnel tests have shown that steering by the lee may help (provided there is no tendency to knockdown or to collapse the 'chute from blanketing), but be sure to rig a preventer to avoid an accidental jib. A tall, narrow, staysail rigged to windward as described earlier may damp the rolling. If the boat cannot be controlled, use a boomed-out jib instead of the spinnaker. Setting this sail is usually done most simply by setting the pole to windward, keeping the jib blanketed under the lee of the main, and outhauling the jib's clew to the outboard end of the pole.

(9) HANDING DIFFICULTIES:
Cause-(a) tack shackle jamming from wind pressure, (b) sheet getting away from the man tending it after the tack has been released, (c) halyard getting away from its tender, (d) the 'chute going overboard or blowing aft as it is being lowered.

Avoidance and Rectification-Consider using wide opening snap shackles hinged near the apex to open a full 180 degrees on the guy and sheet (see Figure 103). Fit the shackle pull pins with strong, heavy lanyards. A few boats use a sacrificial rope ring at each clew so that the rope can be cut if the shackle cannot be opened. Another emergency solution is to uncleat the guy and let it run through the pole end.

If the sheet gets away from its tender after the tack is released, the 'chute will stream from the mast head like a flag. This is the reason I prefer to knot the end of the sheet, although some will disagree with me on the grounds that this may not allow the sheet sufficient slack to spill the 'chute completely. However, when the sheet has adequate length (twice the over-all length of the boat is the rule of thumb), a knot at the very end of the line jamming in the lead block should allow ample spillage. If not, the guy can be released or in a real emergency, the sheet or guy could be cut.

As said before, the man who lowers the chute in a breeze should have a turn on the winch or cleat. He must watch the men handing the sail and lower no faster than they can take it in. The sail should be handed by one leech and the foot only to prevent its filling, and it should be smothered and stuffed below immediately. On yawls especially, the 'chute should not be allowed to blow aft as it could descend on the mizzen. To avoid this, the helmsman should head off, if possible, until the sail is lowered.
Rectification—If the sheet should happen to escape from its tender after the tack has been released causing the 'chute to fly free from the masthead, then the best course of action is usually to run dead before the wind to lessen the apparent wind and to blanket the 'chute with the main. Then perhaps a crew member at the stem can hook the loose sheet with a boat hook. If the 'chute should happen to go overboard, haul it back aboard by one corner (the head, tack, or clew) only, because if the sail is pulled by two corners, it will fill with water, drag like a sea anchor, and probably tear.

A final thought on spinnakers: when more than

one of these sails are on board, the one most suited to the wind strength and point of sailing should be set. A light-weight running spinnaker should not be carried on a reach in a fresh breeze nor should a heavy reaching 'chute be carried on a run in light air. If wind conditions change, causing the hoisted 'chute to be inappropriate while you are far from the leeward mark, the spinnaker should probably be changed. In light airs, changing from a heavy to a light 'chute is not much of a problem. The new 'chute (to be set) is properly turtled and attached at its usual hoisting location on the foredeck. A new sheet is bent and pre-trimmed to about the same position as the sheet in use. The new 'chute's tack is carried forward to the headstay. The outboard end of the pole is lowered to within easy reach, and the pole is guyed forward. A man on the bow releases the hoisted 'chute's tack from the guy and then snaps on the new sail's tack. In the meanwhile, a man at the mast is lowering the hoisted 'chute, while another man or two gathers it in. The halyard is quickly exchanged from one sail to the other, and the new 'chute is hoisted and trimmed.

In heavy air conditions when you are caught flying a light running 'chute, it may not pay to change sails if the course can be nearly a dead run. When running of course, the boat's speed is subtracted from the true wind speed to decrease apparent wind velocity. When reaching, however, the Genoa can be hoisted and will usually draw effectively while the light 'chute is handed. In some cases, it may pay to sail with the Genoa in lieu of the spinnaker, but if the boat speed should drop, the heavy 'chute can be hoisted in the usual manner under the lee of the jib.

Crew Organization

Duties assigned to the crew, such as winching, tacking, jibing, and setting, handing, and reefing sails have already been discussed, but a few words should be said about how the skipper organizes his crew for the greatest effectiveness and racing efficiency. Of course, the number of crew and their job specialties will vary with the boat size, rig, and the length of race. The smallest MORC boats sailing short races over simplified courses can be sailed with a crew of three. In fact, it is even possible to race these boats singlehanded with certain modifications to the running rigging such as leading the halyards, pole lift, and pole downhaul back to the cockpit. However, for maximum racing efficiency

most small, sloop-rigged, racing-cruisers should probably carry a crew of four. Slightly larger boats will normally need a crew of five racing 'round-the-buoys, but a crew of six for night races and when a boat has more than one mast, especially when racing in fresh winds. Boats in the forty to fifty foot range might need a crew of from six to ten depending on the rig and the race length. Obviously the larger and more complicated the rig, the more crew will be required, and distance races involving night sailing require a sizeable crew to combat fatigue. On most overnight races a boat should be manned with sufficient crew to permit half the members to sleep below while the other half handles the boat and stands watch on deck. It should not be necessary to rouse the watch below for normal maneuvers and sail changes except in emergency situations.

The racing crew may be divided into two general groups: the foredeck, those members who often work forward of the mainmast, whose primary duties are to handle the spinnaker and other headsails, and the after guard, those members concentrated in or near the cockpit area. Of course, most of the crew have primary and secondary jobs, and in some cases their position might shift from forward to aft or vice versa, as, for example, when more crew are needed on the foredeck in heavy weather to jibe or hand the spinnaker. On most medium sized boats, the after guard might consist of: the skipper, who is not only in command but also is the principle tactician and helmsman; one or two winch men, crankers who supply the speed and power to winch operation; a sheet trimmer who specializes in fine adjustments and continually plays the sheets, and a navigator who obviously has a key role in offshore races. On 'round-the-buoy races the navigator often doubles as a winch tailer, tactician, or even relief helmsman if he has the "tiller touch." His navigational duties on a short race may be as follows: to time the start, lay out the courses (draw the courses on the chart and figure the headings in degrees or points), keep the skipper informed of the location of rounding marks, other competitors, and time or distance to the lay line (fetch line), figure handicaps, and when visibility is poor, to keep an approximate *dead reckoning* position (a position derived from recording the course and speed over a known period of time). On most races a skilled sheet trimmer is probably an even greater asset than a good navigator especially on a spinnaker leg in light airs.

The foredeck crew consists of a foredeck captain and one, two, or even more assistants depending on the size of the boat. Small boats should have minimal crew forward, in many cases only one man, in order that the hull remains properly trimmed. Only one man (usually the one in charge of the foredeck) should go forward to prepare the spinnaker for hoisting. Needless to say, the foredeck captain should be experienced in the handling of spinnakers, because his responsibility is to carry out and/or direct the setting, positioning, jibing, changing, and handing of the 'chute. His assistants may include a mast man to handle halyards and/or the lift and perhaps a bow man to give help during jibes or at other hectic moments. Of course, these crew members are also responsible for setting and changing jibs and staysails. When beating to windward, the foredeckers usually man the windward or leeward rail (depending on the strength of wind) nearly amidships to help effect the proper angle of heel. Normally, on all but very small boats, at least one of these men will be needed forward to help the jib around the mast when tacking.

On distance races some additional skills and specialties will be needed. An obviously important specialist is the cook, who often is not required to stand regular watches. It is also advisable that other crew members have special aptitudes or knowledge in weather predictions, medicine or first aid, mechanics, electronics, marlinspike seamanship, and sail repair. Of course the navigator needs to be a specialist in celestial as well as radio navigation and dead reckoning when offshore, and there can never be too many competent helmsmen on a long distance race.

Two-watch systems, requiring half the crew to be on duty while the other half is off, can be comprised of four, five, or six hour watches. When four hour periods are used, it becomes necessary to *dog* or divide one of the four hours in half, customarily from 1600 to 1800 and from 1800 to 2000, to alternate the assignment of watch periods to the crew each day. *Swedish systems* make use of five watches in a twenty four hour period, and this automatically alternates the watches every day. Two popular Swedish systems are as follows: 0200-0600, 0600-1200, 1200-1800, 1800-2200, 2200-0200; and 0000-0400, 0400-0800, 0800-1300, 1300-1900, 1900-2400. With the first method, watches are essentially six hours during

daylight and four hours at night, but with the second method, watches are comprised of four, five, and six hour periods with the shorter watches tending to be at night. Occasionally, for the sake of boat handling continuity, a continually rotating watch system is used. With this system, one man goes off watch and is replaced by a new man coming on watch every hour.

The ideal crew is almost impossible to find, because there simply are not enough highly skilled and experienced members for every boat. Of course it is very desirable to have the same crew team for every race, but most skippers are not so fortunate as to have every member a regular. Many skippers feel that it is better to sign on crew members who will be regular and dependable even if they lack experience. With time and patience most enthusiastic greenhorns can be trained. Good sources of crew supply, for 'round-the-buoy races at least, are sailing program juniors and some women. Many of the fairer sex are not interested in racing and are more of a hindrance than a help, but others make excellent crew, and some are as good as the best men. More and more women are crewing, even on ocean races, and they are capable of handling almost any job except one requiring brute strength such as winching in a Genoa jib in a heavy breeze. Another source of crew supply for racing-cruisers are small boat racers. They are usually skilled and eager but not very regular because of their own racing schedule. Skippers of the larger ocean racers can often obtain crew for special distance races from the skippers and crew of the smaller racing-cruisers that do not normally participate in ocean races.

Beyond what has been said, there can be no hard and fast rules for assigning jobs to the crew, because specific assignments will depend on individual skills and degrees of experience. The crew member who does a particular job best should be given that job as his regular assignment. However, in practice sessions or some informal races, it is often a good idea to trade off or switch jobs for the sake of developing a broader range of skills and greater versatility for emergency substitutions. Needless to say, racing a boat is a team operation, and practice in boat and sail handling is of tremendous value. Most skippers of racing-cruisers, including myself, do not hold practice sessions often enough.

Qualities to look for in a regular crew are: enthusiasm, a willingness to learn and a desire to excell, team spirit and the ability to get along with others, dependable availability, intelligence, and experience.

In my opinion these are listed in approximately the right order of importance. In the long run, if the crew will be regular, it is probably better to sign on the person who has a strong desire to learn and win even if he is inexperienced rather than have a crew of high intelligence and experience but one that is half-hearted and lacking in competitive spirit. Of course, in distance ocean races experience and all-around proficiency in seamanship become quite important. Other desirable qualities for the offshore sailor are perseverance, neatness, and resistance to seasickness. A good sense of humor is always a great help.

10
Strategy and Tactics

A distinction will be made between strategy and tactics. Strategy is the general, over-all plan for the race with consideration for wind, current, and waves but discounting the presence of competitors. Tactics, however, is boat-vs-boat competition, your plan of attack or defense with regard to the presence and proximity of other boats. Unless a race is very short and extremely crowded, strategy is usually of much greater importance to the outcome of the race than tactics. This is especially true with handicap racing because of the unequal speed of many boats. However, tactics are nearly always involved near the starting line, around turning marks, and whenever boats crowd together in 'round-the-buoys racing. Also boat-vs-boat tactics are involved when one or two competitors become more important than others as for example, near the end of a race series.

Wind Strategy

As suggested in Chapter 8, it is always wise to plan, well before the start, the general course strategy based on observation and prediction of weather, current, and sea conditions. The start can be considered successful when the starter is free to pursue this strategy in the least amount of time after the starting signal. In most areas where currents are moderate, the strategy should be based primarily on weather expectations. The reason for this is that wind strength dictates what sails are carried, wind direction and strength (together with current) indicate the location of rough and smooth water, wind strength can vary in different locations and at different times, and wind shifts can completely change the relative positions of boats with respect to sailing time to the finish. Of course, consideration of current is very important, but many races have been lost in areas of weak current

by basing the strategy on current alone and not considering the more significant effects of changes in strength and direction of the wind. There are very few racing areas in this country where winds, regardless their direction, are absolutely consistent and steady.

It might be convenient to consider that there are three types of wind shifts: (1) *general,* where the wind shifts about the same amount over the entire racing area; (2) *oscillating,* when the wind shifts back and forth, varying in behavior from one location to the next within the racing area; and (3) *bending shifts* when the wind flow is distorted or bent near shore by the geography and topography of the land. The general shift results from the combination and domination in respect to: the prevailing wind (westerly in the middle latitudes), weather system winds (highs, lows, fronts, etc. moving in an easterly direction in the middle latitudes), and the thermal land-sea breezes.

Weather system winds to a great extent result from the movement and location of highs and lows (high or low barometric pressure). In the Northern Hemisphere winds swing around a high in a clockwise, outward direction, but they move counterclockwise and inwards around a low. The general flow of air moves from a high to a nearby low. When a low passes to the south of you, it produces backing winds (shifting counterclockwise) and on the east coast there is often a lengthy period of wet, sometimes stormy weather (the wet northeaster). A low passing to the north, however, brings a strong veering (clockwise) shift. Compared with lows, highs move much slower, and their winds are often light. When a high passes to the south, the wind backs, but there are occasions when an approaching high will bring a light northerly that will die (usually when it is opposed by an easterly sea breeze) and the wind will often fill in from the south after the high has passed. When a high passes to the north, however, the wind will veer. Frontal passages (either warm or cold) nearly always produce veering winds.

Land-sea breezes are due to differences in temperature of the land and water. In mid-morning of a hot summer's day, the land heats much faster than the water which causes the air over the land to rise. This leaves a partial void into which the cooler air over the water is sucked; thus a sea breeze is created. The sea breeze may begin in the late morning but usually reaches its peak or highest

FIGURE 109: VEERING OF NORMAL GUSTS

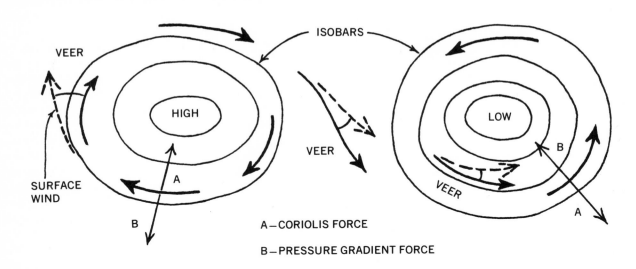

VEER

ISOBARS

HIGH

LOW

VEER

VEER

VEER

SURFACE WIND

A

B

B

A

A—CORIOLIS FORCE

B—PRESSURE GRADIENT FORCE

FIGURE 110: BENDING WIND

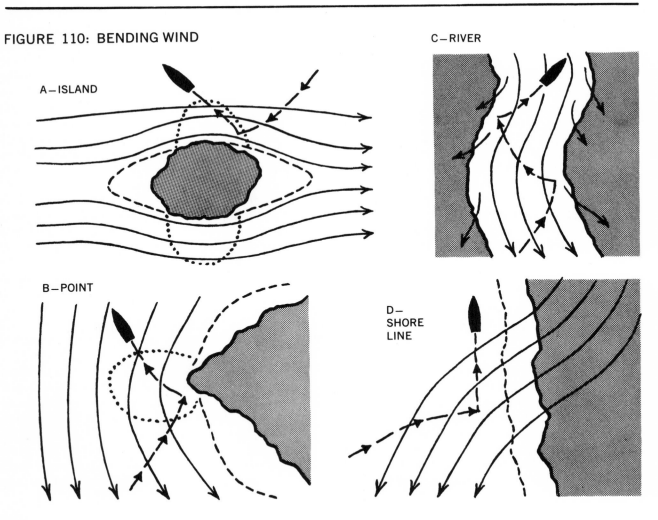

C—RIVER

A—ISLAND

B—POINT

D—SHORE LINE

velocity in the mid-afternoon. At night, however, when the land has cooled but water temperatures have changed very little, the thermal activity is reversed, and there is a breeze off the land. This wind often reaches its peak early in the morning before dawn and continues until gradually subsiding in the early hours of daylight. The strength of a land-sea breeze will depend on temperature, clearness of the weather, character of the land (fields, plains, and beaches heat up faster than wooded areas), and the strength of the prevailing or dominating wind system. The land-sea breeze may cause a shift in the dominating weather system wind, as for example, when an east coast southerly is influenced by a sea breeze to create a southeaster. Then again, the weather system wind may be calmed or increased when it is opposed or re-enforced by the land-sea breeze.

Oscillating shifts may be caused on calm days by small isolated thermals along an irregular shore directly exposed to the sun. These thermals are similar to bubbles or cells of heated air which periodically break away and rise from the ground allowing the air to drift into the void beneath the bubble, and this may cause periodic shifts over small, local areas near shore. Isolated oscillating shifts often occur on windy days when the air is vertically unstable with a cool wind flowing over irregularly heated land, such as during the typical east coast northwester. In these conditions, the winds are gusty when the cool, strong wind aloft drops down to the surface. Puffs in themselves cause oscillating shifts, because the increase in wind velocity causes the apparent wind to draw further aft, and also some gusts are the catspaw type that radiate or fan out slightly from the center. Aside from this, gusts descending from the strong winds aloft are slowed by surface friction, and this normally makes them veer. The wind aloft closely follows the direction of the isobars, because there is a balance between *pressure gradient force,* the tendency of the air to flow directly into a low or out of a high, and the *Coriolis force,* the deflection of air motion (to the right in the Northern Hemisphere) due to the earth's rotation. At the surface, however, the Coriolis force is less due to the slower wind velocity, and this causes the wind to angle (about ten degrees over water) into a low or out of a high (see Figure 109). Thus boats are normally lifted by gusts of this type on the starboard tack but are headed on the port tack. The English

meteorologist and small boat sailor, Alan Watts, gives a complete and more technical explanation of the phenomenon in his book, *Wind and Sailing Boats.*

The remaining wind shift that we have not yet discussed, is the bending shift caused by the geography and topography of the land. Examples of how the surface winds can be affected by the land are illustrated in Figure 110. A bent wind, sometimes called a shore slant when the bend is favorable, is actually not a true shift but an apparent one; because although the general, over-all wind appears to change its direction when a boat sails into a bend, the change of direction is only a result of the distorted flow lines near shore. Four typical situations are shown in Figure 110. The long arrows show the flow lines, the areas enclosed by dotted lines show the approximate regions of fast wind speed, while the areas enclosed by dashed lines indicate slow wind speed, either from the effects of blanket or rebound. The wind bends in order to pass around islands or peninsulas, as shown in situations A and B, and it tends to be channeled down a river, as in situation C, or to follow the axis of a long body of water. When the wind blows obliquely across a fairly regular shore line, the bend is such that the flow lines tend to cross the shore at right angles (situation D). It can be seen that advantage can be taken of the bending flow lines when beating, often by tacking close to the shore towards the center of the wind's rotation but avoiding the lee of the land, as suggested by the broken arrow courses of the boats in the diagram. Although it often pays to tack almost immediately on prolonged headers of the general or oscillating type; it nearly always pays to sail well into a wind bend header before tacking. Of course, bent winds are affected by such factors as the altitude of the shore, gaps along the shore through which the wind can funnel, thermal conditions and the dominance of weather system winds.

Wind shifts and variations of wind strength are often very difficult to predict. The study of a late weather map can be helpful, and the racing skipper should listen to a good marine weather broadcast before and usually during every race. Especially helpful are the Weather Bureau's continuous VHF broadcasts on static free FM, 162.55 megahertz. It is important to have some idea of the general weather pattern (the location of highs, lows, fronts, etc.), and good broadcasts give the strength, direction, and probable shifting of the general winds, the likelihood of thunderstorms, and so forth.

The longer the race, the greater the significance of general weather forecasts. In short races, sailors are concerned with weather in a very limited area over a limited period of time, and obviously weather reports are not so detailed as to cover small specific localities. Furthermore, meteorologists can seldom predict with any accuracy the exact time of a weather change. The 'round-the-buoys sailor should be informed of the general weather picture, but he must also draw on his local knowledge and use his powers of observation to attempt a prediction of weather in his exact locality. He should keep records of local weather behavior and learn the influence of local geography on the wind through thermal activity and wind bending. He should also observe the general characteristics of each directional wind in his region (for instance that a northwester is puffy and shifty, or that a southerly is fairly steady, or that a northerly may die, and so forth.)

Careful and continual observation can be helpful in predicting weather changes. Of course, visual signs of wind changes are wind streaks on the water, the activity of smoke and flags, the movement of lower clouds, distant sailboats, and so forth. Certain clouds such as high altitude cirrocumulus (mackerel sky), altostratus, or altocumulus can warn of approaching fronts, while cumulonimbus (thunderheads) can warn of an imminent thunderstorm either of the frontal or isolated air mass type, while cumulus clouds can predict fair weather and perhaps the presence of sea breeze or other thermal wind activity. As said before, fronts should produce veering winds, but an approaching, isolated, counterclockwise moving storm passing to the south should produce backing winds. A fluctuating barometer can be helpful in predicting these shifts and the usual increase in wind velocity associated with the approach and passage of a front or low. A falling glass will usually announce the approach of these disturbances, and the glass will often rise rapidly and indicate that the wind will further increase temporarily after the passage of a cold front.

Wind changes can even be affected by the tide. The wind often tends to come up (freshen) and go down with the tide. This has been recognized for a long time by many experienced sailors, but I've never heard any entirely satisfactory explanation of why it is true. The meterologist Alan Watts offers a possible explanation that the wind increase may be due to the "flattening of the surroundings," but he admits that "the reason is obscure." Nevertheless, the wind will often begin to freshen at the start of the flood tide, but the wind will often slacken at the start of the ebb, and this also can herald a wind shift.

Although the time and extent of a wind shift is difficult to predict, we can try to place our boat in the right location so as to receive maximum benefit or the least harm from any shift. As pointed out many years ago by Trevor and Calahan (in their book, *Wind and Tide in Yacht Racing*) and by Dr. Manfred Curry, the gains from being in an advantageous location during a wind shift can be enormous. The following is a list of general rules that usually hold true when beating in shifty winds:

(1) *Tack on prolonged or significant headers.* On oscillating wind shifts, small boats should tack almost immediately, but racing-cruisers should not tack with very rapid oscillations especially in light airs because of the time and way lost when tacking. All boats should sail well into a wind bend before tacking, but all boats usually should tack at once on a severe, heading, general shift.

(2) *When sailing towards an expected header, foot (don't point), but point towards an expected lift unless there is a possibility of overstanding.* The boat that foots out but sags to leeward of a competitor gains in a heading shift, because this puts the competitor behind in the footing boat's wake, but when the shift is lifting, the boat behind but to windward decreases the distance she is behind and increases her distance to windward. In a distance race when nearly fetching the mark, it usually pays to foot, because the odds are that there will be a general wind shift sooner or later. A header will put the footing boat ahead, and a significant lift may allow her to fetch, while the boat that has pointed will be behind on the header and will have overstood on the significant lift.

(3) *When the windward mark lies dead to windward, tack towards the heading side of the course.* Sail towards the expected header, to the right side of the course when

170

FIGURE 111: MARK DEAD TO WINDWARD

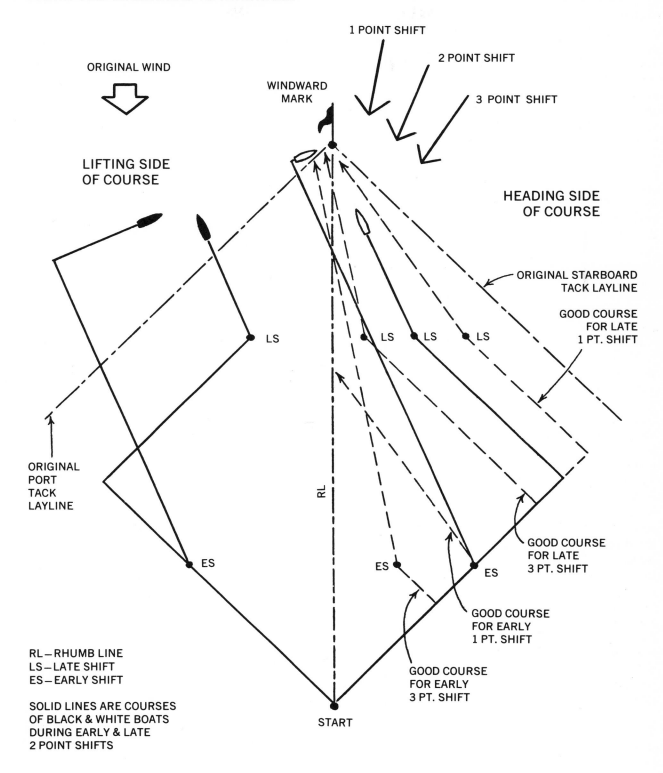

1 POINT SHIFT

2 POINT SHIFT

3 POINT SHIFT

ORIGINAL WIND

WINDWARD MARK

LIFTING SIDE OF COURSE

HEADING SIDE OF COURSE

ORIGINAL STARBOARD TACK LAYLINE

GOOD COURSE FOR LATE 1 PT. SHIFT

LS   LS   LS   LS

ORIGINAL PORT TACK LAYLINE

RL

ES   ES   ES

GOOD COURSE FOR LATE 3 PT. SHIFT

GOOD COURSE FOR EARLY 1 PT. SHIFT

GOOD COURSE FOR EARLY 3 PT. SHIFT

RL—RHUMB LINE
LS—LATE SHIFT
ES—EARLY SHIFT

SOLID LINES ARE COURSES OF BLACK & WHITE BOATS DURING EARLY & LATE 2 POINT SHIFTS

START

171

expecting veering winds or to the left side of the course when expecting backing winds. The antithetic corollary to this rule is: don't sail towards a general shift that is expected to lift. This can be seen by studying Figure 111. Notice that a boat on the lifted side of the course (to the left of the rhumb line on a veering shift) has a much greater distance to sail than one on the headed side of the course experiencing the same shift. The reason for this is that the headed boat may come about and fetch (or nearly fetch) the mark on the opposite tack, while the lifted boat cannot fetch on either tack. Of course, the amount the headed boat gains over the lifted one will depend on the time and degree of shifting (see rule 5).

(4) *When the mark lies nearly dead to windward and the wind's shifting is entirely unpredictable, keep as close to the rhumb line course as is consistent with non-excessive tacking.* The reasoning behind this rule is that no matter which way the wind shifts, the boat near the rhumb line cannot lose drastically. However, she will obviously lose some ground if she sails into a lifting shift; thus the first tack should be towards the most probable header. When the general shifting is completely unpredictable and neither tack is favored by favorable current, seas, bending winds or thermal winds, the port tack should usually be taken first because more often than not, a general shift will veer rather than back in normal, fair weather (in the northern hemisphere).

(5) *Distance from the rhumb line should be minimal when the shift is expected to be major or early, but the distance should be greater when the shift is expected to be minor or late.* This is a corollary of rule 4, and it is explained in Figure 111.

(6) *When the mark definitely does not lie dead to windward, take the close tack until the opposite tack is definitely closer.* The *close tack* may be defined as the tack that allows you to head closest to the windward mark when sailing close-hauled, whereas the *far tack* is the opposite tack. The reasoning behind this rule is that almost any shift will favor a boat on the close tack by allowing

her to fetch or nearly fetch the mark on a lifting shift, but in a severe heading shift she can come about and come close to fetching on the opposite tack. On the other hand, the boat taking the far tack first is hurt by a lift because this will put the mark almost dead to windward while a header will usually mean that she has overstood and wasted time on her initial tack. This is explained in figure 112. About the only exception to this rule is when a boat on the far tack sails into a slight, early header that just allows her to fetch on the opposite tack. This is illustrated by the dashed course lines shown in Figure 112.

(7) *Don't sail out to the lay line until close to the windward mark.* The reason for this is that any wind shift can be harmful to a boat on the *lay line,* the line on which a boat can fetch the windward mark (also called fetch line). When she is aimed for the mark on this line, a lifting shift will mean that she has overstood while a heading shift will mean that her tacking angle is less than ninety degrees (assuming the boat can "sail square" or sail a course that is forty-five degrees from the true wind). An important exception to this rule is that it often pays to keep to one side of the course when sailing in very light airs, partly because thermal winds frequently occur near a shore, and also because excessive tacking, required to stay near the rhumb line, can be very costly in light airs.

(8) *Consider tacking when on port tack during puffs and when on starboard tack during lulls in normal, vertically unstable winds.* This rule is based on the previously mentioned principle that normal gusts tend to veer (see Figure 109). The rule might be considered a corollary to rule 1, and both of these rules are more appropriate for small, light displacement boats. However, under certain circumstances, it could well pay for a small racing-cruiser to tack during prolonged gusts, lulls, or oscillating shifts. Quite often a gusting header on the port tack will not appear to be a header because of the neutralizing effect of the increased wind velocity tending to draw the apparent wind aft. However, on the opposite tack

FIGURE 112: MARK DEFINITELY NOT DEAD TO WINDWARD

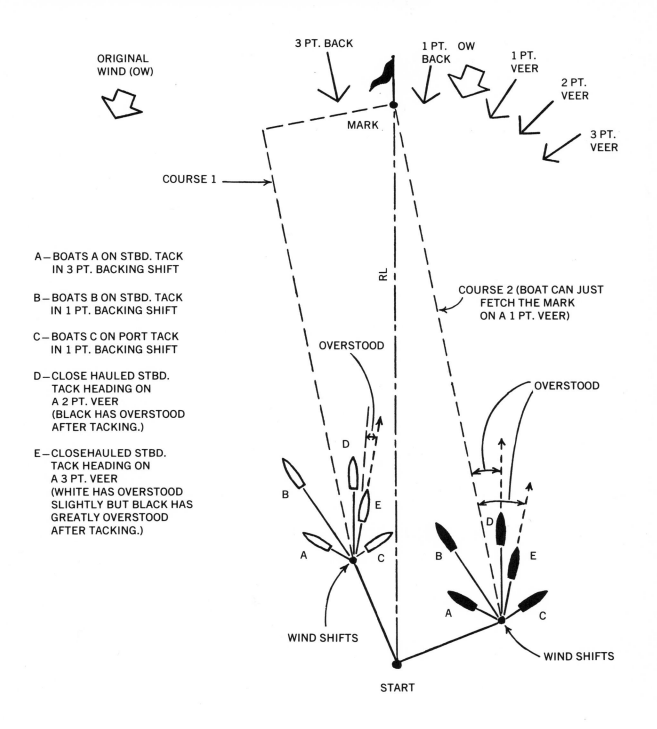

ORIGINAL
WIND (OW)

3 PT. BACK

1 PT. OW
BACK

1 PT.
VEER

2 PT.
VEER

3 PT.
VEER

MARK

COURSE 1

RL

COURSE 2 (BOAT CAN JUST
FETCH THE MARK
ON A 1 PT. VEER)

A — BOATS A ON STBD. TACK
IN 3 PT. BACKING SHIFT

B — BOATS B ON STBD. TACK
IN 1 PT. BACKING SHIFT

C — BOATS C ON PORT TACK
IN 1 PT. BACKING SHIFT

D — CLOSE HAULED STBD.
TACK HEADING ON
A 2 PT. VEER
(BLACK HAS OVERSTOOD
AFTER TACKING.)

E — CLOSEHAULED STBD.
TACK HEADING ON
A 3 PT. VEER
(WHITE HAS OVERSTOOD
SLIGHTLY BUT BLACK HAS
GREATLY OVERSTOOD
AFTER TACKING.)

OVERSTOOD

OVERSTOOD

D

E

B

A

C

D

B

E

A

C

WIND SHIFTS

WIND SHIFTS

START

COURSE 1 IS LONGER THAN COURSE 2
(EXCEPTION TO THE CLOSE TACK RULE)

WHITE BOATS ARE
AHEAD OF BLACK BOATS

FIGURE 113: CHART FOR BEATING IN SHIFTY WINDS

SITUATION	CONDITION	RULE	PARTICULAR EXCEPTION	GENERAL EXCEPTIONS
MARK DEAD TO WINDWARD	SEVERE GENERAL SHIFT EXPECTED DIRECTION FAIRLY CERTAIN	KEEP TO HEADING SIDE OF COURSE DON'T GO FAR FROM RHUMB LINE	LATE SHIFT (IT CAN PAY TO CROSS R.L. SLIGHTLY TO LIFTING SIDE IF SHIFT WILL BE LATE)	
	SLIGHT GENERAL SHIFT EXPECTED (DIRECTION FAIRLY CERTAIN)	KEEP TO HEADING SIDE OF COURSE SAIL FURTHER FROM R.L. INITIALLY ESPECIALLY ON LATE SHIFT	WHEN SHIFTING IS UNCERTAIN IT IS RISKY TO SAIL MUCH FURTHER THAN HALF WAY TO LAY LINE	
	OSCILLATING &/OR GUSTY WIND	TACK TOWARD NEXT PROBABLE HEADER TACK ON DEFINITE PROLONGED HEADERS	YOU ARE TACKING TOO OFTEN & BOAT IS SLOW IN STAYS	IF CURRENT, SMOOTH WATER, WIND BENDING, THERMALS, GREATER WIND STRENGTH, OR PLACEMENT OF COMPETITORS JUSTIFIES OTHER COURSE
	SHIFTING UNKNOWN	TACK TOWARD MOST PROBABLE HEADER DON'T GO FAR FROM R.L. IF NO THERMAL OR BENDING WIND, KEEP TO RIGHT OF R.L.	IN LIGHT AIRS (AVOID TACKING & KEEP TO ONE SIDE OF COURSE— IN THE MOST WIND)	
MARK DEFINITELY NOT DEAD TO WINDWARD	SHIFTING UNKNOWN OR OSCILLATING	TAKE CLOSE TACK TO THE MARK FIRST TACK ON HEADERS	YOU ARE SAILING BEYOND THE POINT WHERE OPPOSITE TACK IS CLOSER	
	CLOSE TACK WILL TAKE YOU INTO A HEADER	DITTO ABOVE	ON A VERY SLIGHT HEADER IT MAY PAY NOT TO TACK	
	CLOSE TACK WILL TAKE YOU INTO A MINOR LIFT	DON'T TAKE CLOSE TACK FIRST. TAKE SHORT TACK TOWARD HEADING SIDE.	YOU CAN ALMOST FETCH ON CLOSE TACK	
	CLOSE TACK WILL TAKE YOU INTO A MAJOR LIFT	TAKE CLOSE TACK	IF SHIFT WILL BE LATE & NOT EXTREME, KEEP ON HEADING SIDE NEAR R.L.	

174

the wind veer and the normal puff lift can re-enforce each other to create a significant lift. The same principle applies to lulls when on the starboard tack.

(9) *In light airs, work into the nearest wind streak regardless of which way it will shift. When expecting a new general shifted wind, try to stay with the old wind as long as possible, but at the same time, work towards the direction of the expected new breeze. Don't tack in a calm spot.* When sailing in light airs, you are primarily concerned with keeping the boat moving even if it is not in the direction closest to the next mark, partly because a moving boat creates her own apparent wind. Also we are concerned with staying in the most breeze, the last of a dying breeze, and in being the first to reach a new breeze. This later principle also applies to the calm before a storm. Advantage can often be taken of the light breeze that is sucked into a thunderstorm in order to sail towards the storm and be one of the first boats to get the shift and strong winds. Naturally this must be done cautiously with sheets ready to run and sails ready to be lowered at a moment's notice, because thunderstorm winds can be dangerous. If the storm is an ominous frontal type, sails should be shortened or lowered early.

(10) *In bending winds sail well into the bend before tacking, and in most cases head for shore towards the center of the wind's rotation, but be careful to avoid the land's blanket.* This has already been discussed and illustrated in Figure 110. One further suggestion is that it will be helpful to plot the estimated wind bend on a chart in order that you can plan your course to take maximum advantage of the shift.

Of course, as with any rules, there may be exceptions to any of the ten wind shift rules. They must be considered along with other factors such as the presence of other competitors, disturbed wind, and the current. The racing sailor must be flexible, keep an open mind, and look at the whole picture, taking into account every influencing factor. At times, it may seem that to be successful the skipper needs a computer to interpret all the available data. In an attempt to simplify slightly the complicated matter of choosing the correct course on a beat, especially in shifty, non-bending winds, a chart has been prepared (Figure 113) which gives the two possible general situations (the mark dead to windward or definitely not dead to windward), the particular wind shift conditions, the appropriate rule, the particular exceptions, and the general exceptions.

Many of the strategic principles for beating in shifting winds also apply to sailing downwind. As mentioned in Chapter 9, it often pays to tack downwind in order to avoid sailing with the wind dead aft. Figure 114, which uses the same speed curves as in Figure 96, illustrates the advantage of tacking downwind in light airs. Boat B, sailing with the true wind on her quarter has about a third of A's distance to the leeward mark further to sail, but B sails almost twice as fast. This is partly due to the fact that all of A's speed is subtracted from the true wind speed whereas only part of B's speed is subtracted; thus A is sailing in less apparent wind than B. Notice, however, that it does not pay to tack downwind to any great extent in heavy winds in a displacement boat; because the boat cannot be pushed appreciably above her hull speed. Of course, speed curves will vary with individual boats, but those illustrated are approximations of a very fast, non-planing, racing-cruiser. Obviously a planing boat should be sailed high enough to allow planing.

General rules for sailing downwind in shifty winds are as follows:

(1) *Tack downwind in light airs, and avoid sailing with the wind dead aft.* This is especially true if the current is favorable because of the low apparent wind strength. The exception to this rule is in heavy wind sailing and when the boat is tending to heel to leeward.

(2) *Bear off in gusts and head up in lulls.* This was discussed in Chapter 9.

(3) *When the mark does not lie dead to leeward, take the close tack first.* This involves the same principle as in rule 6 for upwind sailing. A boat with her spinnaker set, bound for a mark not quite dead to leeward should be put on her optimum downwind heading (perhaps with the wind slightly abaft her quarter if the air is light) and she should start out on the tack that brings her closest to the mark. If the wind shifts so that it is blowing from dead astern, the boat can jibe and approach

FIGURE 114: TACKING DOWNWIND

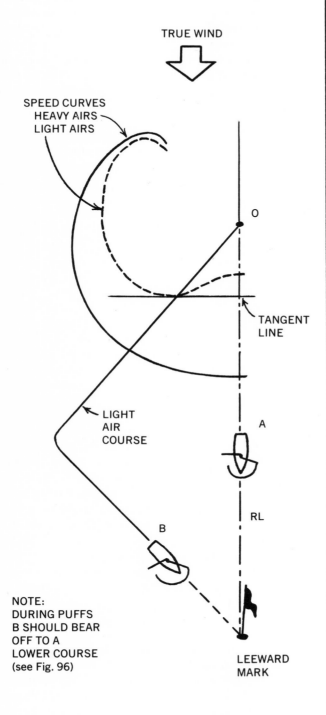

TRUE WIND

SPEED CURVES
HEAVY AIRS
LIGHT AIRS

O

TANGENT LINE

LIGHT AIR COURSE

A

RL

B

NOTE:
DURING PUFFS
B SHOULD BEAR
OFF TO A
LOWER COURSE
(see Fig. 96)

LEEWARD MARK

FIGURE 115: DOWNWIND STRATEGY IN SHIFTY WINDS

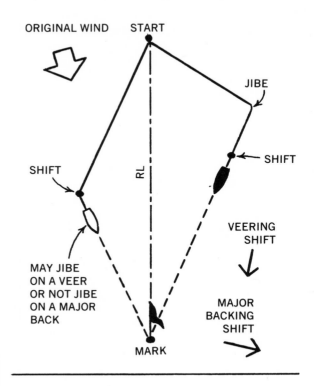

ORIGINAL WIND   START

JIBE

SHIFT   SHIFT

RL

VEERING SHIFT

MAY JIBE
ON A VEER
OR NOT JIBE
ON A MAJOR
BACK

MAJOR BACKING SHIFT

MARK

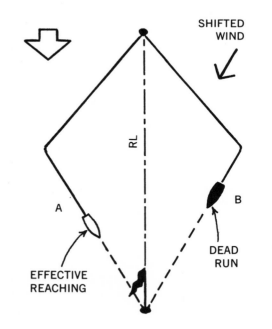

SHIFTED WIND

RL

A

B

EFFECTIVE REACHING

DEAD RUN

the mark on an efficient sailing angle on the opposite tack. If the wind shifts the opposite way, however, with the wind much further ahead (more on the beam) the boat may bear off and come close to or make the mark on a good sailing angle without jibing. The boat taking the far tack first, on the other hand, will either have a greater distance to sail to the mark when the wind shifts one way, or be caught with the wind almost dead aft when the shift is in the opposite direction. This is explained in Figure 115.

(4) *When the leeward mark lies dead to leeward, sail away from the direction of the expected shift*. This is also explained in Figure 115. Boat A sails away from the direction of the expected shift. When the shift occurs she has the wind dead aft, but she may jibe and approach the mark at an efficient sailing angle. Boat B, however, becomes caught with the wind dead aft. She cannot jibe onto either tack and head directly for the mark on an efficient point of sailing.

Of course, these rules are also subject to exceptions due to the influence of current, wind bend, and the whereabouts of other competitors.

Current strategy

In most yachting areas, current is sufficiently strong to be a very important factor when racing. It is often difficult to decide whether the overall strategy should be based primarily on the wind or the current. Of course, wind and current strategy often coincide, but when they conflict, the choice between the two should be influenced by such considerations as: the strength of the current in the racing area, strength of the wind, direction of flow, time of maximum flow and slack water, regions of greatest velocity, the degree of weather certainty, predictability of wind shifts, character of the wind (gusty, shifty, bending, or light and flukey), effect of wind on the current, and so forth. Obviously, if the current is weak in the racing area, strategy based on the current should not be emphasized to the extent it would be were the flow of greater strength. Also current strategy gains importance in light, steady winds. Perhaps a greater emphasis should be put on current strategy when the flow is adverse rather than favorable partly because of the longer exposure to the current when it is against

you. Current should usually be a minor consideration when it is slack while sailing a short leg, but great consideration should be given to being in or away from the location where the flow will first begin to change. If the weather is very unpredictable, it may pay to emphasize current strategy especially if the flow is strong. It will nearly always pay to tack towards shore beating against a current when wind bending or shore thermals can be utilized. Generally speaking, in offshore races that are beyond coastal currents or in areas of favorable current where the depth of water is fairly uniform, it usually pays to put the emphasis on wind strategy. Wind may have a considerable effect on current, because it can affect the strength and direction of flow and time of changing.

Fortunately, current is usually a lot more predictable than wind. Of great assistance to racing skippers are the "Tidal Current Tables" (for Atlantic and Pacific Coasts of North America) published by the U. S. Department of Commerce. These tables are published every year and can be obtained from almost any good yachting supply store, the Coast and Geodetic Survey and its sales agents, or the U. S. Government Printing Office. The tables give the direction, velocity, and time of maximum current from numerous coastal stations. It is not wise, however, always to rely on the exact figures in the tables, because certain conditions of the wind and weather can cause inaccuracies. Current flow should continually be checked visually during a race by watching the leaning of tall buoys, the wakes of crab or lobster pots, wakes of channel markers or fish stakes, boats at anchor, and by keeping track of the boat's lateral movement (excluding leeway) with bearings when crossing a current. It often pays in very light airs to ease over the side a light anchor when in shallow water to check movement made good or lost over the bottom. It may pay at certain times to make a slight course alteration in the interest of passing close to a buoy or other stationary object to "read" or interpret the flow.

A list of basic rules for sailing in current are as follows:

(1) *Stay in shoal water and out of channels when the current is foul, but stay in channels and in deep water when the current is fair*. Friction over the bottom tends to slow the current, thus it flows faster in deep water and in channels than over shoals.

177

(2) It can be beneficial to stay offshore in deep water initially when the current first changes from fair to foul and conversely to stay inshore in shoal water initially when the flow changes from foul to fair. The reason for this is that the current changes first in shallow waters where it has the least momentum; thus it is usually wise to keep in shallow water when the change is favorable until the flow changes in deep water. When the change is adverse, however, it is usually wise to stay in deep water until the current becomes slack in that location in order to benefit from the favorable flow for the greatest length of time.

(3) Crossing a current at or nearly at right angles to the flow, allowance must be made for its lateral push by heading slightly above or up current of the rhumb line course. This is an obvious rule, but current is often misinterpreted, and surprisingly, the rule is sometimes not observed at all. The current's lateral push can be estimated by noting the velocity and direction of the flow in the current tables and by visually judging the flow past turning marks, crab pots, and so forth. Also the boat's lateral movement can be judged by utilizing a range such as the next turning mark lined up against an object on shore. A boat's proper heading can be determined by drawing a simple vector diagram when the boat's speed and the current's speed and direction are known. For example, if the boat were making two knots in a northerly direction and the current flowing two knots towards the west, the boat should be headed northeast to counteract the current's lateral push.

(4) Whenever possible, plan your course to take advantage of a lee bow current. There are times when a close-hauled course can be planned to angle the direction of flow against the lee bow. This will naturally set the boat to windward and be advantageous when competitors are sailing in a current of *differing* direction that angles the flow against their windward bows. It may pay to tack into the mouth of a river to pick up a lee bow current. This is illustrated in Figure 116 which shows the case of a boat

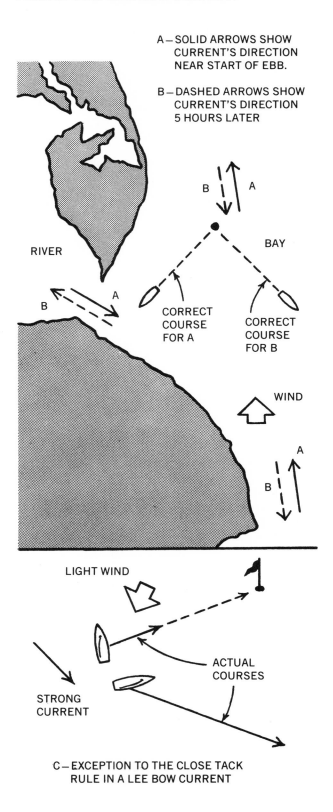

FIGURE 116: LEE BOW CURRENT

A — SOLID ARROWS SHOW CURRENT'S DIRECTION NEAR START OF EBB.

B — DASHED ARROWS SHOW CURRENT'S DIRECTION 5 HOURS LATER

RIVER

BAY

B   A

B   A

CORRECT COURSE FOR A

CORRECT COURSE FOR B

WIND

A

B

LIGHT WIND

STRONG CURRENT

ACTUAL COURSES

C — EXCEPTION TO THE CLOSE TACK RULE IN A LEE BOW CURRENT

tacking towards the river for lee bow benefits in situation A, but notice that five hours later in situation B (based on actual current studies of the area), the current at the river's mouth has changed so that it is on the windward bow; therefore in this case, it would be wrong to tack inshore. Situation C, Figure 116, shows the part a strong lee bow current can play in light airs. Notice that although the port tack boat is headed close to the windward mark, she is swept away from the mark, while the starboard tack boat taking the far tack (heading away from the mark) is swept directly to the mark so that she can round it without tacking. Taking an extra tack can be disastrous in very light air. Also, there is a danger that the port tack boat will overstand or understand. There are occasions when a boat working to windward will head almost directly into an adverse current, and the question often arises as to whether or not it will pay to pinch up slightly in order to bring the current on the lee bow. Except, perhaps, when pinching to fetch a mark without tacking, it will not pay to pinch when the boat's speed is noticeably lessened. The often misunderstood "lee bow effect" is not a result of added hydrodynamic lift, the effect is merely the vectorial movement of the boat in the direction towards which the current is flowing. The distance to windward gained by a boat pinching (with the current on her lee bow) over a boat footing (with the same current on her windward bow) will be the same as if the two boats were sailing on identical courses during the same period of time in no current. The direction of flow can be obtained at current stations from the tables; but for some areas, detailed current charts are published, and obviously these can be most helpful.

(5) *Consider the benefits or detriments of the accelerated current past a point of land and the possible eddy behind the point.* Current often speeds up when it flows past a point or the constricted area between two opposite points in a river or bay when there is a venturi force. Also there is often a relatively weak counter current close to shore behind (under the current-sheltered side of) the point. Obviously, it pays to avoid the eddy or accelerated current when they are adverse but to sail into them when they are favorable, provided this plan does not oppose other important strategic considerations.

(6) *Watch for tide rips and stay on their favorable side.* Tide rips are streaks of ruffled water agitated by the friction of two opposing currents or a slow and fast current moving in the same direction. Of course, it is beneficial to keep on the most favorable side of a rip. Although it is sometimes difficult to tell which side is favorable, this can usually be determined by noting the water's depth, the time of the current's changing from the tables, direction of flow from the tables or a current chart, and by comparing the speeds of boats on both sides of the rip.

Competition Tactics

As previously mentioned, there should be a slightly different emphasis put on competition (boat-vs-boat) tactics in large boat, handicaps racing as compared with small class-boat or one-design racing, because there are usually differences in the way big and little boats should be handled, and also the performance characteristics of handicap racers are often dissimilar. A list of general tactical rules noting differences between large and small boat tactics is as follows:

(1) *In most cases, loose cover your most dangerous competition.* By *loose covering,* it is meant that you keep yourself in a relatively advantageous tactical position with respect to the competition. This is a defensive technique that can be used when you are ahead of or at least even with the competitor. The main principle behind the defense is, in most cases, to stay between your competitor and the next mark of the course, in order that he will not get any special benefits from wind or current that you will not get also. An exception to the rule exists when you are directly to leeward of the windward mark and your competitor is dead to leeward of you. In this position any wind shift will theoretically benefit your competitor, as a lift will short-

en the windward distance between the two boats, and a header will shorten the distance the leading boat is ahead of the other.

(2) *Do not use tight covering tactics unless match racing or unless you must beat a particular rival to win a series.* By *tight covering,* it is meant that the leading boat stays close to her competitor in such a way that the competitor is blanketed or backwinded. Of course, the boat being covered tries to break away by tacking, jibing, or other maneuvering to get her wind clear. These tactics often develop into luffing matches or *tacking duels* (where the covered boat takes many rapid tacks or feigns tacking in order to break away from her cover while the covering boat tries to stay on top of her competitor), but by and large, all this maneuvering is very costly with respect to the rest of the competition in a fleet race. It is especially important when handicap racing large boats not to become overly preoccupied with one competitor except under the special circumstances of match racing or the consideration of series standings.

(3) *Make every attempt to clear your wind when you are covered, and try to break into the covering boat's zone of wind deflection when it is favorable to you.* If you are being covered, you must try to break the cover or at least take the tack of least wind interference when beating. When to leeward you may be able to dodge your competitor's wind shadow by bearing off and footing; or if you are to windward, you may be able to pinch clear of your competitor's backwind. The approximate area of relative wind disturbance is illustrated in Figure 117. Notice that although neither boat, A or B, is hurting the other (because B is ahead of A's backwind and A is ahead of B's windshadow), B is helping A because of the wind deflection or bend that allows A to sail in a lift. Thus if A were being covered by B, and A succeeded in breaking through B's blanket fairly close aboard, the leeward boat would have the advantage of the wind deflection. If A were slightly further astern in B's blanket, she might be able to come about and clear B's wind

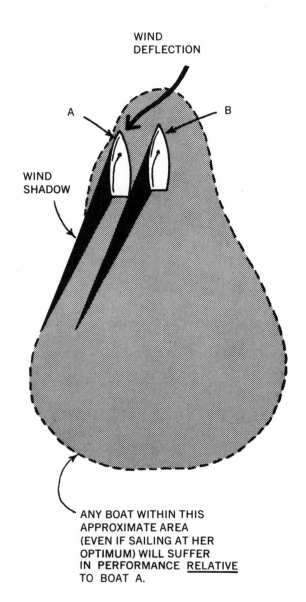

FIGURE 117: RELATIVE DISTURBANCE OF THE WIND

WIND DEFLECTION

A

B

WIND SHADOW

ANY BOAT WITHIN THIS APPROXIMATE AREA (EVEN IF SAILING AT HER OPTIMUM) WILL SUFFER IN PERFORMANCE RELATIVE TO BOAT A.

NOTE: BOAT B IS NOT BEING HURT BY BOAT A, BUT A IS BEING HELPED BY B.

180

shadow on the opposite tack. Be sure to study the wind indicators when judging the direction of wind shadows. Never follow closely behind another boat because of the adverse effect of wind deflection, backwind, and wake.

(4) *When covering on a beat, try to force your competitor into making a strategic mistake by allowing him to split tacks with you when his tack will take him towards the lay line, towards a general lifting shift, on the far tack from the mark, or into a region of less wind or worse current.* If you have a competitor effectively covered, consider letting him escape by splitting tacks with you when his tack will take him into harmful conditions of wind or current. Remember that he will be hurt by a future lifting shift, by almost all shifts when on the far tack from the mark, and by any shift on the lay line. (See rules 3, 6, and 7 for beating in shifty winds.)

(5) *If ahead and to leeward of a competitor, foot for a header but pinch for a lift.* This principle has been explained in rule 3 for beating in shifty winds. It usually pays for the boat behind and to windward to pinch slightly if she is close winded or else tack for the sake of clearing her wind.

(6) *When converging with another boat on opposite tacks, bear off and pass under her stern if your boat is comparatively heavy and slow, but consider tacking under the other's lee bow when your boat is comparatively fast and lively.* A common practice in small boat racing is tacking under a rival's lee bow in the so called *safe leeward position* in order to backwind the rival and/or to profit by wind deflection. However, this can be a dangerous practice in a large, heavy handicap racer, because the tacking boat's lack of acceleration and the other's momentum may allow the windward boat to forge ahead to the point where she can blanket the boat that has just tacked. Whether or not you should tack under a rival's lee bow will depend on the speed of your boat in stays, how fast she will pick up speed, and the relative size of the boats (obviously it would be foolish to tack under a larger faster boat that is

bound to "run over" you). Furthermore, the strategic situation must be considered. You don't want to tack under a lee bow if you will sail into a lift or if you are close to and will be headed for the lay line. Remember that crossing under the stern will allow you subsequent maneuvering freedom.

(7) *On a beat consider consolidating your position with a short tack that will place you dead ahead of a rival who is far behind but slightly to windward of you if that rival is out performing you to windward as a result of having a better wind.* This tactic is often effective when covering a rival, but it is usually not advisable unless the other boat is in a better wind. In racing-cruisers avoid extra tacks in very light airs, and don't tack ahead of a much larger, faster boat.

(8) *On a reaching leg, plan your course so as to be on an optimal point of sailing during the latter part of the leg.* This usually means sailing low initially and then sailing higher near the end of the leg. It is important that a boat be on an optimal point of sailing as she approaches the turning mark and converges with competitors. An exception to this rule might be in the case where it is necessary to sail high initially in order to carry a spinnaker at the end of the leg when the next leg is a course that requires the use of a spinnaker. This is especially true for a large boat with an inexperienced crew when setting the 'chute may take time.

(9) *In most cases, approach a windward mark to be left to port on the starboard tack, but approach a mark to be left to starboard on the port tack.* When leaving the mark to port, it is important to have the right of way when converging on the mark with other boats. However, when leaving the mark to starboard, a boat approaching on the port tack can usually beat a converging starboard tack rival around the mark for the simple reason that the starboard tacker must come about to round. This is especially true with large, heavy boats that are slow in stays.

(10) *When rounding a mark don't turn so fast that you kill way, sail closest to the mark after nearly completing the turn, and, if*

strategy allows, avoid tacking as you round. A sharp turn, especially in a large, heavy boat will kill her way. Usually it is best to make a wide approach so that an easy turn will bring you close to the mark after you have rounded it. This is done to backwind following competitors and to attempt avoidance of disturbed air from rivals ahead of you. If turning onto a windward leg try to avoid tacking immediately (unless an instant tack is necessary for strategic purposes), because a tack made while rounding kills headway more than if the boat were allowed to pick up full speed before coming about.

(11) *In most cases, try for the inside position when rounding a mark, and try to maneuver into a position where you can backwind or blanket your nearby competition.* This usually means that you hold high when turning onto a windward leg, and that you keep directly to windward of competitors when turning onto a downwind leg. It is usually advantageous to be on the inside at the mark when rounding, but be careful not to establish your overlap when closer than two boat lengths from the mark (see Chapter 7 and NAYRU Rule 42.3).

(12) *At the finish, try to be on the starboard tack, head for the close end of the line, and finish between your competition and the committee boat.* It is advisable to have the right of way when converging on the finish line with other boats, and when the line is not exactly square to the last leg of the course, it is obviously desirable to head for the line's end that is closest to you. In the case of a near "photo finish" with a competitor, it may be helpful to you if you finish between the competitor and the committee boat.

These rules incorporate the main competition tactical principles used on the course and when rounding buoys. Starting tactics were dealt with in Chapter 8. As a final bit of advice on tactics, remember to look at the over-all strategic picture before involving yourself in boat-for-boat tactics, stay clear of trouble by avoiding congestions of boats, try to anticipate conditions that could lead to collisions or entanglements, learn the racing rules, and never gamble by splitting with your main competition unless you feel certain the odds are in your favor.

A big difference between class-boat racing and handicap racing is dissimilarities in boat performance. In class-boat racing, it is important for the skipper to size up his competition by considering the human element such as: whether or not a rival skipper likes to pinch his boat or sail her full and by, whether or not another skipper is inclined to luff a boat passing him to windward, whether another skipper will fight for an inside position at the mark, and so forth. A handicap skipper must consider the human element also, but, in addition, he must learn the performance characteristics of his rivals' boats. These characteristics can affect his tactical judgment in the following ways: when a competitor is very close winded, it might be a mistake to start to windward of her or to attempt passing her to windward. If a rival's boat is slowed by choppy head seas, you might be able to escape her cover by tacking offshore into a chop, especially when the current is against the wind. When your boat is a centerboarder, you might be able to elude a deep keel covering boat by heading for shoal water. If your rival has a soft fore-foot or a shallow keel and falls off the wind after tacking, you might profit by a brief tacking duel to escape her cover. When your boat has a short fin and spade rudder (or double rudders), you may be able to outmaneauver a competitor with a long keel and forward rudder when starting or rounding buoys. If your boat is heavy, you may be able to tack sooner than a light competitor to fetch the windward mark by relying on your ability to luff and forereach around the mark. These are just a few examples of how it can help to size up the boats of your racing rivals. The curious thing about handicap racing is that sister boats sometimes do not have close races, but boats of entirely different lines, even based on opposite design concepts (but with similar ratings) often engage in extremely close boat-for-boat racing. But this is another intriguing aspect of the sport.

Appendix I[*]

1969 NAYRU Yacht Racing Rules (Parts I and IV)

Part I Definitions

When a term defined in Part I is used in its defined sense it is printed in **bold** type. All definitions and italicized notes rank as rules.

Racing—A yacht is **racing** from her preparatory signal until she has either **finished** and cleared the finishing line and finishing **marks** or retired, or until the race has been **cancelled, postponed** or **abandoned,** except that in match or team races, the sailing instructions may prescribe that a yacht is **racing** from any specified time before the preparatory signal.

Starting—A yacht **starts** when, after her starting signal, any part of her hull, crew or equipment first crosses the starting line in the direction of the first mark.

Finishing—A yacht **finishes** when any part of her hull, or of her crew or equipment in normal position, crosses the finishing line from the direction of the last mark.

Luffing—Altering course towards the wind until head to wind.

Tacking—A yacht is **tacking** from the moment she is beyond head to wind until she has **borne away,** if beating to windward, to a **close-hauled** course; if not beating to windward, to the course on which her mainsail has filled.

Bearing Away—Altering course away from the wind until a yacht begins to **jibe.**

Jibing—A yacht begins to **jibe** at the moment when, with the wind aft, the foot of her mainsail crosses her centre line and completes the **jibe** when the mainsail has filled on the other **tack.**

On a Tack—A yacht is **on a tack** except when she is **tacking** or **jibing.** A yacht is on the **tack (starboard** or **port)** corresponding to her **windward** side.

Close-hauled—A yacht is **close-hauled** when sailing by the wind as close as she can lie with advantage in working to windward.

Clear Astern and **Clear Ahead; Overlap**—A yacht is **clear astern** of another when her hull and equipment in normal position are abaft an imaginary line projected abeam from the aftermost point of the other's hull and equipment in normal position. The other yacht is **clear ahead.** The yachts **overlap** if neither is **clear astern;** or if, although one is **clear astern,** an intervening yacht **overlaps** both of them. The terms **clear astern, clear ahead** and **overlap** apply to yachts on opposite **tacks** only when they are subject to rule 42, Rounding or Passing Marks and Obstructions.

Leeward and **Windward**—The **leeward** side of a yacht is that on which she is, or, if **luffing** head to wind, was, carrying her mainsail. The opposite side is the **windward** side.

When neither of two yachts on the same **tack** is **clear astern,** the one on the **leeward** side of the other is the **leeward yacht.** The other is the **windward yacht.**

Proper course—A **proper course** is any course which a yacht might sail after the starting signal, in the absence of the other yacht or yachts affected, to **finish** as quickly as possible. The course sailed before **luffing** or **bearing away** is presumably, but not necessarily, that yacht's **proper course.** There is no **proper course** before the starting signal.

Mark—A **mark** is any object specified in the sailing instructions which a yacht must round or pass on a required side.

*To obtain complete NAYRU rules see page 130.

Obstruction—An **obstruction** is any object, including craft under way, large enough to require a yacht, if not less than one overall length away from it, to make a substantial alteration of course to pass on one side or the other, or any object which can be passed on one side only, including a buoy when the yacht in question cannot safely pass between it and the shoal or object which it marks.

Cancellation—A **cancelled** race is one which the race committee decides will not be sailed thereafter.

Postponement—A **postponed** race is one which is not started at its scheduled time and which can be sailed at any time the race committee may decide.

Abandonment—An **abandoned** race is one which the race committee declares void at any time after the starting signal, and which can be re-sailed at its discretion.

Part IV

Sailing Rules When Yachts Meet

Helmsman's Rights and Obligations Concerning Right of Way

The rules of Part IV apply only between yachts which either are intending to **race** or are **racing** in the same or different races, and, except when rule 3.2(b)(ii)*applies, replace the International Regulations for Preventing Collisions at Sea or Government Right-of-Way Rules applicable to the area concerned, from the time a yacht intending to **race** begins to sail about in the vicinity of the starting line until she has either **finished** or retired and has left the vicinity of the course.

Section A—Rules Which Always Apply

31—Disqualification

1. A yacht may be disqualified for infringing a rule of Part IV only when the infringement occurs while she is **racing,** whether or not a collision results.

2. A yacht may be disqualified before or after she is **racing** for seriously hindering a yacht which is **racing,** or for infringing the sailing instructions.

32—Avoiding Collisions

A right-of-way yacht which makes no attempt to avoid a collision resulting in serious damage may be disqualified as well as the other yacht.

33—Retiring from Race

A yacht which realizes she has infringed a racing rule or a sailing instruction should retire promptly; but, when she persists in **racing,** other yachts shall continue to accord her such rights as she may have under the rules of Part IV.

34—Limitations on the Right-of-Way Yacht to Alter Course

When one yacht is required to keep clear of another, the right-of-way yacht shall not (except to the extent permitted by rule 38.1, Right-of-way Yacht Luffing after Starting), so alter course as to prevent the other yacht from keeping clear; or to obstruct her while so doing.

*3.2(b)(ii) When the race is to continue after sunset, the time or place, if any, at which the International Regulations for Preventing Collisions at Sea, or Government Right-of-Way Rules, shall replace the corresponding rules of Part IV, and the night signals the committee boat will display.

35 — Hailing

A right-of-way yacht, except when **luffing** under rule 38.1, Luffing after Starting, should hail before or when making an alteration of course which may not be foreseen by the other yacht or when claiming the establishment or termination of an **overlap** at a **mark** or **obstruction.**

Section B — Opposite Tack Rule

36 — Fundamental Rule

A **port-tack** yacht shall keep clear of a **starboard-tack** yacht.

Section C — Same Tack Rules

37 — Fundamental Rules

1. A **windward yacht** shall keep clear of a **leeward yacht.**
2. A yacht **clear astern** shall keep clear of a yacht **clear ahead.**
3. A yacht which establishes an **overlap** to **leeward** from **clear astern** shall allow the **windward yacht** ample room and opportunity to keep clear, and during the existence of that **overlap** the **leeward yacht** shall not sail above her **proper course.**

38 — Right-of-Way Yacht Luffing after Starting

1. **Luffing Rights and Limitations.** After she has **started** and cleared the starting line, a yacht **clear ahead** or a **leeward yacht** may **luff** as she pleases, except that: —

   A **leeward yacht** shall not sail above her **proper course** while an **overlap** exists if, at any time during its existence, the helmsman of the **windward yacht** (when sighting abeam from his normal **station** and sailing no higher than the **leeward yacht)** has been abreast or forward of the mainmast of the **leeward yacht.**

2. **Overlap Limitations.** For the purpose of this rule: An **overlap** does not exist unless the yachts are clearly within two overall lengths of the longer yacht; and an **overlap** which exists between two yachts when the leading yacht **starts,** or when one or both of them completes a **tack** or **jibe,** shall be regarded as a new **overlap** beginning at that time.

3. **Hailing to Stop or Prevent a Luff.** When there is doubt, the **leeward yacht** may assume that she has the right to **luff** unless the helmsman of the **windward yacht** has hailed "Mast Abeam," or words to that effect. The **leeward yacht** shall be governed by such hail, and, if she deems it improper, her only remedy is to protest.

4. **Curtailing a Luff.** The **windward yacht** shall not cause a **luff** to be curtailed because of her proximity to the **leeward yacht** unless an **obstruction,** a third yacht or other object restricts her ability to respond.

5. **Luffing Two or More Yachts.** A yacht shall not **luff** unless she has the right to **luff** all yachts which would be affected by her **luff,** in which case they shall all respond even if an intervening yacht or yachts would not otherwise have the right to **luff.**

39 — Sailing Below a Proper Course

A yacht which is on a free leg of the course shall not sail below her **proper course** when she is clearly within three of her overall lengths of either a **leeward yacht** or a yacht **clear astern** which is steering a course to pass to **leeward.**

40 — Right-of-Way Luffing before Starting

Before a yacht has **started** and cleared the starting line, any **luff** on her part which causes another yacht to have to alter course to avoid a collision shall be carried out slowly and in such a way so as to give the **windward yacht** room and opportunity to keep clear, but before her starting signal, the **leeward yacht** shall not so **luff** above a **close-hauled** course, unless the helmsman of the **windward yacht** (sighting abeam from his normal station) is abaft the mainmast of the **leeward yacht.** Rules 38.3, Hailing to Stop or Prevent a Luff; 38.4, Curtailing a Luff; and 38.5, Luffing Two or more Yachts, also apply.

Section D—Changing Tack Rules

41—Tacking or Jibing

1. A yacht which is either **tacking** or **jibing** shall keep clear of a yacht **on a tack.**

2. A yacht shall neither **tack** nor **jibe** into a position which will give her right of way unless she does so far enough from a yacht **on a tack** to enable this yacht to keep clear without having to begin to alter her course until after the **tack** or **jibe** has been completed.

3. A yacht which **tacks** or **jibes** has the onus of satisfying the race committee that she completed her **tack** or **jibe** in accordance with rule 41.2.

4. When two yachts are both **tacking** or both **jibing** at the same time, the one on the other's **port** side shall keep clear.

Section E—Rules of Exception and Special Application

When a rule of this section applies, to the extent to which it explicitly provides rights and obligations, it over-rides any conflicting rule of Part IV which precedes it except the rules of Section A—Rules Which Always Apply.

42—Rounding or Passing Marks and Obstructions

When yachts either on the same **tack** or, after **starting** and clearing the starting line, on opposite **tacks,** are about to round or pass a **mark** on the same required side or an **obstruction** on the same side:—

When Overlapped

1. (a) An outside yacht shall give each yacht **overlapping** her on the inside, room to round or pass it, except as provided in rules 42.1(c),(d) and (e). Room includes room to **tack** or **jibe** when either is an integral part of the rounding or passing manoeuvre.

   (b) When an inside yacht of two or more **overlapped** yachts on opposite **tacks** will have to **jibe** in rounding a **mark** in order most directly to assume a **proper course** to the next **mark,** she shall **jibe** at the first reasonable opportunity.

   (c) When two yachts on opposite **tacks** are on a beat or when one of them will have to **tack** either to round the **mark** or to avoid the **obstruction,** as between each other rule 42.1(a) shall not apply and they are subject to rules 36, Opposite Tack Fundamental Rule, and 41, Tacking or Jibing.

   (d) An outside **leeward yacht** with luffing rights may take an inside yacht to windward of a **mark** provided that she hails to that effect and begins to **luff** before she is within two of her overall lengths of the **mark** and provided that she also passes to windward of it.

   (e) When approaching the starting line to **start,** a **leeward yacht** shall be under no obligation to give any **windward yacht** room to pass to leeward of a starting **mark** surrounded by navigable water; but, after the starting signal, a **leeward yacht** shall not deprive a **windward yacht** of room at such a **mark** by sailing either above the first **mark** or above **close-hauled.**

When Clear Astern and Clear Ahead

2. (a) A yacht **clear astern** shall keep clear in anticipation of and during the rounding or passing manoeuvre when the yacht **clear ahead** remains on the same **tack** or **jibes.**

   (b) A yacht **clear ahead** which **tacks** to round a **mark** is subject to rule 41, Tacking or Jibing, but a yacht **clear astern** shall not **luff** above **close-hauled** so as to prevent the yacht **clear ahead** from **tacking.**

Restrictions on Establishing and Maintaining an Overlap

3. (a) A yacht **clear astern** shall not establish an inside **overlap** and be entitled to room under rule 42.1(a) when the yacht **clear ahead:**—

 (i) is within two of her overall lengths of the **mark** or **obstruction,** except as provided in rules 42.3(b) and 42.3(c); or

 (ii) is unable to give the required room.

 (b) The two lengths determinative of rule 42.3(a) (i) shall not apply to yachts, of which one has **tacked** in the vicinity of a **mark,** unless when the **tack** is completed the yachts are clearly more than two overall lengths from the **mark.**

 (c) A yacht **clear astern** may establish an **overlap** between the yacht **clear ahead** and a continuing **obstruction** such as a shoal or the shore, only when there is room for her to do so in safety.

 (d) (i) A yacht **clear ahead** shall be under no obligation to give room to a yacht **clear astern** before an **overlap** is established.

 (ii) A yacht which claims an inside **overlap** has the onus of satisfying the race committee that the **overlap** was established on proper time.

 (e) (i) When an outside yacht is **overlapped** at the time she comes within two of her overall lengths of a **mark,** she shall continue to be bound by rule 42.1(a) to give room as required even though the **overlap** may thereafter be broken.

 (ii) An outside yacht which claims to have broken an **overlap** has the onus of satisfying the race committee that she became **clear ahead** when she was more than two of her overall lengths from the **mark.**

43 — Close-Hauled, Hailing for Room to Tack at Obstructions

1. **Hailing.** When two **close-hauled** yachts are on the same **tack** and safe pilotage requires the yacht **clear ahead** or the **leeward yacht** to make a substantial alteration of course to clear an **obstruction,** and if she intends to **tack,** but cannot **tack** without colliding with the other yacht, she shall hail the other yacht for room to **tack,** but she shall not hail and **tack** simultaneously.

2. **Responding.** The hailed yacht at the earliest possible moment after the hail shall either:—

 (a) **tack,** in which case, the hailing yacht shall begin to **tack,** either:—

 (i) before the hailed yacht has completed her **tack,** or

 (ii) if she cannot then **tack** without colliding with the hailed yacht, immediately she is able to **tack, or**

 (b) reply "You **tack,**" or words to that effect, if in her opinion she can keep clear without **tacking** or after postponing her **tack.** In this case:—

 (i) the hailing yacht shall immediately **tack** and

 (ii) the hailed yacht shall keep clear.

 (iii) The onus shall lie on the hailed yacht which replied "You **tack**" to satisfy the race committee that she kept clear.

3. **Limitation on Right to Room**

 (a) When the **obstruction** is a **mark** which the hailed yacht can fetch, the hailing yacht shall not be entitled to room to **tack** and the hailed yacht shall immediately so inform the hailing yacht.

 (b) If, thereafter, the hailing yacht again hails for room to **tack,** she shall, after receiving it, retire immediately.

 (c) If, after having refused to respond to a hail under rule 43.3(a), the hailed yacht fails to fetch, she shall retire immediately.

44 — Yachts Returning to Start

1.(a) A premature starter when returning to **start,** or a yacht working into position from the wrong side of the starting line or its extensions, when the starting signal is made, shall keep clear of all yachts which are **starting,** or have **started,** correctly, until she is wholly on the right side of the starting line or its extensions.

(b) Thereafter, she shall be accorded the rights under the rules of Part IV of a yacht which is **starting** correctly; but if she thereby acquires right of way over another yacht which is **starting** correctly, she shall allow that yacht ample room and opportunity to keep clear.

2. A premature starter while continuing to sail the course and until it is obvious that she is returning to **start,** shall be accorded the rights under the rules of Part IV of a yacht which has **started.**

45 — Yachts Re-rounding after Touching a Mark

1. A yacht which has touched a **mark** and is about to correct her error in accordance with rule 52.1, Touching a Mark, shall keep clear of all other yachts which are about to round or pass it or have rounded or passed it correctly, until she has rounded it completely and **has** cleared it and is on a **proper course** to the next **mark.**

2. A yacht which has touched a **mark,** while continuing to sail the course and until it is obvious that she is returning to round it completely in accordance with rule 52.1, Touching a Mark, shall be accorded rights under the rules of Part IV.

Section F — When Not Under Way

46 — Anchored, Aground or Capsized

1. A yacht under way shall keep clear of another yacht **racing** which is anchored, aground or capsized. Of two anchored yachts, the one which anchored later shall keep clear, except that a yacht which is dragging shall keep clear of one which is not.

2. A yacht anchored or aground shall indicate the fact to any yacht which may be in danger of fouling her. Unless the size of the yachts or the weather conditions make some other signal necessary a hail is sufficient indication.

3. A yacht shall not be penalized for fouling a yacht in distress which she is attempting to assist or a yacht which goes aground or capsizes immediately ahead of her.

---

*52 — Touching a Mark

1. A yacht which either: —
  (a) touches: —
    (i) a starting **mark** before **starting;**
    (ii) a **mark** which begins, bounds or ends the leg of the course on which she is sailing; or
    (iii) a finishing **mark** after **finishing,** or
  (b) causes a **mark** vessel to shift to avoid being touched,

shall retire immediately, unless she claims that she was wrongfully compelled to touch it by another yacht, in which case she shall protest. However, unless otherwise prescribed in the sailing instructions, when the **mark** is surrounded by navigable water, a yacht may correct her error by making one complete rounding of the **mark,** leaving it on the required side without touching it, in addition to rounding or passing it as required to sail the course. In the case of a **mark** at the starboard end of the starting or finishing line, such complete rounding shall be clockwise, and at the port end of a starting or finishing line anti-clockwise.

Appendix II

The calculation of time allowances and corrected times for Cruising Class Races has long been an onerous burden to all Race Committees. When this work has had to be done under adverse conditions, or the Committees have lacked experience, the accuracy of the results, as well as the delays in posting them, have sometimes been justly criticized.

In a search for "a better way," these Tables have been devised by the Fishing Bay Yacht Club to reduce the calculations required of the Race Committee to an absolute minimum.

The Time Allowance for each Entry in a race of a given distance may be read directly from these Tables and requires no calculation whatever. The 15' to 44.9' range of Ratings with columns for races of 10 mi. to 32 mi. in length, cover 98% of the cases in Chesapeake Bay Yacht Racing Association races last year.

These Tables are derived from the standard NAYRU Allowance Tables, and the differentials between corrected times of yachts, as determined from these Tables, is always identical with those obtained by other methods of calculation.

A unique feature is the assumption that **the "Scratch Yacht" is always a hypothetical entry with a Rating of 30.0'**. This requires a slight change of thinking in the application of time allowances for entries rating above 30.0', in that time allowances for such entries must be **added** to elapsed time, instead of subtracted.

The advantages provided by these Tables are:

a. Subtraction of the Scratch Yacht's allowance from that of each yacht is eliminated.

b. Multiplication of allowance by distance for each yacht is eliminated.

c. It is unnecessary to wait until the entries are complete to determine the Scratch Yacht. Consequently, the time allowances for each yacht for the race can be taken directly from the Tables as soon as the entry form comes in. Thus, much of the Committee's work may be done ashore before the start of the race.

d. "Scratch Sheets" listing yachts and time allowances can be more readily prepared in advance for distribution to skippers before the start.

e. Selection of the Scratch Yacht in the center of the range of ratings covered by these Tables reduces the magnitude of the numbers to be dealt with, thus reducing chances for error and speeding up the Committee's work.

The only special precaution required is to remember that **Time Allowances for yachts rating OVER 30.0' must be ADDED to their Elapsed Time** to determine their Corrected Time.

For races longer or shorter than those covered by the Tables, time allowances may still be determined readily from those given in the Tables by addition or subtraction. For example, the time allowance of any yacht in a 41 mile race is her allowance for 30 miles **plus** her allowance for 11 miles. Similarly, the time allowance of any yacht in an eight mile race is her allowance for 18 miles **less** her allowance for 10 miles.

These Tables will also be most useful to the skipper who wants to know quickly, "how much time" another yacht must give him, or "how much time" he must give to another yacht. One simple subtraction (or, if one of the yachts rates above 30.0', an addition) gives the answer. By timing his own, and the other yachts' roundings of an intermediate mark of known distance from the start, a skipper can easily determine his corrected time position in the race at any such mark of the course.

It is hoped that these Tables will prove a worthwhile contribution to the sport.

Reid A. Dunn
Fleet Captain
Fishing Bay Yacht Club

EXAMPLES

1. In a 20 Mile Race
    YACHT "A" — Rating 21.2'
         Time Allowance — taken from the 20 Mile Column of the Tables =   (−) 24:55
                       Elapsed Time for Yacht "A" was   4:36:59
              SUBTRACTING — (rating below 30.0') — Time Allowance   (−)   24:55

                              Corrected Time   =   4:12:04

    YACHT "B" — Rating 31.5'
         Time Allowance — taken from the 20 Mile Column of the Tables =   (+) 03:10
                       Elapsed Time for Yacht "B" was   4:04:16
              ADDING — (rating above 30.0') — Time Allowance   (+)   03:10
                              Corrected Time   =   4:07:26

2. How much time must a yacht rating 25.4' give to one rating 22.3' in a 15 Mile Race?
        From the 15 Mile Column in the Tables:
              The Time Allowance for a rating of 22.3' =   (−)   15:46
                         and for a rating of 25.4' =   (−)   08:33

        Since both yachts rate below 30.0' —
        Answer is the **DIFFERENCE**   =   07:13

3. How much time must a yacht rating 35.6' give to one rating 30.5' in a 20 Mile Race?
        From the 20 Mile Column in the Tables:
              The Time Allowance for a rating of 35.6' =   (+)   10:47
                         and for a rating of 30.5' =   (+)   01:05

        Since both yachts rate above 30.0' —
        Answer is the **DIFFERENCE**   =   09:42

4. How much time must a yacht rating 31.3' give to one rating 21.1' in an 18 Mile Race?
        From the 18 Mile Column in the Tables:
              The Time Allowance for a rating of 31.3' =   (+)   02:29
                         and for a rating of 21.1' =   (−)   22:46

        Since one yacht rates above 30.0' and the
        other rates below 30.0' — **Answer** is the **SUM**   =   25:15

When one yacht rates **above** the Scratch Yacht rating of 30.0' (zero time allowance) and the other rates **below,** the time allowance of the larger yacht is (+) while that of the smaller is (−). The difference between the two is equal to the numerical total of these two time allowances, added without regard to sign.

191

Rating	Sec/Mi	10 Mi	11 Mi	12 Mi	13 Mi	14 Mi	15 Mi	16 Mi	17 Mi	18 Mi	19 Mi	20 Mi	Rating
15.0	163.35	27-14	29-57	32-40	35-24	38-07	40-50	43-34	46-17	49-00	51-44	54-27	**15.0**
15.1	161.49	26-55	29-36	32-18	34-59	37-41	40-22	43-04	45-45	48-27	51-08	53-50	**15.1**
15.2	159.65	26-36	29-16	31-56	34-35	37-15	39-55	42-34	45-14	47-54	50-33	53-13	**15.2**
15.3	157.83	26-18	28-56	31-34	34-12	36-50	39-27	42-05	44-43	47-21	49-59	52-37	**15.3**
15.4	156.03	26-00	28-36	31-12	33-48	36-24	39-00	41-36	44-12	46-49	49-25	52-01	**15.4**
15.5	154.26	25-43	28-17	30-51	33-25	35-60	38-34	41-08	43-42	46-17	48-51	51-25	**15.5**
15.6	152.50	25-25	27-57	30-30	33-02	35-35	38-08	40-40	43-12	45-45	48-17	50-50	**15.6**
15.7	150.76	25-08	27-38	30-09	32-40	35-11	37-41	40-12	42-43	45-14	47-44	50-15	**15.7**
15.8	149.03	24-50	27-19	29-48	32-17	34-46	37-15	39-44	42-14	44-43	47-12	49-41	**15.8**
15.9	147.31	24-33	27-00	29-28	31-55	34-22	36-50	39-17	41-44	44-12	46-39	49-06	**15.9**
16.0	145.64	24-16	26-42	29-08	31-33	33-59	36-25	38-50	41-16	43-42	46-07	48-33	**16.0**
16.1	143.97	23-60	26-24	28-48	31-12	33-36	35-60	38-24	40-47	43-11	45-35	47-59	**16.1**
16.2	142.31	23-43	26-05	28-28	30-50	33-12	35-35	37-57	40-19	42-42	45-04	47-26	**16.2**
16.3	140.66	23-27	25-47	28-08	30-29	32-49	35-10	37-31	39-51	42-12	44-33	46-53	**16.3**
16.4	139.02	23-10	25-29	27-48	30-07	32-26	34-45	37-04	39-23	41-42	44-01	46-20	**16.4**
16.5	137.39	22-54	25-11	27-29	29-46	32-03	34-21	36-38	38-56	41-13	43-30	45-48	**16.5**
16.6	135.79	22-38	24-54	27-09	29-25	31-41	33-57	36-13	38-28	40-44	43-00	45-16	**16.6**
16.7	134.21	22-22	24-36	26-51	29-05	31-19	33-33	35-47	38-02	40-16	42-30	44-44	**16.7**
16.8	132.64	22-06	24-19	26-32	28-44	30-57	33-10	35-22	37-35	39-48	42-00	44-13	**16.8**
16.9	131.08	21-51	24-02	26-13	28-24	30-35	32-46	34-57	37-08	39-19	41-30	43-42	**16.9**
17.0	129.52	21-35	23-45	25-54	28-04	30-13	32-23	34-32	36-42	38-51	41-01	43-10	**17.0**
17.1	127.99	21-20	23-28	25-36	27-44	29-52	31-60	34-08	36-16	38-24	40-32	42-40	**17.1**
17.2	126.47	21-05	23-11	25-18	27-24	29-31	31-37	33-44	35-50	37-56	40-03	42-09	**17.2**
17.3	124.96	20-50	22-55	24-60	27-04	29-09	31-14	33-19	35-24	37-29	39-34	41-39	**17.3**
17.4	123.46	20-35	22-38	24-42	26-45	28-48	30-52	32-55	34-59	37-02	39-06	41-09	**17.4**
17.5	121.97	20-20	22-22	24-24	26-26	28-28	30-30	32-32	34-33	36-35	38-37	40-39	**17.5**
17.6	120.50	20-05	22-05	24-06	26-06	28-07	30-08	32-08	34-08	36-09	38-09	40-10	**17.6**
17.7	119.04	19-50	21-49	23-48	25-48	27-47	29-46	31-45	33-44	35-43	37-42	39-41	**17.7**
17.8	117.60	19-36	21-34	23-31	25-29	27-26	29-24	31-22	33-19	35-17	37-14	39-12	**17.8**
17.9	116.17	19-22	21-18	23-14	25-10	27-06	29-03	30-59	32-55	34-51	36-47	38-43	**17.9**
18.0	114.75	19-08	21-02	22-57	24-52	26-47	28-41	30-36	32-31	34-26	36-20	38-15	**18.0**
18.1	113.33	18-53	20-47	22-40	24-33	26-27	28-20	30-13	32-07	33-60	35-53	37-47	**18.1**
18.2	111.93	18-39	20-31	22-23	24-15	26-07	27-59	29-51	31-43	33-35	35-27	37-19	**18.2**
18.3	110.54	18-25	20-16	22-06	23-57	25-48	27-38	29-29	31-19	33-10	35-00	36-51	**18.3**
18.4	109.17	18-12	20-01	21-50	23-39	25-28	27-18	29-07	30-56	32-45	34-34	36-23	**18.4**
18.5	107.83	17-58	19-46	21-34	23-22	25-10	26-57	28-45	30-33	32-21	34-09	35-57	**18.5**
18.6	106.48	17-45	19-31	21-18	23-04	24-51	26-37	28-24	30-10	31-57	33-43	35-30	**18.6**
18.7	105.14	17-31	19-17	21-02	22-47	24-32	26-17	28-02	29-47	31-33	33-18	35-03	**18.7**
18.8	103.82	17-18	19-02	20-46	22-30	24-13	25-57	27-41	29-25	31-09	32-53	34-36	**18.8**
18.9	102.50	17-05	18-47	20-30	22-12	23-55	25-38	27-20	29-02	30-45	32-27	34-10	**18.9**
19.0	101.19	16-52	18-33	20-14	21-55	23-37	25-18	26-59	28-40	30-21	32-03	33-44	**19.0**
19.1	099.89	16-39	18-19	19-59	21-39	23-18	24-58	26-38	28-18	29-58	31-38	33-18	**19.1**
19.2	098.60	16-26	18-05	19-43	21-22	23-00	24-39	26-18	27-56	29-35	31-13	32-52	**19.2**
19.3	097.32	16-13	17-51	19-28	21-05	22-42	24-20	25-57	27-34	29-12	30-49	32-26	**19.3**
19.4	096.05	16-00	17-37	19-13	20-49	22-25	24-01	25-37	27-13	28-49	30-25	32-01	**19.4**
19.5	094.78	15-48	17-23	18-57	20-32	22-07	23-42	25-16	26-51	28-26	30-01	31-36	**19.5**
19.6	093.53	15-35	17-09	18-42	20-16	21-49	23-23	24-56	26-30	28-04	29-37	31-11	**19.6**
19.7	092.29	15-23	16-55	18-27	19-60	21-32	23-04	24-37	26-09	27-41	29-14	30-46	**19.7**
19.8	091.06	15-11	16-42	18-13	19-44	21-15	22-46	24-17	25-48	27-19	28-50	30-21	**19.8**
19.9	089.84	14-58	16-28	17-58	19-28	20-58	22-28	23-57	25-27	26-57	28-27	29-57	**19.9**
Rating	**Sec/Mi**	**10 Mi**	**11 Mi**	**12 Mi**	**13 Mi**	**14 Mi**	**15 Mi**	**16 Mi**	**17 Mi**	**18 Mi**	**19 Mi**	**20 Mi**	**Rating**

SUBTRACT time allowances on this page from Elapsed Time

192

Rating	21 Mi	22 Mi	23 Mi	24 Mi	25 Mi	26 Mi	27 Mi	28 Mi	29 Mi	30 Mi	31 Mi	32 Mi	Rating
15.0	57-10	59-54	62-37	65-20	68-04	70-47	73-30	76-14	78-57	81-41	84-24	87-07	15.0
15.1	56-31	59-13	61-54	64-36	67-17	69-59	72-40	75-22	78-03	80-45	83-26	86-08	15.1
15.2	55-53	58-32	61-12	63-52	66-31	69-11	71-51	74-30	77-10	79-50	82-29	85-09	15.2
15.3	55-14	57-52	60-30	63-08	65-46	68-24	71-01	73-39	76-17	78-55	81-33	84-11	15.3
15.4	54-37	57-13	59-49	62-25	65-01	67-37	70-13	72-49	75-25	78-01	80-37	83-13	15.4
15.5	53-59	56-34	59-08	61-42	64-17	66-51	69-25	71-59	74-34	77-08	79-42	82-16	15.5
15.6	53-23	55-55	58-27	61-00	63-32	66-05	68-38	71-10	73-42	76-15	78-47	81-20	15.6
15.7	52-46	55-17	57-47	60-18	62-49	65-20	67-51	70-21	72-52	75-23	77-54	80-24	15.7
15.8	52-10	54-39	57-08	59-37	62-06	64-35	67-04	69-33	72-02	74-31	76-60	79-29	15.8
15.9	51-33	54-01	56-28	58-55	61-23	63-50	66-17	68-45	71-12	73-39	76-07	78-34	15.9
16.0	50-58	53-24	55-50	58-15	60-41	63-07	65-32	67-58	70-24	72-49	75-15	77-40	16.0
16.1	50-23	52-47	55-11	57-35	59-59	62-23	64-47	67-11	69-35	71-59	74-23	76-47	16.1
16.2	49-48	52-11	54-33	56-55	59-18	61-40	64-02	66-25	68-47	71-09	73-32	75-54	16.2
16.3	49-14	51-35	53-55	56-16	58-36	60-57	63-18	65-38	67-59	70-20	72-40	75-01	16.3
16.4	48-39	50-58	53-17	55-36	57-56	60-15	62-34	64-53	67-12	69-31	71-50	74-09	16.4
16.5	48-05	50-23	52-40	54-57	57-15	59-32	61-50	64-07	66-24	68-42	70-59	73-16	16.5
16.6	47-32	49-47	52-03	54-19	56-35	58-51	61-06	63-22	65-38	67-54	70-09	72-25	16.6
16.7	46-58	49-13	51-27	53-41	55-55	58-09	60-24	62-38	64-52	67-06	69-20	71-35	16.7
16.8	46-25	48-38	50-51	53-03	55-16	57-29	59-41	61-54	64-07	66-19	68-32	70-44	16.8
16.9	45-53	48-04	50-15	52-26	54-37	56-48	58-59	61-10	63-21	65-32	67-43	69-55	16.9
17.0	45-20	47-29	49-39	51-48	53-58	56-08	58-17	60-27	62-36	64-46	66-55	69-05	17.0
17.1	44-48	46-56	49-04	51-12	53-20	55-28	57-36	59-44	61-52	63-60	66-08	68-16	17.1
17.2	44-16	46-22	48-29	50-35	52-42	54-48	56-55	59-01	61-08	63-14	65-21	67-27	17.2
17.3	43-44	45-49	47-54	49-59	52-04	54-09	56-14	58-19	60-24	62-29	64-34	66-39	17.3
17.4	43-13	45-16	47-20	49-23	51-26	53-30	55-33	57-37	59-40	61-44	63-47	65-51	17.4
17.5	42-41	44-43	46-45	48-47	50-49	52-51	54-53	56-55	58-57	60-59	63-01	65-03	17.5
17.6	42-11	44-11	46-11	48-12	50-12	52-13	54-14	56-14	58-14	60-15	62-15	64-16	17.6
17.7	41-40	43-39	45-38	47-37	49-36	51-35	53-34	55-33	57-32	59-31	61-30	63-29	17.7
17.8	41-10	43-07	45-05	47-02	49-00	50-58	52-55	54-53	56-50	58-48	60-46	62-43	17.8
17.9	40-40	42-36	44-32	46-28	48-24	50-20	52-17	54-13	56-09	58-05	60-01	61-57	17.9
18.0	40-10	42-05	43-59	45-54	47-49	49-44	51-38	53-33	55-28	57-23	59-17	61-12	18.0
18.1	39-40	41-33	43-27	45-20	47-13	49-07	50-60	52-53	54-47	56-40	58-33	60-27	18.1
18.2	39-11	41-02	42-54	44-46	46-38	48-30	50-22	52-14	54-06	55-58	57-50	59-42	18.2
18.3	38-41	40-32	42-22	44-13	46-03	47-54	49-45	51-35	53-26	55-16	57-07	58-57	18.3
18.4	38-13	40-02	41-51	43-40	45-29	47-18	49-08	50-57	52-46	54-35	56-24	58-13	18.4
18.5	37-44	39-32	41-20	43-08	44-56	46-44	48-31	50-19	52-07	53-55	55-43	57-31	18.5
18.6	37-16	39-03	40-49	42-36	44-22	46-08	47-55	49-41	51-28	53-14	55-01	56-47	18.6
18.7	36-48	38-33	40-18	42-03	43-48	45-34	47-19	49-04	50-49	52-34	54-19	56-04	18.7
18.8	36-20	38-04	39-48	41-32	43-15	44-59	46-43	48-27	50-11	51-55	53-38	55-22	18.8
18.9	35-53	37-35	39-17	41-00	42-42	44-25	46-08	47-50	49-32	51-15	52-57	54-40	18.9
19.0	35-25	37-06	38-47	40-29	42-10	43-51	45-32	47-13	48-54	50-36	52-17	53-58	19.0
19.1	34-58	36-38	38-17	39-57	41-37	43-17	44-57	46-37	48-17	49-57	51-37	53-16	19.1
19.2	34-31	36-09	37-48	39-26	41-05	42-44	44-22	46-01	47-39	49-18	50-57	52-35	19.2
19.3	34-04	35-41	37-18	38-56	40-33	42-10	43-48	45-25	47-02	48-40	50-17	51-54	19.3
19.4	33-37	35-13	36-49	38-25	40-01	41-37	43-13	44-49	46-25	48-02	49-38	51-14	19.4
19.5	33-10	34-45	36-20	37-55	39-29	41-04	42-39	44-14	45-49	47-23	48-58	50-33	19.5
19.6	32-44	34-18	35-51	37-25	38-58	40-32	42-05	43-39	45-12	46-46	48-19	49-53	19.6
19.7	32-18	33-50	35-23	36-55	38-27	39-60	41-32	43-04	44-36	46-09	47-41	49-13	19.7
19.8	31-52	33-23	34-54	36-25	37-56	39-28	40-59	42-30	44-01	45-32	47-03	48-34	19.8
19.9	31-27	32-56	34-26	35-56	37-26	38-56	40-26	41-56	43-25	44-55	46-25	47-55	19.9
Rating	21 Mi	22 Mi	23 Mi	24 Mi	25 Mi	26 Mi	27 Mi	28 Mi	29 Mi	30 Mi	31 Mi	32 Mi	Rating

SUBTRACT time allowances on this page from Elapsed Time

Rating	Sec/Mi	10 Mi	11 Mi	12 Mi	13 Mi	14 Mi	15 Mi	16 Mi	17 Mi	18 Mi	19 Mi	20 Mi	Rating
20.0	088.62	14-46	16-15	17-43	19-12	20-41	22-09	23-38	25-07	26-35	28-04	29-32	20.0
20.1	087.42	14-34	16-02	17-29	18-56	20-24	21-51	23-19	24-46	26-14	27-41	29-08	20.1
20.2	086.24	14-22	15-49	17-15	18-41	20-07	21-34	22-60	24-26	25-52	27-19	28-45	20.2
20.3	085.05	14-11	15-36	17-01	18-26	19-51	21-16	22-41	24-06	25-31	26-56	28-21	20.3
20.4	083.87	13-59	15-23	16-46	18-10	19-34	20-58	22-22	23-46	25-10	26-33	27-57	20.4
20.5	082.71	13-47	15-10	16-33	17-55	19-18	20-41	22-03	23-26	24-49	26-11	27-34	20.5
20.6	081.54	13-35	14-57	16-18	17-40	19-02	20-23	21-45	23-06	24-28	25-49	27-11	20.6
20.7	080.39	13-24	14-44	16-05	17-25	18-45	20-06	21-26	22-47	24-07	25-27	26-48	20.7
20.8	079.25	13-12	14-32	15-51	17-10	18-29	19-49	21-08	22-27	23-47	25-06	26-25	20.8
20.9	078.11	13-01	14-19	15-37	16-55	18-14	19-32	20-50	22-08	23-26	24-44	26-02	20.9
21.0	076.98	12-50	14-07	15-24	16-41	17-58	19-15	20-32	21-49	23-06	24-23	25-40	21.0
21.1	075.87	12-39	13-55	15-10	16-26	17-42	18-58	20-14	21-30	22-46	24-02	25-17	21.1
21.2	074.76	12-28	13-42	14-57	16-12	17-27	18-41	19-56	21-11	22-26	23-40	24-55	21.2
21.3	073.65	12-17	13-30	14-44	15-57	17-11	18-25	19-38	20-52	22-06	23-19	24-33	21.3
21.4	072.56	12-06	13-18	14-31	15-43	16-56	18-08	19-21	20-33	21-46	22-59	24-11	21.4
21.5	071.48	11-55	13-06	14-18	15-29	16-41	17-52	19-04	20-15	21-27	22-38	23-50	21.5
21.6	070.40	11-44	12-54	14-05	15-15	16-26	17-36	18-46	19-57	21-07	22-18	23-28	21.6
21.7	069.33	11-33	12-43	13-52	15-01	16-11	17-20	18-29	19-39	20-48	21-57	23-07	21.7
21.8	068.26	11-23	12-31	13-39	14-47	15-56	17-04	18-12	19-20	20-29	21-37	22-45	21.8
21.9	067.20	11-12	12-19	13-26	14-34	15-41	16-48	17-55	19-02	20-10	21-17	22-24	21.9
22.0	066.15	11-02	12-08	13-14	14-20	15-26	16-32	17-38	18-45	19-51	20-57	22-03	22.0
22.1	065.10	10-51	11-56	13-01	14-06	15-11	16-17	17-22	18-27	19-32	20-37	21-42	22.1
22.2	064.07	10-41	11-45	12-49	13-53	14-57	16-01	17-05	18-09	19-13	20-17	21-21	22.2
22.3	063.04	10-30	11-33	12-36	13-39	14-43	15-46	16-49	17-52	18-55	19-58	21-01	22.3
22.4	062.02	10-20	11-22	12-24	13-26	14-28	15-30	16-32	17-34	18-36	19-38	20-40	22.4
22.5	061.00	10-10	11-11	12-12	13-13	14-14	15-15	16-16	17-17	18-18	19-19	20-20	22.5
22.6	059.99	09-60	10-60	11-60	12-60	13-60	14-60	15-60	16-60	17-60	18-60	19-60	22.6
22.7	058.99	09-50	10-49	11-48	12-47	13-46	14-45	15-44	16-43	17-42	18-41	19-40	22.7
22.8	058.00	09-40	10-38	11-36	12-34	13-32	14-30	15-28	16-26	17-24	18-22	19-20	22.8
22.9	057.01	09-30	10-27	11-24	12-21	13-18	14-15	15-12	16-09	17-06	18-03	19-00	22.9
23.0	056.03	09-20	10-16	11-12	12-08	13-04	14-00	14-56	15-53	16-49	17-45	18-41	23.0
23.1	055.06	09-11	10-06	11-01	11-56	12-51	13-46	14-41	15-36	16-31	17-26	18-21	23.1
23.2	054.09	09-01	09-55	10-49	11-43	12-37	13-31	14-25	15-20	16-14	17-08	18-02	23.2
23.3	053.13	08-51	09-44	10-38	11-31	12-24	13-17	14-10	15-03	15-56	16-49	17-43	23.3
23.4	052.17	08-42	09-34	10-26	11-18	12-10	13-03	13-55	14-47	15-39	16-31	17-23	23.4
23.5	051.22	08-32	09-23	10-15	11-06	11-57	12-48	13-39	14-31	15-22	16-13	17-04	23.5
23.6	050.27	08-23	09-13	10-03	10-53	11-44	12-34	13-24	14-15	15-05	15-55	16-45	23.6
23.7	049.33	08-13	09-03	09-52	10-41	11-31	12-20	13-09	13-59	14-48	15-37	16-27	23.7
23.8	048.40	08-04	08-52	09-41	10-29	11-18	12-06	12-54	13-43	14-31	15-20	16-08	23.8
23.9	047.48	07-55	08-42	09-30	10-17	11-05	11-52	12-40	13-27	14-15	15-02	15-50	23.9
24.0	046.55	07-45	08-32	09-19	10-05	10-52	11-38	12-25	13-11	13-58	14-44	15-31	24.0
24.1	045.64	07-36	08-22	09-08	09-53	10-39	11-25	12-10	12-56	13-42	14-27	15-13	24.1
24.2	044.73	07-27	08-12	08-57	09-41	10-26	11-11	11-56	12-40	13-25	14-10	14-55	24.2
24.3	043.82	07-18	08-02	08-46	09-30	10-13	10-57	11-41	12-25	13-09	13-53	14-36	24.3
24.4	042.92	07-09	07-52	08-35	09-18	10-01	10-44	11-27	12-10	12-53	13-35	14-18	24.4
24.5	042.03	07-00	07-42	08-24	09-06	09-48	10-30	11-12	11-54	12-37	13-19	14-01	24.5
24.6	041.14	06-51	07-33	08-14	08-55	09-36	10-17	10-58	11-39	12-21	13-02	13-43	24.6
24.7	040.26	06-43	07-23	08-03	08-43	09-24	10-04	10-44	11-24	12-05	12-45	13-25	24.7
24.8	039.38	06-34	07-13	07-53	08-32	09-11	09-51	10-30	11-09	11-49	12-28	13-08	24.8
24.9	038.51	06-25	07-04	07-42	08-21	08-59	09-38	10-16	10-55	11-33	12-12	12-50	24.9
Rating	Sec/Mi	10 Mi	11 Mi	12 Mi	13 Mi	14 Mi	15 Mi	16 Mi	17 Mi	18 Mi	19 Mi	20 Mi	Rating

SUBTRACT time allowances on this page from Elapsed Time

194

Rating	21 Mi	22 Mi	23 Mi	24 Mi	25 Mi	26 Mi	27 Mi	28 Mi	29 Mi	30 Mi	31 Mi	32 Mi	Rating
20.0	31-01	32-30	33-58	35-27	36-56	38-24	39-53	41-21	42-50	44-19	45-47	47-16	20.0
20.1	30-36	32-03	33-31	34-58	36-26	37-53	39-20	40-48	42-15	43-43	45-10	46-37	20.1
20.2	30-11	31-37	33-03	34-30	35-56	37-22	38-48	40-15	41-41	43-07	44-33	45-60	20.2
20.3	29-46	31-11	32-36	34-01	35-26	36-51	38-16	39-41	41-06	42-32	43-57	45-22	20.3
20.4	29-21	30-45	32-09	33-33	34-57	36-21	37-44	39-08	40-32	41-56	43-20	44-44	20.4
20.5	28-57	30-20	31-42	33-05	34-28	35-50	37-13	38-36	39-59	41-21	42-44	44-07	20.5
20.6	28-32	29-54	31-15	32-37	33-59	35-20	36-42	38-03	39-25	40-46	42-08	43-29	20.6
20.7	28-08	29-29	30-49	32-09	33-30	34-50	36-11	37-31	38-51	40-12	41-32	42-52	20.7
20.8	27-44	29-03	30-23	31-42	33-01	34-20	35-40	36-59	38-18	39-38	40-57	42-16	20.8
20.9	27-20	28-38	29-57	31-15	32-33	33-51	35-09	36-27	37-45	39-03	40-21	41-39	20.9
21.0	26-57	28-14	29-31	30-48	32-05	33-21	34-38	35-55	37-12	38-29	39-46	41-03	21.0
21.1	26-33	27-49	29-05	30-21	31-37	32-53	34-08	35-24	36-40	37-56	39-12	40-28	21.1
21.2	26-10	27-25	28-39	29-54	31-09	32-24	33-39	34-53	36-08	37-23	38-38	39-52	21.2
21.3	25-47	27-00	28-14	29-28	30-41	31-55	33-09	34-22	35-36	36-50	38-03	39-17	21.3
21.4	25-24	26-36	27-49	29-01	30-14	31-27	32-39	33-52	35-04	36-17	37-29	38-42	21.4
21.5	25-01	26-13	27-24	28-36	29-47	30-58	32-10	33-21	34-33	35-44	36-56	38-07	21.5
21.6	24-38	25-49	26-59	28-10	29-20	30-30	31-41	32-51	34-02	35-12	36-22	37-33	21.6
21.7	24-16	25-25	26-35	27-44	28-53	30-03	31-12	32-21	33-31	34-40	35-49	36-59	21.7
21.8	23-53	25-02	26-10	27-18	28-26	29-35	30-43	31-51	32-60	34-08	35-16	36-24	21.8
21.9	23-31	24-38	25-46	26-53	28-00	29-07	30-14	31-22	32-29	33-36	34-43	35-50	21.9
22.0	23-09	24-15	25-21	26-28	27-34	28-40	29-46	30-52	31-58	33-05	34-11	35-17	22.0
22.1	22-47	23-52	24-57	26-02	27-08	28-13	29-18	30-23	31-28	32-33	33-38	34-43	22.1
22.2	22-25	23-30	24-34	25-38	26-42	27-46	28-50	29-54	30-58	32-02	33-06	34-10	22.2
22.3	22-04	23-07	24-10	25-13	26-16	27-19	28-22	29-25	30-28	31-31	32-34	33-37	22.3
22.4	21-42	22-44	23-46	24-48	25-50	26-53	27-55	28-57	29-59	31-01	32-03	33-05	22.4
22.5	21-21	22-22	23-23	24-24	25-25	26-26	27-27	28-28	29-29	30-30	31-31	32-32	22.5
22.6	20-60	21-60	22-60	23-60	24-60	25-60	26-60	27-60	28-60	29-60	30-60	31-60	22.6
22.7	20-39	21-38	22-37	23-36	24-35	25-34	26-33	27-32	28-31	29-30	30-29	31-28	22.7
22.8	20-18	21-16	22-14	23-12	24-10	25-08	26-06	27-04	28-02	29-00	29-58	30-56	22.8
22.9	19-57	20-54	21-51	22-48	23-45	24-42	25-39	26-36	27-33	28-30	29-27	30-24	22.9
23.0	19-37	20-33	21-29	22-25	23-21	24-17	25-13	26-09	27-05	28-01	28-57	29-53	23.0
23.1	19-16	20-11	21-06	22-01	22-56	23-52	24-47	25-42	26-37	27-32	28-27	29-22	23.1
23.2	18-56	19-50	20-44	21-38	22-32	23-26	24-20	25-15	26-09	27-03	27-57	28-51	23.2
23.3	18-36	19-29	20-22	21-15	22-08	23-01	23-54	24-48	25-41	26-34	27-27	28-20	23.3
23.4	18-16	19-08	19-60	20-52	21-44	22-36	23-29	24-21	25-13	26-05	26-57	27-49	23.4
23.5	17-56	18-47	19-38	20-29	21-20	22-12	23-03	23-54	24-45	25-37	26-28	27-19	23.5
23.6	17-36	18-26	19-16	20-06	20-57	21-47	22-37	23-28	24-18	25-08	25-58	26-49	23.6
23.7	17-16	18-05	18-55	19-44	20-33	21-23	22-12	23-01	23-51	24-40	25-29	26-19	23.7
23.8	16-56	17-45	18-33	19-22	20-10	20-58	21-47	22-35	23-24	24-12	25-00	25-49	23.8
23.9	16-37	17-25	18-12	18-60	19-47	20-34	21-22	22-09	22-57	23-44	24-32	25-19	23.9
24.0	16-18	17-04	17-51	18-37	19-24	20-10	20-57	21-43	22-30	23-17	24-03	24-50	24.0
24.1	15-58	16-44	17-30	18-15	19-01	19-47	20-32	21-18	22-04	22-49	23-35	24-20	24.1
24.2	15-39	16-24	17-09	17-54	18-38	19-23	20-08	20-52	21-37	22-22	23-07	23-51	24.2
24.3	15-20	16-04	16-48	17-32	18-15	18-59	19-43	20-27	21-11	21-55	22-38	23-22	24.3
24.4	15-01	15-44	16-27	17-10	17-53	18-36	19-19	20-02	20-45	21-28	22-11	22-53	24.4
24.5	14-43	15-25	16-07	16-49	17-31	18-13	18-55	19-37	20-19	21-01	21-43	22-25	24.5
24.6	14-24	15-05	15-46	16-27	17-08	17-50	18-31	19-12	19-53	20-34	21-15	21-56	24.6
24.7	14-05	14-46	15-26	16-06	16-47	17-27	18-07	18-47	19-28	20-08	20-48	21-28	24.7
24.8	13-47	14-26	15-06	15-45	16-24	17-04	17-43	18-23	19-02	19-41	20-21	21-00	24.8
24.9	13-29	14-07	14-46	15-24	16-03	16-41	17-20	17-58	18-37	19-15	19-54	20-32	24.9
Rating	21 Mi	22 Mi	23 Mi	24 Mi	25 Mi	26 Mi	27 Mi	28 Mi	29 Mi	30 Mi	31 Mi	32 Mi	Rating

SUBTRACT time allowances on this page from Elapsed Time

Rating	Sec/Mi	10 Mi	11 Mi	12 Mi	13 Mi	14 Mi	15 Mi	16 Mi	17 Mi	18 Mi	19 Mi	20 Mi	Rating
25.0	037.65	06-17	06-54	07-32	08-09	08-47	09-25	10-02	10-40	11-18	11-55	12-33	25.0
25.1	036.78	06-08	06-45	07-21	07-58	08-35	09-12	09-48	10-25	11-02	11-39	12-16	25.1
25.2	035.92	05-59	06-35	07-11	07-47	08-23	08-59	09-35	10-11	10-47	11-22	11-58	25.2
25.3	035.07	05-51	06-26	07-01	07-36	08-11	08-46	09-21	09-56	10-31	11-06	11-41	25.3
25.4	034.23	05-42	06-17	06-51	07-25	07-59	08-33	09-08	09-42	10-16	10-50	11-25	25.4
25.5	033.39	05-34	06-07	06-41	07-14	07-47	08-21	08-54	09-28	10-01	10-34	11-08	25.5
25.6	032.55	05-26	05-58	06-31	07-03	07-36	08-08	08-41	09-13	09-46	10-18	10-51	25.6
25.7	031.72	05-17	05-49	06-21	06-52	07-24	07-56	08-27	08-59	09-31	10-03	10-34	25.7
25.8	030.89	05-09	05-40	06-11	06-42	07-12	07-43	08-14	08-45	09-16	09-47	10-18	25.8
25.9	030.07	05-01	05-31	06-01	06-31	07-01	07-31	08-01	08-31	09-01	09-31	10-01	25.9
26.0	029.25	04-53	05-22	05-51	06-20	06-50	07-19	07-48	08-17	08-47	09-16	09-45	26.0
26.1	028.44	04-44	05-13	05-41	06-10	06-38	07-07	07-35	08-03	08-32	09-00	09-29	26.1
26.2	027.63	04-36	05-04	05-32	05-59	06-27	06-54	07-22	07-50	08-17	08-45	09-13	26.2
26.3	026.82	04-28	04-55	05-22	05-49	06-15	06-42	07-09	07-36	08-03	08-30	08-56	26.3
26.4	026.02	04-20	04-46	05-12	05-38	06-04	06-30	06-56	07-22	07-48	08-14	08-40	26.4
26.5	025.23	04-12	04-38	05-03	05-28	05-53	06-18	06-44	07-09	07-34	07-59	08-25	26.5
26.6	024.44	04-04	04-29	04-53	05-18	05-42	06-07	06-31	06-55	07-20	07-44	08-09	26.6
26.7	023.66	03-57	04-20	04-44	05-08	05-31	05-55	06-19	06-42	07-06	07-30	07-53	26.7
26.8	022.88	03-49	04-12	04-35	04-57	05-20	05-43	06-06	06-29	06-52	07-15	07-38	26.8
26.9	022.10	03-41	04-03	04-25	04-47	05-09	05-32	05-54	06-16	06-38	06-60	07-22	26.9
27.0	021.33	03-33	03-55	04-16	04-37	04-59	05-20	05-41	06-03	06-24	06-45	07-07	27.0
27.1	020.56	03-26	03-46	04-07	04-27	04-48	05-08	05-29	05-50	06-10	06-31	06-51	27.1
27.2	019.79	03-18	03-38	03-57	04-17	04-37	04-57	05-17	05-36	05-56	06-16	06-36	27.2
27.3	019.03	03-10	03-29	03-48	04-07	04-26	04-45	05-04	05-23	05-43	06-02	06-21	27.3
27.4	018.27	03-03	03-21	03-39	03-57	04-16	04-34	04-52	05-11	05-29	05-47	06-05	27.4
27.5	017.52	02-55	03-13	03-30	03-48	04-05	04-23	04-40	04-58	05-15	05-33	05-50	27.5
27.6	016.78	02-48	03-05	03-21	03-38	03-55	04-12	04-28	04-45	05-02	05-19	05-36	27.6
27.7	016.04	02-40	02-56	03-12	03-29	03-45	04-01	04-17	04-33	04-49	05-05	05-21	27.7
27.8	015.30	02-33	02-48	03-04	03-19	03-34	03-50	04-05	04-20	04-35	04-51	05-06	27.8
27.9	014.57	02-26	02-40	02-55	03-09	03-24	03-39	03-53	04-08	04-22	04-37	04-51	27.9
28.0	013.84	02-18	02-32	02-46	02-60	03-14	03-28	03-41	03-55	04-09	04-23	04-37	28.0
28.1	013.11	02-11	02-24	02-37	02-50	03-04	03-17	03-30	03-43	03-56	04-09	04-22	28.1
28.2	012.39	02-04	02-16	02-29	02-41	02-53	03-06	03-18	03-31	03-43	03-55	04-08	28.2
28.3	011.67	01-57	02-08	02-20	02-32	02-43	02-55	03-07	03-18	03-30	03-42	03-53	28.3
28.4	010.95	01-50	02-00	02-11	02-22	02-33	02-44	02-55	03-06	03-17	03-28	03-39	28.4
28.5	010.24	01-42	01-53	02-03	02-13	02-23	02-34	02-44	02-54	03-04	03-15	03-25	28.5
28.6	009.53	01-35	01-45	01-54	02-04	02-13	02-23	02-32	02-42	02-52	03-01	03-11	28.6
28.7	008.82	01-28	01-37	01-46	01-55	02-03	02-12	02-21	02-30	02-39	02-48	02-56	28.7
28.8	008.12	01-21	01-29	01-37	01-46	01-54	02-02	02-10	02-18	02-26	02-34	02-42	28.8
28.9	007.43	01-14	01-22	01-29	01-37	01-44	01-51	01-59	02-06	02-14	02-21	02-29	28.9
29.0	006.74	01-07	01-14	01-21	01-28	01-34	01-41	01-48	01-55	02-01	02-08	02-15	29.0
29.1	006.05	01-00	01-07	01-13	01-19	01-25	01-31	01-37	01-43	01-49	01-55	02-01	29.1
29.2	005.37	00-54	00-59	01-04	01-10	01-15	01-21	01-26	01-31	01-37	01-42	01-47	29.2
29.3	004.68	00-47	00-51	00-56	01-01	01-06	01-10	01-15	01-20	01-24	01-29	01-34	29.3
29.4	004.00	00-40	00-44	00-48	00-52	00-56	01-00	01-04	01-08	01-12	01-16	01-20	29.4
29.5	003.33	00-33	00-37	00-40	00-43	00-47	00-50	00-53	00-57	00-60	01-03	01-07	29.5
29.6	002.66	00-27	00-29	00-32	00-35	00-37	00-40	00-43	00-45	00-48	00-51	00-53	29.6
29.7	001.99	00-20	00-22	00-24	00-26	00-28	00-30	00-32	00-34	00-36	00-38	00-40	29.7
29.8	001.32	00-13	00-15	00-16	00-17	00-18	00-20	00-21	00-22	00-24	00-25	00-26	29.8
29.9	000.66	00-07	00-07	00-08	00-09	00-09	00-10	00-11	00-11	00-12	00-13	00-13	29.9
Rating	Sec/Mi	10 Mi	11 Mi	12 Mi	13 Mi	14 Mi	15 Mi	16 Mi	17 Mi	18 Mi	19 Mi	20 Mi	Rating

SUBTRACT time allowances on this page from Elapsed Time

Rating	21 Mi	22 Mi	23 Mi	24 Mi	25 Mi	26 Mi	27 Mi	28 Mi	29 Mi	30 Mi	31 Mi	32 Mi	Rating
25.0	13-11	13-48	14-26	15-04	15-41	16-19	16-57	17-34	18-12	18-50	19-27	20-05	25.0
25.1	12-52	13-29	14-06	14-43	15-20	15-56	16-33	17-10	17-47	18-23	19-00	19-37	25.1
25.2	12-34	13-10	13-46	14-22	14-58	15-34	16-10	16-46	17-22	17-58	18-33	19-09	25.2
25.3	12-16	12-52	13-27	14-02	14-37	15-12	15-47	16-22	16-57	17-32	18-07	18-42	25.3
25.4	11-59	12-33	13-07	13-42	14-16	14-50	15-24	15-58	16-33	17-07	17-41	18-15	25.4
25.5	11-41	12-15	12-48	13-21	13-55	14-28	15-02	15-35	16-08	16-42	17-15	17-48	25.5
25.6	11-24	11-56	12-29	13-01	13-34	14-06	14-39	15-11	15-44	16-17	16-49	17-22	25.6
25.7	11-06	11-38	12-10	12-41	13-13	13-45	14-16	14-48	15-20	15-52	16-23	16-55	25.7
25.8	10-49	11-20	11-50	12-21	12-52	13-23	13-54	14-25	14-56	15-27	15-58	16-28	25.8
25.9	10-31	11-02	11-32	12-02	12-32	13-02	13-32	14-02	14-32	15-02	15-32	16-02	25.9
26.0	10-14	10-44	11-13	11-42	12-11	12-41	13-10	13-39	14-08	14-38	15-07	15-36	26.0
26.1	09-57	10-26	10-54	11-23	11-51	12-19	12-48	13-16	13-45	14-13	14-42	15-10	26.1
26.2	09-40	10-08	10-35	11-03	11-31	11-58	12-26	12-54	13-21	13-49	14-17	14-44	26.2
26.3	09-23	09-50	10-17	10-44	11-11	11-37	12-04	12-31	12-58	13-25	13-51	14-18	26.3
26.4	09-06	09-32	09-58	10-24	10-50	11-17	11-43	12-09	12-35	13-01	13-27	13-53	26.4
26.5	08-50	09-15	09-40	10-06	10-31	10-56	11-21	11-46	12-12	12-37	13-02	13-27	26.5
26.6	08-33	08-58	09-22	09-47	10-11	10-35	10-60	11-24	11-49	12-13	12-38	13-02	26.6
26.7	08-17	08-41	09-04	09-28	09-51	10-15	10-39	11-02	11-26	11-50	12-13	12-37	26.7
26.8	08-00	08-23	08-46	09-09	09-32	09-55	10-18	10-41	11-03	11-26	11-49	12-12	26.8
26.9	07-44	08-06	08-28	08-50	09-12	09-35	09-57	10-19	10-41	11-03	11-25	11-47	26.9
27.0	07-28	07-49	08-11	08-32	08-53	09-15	09-36	09-57	10-19	10-40	11-01	11-23	27.0
27.1	07-12	07-32	07-53	08-13	08-34	08-55	09-15	09-36	09-56	10-17	10-37	10-58	27.1
27.2	06-56	07-15	07-35	07-55	08-15	08-35	08-54	09-14	09-34	09-54	10-13	10-33	27.2
27.3	06-40	06-59	07-18	07-37	07-56	08-15	08-34	08-53	09-12	09-31	09-50	10-09	27.3
27.4	06-24	06-42	07-00	07-18	07-37	07-55	08-13	08-32	08-50	09-08	09-26	09-45	27.4
27.5	06-08	06-25	06-43	07-00	07-18	07-36	07-53	08-11	08-28	08-46	09-03	09-21	27.5
27.6	05-52	06-09	06-26	06-43	06-59	07-16	07-33	07-50	08-07	08-23	08-40	08-57	27.6
27.7	05-37	05-53	06-09	06-25	06-41	06-57	07-13	07-29	07-45	08-01	08-17	08-33	27.7
27.8	05-21	05-37	05-52	06-07	06-23	06-38	06-53	07-08	07-24	07-39	07-54	08-10	27.8
27.9	05-06	05-21	05-35	05-50	06-04	06-19	06-33	06-48	07-03	07-17	07-32	07-46	27.9
28.0	04-51	05-04	05-18	05-32	05-46	05-60	06-14	06-27	06-41	06-55	07-09	07-23	28.0
28.1	04-35	04-48	05-02	05-15	05-28	05-41	05-54	06-07	06-20	06-33	06-46	06-60	28.1
28.2	04-20	04-33	04-45	04-57	05-10	05-22	05-35	05-47	05-59	06-12	06-24	06-36	28.2
28.3	04-05	04-17	04-28	04-40	04-52	05-03	05-15	05-27	05-38	05-50	06-02	06-13	28.3
28.4	03-50	04-01	04-12	04-23	04-34	04-45	04-56	05-07	05-18	05-29	05-39	05-50	28.4
28.5	03-35	03-45	03-56	04-06	04-16	04-26	04-36	04-47	04-57	05-07	05-17	05-28	28.5
28.6	03-20	03-30	03-39	03-49	03-58	04-08	04-17	04-27	04-36	04-46	04-55	05-05	28.6
28.7	03-05	03-14	03-23	03-32	03-41	03-49	03-58	04-07	04-16	04-25	04-33	04-42	28.7
28.8	02-51	02-59	03-07	03-15	03-23	03-31	03-39	03-47	03-55	04-04	04-12	04-20	28.8
28.9	02-36	02-43	02-51	02-58	03-06	03-13	03-21	03-28	03-35	03-43	03-50	03-58	28.9
29.0	02-22	02-28	02-35	02-42	02-48	02-55	03-02	03-09	03-15	03-22	03-29	03-36	29.0
29.1	02-07	02-13	02-19	02-25	02-31	02-37	02-43	02-49	02-55	03-02	03-08	03-14	29.1
29.2	01-53	01-58	02-03	02-09	02-14	02-20	02-25	02-30	02-36	02-41	02-46	02-52	29.2
29.3	01-38	01-43	01-48	01-52	01-57	02-02	02-06	02-11	02-16	02-20	02-25	02-30	29.3
29.4	01-24	01-28	01-32	01-36	01-40	01-44	01-48	01-52	01-56	02-00	02-04	02-08	29.4
29.5	01-10	01-13	01-17	01-20	01-23	01-27	01-30	01-33	01-37	01-40	01-43	01-47	29.5
29.6	00-56	00-59	01-01	01-04	01-06	01-09	01-12	01-14	01-17	01-20	01-22	01-25	29.6
29.7	00-42	00-44	00-46	00-48	00-50	00-52	00-54	00-56	00-58	00-60	01-02	01-04	29.7
29.8	00-28	00-29	00-30	00-32	00-33	00-34	00-36	00-37	00-38	00-40	00-41	00-42	29.8
29.9	00-14	00-15	00-15	00-16	00-17	00-17	00-18	00-18	00-19	00-20	00-20	00-21	29.9
Rating	21 Mi	22 Mi	23 Mi	24 Mi	25 Mi	26 Mi	27 Mi	28 Mi	29 Mi	30 Mi	31 Mi	32 Mi	Rating

SUBTRACT time allowances on this page from Elapsed Time

Rating	Sec/Mi	10 Mi	11 Mi	12 Mi	13 Mi	14 Mi	15 Mi	16 Mi	17 Mi	18 Mi	19 Mi	20 Mi	Rating
30.0	000.00	00-00	00-00	00-00	00-00	00-00	00-00	00-00	00-00	00-00	00-00	00-00	30.0
30.1	000.66	00-07	00-07	00-08	00-09	00-09	00-10	00-11	00-11	00-12	00-13	00-13	30.1
30.2	001.30	00-13	00-14	00-16	00-17	00-18	00-20	00-21	00-22	00-23	00-25	00-26	30.2
30.3	001.95	00-20	00-21	00-23	00-25	00-27	00-29	00-31	00-33	00-35	00-37	00-39	30.3
30.4	002.60	00-26	00-29	00-31	00-34	00-36	00-39	00-42	00-44	00-47	00-49	00-52	30.4
30.5	003.25	00-32	00-36	00-39	00-42	00-45	00-49	00-52	00-55	00-59	01-02	01-05	30.5
30.6	003.89	00-39	00-43	00-47	00-51	00-54	00-58	01-02	01-06	01-10	01-14	01-18	30.6
30.7	004.52	00-45	00-50	00-54	00-59	01-03	01-08	01-12	01-17	01-21	01-26	01-30	30.7
30.8	005.15	00-51	00-57	01-02	01-07	01-12	01-17	01-22	01-28	01-33	01-38	01-43	30.8
30.9	005.77	00-58	01-03	01-09	01-15	01-21	01-27	01-32	01-38	01-44	01-50	01-55	30.9
31.0	006.39	01-04	01-10	01-17	01-23	01-29	01-36	01-42	01-49	01-55	02-01	02-08	31.0
31.1	007.02	01-10	01-17	01-24	01-31	01-38	01-45	01-52	01-59	02-06	02-13	02-20	31.1
31.2	007.64	01-16	01-24	01-32	01-39	01-47	01-55	02-02	02-10	02-18	02-25	02-33	31.2
31.3	008.26	01-23	01-31	01-39	01-47	01-56	02-04	02-12	02-20	02-29	02-37	02-45	31.3
31.4	008.89	01-29	01-38	01-47	01-56	02-04	02-13	02-22	02-31	02-40	02-49	02-58	31.4
31.5	009.50	01-35	01-44	01-54	02-03	02-13	02-23	02-32	02-41	02-51	03-00	03-10	31.5
31.6	010.11	01-41	01-51	02-01	02-11	02-22	02-32	02-42	02-52	03-02	03-12	03-22	31.6
31.7	010.72	01-47	01-58	02-09	02-19	02-30	02-41	02-51	03-02	03-13	03-24	03-34	31.7
31.8	011.32	01-53	02-05	02-16	02-27	02-38	02-50	03-01	03-12	03-24	03-35	03-46	31.8
31.9	011.92	01-59	02-11	02-23	02-35	02-47	02-59	03-11	03-23	03-35	03-46	03-58	31.9
32.0	012.52	02-05	02-18	02-30	02-43	02-55	03-08	03-20	03-33	03-45	03-58	04-10	32.0
32.1	013.12	02-11	02-24	02-37	02-51	03-04	03-17	03-30	03-43	03-56	04-09	04-22	32.1
32.2	013.71	02-17	02-31	02-45	02-58	03-12	03-26	03-39	03-53	04-07	04-20	04-34	32.2
32.3	014.30	02-23	02-37	02-52	03-06	03-20	03-35	03-49	04-03	04-17	04-32	04-46	32.3
32.4	014.89	02-29	02-44	02-59	03-14	03-28	03-43	03-58	04-13	04-28	04-43	04-58	32.4
32.5	015.48	02-35	02-50	03-06	03-21	03-37	03-52	04-08	04-23	04-39	04-54	05-10	32.5
32.6	016.06	02-41	02-57	03-13	03-29	03-45	04-01	04-17	04-33	04-49	05-05	05-21	32.6
32.7	016.64	02-46	03-03	03-20	03-36	03-53	04-10	04-26	04-43	04-60	05-16	05-33	32.7
32.8	017.21	02-52	03-09	03-27	03-44	04-01	04-18	04-35	04-53	05-10	05-27	05-44	32.8
32.9	017.78	02-58	03-16	03-33	03-51	04-09	04-27	04-44	05-02	05-20	05-38	05-56	32.9
33.0	018.35	03-03	03-22	03-40	03-59	04-17	04-35	04-54	05-12	05-30	05-49	06-07	33.0
33.1	018.92	03-09	03-28	03-47	04-06	04-25	04-44	05-03	05-22	05-41	05-59	06-18	33.1
33.2	019.49	03-15	03-34	03-54	04-13	04-33	04-52	05-12	05-31	05-51	06-10	06-30	33.2
33.3	020.05	03-20	03-41	04-01	04-21	04-41	05-01	05-21	05-41	06-01	06-21	06-41	33.3
33.4	020.61	03-26	03-47	04-07	04-28	04-49	05-09	05-30	05-50	06-11	06-32	06-52	33.4
33.5	021.17	03-32	03-53	04-14	04-35	04-56	05-18	05-39	05-60	06-21	06-42	07-03	33.5
33.6	021.73	03-37	03-59	04-21	04-42	05-04	05-26	05-48	06-09	06-31	06-53	07-15	33.6
33.7	022.28	03-43	04-05	04-27	04-50	05-12	05-34	05-56	06-19	06-41	07-03	07-26	33.7
33.8	022.83	03-48	04-11	04-34	04-57	05-20	05-42	06-05	06-28	06-51	07-14	07-37	33.8
33.9	023.37	03-54	04-17	04-40	05-04	05-27	05-51	06-14	06-37	07-01	07-24	07-47	33.9
34.0	023.91	03-59	04-23	04-47	05-11	05-35	05-59	06-23	06-46	07-10	07-34	07-58	34.0
34.1	024.46	04-05	04-29	04-54	05-18	05-42	06-07	06-31	06-56	07-20	07-45	08-09	34.1
34.2	025.00	04-10	04-35	05-00	05-25	05-50	06-15	06-40	07-05	07-30	07-55	08-20	34.2
34.3	025.54	04-15	04-41	05-06	05-32	05-58	06-23	06-49	07-14	07-40	08-05	08-31	34.3
34.4	026.08	04-21	04-47	05-13	05-39	06-05	06-31	06-57	07-23	07-49	08-15	08-42	34.4
34.5	026.62	04-26	04-53	05-19	05-46	06-13	06-39	07-06	07-33	07-59	08-26	08-52	34.5
34.6	027.15	04-32	04-59	05-26	05-53	06-20	06-47	07-14	07-42	08-09	08-36	09-03	34.6
34.7	027.68	04-37	05-04	05-32	05-60	06-27	06-55	07-23	07-51	08-18	08-46	09-14	34.7
34.8	028.21	04-42	05-10	05-39	06-07	06-35	07-03	07-31	07-60	08-28	08-56	09-24	34.8
34.9	028.72	04-47	05-16	05-45	06-13	06-42	07-11	07-39	08-08	08-37	09-06	09-34	34.9
Rating	Sec/Mi	10 Mi	11 Mi	12 Mi	13 Mi	14 Mi	15 Mi	16 Mi	17 Mi	18 Mi	19 Mi	20 Mi	Rating

ADD time allowances on this page to Elapsed Time

Rating	21 Mi	22 Mi	23 Mi	24 Mi	25 Mi	26 Mi	27 Mi	28 Mi	29 Mi	30 Mi	31 Mi	32 Mi	Rating
30.0	00-00	00-00	00-00	00-00	00-00	00-00	00-00	00-00	00-00	00-00	00-00	00-00	30.0
30.1	00-14	00-15	00-15	00-16	00-17	00-17	00-18	00-18	00-19	00-20	00-20	00-21	30.1
30.2	00-27	00-29	00-30	00-31	00-32	00-34	00-35	00-36	00-38	00-39	00-40	00-42	30.2
30.3	00-41	00-43	00-45	00-47	00-49	00-51	00-53	00-55	00-57	00-59	01-00	01-02	30.3
30.4	00-55	00-57	00-60	01-02	01-05	01-08	01-10	01-13	01-15	01-18	01-21	01-23	30.4
30.5	01-08	01-11	01-15	01-18	01-21	01-24	01-28	01-31	01-34	01-38	01-41	01-44	30.5
30.6	01-22	01-26	01-29	01-33	01-37	01-41	01-45	01-49	01-53	01-57	02-01	02-04	30.6
30.7	01-35	01-39	01-44	01-48	01-53	01-57	02-02	02-07	02-11	02-16	02-20	02-25	30.7
30.8	01-48	01-53	01-58	02-04	02-09	02-14	02-19	02-24	02-29	02-35	02-40	02-45	30.8
30.9	02-01	02-07	02-13	02-18	02-24	02-30	02-36	02-42	02-47	02-53	02-59	03-05	30.9
31.0	02-14	02-21	02-27	02-33	02-40	02-46	02-53	02-59	03-05	03-12	03-18	03-24	31.0
31.1	02-27	02-34	02-41	02-48	02-56	03-03	03-10	03-17	03-24	03-31	03-38	03-45	31.1
31.2	02-40	02-48	02-56	03-03	03-11	03-19	03-26	03-34	03-42	03-49	03-57	04-04	31.2
31.3	02-53	03-02	03-10	03-18	03-26	03-35	03-43	03-51	03-60	04-08	04-16	04-24	31.3
31.4	03-07	03-16	03-24	03-33	03-42	03-51	04-00	04-09	04-18	04-27	04-36	04-44	31.4
31.5	03-20	03-29	03-38	03-48	03-57	04-07	04-17	04-26	04-35	04-45	04-54	05-04	31.5
31.6	03-32	03-42	03-53	04-03	04-13	04-23	04-33	04-43	04-53	05-03	05-13	05-24	31.6
31.7	03-45	03-56	04-07	04-17	04-28	04-39	04-49	05-00	05-11	05-22	05-32	05-43	31.7
31.8	03-58	04-09	04-20	04-32	04-43	04-54	05-06	05-17	05-28	05-40	05-51	06-02	31.8
31.9	04-10	04-22	04-34	04-46	04-58	05-10	05-22	05-34	05-46	05-58	06-09	06-21	31.9
32.0	04-23	04-35	04-48	05-00	05-13	05-26	05-38	05-51	06-03	06-16	06-28	06-41	32.0
32.1	04-36	04-49	05-02	05-15	05-28	05-41	05-54	06-07	06-20	06-34	06-47	06-60	32.1
32.2	04-48	05-02	05-15	05-29	05-43	05-56	06-10	06-24	06-38	06-51	07-05	07-19	32.2
32.3	05-00	05-15	05-29	05-43	05-57	06-12	06-26	06-40	06-55	07-09	07-23	07-38	32.3
32.4	05-13	05-28	05-42	05-57	06-12	06-27	06-42	06-57	07-12	07-27	07-42	07-56	32.4
32.5	05-25	05-41	05-56	06-12	06-27	06-42	06-58	07-13	07-29	07-44	07-60	08-15	32.5
32.6	05-37	05-53	06-09	06-25	06-41	06-58	07-14	07-30	07-46	08-02	08-18	08-34	32.6
32.7	05-49	06-06	06-23	06-39	06-56	07-13	07-29	07-46	08-03	08-19	08-36	08-52	32.7
32.8	06-01	06-19	06-36	06-53	07-10	07-27	07-45	08-02	08-19	08-36	08-53	09-11	32.8
32.9	06-13	06-31	06-49	07-07	07-24	07-42	08-00	08-18	08-36	08-53	09-11	09-29	32.9
33.0	06-25	06-44	07-02	07-20	07-39	07-57	08-15	08-34	08-52	09-11	09-29	09-47	33.0
33.1	06-37	06-56	07-15	07-34	07-53	08-12	08-31	08-50	09-09	09-28	09-47	10-05	33.1
33.2	06-49	07-09	07-28	07-48	08-07	08-27	08-46	09-06	09-25	09-45	10-04	10-24	33.2
33.3	07-01	07-21	07-41	08-01	08-21	08-41	09-01	09-21	09-41	10-02	10-22	10-42	33.3
33.4	07-13	07-33	07-54	08-15	08-35	08-56	09-16	09-37	09-58	10-18	10-39	10-60	33.4
33.5	07-25	07-46	08-07	08-28	08-49	09-10	09-32	09-53	10-14	10-35	10-56	11-17	33.5
33.6	07-36	07-58	08-20	08-42	09-03	09-25	09-47	10-08	10-30	10-52	11-14	11-35	33.6
33.7	07-48	08-10	08-32	08-55	09-17	09-39	10-02	10-24	10-46	11-08	11-31	11-53	33.7
33.8	07-59	08-22	08-45	09-08	09-31	09-54	10-16	10-39	11-02	11-25	11-48	12-11	33.8
33.9	08-11	08-34	08-57	09-21	09-44	10-08	10-31	10-54	11-18	11-41	12-04	12-28	33.9
34.0	08-22	08-46	09-10	09-34	09-58	10-22	10-46	11-09	11-33	11-57	12-21	12-45	34.0
34.1	08-34	08-58	09-23	09-47	10-11	10-36	11-00	11-25	11-49	12-14	12-38	13-03	34.1
34.2	08-45	09-10	09-35	10-00	10-25	10-50	11-15	11-40	12-05	12-30	12-55	13-20	34.2
34.3	08-56	09-22	09-47	10-13	10-38	11-04	11-30	11-55	12-21	12-46	13-12	13-37	34.3
34.4	09-08	09-34	09-60	10-26	10-52	11-18	11-44	12-10	12-36	13-02	13-28	13-55	34.4
34.5	09-19	09-46	10-12	10-39	11-05	11-32	11-59	12-25	12-52	13-19	13-45	14-12	34.5
34.6	09-30	09-57	10-24	10-52	11-19	11-46	12-13	12-40	13-07	13-35	14-02	14-29	34.6
34.7	09-41	10-09	10-37	11-04	11-32	11-60	12-27	12-55	13-23	13-50	14-18	14-46	34.7
34.8	09-52	10-21	10-49	11-17	11-45	12-13	12-42	13-10	13-38	14-06	14-35	15-03	34.8
34.9	10-03	10-32	11-01	11-29	11-58	12-27	12-55	13-24	13-53	14-22	14-50	15-19	34.9
Rating	21 Mi	22 Mi	23 Mi	24 Mi	25 Mi	26 Mi	27 Mi	28 Mi	29 Mi	30 Mi	31 Mi	32 Mi	Rating

ADD time allowances on this page to Elapsed Time

Rating	Sec/Mi	10 Mi	11 Mi	12 Mi	13 Mi	14 Mi	15 Mi	16 Mi	17 Mi	18 Mi	19 Mi	20 Mi	Rating
35.0	029.24	04-52	05-22	05-51	06-20	06-49	07-19	07-48	08-17	08-46	09-16	09-45	35.0
35.1	029.76	04-58	05-27	05-57	06-27	06-57	07-26	07-56	08-26	08-56	09-25	09-55	35.1
35.2	030.28	05-03	05-33	06-03	06-34	07-04	07-34	08-04	08-35	09-05	09-35	10-06	35.2
35.3	030.80	05-08	05-39	06-10	06-40	07-11	07-42	08-13	08-44	09-14	09-45	10-16	35.3
35.4	031.32	05-13	05-45	06-16	06-47	07-18	07-50	08-21	08-52	09-24	09-55	10-26	35.4
35.5	031.83	05-18	05-50	06-22	06-54	07-26	07-57	08-29	09-01	09-33	10-05	10-37	35.5
35.6	032.35	05-23	05-56	06-28	07-01	07-33	08-05	08-38	09-10	09-42	10-15	10-47	35.6
35.7	032.85	05-29	06-01	06-34	07-07	07-40	08-13	08-46	09-18	09-51	10-24	10-57	35.7
35.8	033.36	05-34	06-07	06-40	07-14	07-47	08-20	08-54	09-27	10-00	10-34	11-07	35.8
35.9	033.86	05-39	06-12	06-46	07-20	07-54	08-28	09-02	09-36	10-09	10-43	11-17	35.9
36.0	034.36	05-44	06-18	06-52	07-27	08-01	08-35	09-10	09-44	10-18	10-53	11-27	36.0
36.1	034.86	05-49	06-23	06-58	07-33	08-08	08-43	09-18	09-53	10-27	11-02	11-37	36.1
36.2	035.36	05-54	06-29	07-04	07-40	08-15	08-50	09-26	10-01	10-36	11-12	11-47	36.2
36.3	035.85	05-59	06-34	07-10	07-46	08-22	08-58	09-34	10-09	10-45	11-21	11-57	36.3
36.4	036.34	06-03	06-40	07-16	07-52	08-29	09-05	09-41	10-18	10-54	11-30	12-07	36.4
36.5	036.84	06-08	06-45	07-22	07-59	08-36	09-13	09-49	10-26	11-03	11-40	12-17	36.5
36.6	037.33	06-13	06-51	07-28	08-05	08-43	09-20	09-57	10-35	11-12	11-49	12-27	36.6
36.7	037.81	06-18	06-56	07-34	08-12	08-49	09-27	10-05	10-43	11-21	11-58	12-36	36.7
36.8	038.29	06-23	07-01	07-39	08-18	08-56	09-34	10-13	10-51	11-29	12-08	12-46	36.8
36.9	038.77	06-28	07-06	07-45	08-24	09-03	09-42	10-20	10-59	11-38	12-17	12-55	36.9
37.0	039.25	06-32	07-12	07-51	08-30	09-09	09-49	10-28	11-07	11-47	12-26	13-05	37.0
37.1	039.73	06-37	07-17	07-57	08-36	09-16	09-56	10-36	11-15	11-55	12-35	13-15	37.1
37.2	040.21	06-42	07-22	08-03	08-43	09-23	10-03	10-43	11-24	12-04	12-44	13-24	37.2
37.3	040.69	06-47	07-28	08-08	08-49	09-30	10-10	10-51	11-32	12-12	12-53	13-34	37.3
37.4	041.17	06-52	07-33	08-14	08-55	09-36	10-18	10-59	11-40	12-21	13-02	13-43	37.4
37.5	041.64	06-56	07-38	08-20	09-01	09-43	10-25	11-06	11-48	12-30	13-11	13-53	37.5
37.6	042.10	07-01	07-43	08-25	09-07	09-49	10-32	11-14	11-56	12-38	13-20	14-02	37.6
37.7	042.57	07-06	07-48	08-31	09-13	09-56	10-39	11-21	12-04	12-46	13-29	14-11	37.7
37.8	043.04	07-10	07-53	08-36	09-20	10-03	10-46	11-29	12-12	12-55	13-38	14-21	37.8
37.9	043.50	07-15	07-59	08-42	09-26	10-09	10-53	11-36	12-20	13-03	13-47	14-30	37.9
38.0	043.96	07-20	08-04	08-48	09-31	10-15	10-59	11-43	12-27	13-11	13-55	14-39	38.0
38.1	044.42	07-24	08-09	08-53	09-37	10-22	11-06	11-51	12-35	13-20	14-04	14-48	38.1
38.2	044.88	07-29	08-14	08-59	09-43	10-28	11-13	11-58	12-43	13-28	14-13	14-58	38.2
38.3	045.33	07-33	08-19	09-04	09-49	10-35	11-20	12-05	12-51	13-36	14-21	15-07	38.3
38.4	045.79	07-38	08-24	09-09	09-55	10-41	11-27	12-13	12-58	13-44	14-30	15-16	38.4
38.5	046.24	07-42	08-29	09-15	10-01	10-47	11-34	12-20	13-06	13-52	14-39	15-25	38.5
38.6	046.70	07-47	08-34	09-20	10-07	10-54	11-41	12-27	13-14	14-01	14-47	15-34	38.6
38.7	047.16	07-52	08-39	09-26	10-13	11-00	11-47	12-35	13-22	14-09	14-56	15-43	38.7
38.8	047.60	07-56	08-44	09-31	10-19	11-06	11-54	12-42	13-29	14-17	15-04	15-52	38.8
38.9	048.04	08-00	08-48	09-36	10-24	11-13	12-01	12-49	13-37	14-25	15-13	16-01	38.9
39.0	048.48	08-05	08-53	09-42	10-30	11-19	12-07	12-56	13-44	14-33	15-21	16-10	39.0
39.1	048.92	08-09	08-58	09-47	10-36	11-25	12-14	13-03	13-52	14-41	15-29	16-18	39.1
39.2	049.36	08-14	09-03	09-52	10-42	11-31	12-20	13-10	13-59	14-48	15-38	16-27	39.2
39.3	049.81	08-18	09-08	09-58	10-48	11-37	12-27	13-17	14-07	14-57	15-46	16-36	39.3
39.4	050.25	08-23	09-13	10-03	10-53	11-44	12-34	13-24	14-14	15-05	15-55	16-45	39.4
39.5	050.69	08-27	09-18	10-08	10-59	11-50	12-40	13-31	14-22	15-12	16-03	16-54	39.5
39.6	051.12	08-31	09-22	10-13	11-05	11-56	12-47	13-38	14-29	15-20	16-11	17-02	39.6
39.7	051.55	08-35	09-27	10-19	11-10	12-02	12-53	13-45	14-36	15-28	16-19	17-11	39.7
39.8	051.98	08-40	09-32	10-24	11-16	12-08	12-60	13-52	14-44	15-36	16-28	17-20	39.8
39.9	052.40	08-44	09-36	10-29	11-21	12-14	13-06	13-58	14-51	15-43	16-36	17-28	39.9
Rating	Sec/Mi	10 Mi	11 Mi	12 Mi	13 Mi	14 Mi	15 Mi	16 Mi	17 Mi	18 Mi	19 Mi	20 Mi	Rating

ADD time allowances on this page to Elapsed Time

Rating	21 Mi	22 Mi	23 Mi	24 Mi	25 Mi	26 Mi	27 Mi	28 Mi	29 Mi	30 Mi	31 Mi	32 Mi	Rating
35.0	10-14	10-43	11-12	11-42	12-11	12-40	13-09	13-39	14-08	14-37	15-06	15-36	35.0
35.1	10-25	10-55	11-24	11-54	12-24	12-54	13-24	13-53	14-23	14-53	15-23	15-52	35.1
35.2	10-36	11-06	11-36	12-07	12-37	13-07	13-38	14-08	14-38	15-08	15-39	16-09	35.2
35.3	10-47	11-18	11-48	12-19	12-50	13-21	13-52	14-22	14-53	15-24	15-55	16-26	35.3
35.4	10-58	11-29	12-00	12-32	13-03	13-34	14-06	14-37	15-08	15-40	16-11	16-42	35.4
35.5	11-08	11-40	12-12	12-44	13-16	13-48	14-19	14-51	15-23	15-55	16-27	16-59	35.5
35.6	11-19	11-52	12-24	12-56	13-29	14-01	14-33	15-06	15-38	16-11	16-43	17-15	35.6
35.7	11-30	12-03	12-36	13-08	13-41	14-14	14-47	15-20	15-53	16-26	16-58	17-31	35.7
35.8	11-41	12-14	12-47	13-21	13-54	14-27	15-01	15-34	16-07	16-41	17-14	17-48	35.8
35.9	11-51	12-25	12-59	13-33	14-06	14-40	15-14	15-48	16-22	16-56	17-30	18-03	35.9
36.0	12-02	12-36	13-10	13-45	14-19	14-53	15-28	16-02	16-36	17-11	17-45	18-20	36.0
36.1	12-12	12-47	13-22	13-57	14-32	15-06	15-41	16-16	16-51	17-26	18-01	18-36	36.1
36.2	12-23	12-58	13-33	14-09	14-44	15-19	15-55	16-30	17-05	17-41	18-16	18-51	36.2
36.3	12-33	13-09	13-45	14-20	14-56	15-32	16-08	16-44	17-20	17-56	18-31	19-07	36.3
36.4	12-43	13-19	13-56	14-32	15-08	15-45	16-21	16-57	17-34	18-10	18-47	19-23	36.4
36.5	12-54	13-30	14-07	14-44	15-21	15-58	16-35	17-12	17-48	18-25	19-02	19-39	36.5
36.6	13-04	13-41	14-19	14-56	15-33	16-11	16-48	17-25	18-03	18-40	19-17	19-55	36.6
36.7	13-14	13-52	14-30	15-07	15-45	16-23	17-01	17-39	18-16	18-54	19-32	20-10	36.7
36.8	13-24	14-02	14-41	15-19	15-57	16-36	17-14	17-52	18-30	19-09	19-47	20-25	36.8
36.9	13-34	14-13	14-52	15-30	16-09	16-48	17-27	18-06	18-44	19-23	20-02	20-41	36.9
37.0	13-44	14-23	15-03	15-42	16-21	17-00	17-40	18-19	18-58	19-38	20-17	20-56	37.0
37.1	13-54	14-34	15-14	15-54	16-33	17-13	17-53	18-32	19-12	19-52	20-32	21-11	37.1
37.2	14-04	14-45	15-25	16-05	16-45	17-25	18-06	18-46	19-26	20-06	20-47	21-27	37.2
37.3	14-14	14-55	15-36	16-17	16-57	17-38	18-19	18-59	19-40	20-21	21-01	21-42	37.3
37.4	14-25	15-06	15-47	16-28	17-09	17-50	18-32	19-13	19-54	20-35	21-16	21-57	37.4
37.5	14-34	15-16	15-58	16-39	17-21	18-03	18-44	19-26	20-08	20-49	21-31	22-12	37.5
37.6	14-44	15-26	16-08	16-50	17-32	18-15	18-57	19-39	20-21	21-03	21-45	22-27	37.6
37.7	14-54	15-37	16-19	17-02	17-44	18-27	19-09	19-52	20-35	21-17	21-60	22-42	37.7
37.8	15-04	15-47	16-30	17-13	17-56	18-39	19-22	20-05	20-48	21-31	22-14	22-57	37.8
37.9	15-14	15-57	16-41	17-24	18-08	18-51	19-35	20-18	21-02	21-45	22-29	23-12	37.9
38.0	15-23	16-07	16-51	17-35	18-19	19-03	19-47	20-31	21-15	21-59	22-43	23-27	38.0
38.1	15-33	16-17	17-02	17-46	18-30	19-15	19-59	20-44	21-28	22-13	22-57	23-41	38.1
38.2	15-42	16-27	17-12	17-57	18-42	19-27	20-12	20-57	21-42	22-26	23-11	23-56	38.2
38.3	15-52	16-37	17-23	18-08	18-53	19-39	20-24	21-09	21-55	22-40	23-25	24-11	38.3
38.4	16-02	16-47	17-33	18-19	19-05	19-51	20-36	21-22	22-08	22-54	23-39	24-25	38.4
38.5	16-11	16-57	17-44	18-30	19-16	20-02	20-48	21-35	22-21	23-07	23-53	24-40	38.5
38.6	16-21	17-07	17-54	18-41	19-27	20-14	21-01	21-48	22-34	23-21	24-08	24-54	38.6
38.7	16-30	17-18	18-05	18-52	19-39	20-26	21-13	22-00	22-48	23-35	24-22	25-09	38.7
38.8	16-40	17-27	18-15	19-02	19-50	20-38	21-25	22-13	23-00	23-48	24-36	25-23	38.8
38.9	16-49	17-37	18-25	19-13	20-01	20-49	21-37	22-25	23-13	24-01	24-49	25-37	38.9
39.0	16-58	17-47	18-35	19-24	20-12	21-00	21-49	22-37	23-26	24-14	25-03	25-51	39.0
39.1	17-07	17-56	18-45	19-34	20-23	21-12	22-01	22-50	23-39	24-28	25-17	26-05	39.1
39.2	17-17	18-06	18-55	19-45	20-34	21-23	22-13	23-02	23-51	24-41	25-30	26-20	39.2
39.3	17-26	18-16	19-06	19-55	20-45	21-35	22-25	23-15	24-04	24-54	25-44	26-34	39.3
39.4	17-35	18-26	19-16	20-06	20-56	21-47	22-37	23-27	24-17	25-08	25-58	26-48	39.4
39.5	17-44	18-35	19-26	20-17	21-07	21-58	22-49	23-39	24-30	25-21	26-11	27-02	39.5
39.6	17-54	18-45	19-36	20-27	21-18	22-09	23-00	23-51	24-42	25-34	26-25	27-16	39.6
39.7	18-03	18-54	19-46	20-37	21-29	22-20	23-12	24-03	24-55	25-47	26-38	27-30	39.7
39.8	18-12	19-04	19-56	20-48	21-39	22-31	23-23	24-15	25-07	25-59	26-51	27-43	39.8
39.9	18-20	19-13	20-05	20-58	21-50	22-42	23-35	24-27	25-20	26-12	27-04	27-57	39.9
Rating	21 Mi	22 Mi	23 Mi	24 Mi	25 Mi	26 Mi	27 Mi	28 Mi	29 Mi	30 Mi	31 Mi	32 Mi	Rating

ADD time allowances on this page to Elapsed Time

Rating	Sec/Mi	10 Mi	11 Mi	12 Mi	13 Mi	14 Mi	15 Mi	16 Mi	17 Mi	18 Mi	19 Mi	20 Mi	Rating
40.0	052.82	08-48	09-41	10-34	11-27	12-19	13-12	14-05	14-58	15-51	16-44	17-36	40.0
40.1	053.25	08-53	09-46	10-39	11-32	12-26	13-19	14-12	15-05	15-59	16-52	17-45	40.1
40.2	053.68	08-57	09-50	10-44	11-38	12-32	13-25	14-19	15-13	16-06	16-60	17-54	40.2
40.3	054.12	09-01	09-55	10-49	11-44	12-38	13-32	14-26	15-20	16-14	17-08	18-02	40.3
40.4	054.54	09-05	09-60	10-54	11-49	12-44	13-38	14-33	15-27	16-22	17-16	18-11	40.4
40.5	054.96	09-10	10-05	10-60	11-54	12-49	13-44	14-39	15-34	16-29	17-24	18-19	40.5
40.6	055.38	09-14	10-09	11-05	11-60	12-55	13-51	14-46	15-41	16-37	17-32	18-28	40.6
40.7	055.79	09-18	10-14	11-09	12-05	13-01	13-57	14-53	15-48	16-44	17-40	18-36	40.7
40.8	056.20	09-22	10-18	11-14	12-11	13-07	14-03	14-59	15-55	16-52	17-48	18-44	40.8
40.9	056.61	09-26	10-23	11-19	12-16	13-13	14-09	15-06	16-02	16-59	17-56	18-52	40.9
41.0	057.02	09-30	10-27	11-24	12-21	13-18	14-15	15-12	16-09	17-06	18-03	19-00	41.0
41.1	057.44	09-34	10-32	11-29	12-27	13-24	14-22	15-19	16-16	17-14	18-11	19-09	41.1
41.2	057.85	09-38	10-36	11-34	12-32	13-30	14-28	15-26	16-23	17-21	18-19	19-17	41.2
41.3	058.26	09-43	10-41	11-39	12-37	13-36	14-34	15-32	16-30	17-29	18-27	19-25	41.3
41.4	058.66	09-47	10-45	11-44	12-43	13-41	14-40	15-39	16-37	17-36	18-35	19-33	41.4
41.5	059.07	09-51	10-50	11-49	12-48	13-47	14-46	15-45	16-44	17-43	18-42	19-41	41.5
41.6	059.48	09-55	10-54	11-54	12-53	13-53	14-52	15-52	16-51	17-51	18-50	19-50	41.6
41.7	059.88	09-59	10-59	11-59	12-58	13-58	14-58	15-58	16-58	17-58	18-58	19-58	41.7
41.8	060.27	10-03	11-03	12-03	13-03	14-04	15-04	16-04	17-05	18-05	19-05	20-05	41.8
41.9	060.67	10-07	11-07	12-08	13-09	14-09	15-10	16-11	17-11	18-12	19-13	20-13	41.9
42.0	061.07	10-11	11-12	12-13	13-14	14-15	15-16	16-17	17-18	18-19	19-20	20-21	42.0
42.1	061.47	10-15	11-16	12-18	13-19	14-21	15-22	16-24	17-25	18-26	19-28	20-29	42.1
42.2	061.87	10-19	11-21	12-22	13-24	14-26	15-28	16-30	17-32	18-34	19-36	20-37	42.2
42.3	062.26	10-23	11-25	12-27	13-29	14-32	15-34	16-36	17-38	18-41	19-43	20-45	42.3
42.4	062.65	10-26	11-29	12-32	13-34	14-37	15-40	16-42	17-45	18-48	19-50	20-53	42.4
42.5	063.04	10-30	11-33	12-36	13-39	14-43	15-46	16-49	17-52	18-55	19-58	21-01	42.5
42.6	063.43	10-34	11-38	12-41	13-45	14-48	15-51	16-55	17-58	19-02	20-05	21-09	42.6
42.7	063.81	10-38	11-42	12-46	13-50	14-53	15-57	17-01	18-05	19-09	20-12	21-16	42.7
42.8	064.20	10-42	11-46	12-50	13-55	14-59	16-03	17-07	18-11	19-16	20-20	21-24	42.8
42.9	064.58	10-46	11-50	12-55	13-60	15-04	16-09	17-13	18-18	19-22	20-27	21-32	42.9
43.0	064.96	10-50	11-55	12-60	14-04	15-09	16-14	17-19	18-24	19-29	20-34	21-39	43.0
43.1	065.34	10-53	11-59	13-04	14-09	15-15	16-20	17-25	18-31	19-36	20-41	21-47	43.1
43.2	065.72	10-57	12-03	13-09	14-14	15-20	16-26	17-32	18-37	19-43	20-49	21-54	43.2
43.3	066.10	11-01	12-07	13-13	14-19	15-25	16-32	17-38	18-44	19-50	20-56	22-02	43.3
43.4	066.48	11-05	12-11	13-18	14-24	15-31	16-37	17-44	18-50	19-57	21-03	22-10	43.4
43.5	066.86	11-09	12-15	13-22	14-29	15-36	16-43	17-50	18-57	20-03	21-10	22-17	43.5
43.6	067.24	11-12	12-20	13-27	14-34	15-41	16-49	17-56	19-03	20-10	21-18	22-25	43.6
43.7	067.62	11-16	12-24	13-31	14-39	15-47	16-54	18-02	19-10	20-17	21-25	22-32	43.7
43.8	067.99	11-20	12-28	13-36	14-44	15-52	16-60	18-08	19-16	20-24	21-32	22-40	43.8
43.9	068.35	11-23	12-32	13-40	14-49	15-57	17-05	18-14	19-22	20-30	21-39	22-47	43.9
44.0	068.72	11-27	12-36	13-45	14-53	16-02	17-11	18-20	19-28	20-37	21-46	22-54	44.0
44.1	069.09	11-31	12-40	13-49	14-58	16-07	17-16	18-25	19-35	20-44	21-53	23-02	44.1
44.2	069.46	11-35	12-44	13-54	15-03	16-12	17-22	18-31	19-41	20-50	21-60	23-09	44.2
44.3	069.83	11-38	12-48	13-58	15-08	16-18	17-27	18-37	19-47	20-57	22-07	23-17	44.3
44.4	070.20	11-42	12-52	14-02	15-13	16-23	17-33	18-43	19-53	21-04	22-14	23-24	44.4
44.5	070.57	11-46	12-56	14-07	15-17	16-28	17-39	18-49	19-60	21-10	22-21	23-31	44.5
44.6	070.93	11-49	13-00	14-11	15-22	16-33	17-44	18-55	20-06	21-17	22-28	23-39	44.6
44.7	071.29	11-53	13-04	14-15	15-27	16-38	17-49	19-01	20-12	21-23	22-35	23-46	44.7
44.8	071.65	11-56	13-08	14-20	15-31	16-43	17-55	19-06	20-18	21-30	22-41	23-53	44.8
44.9	072.01	12-00	13-12	14-24	15-36	16-48	18-00	19-12	20-24	21-36	22-48	24-00	44.9
Rating	Sec/Mi	10 Mi	11 Mi	12 Mi	13 Mi	14 Mi	15 Mi	16 Mi	17 Mi	18 Mi	19 Mi	20 Mi	Rating

ADD time allowances on this page to Elapsed Time

Rating	21 Mi	22 Mi	23 Mi	24 Mi	25 Mi	26 Mi	27 Mi	28 Mi	29 Mi	30 Mi	31 Mi	32 Mi	Rating
40.0	18-29	19-22	20-15	21-08	22-00	22-53	23-46	24-39	25-32	26-25	27-17	28-10	40.0
40.1	18-38	19-32	20-25	21-18	22-11	23-05	23-58	24-51	25-44	26-38	27-31	28-24	40.1
40.2	18-47	19-41	20-35	21-28	22-22	23-16	24-09	25-03	25-57	26-50	27-44	28-38	40.2
40.3	18-57	19-51	20-45	21-39	22-33	23-27	24-21	25-15	26-09	27-04	27-58	28-52	40.3
40.4	19-05	19-60	20-54	21-49	22-44	23-38	24-33	25-27	26-22	27-16	28-11	29-05	40.4
40.5	19-14	20-09	21-04	21-59	22-54	23-49	24-44	25-39	26-34	27-29	28-24	29-19	40.5
40.6	19-23	20-18	21-14	22-09	23-05	23-60	24-55	25-51	26-46	27-41	28-37	29-32	40.6
40.7	19-32	20-27	21-23	22-19	23-15	24-11	25-06	26-02	26-58	27-54	28-49	29-45	40.7
40.8	19-40	20-36	21-33	22-29	23-25	24-21	25-17	26-14	27-10	28-06	29-02	29-58	40.8
40.9	19-49	20-45	21-42	22-39	23-35	24-32	25-28	26-25	27-22	28-18	29-15	30-12	40.9
41.0	19-57	20-54	21-51	22-48	23-45	24-42	25-40	26-37	27-34	28-31	29-28	30-25	41.0
41.1	20-06	21-04	22-01	22-59	23-56	24-53	25-51	26-48	27-46	28-43	29-41	30-38	41.1
41.2	20-15	21-13	22-11	23-08	24-06	25-04	26-02	26-60	27-58	28-56	29-53	30-51	41.2
41.3	20-23	21-22	22-20	23-18	24-17	25-15	26-13	27-11	28-10	29-08	30-06	31-04	41.3
41.4	20-32	21-30	22-29	23-28	24-26	25-25	26-24	27-22	28-21	29-20	30-18	31-17	41.4
41.5	20-40	21-40	22-39	23-38	24-37	25-36	26-35	27-34	28-33	29-32	30-31	31-30	41.5
41.6	20-49	21-49	22-48	23-48	24-47	25-46	26-46	27-45	28-45	29-44	30-44	31-43	41.6
41.7	20-57	21-57	22-57	23-57	24-57	25-57	26-57	27-57	28-57	29-56	30-56	31-56	41.7
41.8	21-06	22-06	23-06	24-06	25-07	26-07	27-07	28-08	29-08	30-08	31-08	32-09	41.8
41.9	21-14	22-15	23-15	24-16	25-17	26-17	27-18	28-19	29-19	30-20	31-21	32-21	41.9
42.0	21-22	22-24	23-25	24-26	25-27	26-28	27-29	28-30	29-31	30-32	31-33	32-34	42.0
42.1	21-31	22-32	23-34	24-35	25-37	26-38	27-40	28-41	29-43	30-44	31-46	32-47	42.1
42.2	21-39	22-41	23-43	24-45	25-47	26-49	27-50	28-52	29-54	30-56	31-58	32-60	42.2
42.3	21-47	22-50	23-52	24-54	25-56	26-59	28-01	29-03	30-06	31-08	32-10	33-12	42.3
42.4	21-56	22-58	24-01	25-04	26-06	27-09	28-12	29-14	30-17	31-20	32-22	33-25	42.4
42.5	22-04	23-07	24-10	25-13	26-16	27-19	28-22	29-25	30-28	31-31	32-34	33-37	42.5
42.6	22-12	23-15	24-19	25-22	26-26	27-29	28-33	29-36	30-39	31-43	32-46	33-50	42.6
42.7	22-20	23-24	24-28	25-31	26-35	27-39	28-43	29-47	30-50	31-54	32-58	34-02	42.7
42.8	22-28	23-32	24-37	25-41	26-45	27-49	28-53	29-58	31-02	32-06	33-10	34-14	42.8
42.9	22-36	23-41	24-45	25-50	26-54	27-59	29-04	30-08	31-13	32-17	33-22	34-27	42.9
43.0	22-44	23-49	24-54	25-59	27-04	28-09	29-14	30-19	31-24	32-29	33-34	34-39	43.0
43.1	22-52	23-57	25-03	26-08	27-14	28-19	29-24	30-30	31-35	32-40	33-46	34-51	43.1
43.2	23-00	24-06	25-12	26-17	27-23	28-29	29-34	30-40	31-46	32-52	33-57	35-03	43.2
43.3	23-08	24-14	25-20	26-26	27-32	28-39	29-45	30-51	31-57	33-03	34-09	35-15	43.3
43.4	23-16	24-23	25-29	26-36	27-42	28-48	29-55	31-01	32-08	33-14	34-21	35-27	43.4
43.5	23-24	24-31	25-38	26-45	27-51	28-58	30-05	31-12	32-19	33-26	34-33	35-39	43.5
43.6	23-32	24-39	25-47	26-54	28-01	29-08	30-15	31-23	32-30	33-37	34-44	35-52	43.6
43.7	23-40	24-48	25-55	27-03	28-11	29-18	30-26	31-33	32-41	33-49	34-56	36-04	43.7
43.8	23-48	24-56	26-04	27-12	28-20	29-28	30-36	31-44	32-52	33-60	35-08	36-16	43.8
43.9	23-55	25-04	26-12	27-20	28-29	29-37	30-45	31-54	33-02	34-11	35-19	36-27	43.9
44.0	24-03	25-12	26-21	27-29	28-38	29-47	30-55	32-04	33-13	34-22	35-30	36-39	44.0
44.1	24-11	25-20	26-29	27-38	28-47	29-56	31-05	32-15	33-24	34-33	35-42	36-51	44.1
44.2	24-19	25-28	26-38	27-47	28-56	30-06	31-15	32-25	33-34	34-44	35-53	37-03	44.2
44.3	24-26	25-36	26-46	27-56	29-06	30-16	31-25	32-35	33-45	34-55	36-05	37-15	44.3
44.4	24-34	25-44	26-55	28-05	29-15	30-25	31-35	32-46	33-56	35-06	36-16	37-26	44.4
44.5	24-42	25-53	27-03	28-14	29-24	30-35	31-45	32-56	34-06	35-17	36-28	37-38	44.5
44.6	24-50	26-00	27-11	28-22	29-33	30-44	31-55	33-06	34-17	35-28	36-39	37-50	44.6
44.7	24-57	26-08	27-20	28-31	29-42	30-54	32-05	33-16	34-27	35-39	36-50	38-01	44.7
44.8	25-05	26-16	27-28	28-40	29-51	31-03	32-15	33-26	34-38	35-50	37-01	38-13	44.8
44.9	25-12	26-24	27-36	28-48	30-00	31-12	32-24	33-36	34-48	36-00	37-12	38-24	44.9
Rating	21 Mi	22 Mi	23 Mi	24 Mi	25 Mi	26 Mi	27 Mi	28 Mi	29 Mi	30 Mi	31 Mi	32 Mi	Rating

ADD time allowances on this page to Elapsed Time

Index